REDPATH

THE HISTORY OF A SUGAR HOUSE

THE HISTORY OF A SUGAR HOUSE

RICHARD FELTOE

NATURAL HERITAGE/NATURAL HISTORY INC.

Redpath: The History Of A Sugar House
Published by Natural Heritage/Natural History Inc.
P.O. Box 69, Postal Station H
Toronto, Ontario
M4C 5H7

Editor: Wendy Thomas
Design: Derek Chung Tiam Fook
Printed and bound in Canada by Hignell Printing Limited

Canadian Cataloguing in Publication Data
Feltoe, Richard D., 1954 -
Redpath

Includes bibliographical references and index.
ISBN 0-920474-67-5

1. Redpath Industries – History. 2. Sugar – Manufacture and refining – Canada – History.
I. Title

HD 9114.C24R44 1991 338.7'6336'0971 C91-094846-1

Contents

Acknowledgements

Although it is my name that appears on the cover of this book, I would not wish it to be thought that Redpath, The History of a Sugar House, is the result of my efforts alone. Therefore I would now like to acknowledge the contributions and efforts of those who have supported me in the development of this work.

To start, I must credit Murray McEwen for proposing and advancing the concept of a written history of the company and thank him for allowing me the opportunity to write this book. Likewise my thanks go to Ed Makin and Peter Sharpe for permitting me to take time from my duties as curator of the Redpath Sugar Museum to research the contents of the book and for acting in conjunction with Mr. McEwen as a committee to oversee the entire project.

Next, I wish to express my gratitude to Barry Penhale, Wendy Thomas, and Derek Chung for guiding me through the complexities of producing this book.

Third, my thanks to the many descendants of the Redpath and Drummond families, including: Linda Redpath, Bruce McNiven, Audrey Amsden, Shirley Bartram, Helen Henderson, and many others who supplied me with many of the pictures of the family and inside details which enhanced the text.

Penultimately, my thanks to Karen Posner for acting as a sounding board for my ideas and critic and advisor during my writing of the manuscript and Laura Bellingham for her proofreading of the finished manuscript.

Finally and most deservedly, I would like to express my appreciation and indebtedness to my wife, Diane. Who took my literary meanderings and translated them into legible print. It can honestly be said that without her continuous support and commitment, plus her patience during the numerous drafts, re-writes, editorial changes and last minute adjustments, this book would never have been completed.

To all my heartfelt thanks

Richard Feltoe
Curator and Corporate Archivist - Redpath Sugar Museum
August 1991

Introduction

Dear Reader:

Before you continue, I would like to ask you to look once again at the cover of this book and take note of the word that is printed so boldly across its front. REDPATH, a name that has meant quality sugar on Canadian grocery store shelves and in kitchen cupboards across this country since before Confederation. But few people realize where the name REDPATH comes from, or what it represents as a part of Canada's industrial heritage. It is not only one of the oldest continuously used trade-marks in Canadian business history, but it is also the reproduction of the signature of the company's founder, John Redpath.

Today the corporate descendant of John Redpath's original endeavour is Canada's oldest surviving sugar company and trades under the name of Redpath Sugars. This multi-million dollar corporation purchases raw sugar from sources around the globe, brings it to Canada, where it is processed and cleaned into a pure substance to meet this nation's stringent standards of purity for sugar. It is then distributed to the company's domestic, commercial, and industrial customers in a variety of forms that would have astounded John.

Notwithstanding all these advances in the technologies of modern production, we still retain John's original signature on all our packaging, delivery vehicles, and letterhead, reminding us of our heritage as part of Canada's industrial and commercial history.

This then is our story. Although it cannot be claimed that John Redpath or his successors – Peter Redpath, George Alexander Drummond, and Huntly Redpath Drummond, – affected the course of Canada's national or even provincial history, it will be seen that at times they did help to "adjust" the balance of the scales of decision making within governmental and economic circles.

Finally, as a personal comment, while I naturally studied the business and financial records of the company, I also had the fortunate opportunity to study a wealth of personal letters written by various members of the Redpath and Drummond families. Although most of these latter pieces could not be included in this work, some have been retained in order to allow a glimpse into their lives beyond the confines of the company. In addition, they have allowed me, to some degree, to feel that I have "got to know" these people, not as bygone characters within an historic setting, but as the real people that they were.

As a result, in writing this book I have become convinced that although this is the history of a company, it is also the story of the people who made this history happen, and the economic, political, social, and domestic events in which they participated resulted in the creation of a "sugar house."

The end result is, as you will see, not a "standard" corporate history; but since those who made this history could not be classed merely as "standard," it would be doing them an injustice to confine them to a work of that kind.

Richard Feltoe
Curator and Corporate Archivist
Redpath Sugar Museum
August 1991

YE OLDE SUGAR LOAF

An artist's impression of an early sugar cane mill in India, with the boiling pots for the making of gur in the background.

CHAPTER ONE

"That Sweet Comfit Men Call Sugar"

The beginnings of sugar are generally believed to have been centred in the islands of the South Pacific. In the ancient mythology of the Solomon Islands, sugar cane is credited with the birth of mankind, with the original male and female sprouting from the ripened stalk of a cane. In a similar story from New Britain, two fishermen, To-Kabwana and To-Karvuvu ("To" being the Polynesian for sugar cane) found a piece of cane trapped in their nets. They planted the cane stalk, which grew and brought forth a woman. During the day, she cooked and cared for the men and at night hid herself within the cane. Discovering her nightly secret resting place, the men forced her to remain with them. Eventually she became wife to one of the fishermen and from their union sprang the whole human race.

More prosaically the earliest recorded use of cane for food is found from about 500 B.C. in certain holy scriptures in India, where it was generally used as a vegetable, with the body of the plant being boiled into a pulp. The earliest datable mention of sugar cane comes from 325 B.C., when sugar (and sugar cane, by inference) is recorded by the Macedonian General Nearchus, during his campaigns in the east under Alexander the Great. From the very beginning, efforts were made to produce a distinct concentrate from the cane juice, resulting in the production of the roughest or crudest type of sugar known as Jaggery or Gur.

From the time of the empires of Greece, and later Rome, there are a number of accounts that indicate a knowledge of the existence of sugar cane and its sweet extract. They include Erathosthenes (c 276 - 194 B.C.)

> *The roots of plants [in India], particularly of the great reeds are sweet by nature and decoction.*[1]

and from Seneca the Younger (3 B.C. - 65 A.D.),

> *They say that in India honey has been found on the leaves of certain reeds [produced] by the juice of the reed itself, which has an unusual richness and sweetness.*[2]

Unfortunately, recorded documentation is somewhat less clear about the extent of sugar usage within the average Greek or Roman home, and it is generally thought that honey remained the principal sweetener in those times.

The real credit for the spreading of sugar cane cultivation must go to the Arabs. During their great period of conquests throughout the Mediterranean basin in the latter half of the first millennium A.D., the Arabs discovered or, perhaps more accurately, were introduced to sugar by the

Persians around 600 A.D., and readily assimilated it into their own culture. In turn, they introduced the cultivation of sugar cane to most of their later conquests. Records of the various ruling governors of conquered states indicate the growing of sugar cane in such diverse places as Syria (circa 640 A.D.), Spain (650 A.D.), Palestine (650 A.D.), Egypt (650 A.D.), Sicily (655 A.D.), Cyprus (655 A.D.), Morocco (682 A.D.), Crete (823 A.D.), and Malta (870 A.D.) By the year 1000 A.D., the humble sugar cane had become an economic crop grown throughout the length of the Mediterranean and the Near and Middle East. This widespread use within these countries now led to the next phase of sugar's history – its introduction to the cultures of Northern Europe. For these populations, the only sweetener readily available prior to 1000 A.D. was honey, and most of the royal courts and major religious houses had specialists on staff to keep the beehives and provide honey to the kitchens.

The wave of Islamic conquests brought the counter-reaction of the Christian world for a crusade to retrieve the holy places. With the successive series of invasions of Moslem strongholds by the Crusaders, sugar came to the attention of Western scholars, prompting Fulcherius Carnotensis to write in the early eleventh century: "On the fields of Laodicia [Turkey] we found certain reed like plants called cannamella [reed-honey]"[3] while Jacobus de Vitriaco wrote the following about the Jordan valley:

> *There is a reed from which flows a very sweet juice called cannamelli zachariae; this honey they [the Arabs] eat with bread and melt it with water, and think it more whole-some than the honey of bees ... with the juice of this reed our men at the siege of Acre often stayed their hunger.*[4]

Quick to appreciate the value of this new sweetener, the returning Crusaders not only disseminated the information about the existence of sugar cane, they also brought back samples of cane and semi-processed sugar, much to the delight of those at home. Meanwhile, in the Holy Land itself, groups of Crusaders formed merchant cartels in order to gain control over the sources of production, which they maintained for the following two centuries (thus funding their other, more martial activities). Following the loss of the Holy Land to the Saracens in the late thirteenth century, the centre of sugar cane cultivation gravitated westward through Cyprus, Sicily, and Spain, until by the early fifteenth century the islands of Madeira, Tenerife, and other parts of the Canary group of islands were the major production centres for sugar cane. Meanwhile, within Europe, the introduction of sugar for consumption had wrought some significant social and economic changes.

It may be of some surprise to the modern reader that while today we think of "sugar and spice" as counterpoints in our taste range, to the medieval mind sugar **was** a spice, alongside pepper, nutmeg, ginger, and coriander. Numerous dishes using beef, pork, poultry, and fish were seasoned with combinations of sharp-flavoured spices and sugar, or used sugar-based sauces, but the price of sugar placed its use well beyond the means of any but the most wealthy. In the official records of royal houses such as that of Henry II of England (1154 - 89), we first see the regular purchase of sugar for use in the royal kitchens. By the year 1243, Henry III of England was ordering 300 pounds of "Zucre de Roche" and by 1289 records indicate that the royal household of Edward I consumed more than 6,258 pounds of sugar per year. Expensive as it was, this royal example of sugar consumption was enough to ensure rapid mimicry by the nobility. Throughout the thirteenth and fourteenth centuries, household accounts clearly indicate that in the upper echelons of society, sugar had become a status symbol. It was given as a gift alongside precious metals and spices, or blended with marzipan, oil of almonds, rice, and various gums to create a form of edible clay, from which artistic masterpieces could be created. These sugar sculptures were called "subtleties" and were generally served between major courses, taking the forms of real and fantastic beasts, buildings, heraldic designs, and famous warriors. Entire festive tables would be covered with subtleties and the intense political and social rivalries between the noble houses (coupled with the example of the royal households) led to a profligacy of sugar use that would horrify the modern accountant. At the same time, sugar began to be used extensively as a pharmaceutical product and was touted as the wonder drug of the age. It was claimed that sugar was capable of curing haemorrhoids, stomach ulcers, headaches, and childbirth pain; and by the late fifteenth century the use of sugar in medicine was so well established that a saying "like an apothecary without sugar" meant being totally useless. One quotation from the writer Tabernaemontanus (c1515 - 1590) gives an idea of the feelings towards sugar at that time and indicates that not all "modern" ideas are necessarily new.

Inside the workshop of a medieval apothecary, showing the sugar cones on the shelves.

> *Nice white sugar from Madeira or the Canaries, when taken moderately cleans the blood, strengthens body and mind, especially chest, lungs and throat, but it is bad ... for hot and bilious people for it easily turns into bile, makes the teeth blunt and makes them decay. As a powder it is good for the eyes, as a smoke it is good for the common cold, as flour sprinkled on wounds it heals them ... sugar wine with cinnamon gives vigour to old people.*[5]

The mention of "nice white sugar" is of particular note since it clearly indicates that by this time sugar refining was well established as an industry in its own right.

Although it is known that various degrees of cleaning and concentration of sugar took place simultaneously with the spread of the growing of sugar, refining did not really develop into an industry until the mid-fifteenth century.

When some of the major merchant families of Venice acquired the knowledge of refining by the use of conical drainage moulds, the "sugar cone" had arrived.

Huge incomes were generated for the refining "families" by their sugar "houses," their sales network covering all of Western Europe. Such was the economic and strategic value of this new technology that local laws were passed forbidding, upon pain of death, the exportation of production machinery, technological information, or even trained personnel to other regions. However, as in most such cases, the desire for knowledge and profit outran the legal restrictions. Soon additional refining operations sprang up across Europe. By the mid-sixteenth century, there were more than thirteen refineries in Antwerp alone, with additional production centres in Amsterdam, Augsburg, Bordeaux, Lisbon, Bristol, and London. The technology of this period (i.e., the use of sugar cone moulds and "claying"*) appears to our modern eyes as slow, crude and inefficient. But in terms of the technology of the time, it represented a quantum leap in the production capabilities of the sugar manufacturers. These advances reduced costs and allowed prices to fall, making sugar an even more attractive product – which was just as well, since the wealthy, middle and upper classes had been demanding, in increasing volume, access to the sweet luxury previously enjoyed only by royalty. Furthermore, such was the success of this technology in producing the desired product that from the sixteenth century to the mid-eighteenth century, the art of refining by the sugar cone method changed very little. But in terms of the mainstream history of sugar, our attention must now span the Atlantic with the discovery and development of the New World as the centre for sugar production.

The fill-house of an eighteenth century sugar house, illustrating the rows of sugar cones undergoing refining.

Documentary evidence indicates that it was Christopher Columbus who brought sugar cane to the Americas on his second voyage in October 1493 and that he was significantly impressed by the rapidity with which the transplanted sugar cane germinated and grew. The economic bonanza that sugar production represented to the expansionist powers of Britain, France, Spain, and Portugal led to a race for the establishment of colonies throughout the

* For those of a mechanical inclination, details of the techniques involved are outlined in Appendix 1.

Caribbean Islands, as well as the adjacent coasts of South, Central, and North America. The competition was so fierce that local raids between ships and garrisons of the various powers in the Caribbean escalated into full-scale wars on the European mainland. Entire governmental policies were based on the economic control (and subsequent revenues) that could be derived from the growing and production of sugar. By 1680, the English had succeeded in occupying the Leeward Islands, Barbados, Jamaica, Antigua, Grenada, and Trinidad. Spain held onto Cuba, Porta Rico (Puerto Rico), and Hispaniola (Haiti and the Dominican Republic), as well as mainland colonies. Portugal controlled Brazil and areas of Central America. The French had Martinique and Guadeloupe (having lost most of their original territories to the English), while the Dutch were clinging to their toehold in the New World around their Guiana's colonies. The individual histories of these areas during the next two hundred years is a fascinating story of political and economic intrigue. Unfortunately there is not space here to chronicle that tale. Suffice it to say that fabulous fortunes were made and lost by plantation owners and traders.

As in most cases where there is a rapid production of wealth for a minority, there is a negative impact on the majority, which in this case related to the vast amounts of labour required for the sugar cane fields and mills. Initially some labour was derived from indentured whites and local Carib natives. But as time progressed, the use of imported black African labour came to dominate the workforce, and the "Black Triangle" trade route developed. Under this system, finished goods were loaded into ships in northern European ports and were then shipped to the African slaving centres run by Muhammedan Arabs and coastal black natives, who were eager to exchange captured negroes of the continental interior for the trade goods. The chained and branded slaves were forced aboard the ships and chained to makeshift platforms, with the absolute minimum of space between either individuals or racks of more slaves above and below. During the subsequent voyage to the Caribbean, sanitary conditions were non-existent.

Trading in human misery: the slave trade in West Africa.

Preparing the fields and planting the segments of cane "ratoons."

Harvesting the fully grown sugar cane.

The maggoty food and stale water fed to the slaves led to an average death rate of around 25%. For those who survived, two of every three were sold in auction to work in the plantations. The money earned by the slavers was then used to purchase the sugar (produced by those selfsame slaves), for transport to and sale in Europe, whereupon the cycle began again. But now that we have brought the production of sugar up to the 1700s, we should also look at the changes wrought by its increased consumption during this same period.

With the expansion of the production in the West Indies, the doors were thrown wide open for increased consumption by all levels of society. In Elizabethan England, sugar was sold in penny and two-penny packets. By the reign of Charles II in the 1600s, the growth of coffee and chocolate (sweetened with large amounts of sugar) as social drinks led to the establishment of "clubs" specifically for the enjoyment of these beverages. Further impetus was given to the use of sugar by travellers returning from the continent and demanding dishes experienced while abroad and Spanish Olio, Portugal Cakes, Dutch Biskets, and Italian Puffs became all the rage. In his undated work, *A Collection of Ordinances and Regulations for the Government of the Royal Household*, Braithwaite comments on the employment of continental cooks:

> *In ancient times noblemen contented themselves with such [cooks] as had been bred in their own houses, but of late none could please but some Italians and Frenchmen ... nor*

A cane mill powered by animals.

Inside the boiling house, the raw cane juice is processed into muscovado (raw)sugar.

> *would the old manner of baking, boiling or roasting please them, but the boiled meats must be after the French fashion, the dishes garnished with sugar and preserved plums, the meat covered with orangeade, preserved lemons and ... stuff fetched from the confectioners. More lemons and sugar are spoilt in boiling fish than might well serve the whole expense of the house in a day.*[6]

Sugar, it will be noted, was still being served with meat and fish. It was also increasingly being used as a preservative for fruit and was the main ingredient in the many popular syrups of the day. *The Art of Cookery*, published in 1654, distinguished between the effects of different types of sugar in cooking; while another cook, known only by the initials M.H., writing in 1693, produced a number of recipes using generous quantities of rich ingredients. For example, in "Hypocras," a favourite mixed drink of the period, the ingredients included four quarts of wine, two quarts of milk, one and a half pounds of fine white sugar, and varying quantities of cinnamon, galingale, coriander seeds, and nutmeg, all strained through a linen bag "until fine." A recipe for "an excellent cake" used four pounds of butter, ten pounds of currants, three pounds of sugar, sixteen eggs, and a quart of sack (wine). The icing required another two pounds of sugar, "... beaten very fine and passed through a sieve ... ."[7] Outside of the culinary arts, sugar was making perhaps its most widespread and therefore influential social impact as the inseparable companion to the developing rage for tea drinking. This "social event" of tea drinking developed its own highly stylized forms of etiquette and had its own set of tools, often highly decorated and made in silver or gold as well as more mundane metals. Thus we have the age of the sugar caster, the sugar bowl, nippers, tongs, crushers, and cutters, which today rate as highly collectable antiques.

Throughout the eighteenth century, as production and consumption increased hand-in-hand, cookery books were full of suggestions for sweet dishes. Using all their authors' imaginations to augment the resources that greater trade and food production were supplying, recipes increasingly referred to specific varieties of sugar for certain uses. Thus the terms Crushed, Powdered, Groundcommon, Loaf, Double Refined, and even Treble Refined Loaf sugar became terms the educated cook could recognize. (This last was the finest sugar available at the end of the century and was esteemed for its purity.) Meanwhile, at the other end of the economic and social spectrum, the poorer grades of sugar called Pieces, Bastard, Muscovado, Coarse, and Brown Candy became the provenance of the lower classes. In fact, the whole social outlook on sugar changed as it spread throughout the middle and working classes. By the start of the nineteenth century in England, the sight of a railway or canal navvy with his mug of tea, sweetened with sugar, was as engrained a part of the British social make-up as the upper-class scones and cakes were for high tea. Three quotes may serve to illustrate the point. In a charming small work written by Susanna Whatman between 1776 and 1787, she refers to the storing of sugar in the following manner:

> *Plenty of sugar should always be kept ready broke in the deep sugar drawers ... there is ... one for moist [brown] sugar and two for lump [broken pieces from a larger loaf] sugar. The pieces should be as square as possible and rather small. The sugar that is powdered to fill the silver castor should be kept in a bason in one of the drawers to prevent any insects getting into it and be powdered fine in the mortar and kept ready for use.*[8]

The Scottish theologian Duncan Forbes wrote in 1744:

> *But when the opening [of] a trade with the East Indies ... brought the price of tea ... so low, that the meanest labouring man could compass the purchase of it; ... when sugar, the inseparable companion of tea came to be in the possession of the very poorest housewife, where formally it had been a great rarity the [social] effects were very suddenly and severely felt.*[9]

Finally, an important observer of rural life in England at the end of the eighteenth century, the cleric David Davies, put forward a rather different view of the place of sugar (linked with tea) and attributed the increased use of tea and sugar by the poor not as an aping of their social betters but as the lowest margin above absolute poverty, because no alternative drink such as milk or beer could be afforded.

> *Under these hard circumstances, the dearness of malt, and the difficulty of procuring milk the only thing remaining of them to moisten their bread with was tea ... still you exclaim tea is a luxury. If you mean fine hyson tea sweetened with refined sugar, and softened with cream, I readily admit it to be so. But this is not the tea [or sugar] of the*

poor. Spring water just coloured with a few leaves of the lowest priced tea, and sweetened with the brownest sugar is [their] luxury ... and were they now to be deprived of this they would ... be reduced to bread and water.[10]

Thus by the end of this period the use of sugar had reached every stratum of society. But for the manufacturers of sugar, who seemed to be on top of the world, the changes that occurred within the industry during the next few years, were as dramatic and revolutionary as the social and political revolutions reverberating around the globe at the same time.

Ever since the opening up of the Caribbean Islands and the growth in slavery, there had been voices raised against this "social crime." Locke spoke his mind on the subject, as did Adam Smith, Jeremy Bentham, Dr. Johnson, Montesquieu, and Rousseau. The stigma of slavery was now firmly imprinted on sugar and a movement to boycott sugar as a "tainted article" slowly spread. In 1792, the Anti-Saccharite Society was formed in London and soon developed into a national anti-slavery movement.

In the English Parliament William Fox challenged the public

To abstain from the use of sugar and rum until ... the speedy subversion of slavery ... or until we can ... produce the sugar cane in some other mode unconnected with slavery.[11]

Increasing measures of protection for the slaves under English jurisdiction developed, until in 1833 slavery was abolished by an Act of Parliament. The immediate result was to bankrupt many of the cane growing estates, and the

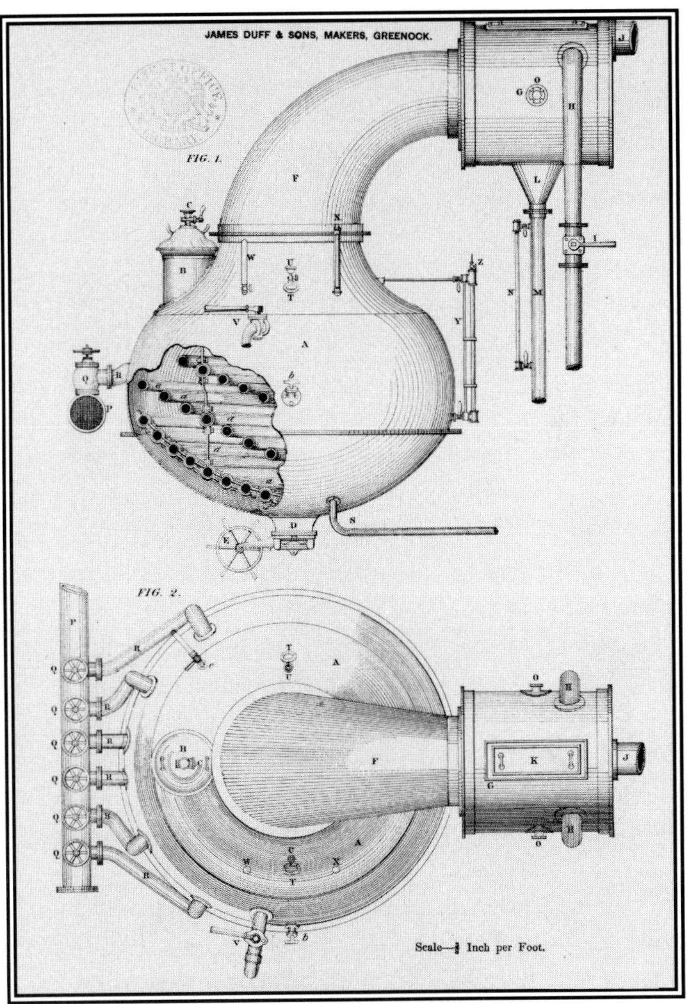

An early vacuum pan.

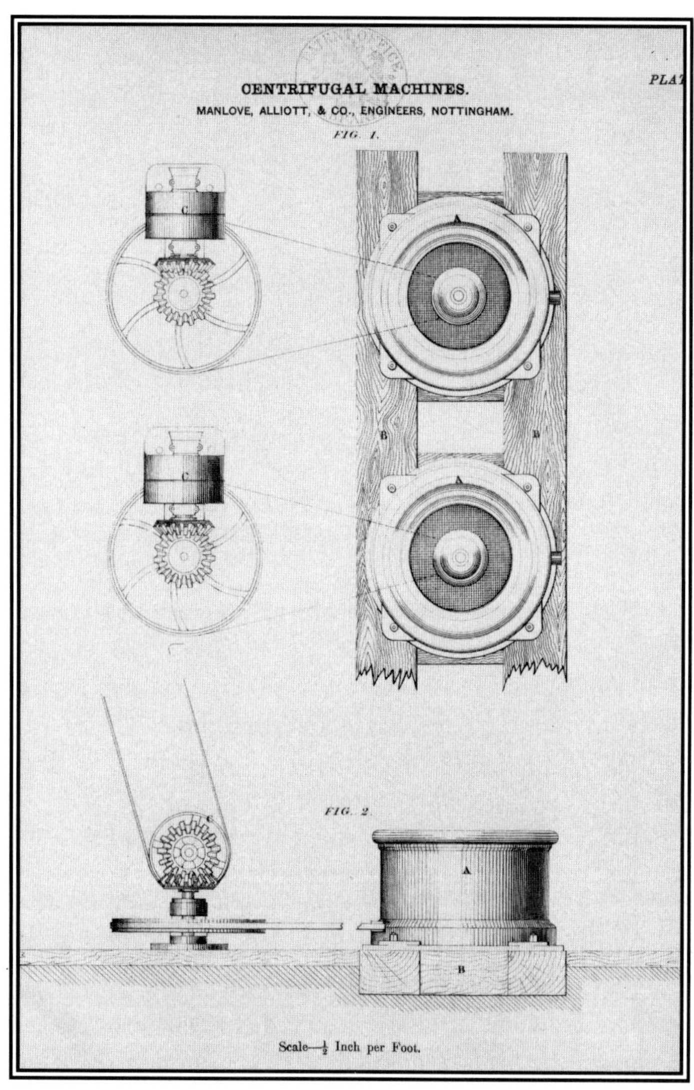

An early centrifugal machine, driven by belts. This type of centrifugal had to be loaded and emptied through the open top.

repercussions on the shipping trade and cane growing industry lingered for years. At the opposite end of the production cycle, the refineries were now faced with potentially disastrous cuts in their supplies of cheap sugar. However, technological developments saved and transformed the refining industry during the next fifty years. The old open-topped boiling pans were replaced by low air pressure vacuum pans (which were developed in 1813.) The use of charcoal (derived from bones) for filtering out impurities was originated in 1812, replacing the top skimming and the large scale use of bullocks' blood. By 1837, the use of large spin dryers originally used in laundries was recognized as a more efficient way of separating the liquid molasses from the sugar than the old cone drainage method. Finished cones were being sliced into regular sized tablets by 1840, thus originating the predecessor of the modern sugar cube. Other technological experiments were not so benign, however, as filtration using alum, sulphurous acid, zinc, lead, and tin salts were tried; fortunately these experimental methods did not take hold. By the 1870s, the sugar industry was effectively modernized and a new standard of technical expertise had taken command, increasing production and dramatically reducing costs. Price cuts made sugar even more available to the domestic market and the growing number of industrial food-processing facilities and ready-made food manufacturers.

Within the Canadian context, until the arrival of the white man, the native populations relied upon honey, maple syrup or an extract from corn to supply their sweetening needs. The incoming European settlers considered these products inferior substitutes to the loaf sugar in use back in Europe. Unfortunately, the governments of both the French and later the British Empires considered the North American colonies as merely sources of raw materials, and there were deliberate pieces of restrictive legislation enacted to specifically prevent the development of industrial capability in the colonies and keep them totally dependent upon the homeland for all finished products.

Therefore, although raw sugar could be obtained directly from the Caribbean, all the refined sugar came from the refineries of France or England and was sold at exorbitant prices to the merchants of Canada, who in turn added their profit margins to create a price nearly ten times that in Europe. For the southern colonies in Virginia, Georgia, etc., the answer was relatively simple, and they developed their own refineries, first on the plantations and later in the major cities including Baltimore, Boston, and other Eastern seaboard cities. In Canada no such investment was made and the population had to purchase either on the open market from England at inflated prices or on the black market from New England.

With the American Revolution, these supplies of U.S. sugar were all but cut off from the Canadian market and the requirement of buying only from Great Britain forced prices to even more unwelcome heights. Following the war, anti-American sentiment effectively forbade the buying of American sugar in those areas settled by Loyalists expelled from the United States. In other areas, especially Upper Canada (Ontario), with the influx of Americans settling throughout the province, virtually all sugar was of U.S. origin until 1812, when once again war caused a virtual ban on imports of U.S. products unless smuggled in and sold at inflated margins. In the area of York (Toronto), sugar prices quadrupled during the war, as supplies were interrupted by various invasions of Canada or supply convoys were captured.

As a direct result of the War of 1812, various commercial interests in the Maritimes decided that there was an opportunity to capitalize on the general anti-American feeling throughout the British North American colonies. As a result, in 1818 a small sugar refinery was established in Halifax by John Moody and a group of local businessmen. Both the nature of the West Indies' trade and the advantageous location of Halifax seemed to indicate its future would be secure. These hopes were not realized, however, as the various trade acts of the 1830s opened the British West Indies to American enterprise, and with the removal of the colonial preference, the Halifax refinery found itself without a market.

Early in 1831, it was announced that the sugar refinery had closed down. Subsequent re-openings kept it going for short periods until 1837 when the company finally collapsed under its accumulated debt load, leaving the various independent provincial colonies to acquire sugar either from the U.S. or Great Britain. Over the next sixteen years, as the population of the Canadas increased, so the demand for a home industry grew, until in 1854 the first successful sugar company in Canada, the Canada Sugar Refinery, was established in Montreal by a local prominent businessman, John Redpath.

But just who was this man? And what qualifications did he have for starting up such a huge concern as a sugar refinery?

Terrace Bank

CHAPTER TWO

The Making Of A Man Of Substance

Of John's date of birth we have no actual records, nor do we know the names of his parents. According to family accounts he was born in the village of Earlston, south of Edinburgh in 1796, although the parish records do not record any baptisms for either John or any other Redpaths during a ten-year period before and after John's supposed year of birth. This is not surprising, as no official records were instituted until1830, and it was up to the parents to register all matters of this kind with the official local parish church. For those who were dissenters or non-members of the "official" church, it was often the case that, on principle, they would refuse to register their children and so we must take John's own word for his place and date of origin. We do know that he had at least four brothers – Robert, George, Peter, and James. There are also indications of at least one sister, Elspeth. Reportedly left as orphans, John and his brothers apprenticed and trained as stone masons in Edinburgh under a builder named George Drummond. In 1816, John and his brothers plus Robert Drummond (George's brother) decided to emigrate to the Americas, landing in Quebec City in mid-summer 1816. According to a source outside the family, John and three of the others travelled up to Montreal, a distance of 160 miles (352 km), walking barefoot in order to save wear on the only pair of shoes each man had.

Notre Dame Church, Montreal.

Upon arrival at Montreal, John obtained work with a building contractor by the name of Couvrette, doing minor construction work. Within four years John had established his own contracting business, married a young woman called Janet McPhee of Glengarry County, Upper Canada (Ontario), and had a daughter, Elizabeth.

In 1821 in order to bypass the Lachine Rapids, the merchants of Montreal decided to construct a canal. This would allow cargo boats to be sailed up river, replacing the laborious method of the past of unloading, hauling overland, and reloading onto another vessel. John bid for and won a contract to build part of this canal in co-operation with another building contractor, Thomas Mackay. Mackay was obviously impressed by Redpath's work, as he brought Redpath in on another major project of the day, the building of Notre Dame

Church, which today stands as an impressive testimony to the stone mason's art. John and Janet also had a second child, whom they christened Peter, after his uncle. Throughout 1822 and 1823 John was busy on the construction of the Lachine Canal and Notre Dame Church, and in November 1823 another daughter, Mary, was born.

He also seems to have had a business partnership with a Mr. Riley that lasted until 1824 when that partnership was dissolved; John then continued in business by himself, doing numerous contracts related to his building and general contracting business including repairing chimneys on houses; constructing walls, brick arches, and foundations; laying hearths and fireplaces; constructing outdoor buildings; digging privy holes and clearing full ones; digging cess pools; and laying paths.

The year 1825 was exceptionally full for John, for as well as participating in the opening of the Lachine Canal, he worked on several large projects for the Royal Engineers Department at the military fortifications on St. Helens Island in the middle of the St. Lawrence River. In the city, he was working for John Molson in the construction of the new Theatre Royal at the corner of St. Denis and St. Paul Streets, and for John Molson & Sons brewery in the demolition of a "large chimney" and the rebuilding of another in its place. The Bank of Montreal then contracted John for repair work to their offices in the city, as did the Free Masons for their hall (again under the Molsons, who were Grand Masters in the lodge.) Another project being developed that was to keep John occupied for the next several years was a military canal, which would run from the Ottawa River, along the Rideau River system, down to Kingston on Lake Ontario. This was to bypass the St. Lawrence River, which was considered by military authorities as too susceptible to attack by hostile U.S. interests in a possible war.

Before John became totally involved in the Rideau Canal, he did make time to have a fourth child, a girl they named Jane, as well as completing several contracts in Montreal such as the Nelson's Column Memorial, the Montreal National School House, McGill University, the Artillery Barracks and Magazine on St. Helens Island, and a billiard room for the Masonic Hall. He was also joined in Canada by his sister Elspeth, her husband Thomas Fairbairn, and their eight children, all of whom lived with John and Janet in their home on Dalhousie Square in Montreal, until the Fairbairns moved into Upper Canada to settle at Jones Falls.

Early in January 1827, John, in partnership with Thomas Mackay, began work on the Rideau Canal with the construction of a stone storehouse measuring 74 feet long, by 34 feet wide and 27 feet high at the entrance of the canal on the Ottawa River. By the end of the year, John had completed the storehouse and moved inland along the route of the canal, to his sister's home at Jones Falls, while Janet returned to Montreal with the children and very shortly thereafter gave birth to their fifth child, Helen. At Jones Falls, John prepared for his biggest challenge to date, the construction of a series of four locks and a dam more than sixty feet high and three hundred and fifty feet long, almost twice the size of any other dam in North America at that time.

In his book on the Rideau Waterway, R. Leggett comments upon the work involved in constructing this massive edifice:

> *In the light of the fact that all the stone was hand cut and hoisted into place by small winches, in the isolation of the Canadian forest, the daring and indeed grandeur of his [Lt. Colonel J. By] conception seem all the more remarkable. Luckily he found a contractor capable of carrying out this great pioneer piece of construction work … John Redpath … the immense quantities of stone required for the dam and locks necessitated an unusually large labour force. A construction camp was therefore the first major undertaking and accommodation for 200 men was provided. When the work was in full swing there were forty masons employed … We know that the dreaded swamp fever was especially severe in this construction camp at Jones Falls … many men died and were buried in a small graveyard … near the great dam.*[1]

According to a later report John also suffered from the "ague" (malaria) caused by the swamp, and its debilitating effects recurred throughout the rest of his life.

Fortunately John's account books for this project still exist and reveal the daily expenditures for materials and wages on the construction of the dam. They also show that Robert, Peter, and James Redpath worked alongside their brother John throughout1827. Similarly, personal account books indicate that upon at least one occasion, Janet joined John on the site. Unfortunately, we also know that in May 1828 they suffered the death of their three-year-old daughter, Jane.

As the dam project advanced into the winter of 1828, conditions became harsher, and to assist the workers in surviving the loneliness of the "bush," Mr. Leggett reveals that

> *The men working at Jones Falls were allowed to have liquor at Mr. Redpath's expense … charged to the Jones Falls account were also such pleasing items as a box of cigars, a bugle and a fiddle. There are also several items listed as "Expenses to Lachine to see the men off" notes which testify once again to the character of the man.*[2]

John continued his work on the canal into 1829 with construction of another dam at Hogs Back, just outside of present-day Ottawa, which was then called Bytown after the project engineer Lieutenant Colonel John By, Royal Engineers. John and Janet also had their sixth child, whom they named Jane Margaret.

Throughout 1830 and 1831, John's entire efforts were directed at completing the canal by the late summer of 1831. Unfortunately, delays in construction prevented this opening occurring on time, and the official ceremonies scheduled for August 21 actually did not occur until the following May. To commemorate the work done on the canal, Lieutenant Colonel By commissioned four silver trophy pieces to be presented to the major contractors, including the partnership of Mackay and Redpath. Their trophy was inscribed with the following list of credits for their work on the canal system, and it is now proudly displayed in the Redpath Sugar Museum in Toronto.

A frontal view of the "great dam" at Jones Falls during construction.

A panoramic view of the Jones Falls complex, showing the lower three locks running from right to left across the centre with the fourth lock set at right angles off to the left. The "great dam" can just be seen in the background [to the right of the military blockhouse set on top of the hill in the upper centre of the picture].

The Gift of Lieut. Colonel John By Commanding Royal Engineer of the Rideau Canal in Upper Canada to Mess'rs Mackay and Redpath. The contractors for the first eight locks at the entrance of the Ottawa. Two locks at Hartwells, Two locks at Hogsback and Four locks and a Dam sixty five feet in height at Jones Falls. As an acknowledgement of the zeal displayed by them in the performance of their contracts and a testimonial of the works above mentioned having been completed to his entire satisfaction.

Presented on the opening of the Rideau Canal the 21st of August 1831.

In the scale of the modern world, the Rideau Canal is considered a small historical waterway used mainly for pleasure boating through a quiet rural environment, and we have lost sight of the huge cost paid in both money and lives that went into carving out the route from virgin forest, rocky wilderness, swamps, and lakes. It is only when one visits sites such as Jones Falls (which even today is isolated well away from Highway15 running from Kingston to Smiths Falls) that one realizes the impressive substance of the work that John, his brothers, and their skilled work teams did on the development of Canada's waterways system.

Following completion of the Rideau Canal, the partnership of Mackay and Redpath was dissolved, as was another partnership agreement between the four major contractors on the project, namely Thomas Phillips, Andrew White, Thomas Mackay, and John Redpath. In this latter agreement all four agreed to divide equally the projected losses or profits for the completed work. In fact, the partners each received a profit of over £20,000*, a huge sum for those days.

Returning to Montreal with his new fortune, John began to make a large number of investments, including shares in the Bank of Montreal and the Ottawa Steamboat Line (run by the Molsons.) He also purchased various lots of land in and around Montreal and in Upper Canada at Nepean. On one of these Montreal lots, John contracted for a new house to be built costing £5,300* into which he moved his growing family at the end of the year.

John's place as a man of substance and a respected businessman led to his holding positions of influence and power in social, business, and political spheres. During the next year, John was appointed to the Committee of Management for the Montreal General Hospital and later became its chairman. He was also appointed an Alderman for the City of Montreal and served eight successive terms. In fact there are stories that the current width of Sherbrooke Street, a broad boulevard, is due entirely to John's efforts in the face of concerted opposition that would have seen it as just another narrow city street. In the religious sphere, he was recognized as a strong leader, acting as deacon, church elder, and lay preacher in a number of congregations over the years.

In 1833, John increased his share holdings in the Bank of Montreal, the Ottawa Steamboat Line, and another Molson project, the Montreal Tow Boat Co. He was also invited to join the Bank of Montreal as a Director of the Board. He was now definitely a man of substance and

(* Prior to 1858 a large mixture of foreign currencies circulated in the Canadian colonies. Official ledger accounts however, generally recorded financial matters in Pounds, Shillings, and Pence shown as £/s/d.)

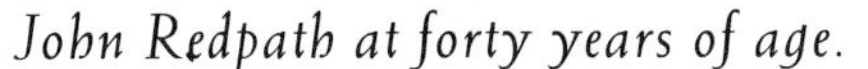

John Redpath at forty years of age.

Jane Redpath (née Drummond).

seemed set for a career of success among his fellow entrepreneurs. Unfortunately, tragedy struck in 1834 when Janet died at age forty-three giving birth to their seventh child, John James. No records of how John reacted to the death of his wife exist, but he and his family spent much of that year in Jones Falls with his sister and then in Kingston with Robert Drummond where John became acquainted with Jane Drummond, Robert's younger sister. In August 1834, Robert Drummond died in the cholera epidemic that swept the entire colony, whereupon John returned to Montreal. The following year in September, the thirty-nine-year-old John Redpath was married to Jane Drummond, who was then twenty years old. The couple lived in Montreal and within a year had their first child whom they named Margaret Pringle Redpath, Pringle being Jane's mother's maiden name. Also in 1836, John purchased a substantial lot of ground from the Des Rivières family on the slopes of Mount Royal amounting to 235 acres and costing £10,000. On this site a huge new home was built, which John named Terrace Bank. Whether his earlier house contained too many memories for John or whether Jane felt the need to be in a new location is not known, but they moved into Terrace Bank even before all the ground work and drives were completed and leased their previous home to John's brother Robert.

While for John Redpath personally the 1830s were generally years of success and prosperity, for Quebec they were a time of economic and political unrest with the growing dissatisfaction of the French-Canadian majority towards the English-speaking minority who effectively controlled the governmental machinery. This led to an increasingly vocal and later militant minority of radical French-Canadian reformers who became know as the *Patriotes* under Louis Joseph Papineau. During the 1834 elections (which were marked by *Patriote* violence and intimidation), the radical elements swept to a major victory in the Assembly. This caused grave concern among the English in Lower Canada, who had always been a minority but who now were deprived of a voice in the elected house. Numerous groups sprang up among the English opposition and one of these, the Constitutional Association, had a strong supporter in John Redpath who helped draft the statement presented to the British authorities

Terrace Bank.

A rear view of Terrace Bank in early springtime, showing the commanding panorama of the city enjoyed by John Redpath and his family.

Looking from Terrace Bank down Redpath Lane,
now called Mountain Street.

The front gates of the Terrace Bank property, located at the present-day site of Sherbrooke Street and Mountain Street.

The conservatory at Terrace Bank.

in England on the concerns of the "English" party:

> *The members of the Constitutional Association claim no privileges over their fellow subjects of another origin; but the experience of the late years has shown a determination on the part of the majority of the Assembly of that origin to make of the power ... an instrument for controlling the Metropolitan Government, and for reducing their fellow subjects of British and Irish origin to a condition of inferiority without regard to the public utility or the principle of equal justice.*[3]

On October 23, 1837, the Loyalist forces held a rally in Place d'Armes in front of the Bank of Montreal, when calls were made for the reinstating of representation for the English-speaking minority in the Assembly. Prominent in the leadership of this event were the Honourable Peter McGill, John Molson Jr., and John Redpath, all members of the board of the bank. In retaliation, two weeks later the *Patriotes* raised a liberty pole in Place d'Armes with a "liberty" or French Revolutionary cap at its summit. This was an open challenge to the government authorities, revealing the true nature of the *Patriotes* and their aim of total separation into a republic of their own. Violence broke out as militant elements of both sides of the argument clashed in the streets of Montreal. Open rebellion now broke out across the colony, with small battles being fought at the villages of St. Denis, St. Charles, and St. Eustache, in which the *Patriotes* "army" was repeatedly defeated, suffering numerous casualties.

John Redpath recognized that this was not the time to keep his family in Montreal, where martial law was in force. Therefore, Jane and most of the children went to stay with Elspeth at Jones Falls, while Peter, at age sixteen, was sent to boarding school in England. John remained in Montreal organizing support for the Loyalist cause. Early in January 1838, John drafted a letter to another member of the Constitutional Association, James Holmes, expressing his dissatisfaction with the current efforts to project the cause of the Loyalist element.

> *I address myself to you as having been the active member of the Committee ... for the editorship of the "Morning Courier". According to my understanding he [Dr. Barber, the editor] was to conduct the paper in accordance with our political views. Of which the declaration put forth by the Constitutional Association was to be the basis. And that he was to advocate at all times the views and interests of the great majority of the Constitutionalists. ... In my*

opinion ever since the commencement of the present rebellion the editorial matter of the paper has been sadly deficient and in many respects directly calculated to injure the Constitutional cause ... instead of warmly advocating our cause he has studiously avoided the question. For fear no doubt of giving offense to his patrons. Such conduct is however unpardonable and will no doubt meet the indignation of every man who wishes to see the country freed from its present thraldom.[4]

The political situation continued to fester throughout the summer and fall of 1838 until November 8, when a *Patriote* force attacked a Loyalist garrison at Odelltown. Following a sharp battle, the *Patriotes* were totally defeated. This marked the end of the rebellion in Lower Canada, as swift reprisals of twelve hangings, fifty-eight deportations,

The headquarters for the Bank of Montreal on Place d'Armes.

and two banishments established a strong element of authority once more. Jane and the children returned to Montreal, and within a year the couple had their second child, named George Drummond Redpath after Jane's father.

In 1840, the British Parliament debated the future of Canada and John Redpath travelled to Britain to speak on behalf of the Constitutional Association before the committee of both houses dealing with an "Act for the Constitution of Canada." After much deliberation, the British government decided to join the separate provinces of Upper and Lower Canada into a single united province in July 1840.

During the next few years, the Redpath family continued to expand with two daughters Wilhemmina (1841) and Isabella (1844), although Wilhemmina died after only nine months; outside the family, John's business activities from 1841 to 1844 seem to have centred on the Bank of Montreal and its business expansions into Canada West (Ontario) at Toronto, Bytown, Kingston, St. Catharines, St. Thomas, and Amherstburg. In 1844, the bank appointed John to a committee to study the feasibility of enlarging the existing headquarters erected in 1818 or building on a new site elsewhere in the city. When the committee reported back in 1845, it recommended that the 1818 building be abandoned and that a new structure be erected nearby. As a result, John was deeply involved with the architect and contractors during all stages of the completion of the new building, which is still in existence today on Place d'Armes.

The start of 1846 brought a mixture of tragedy and happiness to John and Jane when Isabella died in January, and their fifth child, Francis Robert, was born in February. Meanwhile the Canadian economy began to falter when the British Parliament instituted a strong free trade policy and repealed the legislation that gave Canadian corn and wood a preference in importing to Great Britain. But more significantly, it did not repeal the Navigation Laws, which retained exclusive rights of shipping in the St.Lawrence River for vessels of British registry. This combination of action and non-action spelled economic disaster to the merchants and business interests of Montreal, John Redpath included. At the same time, the American authorities established Canada as a separate tariff entity instead of being classed simply as a British outpost. This was accomplished by a drawback law, which permitted foreign goods to enter the U.S. duty free if they were to be re-exported to Canada. This had an immediate effect on Canada with the establishment of the St. Lawrence and Atlantic Railroad to connect Montreal and Portland, Maine, and other similar lines that would allow goods to be shipped to Canada West via the United States instead of by Montreal.

The result was that 1848 brought large financial losses for everyone in either the mercantile or business field in Montreal as the economy continued to worsen under the combined activities of British free trade attitudes and U.S. drawback legislation. Some British banks even refused to issue loans or credit for Canadian investments. The Montreal merchants were certain that the blame for their plight centred on the government in Britain, which seemed to be abandoning Canada. The problem was further compounded in February 1849 when Louis Hippolyte Lafontaine proposed a controversial bill in the assembly to repay the residents of Lower Canada who had suffered financial losses during 1837 and 1838. Unfortunately, the wording of the bill was deliberately designed to allow former rebels to qualify for compensation. When tabled, this bill was greeted with outrage by the Tory opposition. When it actually passed into law later in the year and was approved by the Governor General, word quickly spread throughout the city. That evening a huge crowd gathered at the Parliament buildings, and an extreme element broke into the building and set it ablaze. We know that John was not involved in this incident, being in attendance at the birth of his new son, Charles Andrew (who unfortunately died the following June at fifteen months.) The next day, Parliament convened at the Bonsecours Market and decided to relocate to Toronto.

In this environment of political bitterness and frustration grew a rationale that the time had come for a distinct split of Canada away from the rule of Britain, and an alliance with and annexation by the United States. In October 1849, the *Annexation Manifesto* was published, proposing "... a friendly and peaceful separation from British connections and a union upon equitable terms with the great North American Confederacy of sovereign States ... ."[5] Within ten days, more than 1,000 signatures were on the petition for annexation. Most of the signatures were English in origin and included almost every prominent merchant in Canada East, including the Molsons and John Redpath.

At the inaugural meeting of the association, John Redpath acted as chairman. Following numerous motions, the resolution defining the association's goal of annexation with the United States was passed unanimously. Once published, the *Annexation Manifesto* attracted the official attention of the government. All those who signed the document were called upon to explain themselves, and all concerned were stripped of any titles or offices. As a result, John was forced to resign as a trustee of the Montreal Turnpike Commission but he maintained his unrepentant stand.

Generally the annexation movement of 1849 was confined to Montreal and its immediate vicinity. It gained little support in Canada West and it was staunchly opposed by both the Conservative and Reform elements of the government. Subsequently, support for the movement failed and quickly evaporated with changes in the economy due to a bumper harvest in 1849 and the repeal of the Navigation Laws.

Following the dissolution of the annexation movement and the improvement of the economy, John Redpath recognized that simply relying on various investments would not secure his family's future. Therefore he began to investigate various aspects of manufacturing, with a plan to establish a centre of production in one field or another. Some of the ideas he investigated included a cotton mill, an iron foundry, copper works, and a steamship line. But since each of these already had businesses well established, and John felt that he would be at a disadvantage in starting up in the face of such competition, he struck out at a complete tangent to his previous considerations and looked at a business totally without competition inside Canada, namely sugar refining.

In 1850, he left Jane with their latest child, Augusta Eleanor, while he travelled to Great Britain to study various refineries in operation in London and Greenock, Scotland. He planned to undertake another tour the following year, but on July 9, 1852, a major fire broke out in Montreal's east end. Fanned by brisk winds and made worse by a shortage of water in the city's reservoirs, the conflagration engulfed hundreds of buildings, leaving thousands homeless. Within days, a Committee of Relief was established among the more influential citizens of Montreal, including John Redpath. Such was the effort put in by the committee throughout the rest of the year that the relief fund collected more than was needed to cover the costs, and a small surplus was distributed to local charities.

John Ostell, the architect for the Canada Sugar Refinery.

Determined on his choice of a new industry, John returned to Great Britain in 1853, again leaving Jane to care for their newest child, Emily Jane Bonar. Accompanying John on this trip was his son Peter and Peter's wife, Grace. Together John and Peter finalized details for the production of appropriate machinery to be installed in the factory upon completion. They also visited Edinburgh to see John's old employer, George Drummond, and talked with one of his younger sons, George Alexander Drummond, who was twenty-four years old and completing his education at Edinburgh University. Whether this was the first meeting between John, who was now fifty-seven, and George Alexander, we do not know. But we do know that it resulted in a subsequent life-long partnership.

Meanwhile back in Montreal, John had left John Ostell, a well-known local architect, to draw up plans for the new facility. Ostell had previously worked with John Redpath on the Notre Dame Church project and had been commissioned on his own in earlier years for the Government Custom House, the Court House on Notre Dame Street, St. Jacques Church, and parts of McGill University.

The time had come for the building of a Sugar House.

This panoramic view gives a very good impression of the site chosen by John Redpath for his new enterprise. In the distance, the city of Montreal and St. Lawrence River can be seen.

CHAPTER THREE

The Building Of A Sugar House

Having made the decision of what business manufactury to undertake, John Redpath wasted no time in making preparations. He had long kept in mind the advantageous situation of the land next to the Priests Basin on the Lachine Canal and its adjacent water-driven power plant. In August 1853, John initiated purchases of land from the Gentlemen Ecclesiastics of the Seminary of St. Sulpise of Montreal. More purchases followed in December from John Ostell, who had previously bought the adjacent land areas from the aforementioned gentlemen in June. This necessitated a number of negotiated settlements where traffic access was to be altered from the original "greenfield" plans, and the blocking of the proposed Richmond Street extension had to be agreed to. Further, since John Ostell maintained land on the opposite side of the basin, John had to agree to avoid blocking John Ostell from access to his side of the basin. In return, John Redpath was given the right to erect a wharf on his side of the basin and to deepen the entrance to the basin from the canal (at his own expense). John also lost no time in contacting the authorities and attempted to pull a few strings to gain some relief on the duties payable for the machinery necessary for the fitting out of the refinery. His letter to the Honourable Francis Hincks, Inspector General on December 8,1853, makes interesting reading:

> *Being engaged in the erection of a large manufactory for the making and refining of sugar, which involves and will involve a large outlay of capital, I take the liberty of addressing you on the subject, prompted by the conviction that it is the desire, as it is the interest and duty of the Government, to afford every possible encouragement to such an enterprise, to solicit the government now to allow as much of the Iron and Copper work as may not be suitably obtained here, to be imported at an ad valorem duty of 2½ per cent. I may take leave also to express my expectation, that upon the same grounds of encouragement to Home Manufacturing enterprise, the Government will, on the earliest revision of the tariff of duties, allow a corresponding reduction to be made on the duty payable on the raw material required in the manufacture and refining of sugar.*[1]

Meanwhile the excavations for the sugar house went ahead as long as the ground was unfrozen. Throughout the following months, tenders were submitted and building contracts were agreed upon with several of the larger construction companies within the district. There is little doubt that all of these contractors were well known to John Redpath personally through all his years in the contracting business. Nor is there any doubt whatsoever that John intended to stamp his personal mark of quality upon the enterprise, as the dozens of pages of specifications held by the company archives, covering every detail of the construction testify. Short of reprinting the mass of papers, one cannot fully appreciate the obvious determination of John to have his sugar house stand as a landmark both of construction skills and business daring within the city of Montreal and the country as a whole. However, space forbids such a testament and some extracts must suffice instead. In a contract for the masonry work with Augustin Laberge, some of the specifications included that Laberge would:

> *Perform and execute all the masonry and cut stone work requisite and necessary in the erection of a Sugar House near St. Gabriel Lock on the Lachine Canal, the foundations of which are now built to the ground line, and which consist of two stories of masonry, mass for chimney, cut stone dressings to door openings, cut stone belt course and cut stone pillars for bearing beams in cellars, the whole to be done and executed in the most substantial and workmanlike manner and in strict conformity with the plans thereof made by John Ostell Architect ... The said Laberge further engages and binds himself to proceed at once in procuring the materials and depositing them on the ground and to proceed with his works that the first Tier of joisting shall be all on, and placed before the First day of April next, and the entire work hereby contracted for, completed and delivered by the fifteenth day of the same month of April, it being understood that should the month of March prove too inclement to complete the first storey of masonry, these periods shall be extended for one week ... it being specially understood ... that should the said architect or John Redpath ... deem the progress of the work insufficient to ensure its completion at the time above stipulated they are hereby authorised ... to employ ... other workmen ... to complete the works ... and all expenses ... shall be chargeable ... out of any monies due ... to Laberge by the said John Redpath ... The whole payable every fortnight (two weeks) as the work progresses, less fifteen per cent to be retained until the final completion of all the works.*
> (December 14, 1853)

Even the corner-stones were designated for a specific "Pierre Picque" style of carving to give ornamentation to the structure. The brickwork contract with the company of Peel and Ward is equally detailed.

> *The brickwork proposed to be employed is to be of the best possible description faced on both inside and outside furnished with a neat pat joint, no four courses to rise more than ¼ inch more than the measure of the bricks themselves ... The work outside and inside English Bond and neither outside or inside courses to be at any time carried up more than 3 courses more than the body of the wall, ... all openings throughout the building to be ... perfectly plumb one over the other ... the whole of the brickwork carefully pointed and grouted clear up to the plates.*
> (December 17, 1853)

Not even the mortar between the bricks was exempt from John Redpath's eagle eye as it was to be

> *Compounded of best fresh lime, burnt from good stone, and used in the proportion of one part of lime and two of sand, and made up in small quantities so as to be used fresh and kept covered when any is left over ... The sand is to be River sand, clear and bright and sharp clear pit sand in proportion, half and half.*
> *(December 17, 1853)*

As to the timetable for construction, Peel and Ward were expected to adhere to as tight a schedule as the stone masons were before them:

> *The masonry being completed and finished the bricklayers to commence their work on or before the first day of May next, or whenever the walls are ready ... to proceed and carry on with all possible despatch the Brickwork with sufficient force to finish and complete a storey in every ten days and the whole five storeys shall thus be completed and finished on or before the thirteenth of June ... The chimney shaft to be entirely completed and capped by the fifteenth day of July next.*
> *(December 17, 1853)*

To top matters, even the clean-up work was covered in John's specifications and contracting:

> *All stains on the face of the work resulting from the employment of grout to be carefully removed.*
> *(December 17, 1853)*

Similar treatment was meted out to the contracting companies of George Brown for the painting and glazing work, and to an unspecified company for the provision of wooden beams and planking for the flooring. By the end of January 1854, John was at the point of ordering the major equipment for the sugar house when a response from the customs department to his earlier request for a relaxation of customs duties arrived, but it was not to his liking. It stipulated that no alterations of the current tariff were possible without legislative authority. This forced John to rapidly reconsider his original proposal to bring in foreign equipment throughout and he instead resorted wherever possible to local manufacturers who, although inexperienced with sugar machinery, could be instructed in the appropriate technology and thus avoid the duties. Messrs. Rice and Lombard of Boston (who had originally tendered for the contract on manufacturing the moulds for the loaves) were advised to obtain a local sub-contractor if they wished to keep Redpath's order while Messrs. Rogers and King of a cast iron foundry only a few hundred yards away on the canal bank were given the authority to cast the major cisterns. Not averse to supporting local industries if they could provide material at a quality equal to that available outside the country, John Redpath offered incentives to the local industrialists as shown in his letter to James MacArthur, ordering bronze bag nozzles for the price of two shillings per pound.

> *And if the work is done to my satisfaction I will allow you three pence (3d) per pound extra which will make it equal to the New York prices. You may therefore go on to make me one hundred and fifty (150) in the first place, to be delivered at the rate of not less than one and a half dozen (say eighteen) per week ... each nozzle to weigh two pounds thirteen ounces (2lb 13oz).*

By early February 1854, things had developed sufficiently for John to notify his son, John James (who was working in Toronto), of the development of the refinery. Unfortunately, this letter has not survived but obviously John James was not aware of his father's activities, nor on the face of it could he fathom what his father referred to because he wrote to his elder brother, Peter (who was still in England with his wife). In his reply letter of February 10, 1854, Peter described matters as follows:

> *Now touching the mysterious letter you received from Papa about business. The reason I did not tell you anything about the new enterprise was that when I saw you last, it had scarcely been decided on and as it was possible it might not be carried out I did not think it wise to unsettle your mind in the least. Now however the matter is a fixed fact. Papa is building a Sugar Refinery, and I suppose that both you and I will be connected with it. It will probably be in operation next August. It is a very great undertaking for any one man as it will require a large capital. I hope however it will repay Papa for all the anxiety attendant upon such a serious outlay of money on a new undertaking. The buildings and apparatus will I think not cost less than twenty thousand pounds; very likely a good deal more. This of course you must keep to yourself. I do not know when you will be required, but I think you will have to complete at least two years with Betley & Kay. I will do what I can to cut it short. Learn all that you can where you are. The discipline will be useful too as you will find in after life ... I should have told you that the sugar house is to be on the Canal bank, about two or three hundred yards above the Wellington Bridge, on the side farthest*

John James Redpath

Peter Redpath

from the town. There will be a basin for our own boats.

Meanwhile back on the canal John Redpath was a constant visitor to the site, inspecting and criticizing the quality of the workmanship to the evident distraction of the contractors. Construction had now reached a point where further contracting was required for the roofing material. Initially it was proposed to use sheet tin, but this was subsequently changed to slate, a substantial alteration when one considers that the roof area was estimated at 70,000 square feet. The firm of Reed and Rayner was given the job on May 18 and once again John's past experiences in the building trade led him to be exacting in his demands:

It being understood that the work shall be executed in the most efficient and workmanlike manner and to my satisfaction, that you undertake to maintain the same tight and in good condition for two years ... and that all the nails be either galvanized or soaked in boiled linseed oil ... the description of the slate to be green Vermont in sizes not less than sixteen inches by eight and not larger than twenty inches by eleven.

With the arrival of the better weather, the pace of construction quickened and the growing size of the structure made it a popular site for outings by the residents of Montreal; several prominent local citizens were given guided tours by John and his newly arrived refinery manager, George Alexander Drummond. Research suggests that John had recognized George's talents during his trip to England the previous year, since the offer to come to Canada resulted in George taking out an insurance policy on his life for £200 in 1853. However, as the insurance company was obviously uncertain of life in the wilds of the Americas, there was an endorsement that George had to adhere to, "to live and travel north of the 38th parallel of Latitude (about Washington D.C.) and east of the Mississippi River."

George Alexander Drummond

Fortunately for the company, at this time the governments of British North America and the United States signed the Elgin-Marcey Agreement or reciprocity treaty by which the mutual abolition or reduction of various customs duties was agreed to. This opened the way for export opportunities for the new company as well as providing for its own Canadian market. On August 12, 1854 and without fanfare, the John Redpath Canada Sugar Refinery opened its doors for business and George Drummond, with his greater technical expertise, oversaw the initial training of the new refinery workers and the working-up trials of the plant.

From the historic point of view, it is unfortunate that very few company documents survive to record the early days of the refinery's activities, and we have to look to external documentation to assess the initial functioning of the business. Not deterred by his earlier failure to persuade the authorities of the need to alter the tariffs on machinery, John tried once again. This time he argued the case for adjustments on the tariff on sugars, and he did not waste time going though middlemen. In a memorial to "The Right

The Canada Sugar Refinery 1854

Honourable James Earl of Elgin and Kincardine, Governor General of British North America and Captain General and Governor in Chief in and over the Provinces of Canada, Nova Scotia, New Brunswick and the Island of Prince Edward, and Vice Admiral of the same etc. etc. etc.," John clearly stated:

The Memorial of the undersigned John Redpath of the city of Montreal,

Respectfully sheweth,

1. That your Memorialist has recently erected in the said City of Montreal and is now nearly prepared to put into operation a Sugar Refinery on a large Scale; and that this is the first Sugar Refinery which has been established in Canada.

2. That a Sugar Refinery in Canada must at present be carried on under very serious disadvantages, among which are the following, viz;
The uncertainty and great expense attending the importation of Raw Sugar during the winter months, and the consequent necessity of laying in a very large Stock before the close of the Navigation.
The impossibility of making sales to any considerable amount while the navigation remains closed; the accumulation of Stock during the winter and the consequent locking up of capital to a much larger extent than in countries more favoured by climate.

3. That your Memorialist understands that it is the intention of the Government to propose a reduction of the duty on Sugar during the present session of the Legislature.

4. That inasmuch as the Refined Sugar known as "White Bastard" which is extensively used in Canada is admitted at the same specific duty as Raw Sugar, a nominal but no real protection is afforded to the Refined Article.

5. That your Memorialist at present holds a large Stock of

Raw Sugar for the purpose of Refining during the coming winter and that for reasons before stated he will be unable to dispose of any considerable quantity of Refined Sugar before the opening of the navigation next Spring; at which time your memorialist supposes that the new Tariff will be in operation.

Your Memorialist therefore prays

1. That he be allowed to refine in Bond for Export with such restriction as your Excellency may deem necessary for the protection of the Revenue.

2. That he be not required actually to pay duty on the Raw material until the Sugar Refined from it be removed from the premises of the Refinery.

3. That he be allowed the benefit of the reduced duty on all the Stock, Refined and Raw which he shall hold when such comes into operation, and

4. That in the contemplated alteration of the Tariff the interests of this and other Refineries which may yet be established may receive Your Excellency's favourable consideration.

And your memorialist will ever pray etc. etc. etc.

John Redpath
Montreal November 6, 1854[2]

On the reverse of the original memorial document some unknown bureaucratic official has penned some notes that reveal the official reaction.

The refining of sugar in Bond is not provided for by law ... [which does give] that privilege, to slaughtering, curing and packing cattle or grinding wheat in Bond, nor does the act confer the power on the Government in Council to remake Regulations ... The present application therefore if entertained will I think require legislative action. It certainly appears to be desirable that Government in Council should be vested with some general powers on the subject applications having been made not only to refine sugar in the present instance but to grind drugs and manufacture candles from tallow in Bond.[3]

Fortunately John Redpath's pleas were not in vain, and early in the new year when actual production commenced, John was elated to see that the customs tariffs were changed in favour of the importation of raw sugar for refining over the bringing in of refined sugar, which, in effect, gave the refinery a basic protection of 48 cents per 100 pounds. Things really did begin to look as if they might just work out.

Within the relatively close-knit business community of Montreal, the opening of the sugar house did not go unnoticed and in a major editorial in the Montreal *Witness* dated March 7, 1855, the following glowing account was published:

REDPATH'S SUGAR REFINERY.

Montreal is no longer a mere Commercial City, a buyer and seller of goods. Availing herself of her central position, and her great facilities, she is making rapid strides in manufacturing enterprise. Along the Canal Basin, Factory crowds on Factory, and the busy hum of industry, and the unceasing clank of machinery tells of the activity within. To those who have watched the gradual rise and extension of this branch of trade, there is nothing extraordinary in

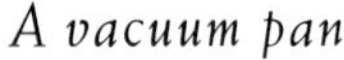

A vacuum pan.

Filling the moulds.

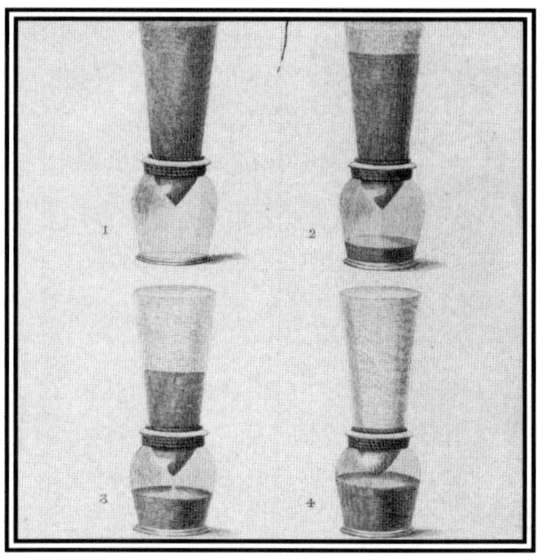

The drainage of the molasses from the sugar by "claying" or "liquoring."

this; but to one returning after a few years of absence, the change appears almost magical.

Among all the enterprises which have been successfully carried out in this locality none is more important in all its bearings, nor more creditable to the projector, than the Sugar Refinery of John Redpath, Esq., which has just commenced operations.

The buildings form a magnificent pile of stone and brick, The main erection measuring one hundred and sixty feet in length, by forty-four, of the same height, exclusive of the boiler house, and charcoal kilns. The whole being by far the largest manufacturing erection in the city. It is designed to manufacture Bastard Sugars from Molasses, and Loaf and Crushed Sugars from Muscovado.

Below the lower story are situated the Molasses Tanks, and dissolving vats, and it is here that the process of Refining commences. Upon entering the spacious room in which the dissolving takes place, we see hogshead after hogshead of Muscovado shovelled into the tank beneath, to be subjected to the joint action of water and steam. Thence the syrup is pumped up to the filters, and being treated with bone charcoal and other chemicals, it parts with its glutinous matter, fecula, and coloring particles. On the second floor of the main building is situated the Steam Pan, in which the syrup is concentrated by being subjected to evaporation at a low temperature.

This pan is a copper sphere of about eight feet, diameter, of the most improved construction, and was manufactured by Benson & Day of New York, at a cost of about $5000: and works four charges a day of 2000 gallons each.

Removing the coarse sugar by "brushing-off" the cone.

Removing any last elements of molasses from the cone by "turning-off."

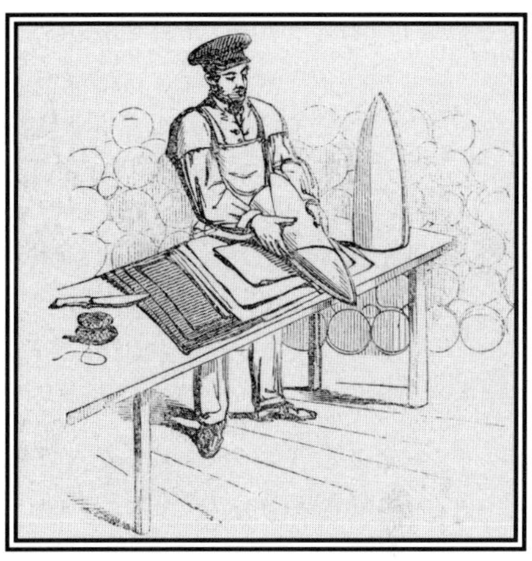

Wrapping the cones with an inside layer of white paper, then an outside layer of blue paper, prior to shipment.

When in full work, the house will require from three to four pans. From the pan, the concentrated syrup falls into sheet iron semi-cylindrical reservoirs on the first flat, where after being vigorously stirred to facilitate its granulation, it is drawn off and emptied into the settling moulds.

These moulds are a very important item of expenditure. They are of sheet iron, rivetted together, of the shape of an over-grown sugar loaf, being near four feet in height, and 16 inches across the base of the cone. There are at present eleven thousand in use, and for full work about thirty thousand will be required. They were manufactured by Mr. Rodden of this city, at a cost over $1 each.

After the syrup has settled in the moulds, they are conveyed by the hoisting apparatus to the floors above, which form each one immense room. The floors are perforated with holes, in which the apex of each conical mould fits. Beneath these holes longitudinal gutters run to convey off the syrup which separates as soon as the plugs are withdrawn.

Here will be seen sugar of every color, from the dark Bastards from Molasses, to the whitest crushed. In each mould will be several shades of color. If it is required purer than the first process leaves it, concentrated syrup is poured on the mass in the moulds, and the coloring matter being more soluble than the sugar, the syrup deposits a portion of its base, as it percolates, and taking up an equivalent of color, runs off as molasses at the bottom.

To promote a rapid granulation, the building has to be kept at a high temperature, which is maintained by means of a series of steam pipes having a diameter of six inches, which pass around each flat; ascending from story to story; these are fed from the boilers, and keep up a degree of heat, rendering any superfluity of clothing very inconvenient. We were shown a quantity of Maple Sugar in course of refining, for the Paris Exhibition; and in point of colour and grain, equal to the best English loaf.

The Refinery is working at the present time forty hogsheads a day, or 70,000 lbs of the value of $3,500 - a quantity, however, far below its capacity; and gives direct employment to eighty men. It is under the superintendence of George Drummond, Esq. The Sugar Boiler is Mr. John Burns, formerly in the Portland Works, a man we are assured, eminently qualified for his position.

The driving power is furnished by an engine of fifty horse power, and the momentum and steam required for the various purposes of "blowing up," supplying the pan and heating the building, produced by four boilers, each 34 feet in length, by 4 feet 4 in. in diameter, having double return flues.

In and adjoining the Boiler House, which is entirely cut off from the rest of the building, are the retorts and kilns in which the bones are converted into charcoal for bleaching the syrup. They require three hundred tons a year, at a cost of from $10 to $16 per ton.

With the exception of the boilers which were built by Bartley and Dunbar, and which are highly creditable to that firm, the whole of the machinery, engine and fittings, were designed, manufactured and erected by Messrs. Milln and Milne, at their works on the Canal Basin.

We cannot conclude this notice without remarking that Mr. Redpath has shown by the immense outlay embarked in this undertaking, and the great capital required for its working, a strong degree of faith in its remunerativeness as a speculation - an opinion which we trust will be more than realized. But there is one measure, not only very necessary to its advantageous working, and at the same time one of general wisdom, and loudly called for by the people - we mean the abolition of the duties upon raw sugars. *And we hope the Ministry will be in a position before long to yield this item of revenue.*

In a subsequent article in the Montreal *Gazette* on March 14, 1855, some further details of the samples for the Paris exhibition mentioned above were revealed in a list of articles selected by judges from the local trades exhibition in Montreal.

Sample of Maple Sugar (brown)
John Redpath & Company, Montreal

Sample of Maple Sugar (white)
John Redpath & Company, Montreal

Sample of Refined (white)
John Redpath & Company, Montreal

Sample of Manilla (white)
John Redpath & Company, Montreal

Sample of sugar made from molasses
John Redpath & Company, Montreal

Sample of Crushed "X" Sugar
John Redpath & Company, Montreal

Sample of Crushed "A" Sugar
John Redpath & Company, Montreal

The next day a follow-up article referred to these samples as follows:

> *The sugars sent by Mr. Redpath deserve the highest praise and show that he has already carried the process of sugar refining to a high degree of excellence. Besides the beautiful white sugars obtained from molasses, and from coarse manilla sugar there were various specimens of refined maple sugar, which possess particular interest as being among our native productions.*

During April, a number of advertisements appeared in newspapers stating quite clearly that the immediate need of the company was ready cash and not long-term credit. This requirement for cash payment in a mercantile system still extensively given over to credit and deferred payments may explain why on the twenty-seventh of March at the Union Sales Room, the first public sale of production of the Canada Sugar Refinery succeeded in selling only one ten-barrel lot of Yellow Bastard sugar for 34 shillings per 100 pounds from a submission of 600 barrels, followed by 20 barrels of molasses from a shipment of 200 at one shilling and five and a half pence per gallon. The rest being withdrawn due to the relative terms of the prices "not being satisfactory" while immediately afterwards a few hogsheads of imported Bright Porta Rico Sugar were sold at 39 shillings and 9 pence per 100 pounds on a discounted bill basis.

Puzzled as to this poor reception for his product, John made some investigations and found out that although the tariff on sugars had been officially changed, the customs inspectors at various importing posts in the country were differing wildly in their interpretation of the new Customs Act's definitions of the various grades of sugar. He immediately despatched an urgent letter to the Commissioner of Customs at Quebec wherein he brought this matter to the attention of the government. Citing the facts that his sales representative had obtained a sample of sugar refined in the West Indies, he wrote

> *But because it was refined ... direct from the cane juice the collector at Toronto considers it to be Raw sugar ... upon the same principle a piece of cotton cloth made on a plantation must be considered raw cotton ... The collector at Toronto further stated ... that all sugars called "White Bastard" would be admitted at 8/6 [8 shillings and 6 pence] but if called "crushed" would be charged 12 [12 shillings]. He takes no account whatever of the clause "other sugar equal in quality to refined Sugar" but looks upon names as the standard for duty.*[4]
> (April 20, 1855)

John then went on to suggest some solutions to the problem, including providing the collectors of customs with instructions on what was to be considered refined sugar, and providing of a standard set of samples for comparison and assessment of the duties.

> *I can see no other mode of ensuring a uniform rate of duty at the different ports, excepting that the rule be established*

> *that all white ... sugars ... shall be considered refined sugar.*[5]
> (*April* 20, 1855)

While waiting for an answer, John received some unexpected support from the Montreal Board of Trade, who complained to Sir Edmund Bond Head, the Governor General of British North America, of similar variations in interpretation between the customs officials at Montreal and the port of Quebec to the detriment of the Montreal importers. Obviously, as in the case of more recent taxation alterations, the new system of classing sugars in 1855 raised more questions than it answered and created much confusion for all concerned. By the end of the year the refinery was running with just over 100 employees and production of 900,000 pounds per month until the closure and draining of the Lachine Canal for the winter suspended the work at the refinery for the season. At the shut-down, the payroll for 1855 was listed as having been £8,000 for the year and the expenses for the plant were listed at £26,500. Stockpiles for the spring season included a full storehouse of 8,000 barrels of refined sugar and 2,500 hogsheads of raw sugar and muscovados.

For the year 1856, literally the only corporate document surviving is a single copy of a letter written by John Redpath to his business neighbour, John Ostell, complaining of the fact that Ostell was trying to bill the refinery for repairs and costs of a pontoon bridge across the entrance to the basin. As John Redpath put it:

> *At the time I purchased your lot on the basin you mentioned that there would be a bridge required ... costing about fifty pounds ... but when you charge me three times that amount for the use of the pontoon bridge for one year–when there is actually no bridge there it becomes a totally different matter, and I am not willing to pay for a bridge that is not in existence.*

Outside of the company, however, John Redpath's activities on behalf of the Bank of Montreal are somewhat better documented. During the year he travelled on behalf of the bank (as the permanent head of the building committee) to inspect the newly purchased sites and buildings for future branches in Canada West (Ontario), including Brockville, Belleville, Coburg, Guelph, and Hamilton. He also supervised the design and construction of many of these sites, some of which still existed up to the mid-1950s.

The refinery continued to develop in a steady fashion during 1857 despite a slump in the Canadian economy, brought on by the effects of a speculative investment "bubble" bursting in New York, which in turn precipitated a major money panic throughout the United States and financial centres of Canada. On June 13, 1857, in recognition of his work done since the start of the company, John took his son Peter into the business as a partner, changing the corporate name to John Redpath & Son, Canada Sugar Refinery, while the business relationship between John Redpath and George Drummond took on a more personal perspective when in September George married John's daughter Helen. Whether this match was a romantic or business union is somewhat uncertain, given the tone of a letter written by George to his elder brother Andrew in Ottawa:

> *It has been arranged that my marriage shall take place on*

George Alexander Drummond in 1868.

Helen Drummond (née Redpath) in 1868.

> *Tuesday 15th inst, rather unexpectedly I must say as I did not anticipate its occurrence so early ... until within the last few days.*

With the arrival of 1858, the long-delayed introduction of decimal currency for Canada came into effect and the methods of keeping books with cross-currency exchange values was eliminated. We are also fortunate that from this point there exists the main corporate ledger for the firm of John Redpath & Son. With its fine red leather cover, gold embossed title, and immaculate copperplate writing, it remains as a testimony to the meticulous records that were kept, recording all aspects of the company activities. For example, at the end of the working year and upon shut-down, the refinery recorded that it had 100 barrels of white sugar in store with 286 sugar loaf moulds of white sugar and 6,181 moulds of Yellow Bastard sugar still in the final stages of drainage. Corporate assets were listed at a value of $176,067.75 and the profit on business for the year at $40,000. As in 1846, happiness and sadness were felt by the Redpath family for in February, Jane gave birth to their last child, William Wood Redpath, followed only three months later by the death of their two-year-old daughter, Harriet Ina Redpath. In a touching memorial to his child, John penned a moving poem:

LITTLE HARRIET

The Lord gave us a beauteous flower
To cherish for a day,
And in the morn His angel sent
To take our flower away.

We prayed the Lord to leave it here
Another little day,
And we would tend and water it,
And keep it from decay.

But Jesus said, 'tis best that I
Ere noon should take it home,
And plant it in my garden fair,
Forever there to bloom.

No chilling blasts nor scorching suns
Shall ever touch it there,
But 'neath my smile this opening bud
Shall blossom ever fair.

Again we prayed that His rich grace
Might unto us be given,
To say, "Lord, let Thy will be done, –
Take our sweet bud to Heaven."

May 28, 1858.

Margaret Redpath with her younger sister Harriet.

The last year of the decade proved to be a bumper year in many respects for both the company and its president. The government readjusted the tariffs, giving a substantial advantage to the company as an indigenous refiner bringing in raw sugar over the commercial wholesale importers of refined and semi-refined sugars. At the Bank of Montreal, John was elected Vice-President to replace Thomas B. Anderson, who had taken up the presidency of the bank upon the retirement of Peter McGill. John was also made President of the Board of Governors for the Montreal General Hospital (and there are several reports of his doing duty in the wards as a lay chaplain tending to the spiritual needs of the sick and dying.) His strong religious convictions also show in his acceptance of the presidencies of the Presbyterian Foreign Mission Society and the Presbyterian Labrador Mission. In August, John received an invitation to address a major meeting of the Mechanics Institute in Great Britain, which he regretfully declined due to pressures of business. (It would have been interesting had he accepted the invitation, since it might have been possible for him to have met Henry Tate, who had just established his own sugar business in the United Kingdom.)

By the close of the year, the accounts reported a healthy profit of $89,546.98, while corporate assets had risen by more than 81% to $285,749.72. Even more amazingly, the total value of sugar and syrups, raw, refined and in process, valued out at a substantial $240,348.78, not bad for a mere five years of production.

The mountainous volumes of ice that blocked the St. Lawrence River in winter, almost block the view of the twin towers of Notre Dame Church.

CHAPTER FOUR

"A Growing Concern"

The success of the Canada Sugar Refinery in the later part of the 1850s and its subsequent growth in the early 1860s paralleled to a large extent the progressive expansion of the country as a whole. By 1869, there was a recognition that the time had come to set down formally the terms upon which future business would be based in the Canada Sugar Refinery. Thus in January 1860, Articles of Partnership were drawn up. This document remains as the earliest recorded statement we know of for the express purpose of stipulating the nature of the business relationships, and in reading it we are left in no doubt whatsoever over just who had run the business and made the major decisions up to that point. It also clearly demonstrates John's determination to remain at the helm for the foreseeable future.

ARTICLES OF PARTNERSHIP

The Canada Sugar Refinery was erected by the undersigned for the purpose of establishing a new branch of manufacture in Canada and also with the view of creating a business for his sons.

The business has now been carried on for five years; during the first two viz, 1855 and 1856 by the undersigned alone; and during the last three, viz 1857, 1858 and 1859 in company with his eldest son Peter Redpath under the firm of John Redpath and Son.

It is intended that George A. Drummond shall be admitted to a partnership at a future period should he desire it; and also that my younger sons shall be admitted as partners as soon as they shall be considered by me, competent for the duties which would devolve upon them. They shall receive such share in the business as may be determined by me.

The business shall be divided into twenty one shares of four thousand pounds each of which Peter Redpath now holds five and the undersigned holds the remaining sixteen.

The Capital and profits of each partner shall be applied first towards acquiring property in the sugar house (that is in the real estate and plant of the establishment) to the extent of one half of their respective shares and that being accomplished the partners shall make up their respective shares in the floating capital.

Profits and losses shall be annually estimated on the 31st December.

The profits of the junior partners shall ... be transferred to the credit of the undersigned until such time as their respective shares ... shall be fully paid up.

No partner shall at any time sell or otherwise dispose of any share or part of a share or any interest in the concern excepting to the other members of the firm and then only with the consent of the majority.

No partner shall on any account whatever use the name of the firm for any purpose not directly connected with the business of the firm; nor shall any partner be engaged in any other business whatever or have any interest in any other business; nor shall any partner sign or endorse bills or otherwise become security for any person whomsoever. The undersigned's excepted from the operation of this rule.

In the event of the decease of a partner ... the share of the deceased partner shall not on any account be disposed of otherwise than to the surviving partners.

In the event of the decease of the undersigned his executors shall have the right to retain the shares ... for the benefit of his younger sons ... his intention being that all his younger sons shall have equal shares if they be considered ... competent for the duties devolving upon them.

Any violation of the spirit will necessitate the immediate withdrawal of the offending partner from the concern if required by the majority of the partners.

Montreal January 1860

John Redpath

By the end of the year, although the assets of the company had dropped slightly due to depreciation of equipment values through wear and tear to $245,907.42, the profits were still rising to a respectable $111,868.06. This very success, however, was about to become a double-edged sword, for at this time the imposed "evil" of income taxes did not exist within the country, and the major source of revenue for the government was through the imposition of levies and duties on all goods being imported to satisfy the rapidly growing consumption demands of the population. To most of us today, benefiting from all the consumer food goods that the industrialized world can provide, sugar is a minor if not almost negligible substance (despite its extensive use in various industries) but in the mid-nineteenth century, sugar was a highly visible staple product upon which households depended for cooking and preservation of fruit and some vegetables. Such was the increase in consumption during this period that the revenues derived from sugar imports exceeded virtually every other category in the customs' manifests. The government was not slow to recognize the value of this "milk cow," and in early 1860 across the board ad valorem duties were imposed on refined sugar at forty percent while raw was assessed at thirty percent. This caused a substantial jump in the costs of production to the Canada Sugar Refinery as well as to the numerous importers of foreign sugars; as a result, almost immediately the wholesale and then the retail price of sugar rose. An outcry from the public was only to be expected, but its ferocity caught even the government off guard, and on June 30, 1860, the rates of duty were lowered to 35% on refined imports and 25% on raw. Slightly mollified, the outraged populace slowly forgot the issue, but for the company it was a portent of things to come.

With the new year came an expansion for the company as John James Redpath (John's last child by his first marriage) and George Alexander Drummond were taken into the business as partners, although the business name "John Redpath & Son" remained in the singular grammatic form.

Following the regular Christmas period shut-down the refinery resumed work in the early part of February 1861, but the annual problem of ice on the St. Lawrence River made it necessary to maintain a close watch because an ice jam could cause a sudden rise in water levels, which would endanger the refinery area. Nothing happened however, and the watch was relaxed. But on April 15, 1861, an ice jam did occur, and water rapidly rose to within inches of the lip of the Lachine Canal and only two feet below the floor level of the main raw sugar shed.

Montreal, 19 Sept 1861

Messrs. Pigeon & Co

Bought of JOHN REDPATH & SON.

—Under ten barrels, Net Cash on delivery; Ten barrels and upwards, 60 days. All credit accounts will be drawn for & Bank Commission added.

4 Barrels Crushed A Sugar

265 18
260 21
245 19
252 17

1022 - 75 = 947 10½ $103 00

Received payment
J Redpath & Son
24 Sept/61 Per Louis Campbell

Another situation that John Redpath felt required close watching was the outbreak of Civil War in the United States. The trade in raw sugar with the islands of the West Indies was now in danger of interruption by the navies from both sides of the conflict. Wanting to clarify his position, John drafted an enquiry to the Honourable Charles Alleyn, the Provincial Secretary at Quebec.

> *Sir*
> *We beg to call the attention of the provincial Government to a matter in which the interests of Canadian importers of West India produce are now subject to serious danger. In consequence of the existing disturbances in the neighbouring states, cargoes of sugar shipped at a West India port in a vessel carrying the United States flag are liable to capture by privateers sailing under the sanction of the "Southern Confederacy" ... we are desirous to know whether in the event of the capture of a cargo belonging to a British Subject a claim for compensation would be allowed by the United States Government ... We have seen in newspapers, a report ... made ... that losses sustained by French subjects ... would be made good by the Federal [U.S.] Government ... It would be satisfactory to us and ... to all other Canadian importers of West India produce if the Provincial Government would ascertain ... the intentions of the U.S. Government ... to matters of this kind and officially make such intentions known.*[1]
> (May 9, 1861)

Other incidents between the United States and Great Britain (such as the Trent Affair when Confederate agents were forcibly taken off a British merchant ship by men of the U.S. warship U.S.S. *San Jacinto*, as well as highly belligerent statements by the U.S. government against Britain for selling goods to the Confederates) led to a worsening of relations. The situation became so serious that war between the U.S. and Great Britain was a distinct possibility, and the threat of an invasion of Canada by Union troops loomed large. This threat resulted in the large-scale shipping of British troops to Canada to defend the border. Within the various and separate provinces, local regiments of militia were raised as they had previously been raised during the War of 1812 and the 1837 rebellion period. George Alexander Drummond quickly signed up with one of these regiments, the Royal Guides. An anonymous friend of George's described this regiment as "a troop of picked cavalry composed of young men mounted on their own horses and all good cross country riders ... and in this troop he did duty." Additionally, John James Redpath served for a time in the Victoria Rifles Regiment, while for the young daughters of the family this was also an exciting time, as:

> *England poured her choicest troops into the City. The streets were bright with uniforms - the scarlet tunics and the bearskin shako's of the Guards, the floating plumes of the Highland Regiments. The dark green, quick stepping columns of the rifles, the blue uniforms of the hussars and the gold lace and dark blue of the horse artillery made the streets flash with colour under the bright blue sky.*[2]

For John Redpath this period represented both an opportunity and an additional expense. The opportunity came in the form of contracts to supply the troops with sugar, and subsequently substantial quantities were supplied to the military commissariat. The additional expense came in the form of marine insurance, for up to that point only the occasional cargo had been covered by insurances. Now all cargoes were required to have not only insurance but also a special war premium that represented more than 25% extra in the way of costs to get the raw sugar. Fortunately, the additional sales to the military allowed the year end profits to accrue to a total of $265,540.52. Allowing for the clauses in the partnership agreement (whereby profit was deducted for the development of the capital of the business), the net profit came to $153,672.46, while the assets rose to $369,424.43.

We are fortunate in having an outsider's view of the "sugar house" and its surroundings at this time, from an article published in *English America or Pictures of Canadian Places and People* by Samuel Phillips Day. Mr. Day was a visitor to Montreal in 1862 as a correspondent for the English newspaper, the London *Herald*. His account of the factories along the Lachine Canal gives a clear impression of the growing industrialization of the area as he described iron works, flour mills, marine foundries, saw mills, candle works, and India rubber works, as well as the refinery of John Redpath & Son.

> *Within the past five or six years ... a variety of manufacturing resources have been developed along the banks of the Lachine Canal ... factories and mills are closely congregated; the machinery of each being altogether worked by means of water power. One leading feature of these establishments is, that machinery is made to do what in the old country is accomplished by human hand. In Canada labour of this description is scarce; and hence ingenuity ... has been exercised to beneficial purpose ...*

The Sugar Refinery is ... an object of interest ... About seven-eights of the white sugar consumed in the Province are produced here; the remainder being imported from various countries when the price happens to fall a little lower than the current value of that article in Montreal. The Capacity of the Works is equal to the requirements of Upper and Lower Canada for several years to come; that is if immigration does not set in very rapidly. The great difficulty experienced consists in the extremely limited market that the country affords for refined sugar. For this reason the manufacture of the commodity is discontinued during two or three months every year. The quantity of raw sugar consumed in Canada is estimated at about seven thousand tons annually; the product being white and yellow sugar, and a moderate quantity of syrup. The refinery establishment of Messrs. Redpath and company is very complete being replete with every modern improvement ... The animal charcoal required in the manufacture is made on the premises, the gas from the bones being used to light the same.[3]

Within the company, the new partners were beginning to stretch their wings, and after considerable discussion and probably a few arguments, it was agreed in June 1862 that a new copy of the Articles of Partnership needed to be written. In studying this version and comparing it to the previous document of 1860, there are signs that although John Redpath was determined to retain overall control of the company, the combined forces of economic changes and the driving personality of George Drummond in particular were having their effects in changing the company. Some of the points included:

1. The business shall be divided into twenty-one shares of which John Redpath shall hold eight; Peter Redpath five, George Alexander Drummond five and John James Redpath three. John Redpath shall have the right to transfer one or more of his shares to any other of the above named partners should he at any time see fit to do so; and also to give any or more of his younger sons an interest in the business by bestowing upon him or them the whole or any portion of his shares.

2. The partnership shall be for the term of seven years from the first day of January 1861.

3. The Working Capital over and above the Sugar House property required to carry on the business satisfactorily is now estimated at £60,000/-/-. On the first day of January last 1862 John Redpath had $207,218.20, Peter Redpath had $7,879.44, George Alexander Drummond had $10,228.01 and John James Redpath had $1,415.38 of working Capital.

4. The Capital and profits of Peter Redpath, George Alexander Drummond and John James Redpath are applied first towards acquiring property or ownership in the real estate and plant of the establishment ...

5. No partner shall on any account whatever use the name of the firm for any purpose not directly connected with the business of the firm; nor shall any partner be engaged in any other business or have any interest in any other business. This article is not to be held as preventing investments of profits over and above the capital required for the business in property or in joint stock companies such as Banks, Insurance Companies, Telegraph Companies or similar enterprises.

> *6. In the event of a partner wishing to withdraw from the business at the expiration of the term of partnership, the remaining partners shall be allowed one year if they require it, before being called upon to pay out the share of working capital of the withdrawing partner.*

It is interesting to note from clause 3, that even at this early date, George had acquired significantly more working capital than the longer-serving Peter Redpath.

Further discussions later in the year persuaded John Redpath to alter the requirements that the monies invested in the actual buildings and machinery should no longer be untouchable, and in future the finances were altered to represent a form of "rental" of the property from the individual owners to the business, for which a "rent" would be assessed for payment to each partner. Thus, net profits for the year of 1862 slipped slightly from those of 1861 to $142,577.70 but the capital assets continued to accrue to just below one half million dollars.

Despite the ongoing uncertainties caused by the American Civil War, the year 1863 was one of decision and change for the company, as George Drummond pushed for, and got, a commitment for a radical expansion and modernization of the refinery. Throughout the year, old equipment was replaced by more efficient pieces and in some cases entirely new innovations were added. The largest investment was in the installation of a much larger vacuum pan than the one originally installed and in a letter to the manufacturers, Messrs. James Duff & Sons, Greenock, George requested:

> *Will you oblige me with an estimate accompanied with full*

John Redpath in 1862, at the age of sixty-six.

detailed specifications on a copper pan 10 ft. 6 inches outside diameter and not more than 3 ft. 3 inches the other way ... the shape may be a little unusual but will present no difficulties in execution ... I am desirous of having it all complete in one piece having coils in it furnished with cocks, fittings, valves of every kind all ready to connect, and for this purpose you will oblige me by enquiring of some of the shipping agents whether a package of that bulk can be safely stored in a ship for this port. No doubt it will require to go on deck. What is wanted is a first class article, so far as working qualities are concerned, every part of sufficient strength, being on the heavy side.
(June 9, 1863)

Another significant investment was in centrifugal machines, which were revolutionizing the sugar industry in Europe. Based upon the large washing machine/spin dryers used in laundries, the centrifugals achieved in minutes the draining of the molasses, which previously took weeks to accomplish using sugar cone moulds. These centrifugals were the way of the future and George knew it, so the initial installation of four units in 1863 was a good start towards the total conversion of the refinery away from the making of loaves, which for the time being continued as well.

On another front, George had less success in the running of the daily business. While George Drummond's relationship with Peter and John Redpath was generally cordial and that with John James exceptionally good, a younger son, George D. Redpath, was being far from satisfactory in his attendance or application to work to the point that George Drummond instructed George Redpath to leave the office. The resulting conference with John Redpath (who was planning to give George Redpath a position as partner) is not recorded but we do know that for some days relationships were extremely strained around the refinery. About a month later, George Drummond wrote a letter to John Redpath on the matter:

I ought to mention to you that I went to George some time ago upon the important question of his re-entering the office ... I hesitated long before doing so ... because I feared my silence would confirm suspicions (on your part) ... that I had a prejudice against his coming back. After a careful consideration of my interests and inclinations I told him in substance that neither of these would in the least degree oppose his return to the office, provided he came back to work and I proceeded to point out the responsibilities which he would require to assume, which would be no sinecure because as a junior partner he would require to devote all his energies to his work. I believe a place could be well filled in this business by some one who would, by giving great attention, relieve Peter from details. Whether George could do this I doubt, and while I carefully abstained from offering him any advice ... there can be no harm, I think, in my telling you that I don't anticipate much good from his coming back to the office. It would certainly be a very lame conclusion to his university career, and as he left avowing that he despised sugar. I fear his experience since will not have changed his mind and that it will be a very dangerous spirit in a future partner ... I believe George would make a good figure in a profession if fairly launched on his own recognisance.
(March 16, 1863)

Apparently John Redpath paid some attention to this letter and the additional talks he had with Peter and George, for shortly thereafter, George D. Redpath dropped out of the business and moved to England where he enrolled in the Church of England as a trainee minister.

As well as the modernization and developments mentioned above, the company was able to expand its local land holdings through the purchase of a number of lots from John Ostell, who had suffered some financial setbacks and was selling off many of his properties. All these expenditures took their toll on the net profits, but boosted the listed assets to substantially break the half-million-dollar mark. Not content with these successes, George Drummond pressed for more modernization and on the eighth of February 1864, he wrote to Manlove Alliot and Company, Nottingham, England, ordering another four 40 inch diameter centrifugal machines and two pairs of engines. However, like John Redpath before him, he was unstinting in his demands to get the best from any expenditure he made and criticized any faults he might find.

> *We beg to call your special attention to the fact that the inner flat bottoms in all the machines you have sent to us have been very imperfectly seamed, in consequence of which it, in almost every machine, has got loose and the sugar getting in-between the bottom, necessitated its removal. Unless therefore you can make the present order very much stronger, be pleased to leave out the inner bottoms ... We wish you also to keep this in view. That we desire to keep pace with all the improvements of the day and if you have made any improvement since the last were got, we wish to have it embodied in them.*

Even outside the refinery, George took his responsibilities of maintaining the area very seriously, and when the problem of the condition of the adjacent Lachine Canal and its locks and bridges was raised by local residents and small businesses, George consulted with John, Peter, and John James Redpath and then proceeded to lobby for an improvement of conditions. As he put it in his letter of March 16, 1864, to General A.A. Dorion, the local Member of Parliament:

> *In consequence of the rapid increase of the population of the area, the foot traffic over the lock gates is yearly increasing and the ... danger, especially after nightfall cannot be overstated. The Corporation of the City defer all improvement in the locality till the location of the [proposed] bridge is decided upon, and consequently the condition of the approaches is simply disgraceful. Not less than five flumes ... have to be crossed at this point on temporary crossings (they cannot be called bridges) of logs and planks put down by the mill owners and in a constant condition of disrepair. Under these circumstances it cannot be a matter of surprise that loss of life is continually occurring, not less than five cases have come to my personal knowledge within the last three or four years ... a large number of our own workmen who supported you at the last election reside in the neighbourhood and daily use the present perilous means of crossing.*

In a related problem, the small bridge across the entrance to the Priests Basin was in a poor state of repair and John Redpath and his neighbour, Mr. Dickson, agreed to split the cost of repairs, while Dickson hired men to do the work. When they didn't turn up, Redpath was asked to supply the men to do the labour, to which he agreed. He later objected, however, when he was also asked to pay half the material costs as well as having supplied all the labour.

With much of the internal renovations complete, the company now turned to the question of improving its supply system for the raw sugar. Enquiries were made of various shipbuilders around Quebec City on the costs of building a ship for the company. In addition, they imported some barrels of beet sugar to investigate its qualities relative to the normal cane raws. George Drummond even went to the extent of privately purchasing some sugar beet processing machinery and beet seeds to try to interest local farmers in establishing a new crop, but in this he had no success, and the matter was dropped. Elsewhere during the year, Peter Redpath was honoured by his election to the Board of Governors for McGill University, establishing a connection that was to last until Peter's death, and that would greatly benefit the university.

In August, tragedy struck the Drummond household when George's young daughter Helen died of hydrocephalus while on vacation with the family at Tadoussac. George was devastated and blamed himself, as he had left the child when he was called away urgently to New York on business. For many weeks, George could hardly face anyone and it was not until December that he unburdened himself in a letter to his sister Agnes in Scotland. Having released his inward guilt and anger, George returned to the business, just in time to engage in another quarrel between the company and Mr. Dickson over the boundary fence situated on Dickson's side of the property. This fence was in a severe state of dilapidation, and when pressed to repair it, to maintain the security and appearance of the area, Dickson moved the fence almost four feet across into Redpath property. Recognizing the need to let George "blow off some steam", John, Peter, and John James let George give Dickson "both barrels" and in a letter of December 22, 1864, George not only "blasted" Dickson for his appropriation of Redpath Company land, but he also criticized Dickson for his poor attitude towards the local area, his monopolistic use of the basin area in contravention of their contract, and the filling of the basin with lengths of lumber for his business. No letter or evidence of a reply from Dickson is known to exist but within a week the fence had been quietly re-located and the basin cleared.

A Redpath family wedding.

CHAPTER FIVE

"Growing Concerns"

On the tenth anniversary of the first production of sugar by the Canada Sugar Refinery, the senior employees submitted a letter of appreciation to the management. This note clearly indicates the normally precarious life of a worker who fell ill during these times when there were no pensions or workers' compensation to fall back on. It also shows that within the company there was a paternalistic consideration by the partners of workers' needs, especially in times of sickness or trouble:

> TO MESSRS. JOHN REDPATH & SON
>
> *Gentlemen,*
>
> *We the Undersigned Employees at the* CANADA SUGAR REFINERY *beg to return you our sincere thanks for the kind present we have each of us received at the commencement of the New Year, and we gladly embrace the opportunity not only to express our gratitude for this particular instance of your liberality, but also for the consideration you have always shown us in continuing to pay us our wages in Bankable Currency, thereby saving us from the loss we should otherwise sustain through the depreciation in the value of silver.*
>
> *Many of us have also to be grateful for the especial acts of kindness of which we have been the recipients, when unable from sickness to attend to our ordinary duties, and we are all desirous of joining our acknowledgments, with the friends of those who have died while in your employment, for the advice and assistance which you are ever ready to afford them.*
>
> *Wishing you a continuance of health and prosperity, and a very happy New Year,*
>
> *We are, Gentlemen,*
>
> *On behalf of the Employees of the Canada Sugar Refinery,*
>
> *Your Obedient Servants,*
>
> *James Robertson, Jas. McMenamin, Thos. Murphy,*
> *John Bennett, Jas. Conolly, Wm. Clarke,*
> *J. W. Grose, Alex. Bower, Frank Corbin,*
> *W. J. Madden, Peter Gillespie, Chas. Sweeny.*
> *(January 2, 1865)*

Early in 1865, after ten years of being Canada's only sugar refinery, the first elements of competition to the firm of John Redpath & Son appeared in the person of George Gordon Dustan of Saint John, New Brunswick. As will be seen in subsequent years, Mr. Dustan was an impulsive entre-preneur who tended to spend first and complain later, and his poor business success rate reflected this attitude. For example, in March of 1865, having already spent $40,000 to establish a refinery at Saint John, he decided that he should have chosen Halifax instead. Unwilling to accept that the financial die was cast, he submitted a memorial to Sir Richard Graves MacDonnell, the Lieutenant Governor for Nova Scotia, whereby he offered to uproot his operation and transfer it to Halifax if Sir Richard would just do him "a few favours," including dropping all duties on the importation of machinery to Halifax from Saint John, giving a bonus to the company if it exported sugar and syrup, and allowing the company to pay a reduced duty on all the sugar it refined. As a carrot to the province, Dustan claimed the capital investment would be $200,000, the consumption of local coal would reach 2,500 tons per year, and sixty men would be employed. As he put it:

> *The large expenditure named, the constant employment of so many hands and the enormous importation of raw material bearing duty would of themselves prove of essential advantage to the Province.*

On its own, this memorial would have certainly failed, but Dustan succeeded in his submission because he played on the inter-provincial jealousies of the governments and the past success of Redpath's efforts in order to goad the Lieutenant Governor by stating:

> *Your memorialist would especially direct your attention to the fact that in the event of free trade in manufactures between the colonies, a manufacture such as the one contemplated could be advantageously worked in this Province and could successfully compete and undersell in the market the older establishment in Canada ... the interception ... of the raw material at Halifax before reaching Canadian manufactories would ... stimulate the trade ... of the Province.*[1]

Shortly thereafter, George Dustan set up the second sugar refinery in Canada when the above mentioned equipment was relocated to Halifax.

In April, the annual spate of flooding at Montreal was causing concerns for the company, as water crept within a short distance of the refinery warehouses. This threat kept George Drummond and the men of the refinery quite busy as the stocks were moved to upper floors of the buildings to prevent damage. Still not completely over the loss of his daughter, George's worries over possible flooding and Dustan's activities in the Maritimes were compounded by the Molson family, who, not content to remain in their brewing, shipping, and banking fields, were actively investigating the construction of a sugar refinery in Montreal to compete with the Redpath facility. Recognizing the economic danger this represented, John Redpath & Son approached the Molson family and offered to open their books to allow the Molsons to see for themselves that if there was only one refinery in Canada it could prosper, two might just survive, but three would be economic suicide. In a letter to J.H. Molson and Bros., George Drummond outlined the status of the Canadian sugar industry at this time.

MEMORANDUM FOR MR. MOLSON

- *The working capacity of our establishment is equal to 400 barrels a day*

- *Last year we produced and sold an average of 148 barrels a day and this was fully up to any previous year*

- *Of this quantity (148 barrels) there were 81 barrels a day of white refined of all qualities and 67 of every other kind*

- *During the first six months of the year the importation of refined sugar amounted to 795 barrels on an average of 10 ½ barrels a day for that period*

- *The returns for the last half of the year are not yet published but the importation of Refined Sugar was almost nil the average for the year is less than 3 barrels a day*

- *The total consumption therefore of the country last year was 84 barrels a day and a larger proportion of imported sugar was prevented by our prices being kept below the cost of bringing it here*

- *The consumption of refined sugar in Canada are found shortly after beginning to be about 60 barrels a day - and it has now got up to 84 in a period of ten years*

The consumption of sugar of every kind (foreign and home made) in Canada has amounted to the quantities in the following table:

Per head of the population - exclusive of Maple Sugar

1854	16½ lbs	1859	14¾ lbs
1855	20½ lbs	1860	11¾ lbs
1856	17¼ lbs	1861	16½ lbs
1857	13 lbs	1862	18 lbs
1858	15½ lbs	1863	14¾ lbs

(April 24, 1865)

And in a covering letter, George continued:

> *Dear Sirs:*
> *In continuation of my conversation with Mr. M. Molson I enclose some figures bearing on the sugar trade of this country. You will be able to verify them by reference to the Board of Trade returns and also by reference to our books - which are open to you for that purpose. This fully bears out I think my assertion - that we are ourselves only half employed - and that there is no reasonable opening for further employment of capital in this business in Canada.*
>
> *Yours Respectfully,*
> *George Alexander Drummond*

Unknown to George, however, the financial outlook for sugar was about to change very rapidly, which subsequently persuaded the Molsons to ignore the advice and enter the sugar business. These changes centred on the continuing war south of the border and the increasing tension between the United States government and the United Kingdom. This made investments highly speculative in nature with the possibility of reaping major gains or suffering total loss. Pressed by its New York agents, the company considered using its profits to invest in gold, diamonds, and raw sugar futures, but George Drummond advocated holding off until things were more settled. As he put it in a letter to Mr. Whitman of the New York office:

> *Our last advices from New York speak of a diamond, gold and sugar boom market ... but neither Peter or I feel safe at this time ... we rather feel disposed to continue our policy of buying for current wants only ... I propose seeing whether sugar can be got from England, at any rate the rates there for refined ... have knocked our price list into a cocked hat.*
> (May 1, 1865)

As the summer wore on, the combination of difficulties of ensuring constant supplies of raw materials and increased war insurance premiums led to a general increase in the prices of raw sugar. This coincided with an exceptionally long and hot summer, which boosted sales considerably and by June, George was notifying Mr. Whitman:

> *Our sales last month were the heaviest we ever had ... our consumption is not less than 1,000 hogsheads a week!*

The time had obviously come to investigate alternative sources to the traditional Caribbean plantations, and Peter Redpath was sent to England to initiate negotiations with some of the major sugar importation syndicates there. During the next few months, George communicated the state of business to Peter in a series of detailed letters that allow us a look at the business thinking of that period.

> *The prices of sugar are going up, it is hard to find good priced raws ... we have now only about 3,000 casks of sugar and 2,200 of meladoes [raw] try to get some.*
> (October 6, 1865)

> *You will find a very excited sugar market reported from New York because you bought at least 250 Tons at the current rate ... well done! ... from this we can realize a profit of from 30¢ to 80¢ per hundred pounds on the prices of today.*
> (October 12, 1865)

> *Prices are now pretty high for sugar but the feeling in New York is that they will be much higher. You know better than I the higher the better ... Excluding war and pestilence or panic from our considerations I am of certainty that prices will go up yet. ... Molsons not yet begun, they bought 500 hogsheads of sugar from us the other day ... [to fulfil orders they had taken but were not able to supply from their own production] ... our prices list has advanced [risen] and now stands*

Loaf Sugar	*12¢ per lb. [wholesale]*
Dry Crushed	*12¾¢ per lb.*
"A" Grade White	*12¼¢ per lb.*
Yellow Grade "2"	*10½¢ per lb.*

> *All efforts to buy raw sugar in New York failed and not a pound can be got there.*
> (October 13, 1865)

On October 16, a rise in the discount rate on bills of exchange stalled the economic trends and precipitated a drop in prices overall.

> *The market is now dull for raws but our sales of refined are*

high we are selling all we make ... our stock of standard syrup is huge I feel inclined to press it off [i.e. sell it cheap to get rid of it] ... no stock whatever of golden syrup ... Today I feel inclined to believe that sugar has seen its highest point.
(October 20, 1865)

Stock increasing ... business of every kind at a standstill ... what a change ... the fact is that our neighbour south of the line have had a little trouble of a financial panic ... which has ... taken the shape of ... an utter cessation of demand for merchandise. You will see all the riders for goods countermanded in England and France.
(October 27, 1865)

The New York market has been shockingly dull, all the fire vanished out of it ... Molson not yet at work he bought another 500 casks.
(November 17, 1865)

We had another drowning in the Canal on Saturday it was Labarge from the stores ... I have managed to sell nearly 700 casks of sugar and molasses here ... all at a fair profit ... our stock of raw sugar today cannot exceed 700 hogsheads. To this must be added our English purchases yet to arrive ... our stock of refined is small, yellows and "A" lows have begun to creep up the last few days.
(November 24, 1865)

Here everything is very dull and our operations at the Refinery are now almost suspended, our sales have gone down nearly to zero ... but there is a good margin yet and I think we can get out very well ... The total sales of refined sugars during the past year have been over seven millions of pounds, an increase of nearly one million pounds in excess of the year before.
(December 1, 1865)

In a final year-end letter to Mr. Whitman, George looked forward to the New Year.

> *Sugars are now pretty well down everywhere and we begin to think that it might not be amiss to contemplate a contract for sugar now ... It will be our intent next season to try to get lots of sugar ranging from fair to good grocery, assuming our duties remain unchanged ... we hope to keep up our business to the old point as no doubt our refinery business will suffer a little from local competition.*
> (December 30, 1865)

The death of the employee mentioned in the letter of November 24 compelled George to try once again to get the poor state of the local area improved by writing to the local Member of Parliament, the Honourable T. D'Arcy McGee:

> *Between the Wellington Bridge and Brewsters Bridge on the Lachine Canal a distance of about a mile - the only means of crossing is at the locks of St. Gabriel where a small path on the gates certainly less than two feet wide with rail on one side, gives the means of crossing. On either side of the lock the ground has been ditched and cut through by the Government or by its tenants to an extent which is almost incredible. To pass from the Joseph Street to the locks it is*

necessary to cross no less than five flumes or ditches - varying from 10 feet to 30 feet wide, and all of them deep and dangerous enough. On the south side of the locks it is little better and before any stores or dwelling house can be reached three more must be crossed.

All these waterways are covered with wood supports and planked - the planking nearly always in a dilapidated and half rotten condition, full of holes - not fenced ... and the whole half lighted up at night.

Within the last nine years populous district has grown up from nothing in the St. Gabriel Farm ... and a very large number of people use this dangerous method of crossing not by day only, but at all hours.

Not a season passes but that there are several deaths from drowning - the last being a poor fellow employed in the Sugar Refinery - whose body was recovered from the lock last Saturday. ... the obvious remedy is a bridge at the locks with sound and well lighted approaches - but failing the immediate construction of a bridge the passage to the locks on both sides ought at once to be got in good condition and a double rail put on the lock gates to diminish the danger of crossing.
(November 29, 1865)

There is no record of any reply to this call for improvements, but we do know that the state of the canal remained unchanged for some years to come.

The end of the American Civil War in 1865 should have meant an end to the threats of invasion to Canada; unfortunately a large proportion of Irish immigrants in the U.S. felt that this was a good time to get revenge for the actions of Cromwell and William III. Using many Irish ex-servicemen from both sides of the previous war, they established a North American Irish army of "Fenians" to punish Great Britain by invading Canada. As a result, more than 10,000 militiamen in Canada were placed under arms in early March in anticipation of an attack on St. Patrick's Day. George Drummond and John James Redpath were therefore gone from the business for some time, while John Redpath became chairman of the Volunteer Relief Fund, which raised funds to pay for equipment and supplies for the volunteers on active service. When George returned in mid-April (John James coming home later), it was to face the fact that the United States government had abrogated the treaty of reciprocity with Canada, and the American refiners were now in a better position to export refined sugar to Canada and compete with Redpath's refinery and the two newer facilities of Molsons and Dustan. To complicate matters even more, the Finance Minister for the Canadas, Mr. Galt, brought in a new tariff level that reduced by almost 40% the level of protection enjoyed by the Canadian refiners. Additional similar clauses in the budget also affected the major industrialists and manufacturers throughout the province, slashing into the economic viability of the country in the name of free trade. This produced an intense opposition throughout the commercial and industrial communities. Newspaper columns were crowded with letters from various manufacturing concerns and boards of trade, but the outcry produced no practical remedy or response from the government. George Drummond recognized that now was the time for a complete re-evaluation of the funding of the refinery and the need to avoid "having all the eggs in one basket."

He therefore pushed for a series of investments in outside businesses, and during the rest of the year purchases were made in stocks of the Rockland Slate Company, Melbourne Slate Company, Montreal Investment Association, Atlantic Telegraph Company, Bank of Montreal, Belvidere Mining Company, Bear Creek Coal Mine, Canada Iron Mining Company, "Capel" Copper Mine, and the Copper Smelting Works to a value of $137,281.87. Additionally, Missouri bonds and Montreal Harbour Commission bonds increased this sum to a grand total of $158,054.37.

Another major investment for the Canada Sugar Refinery was the contracting for the construction of two sailing barques as originally investigated in 1863. The vessels were built in Pointe Levi, Quebec, were launched in August and October 1866, and were named the *Helen Drummond* and the *Grace Redpath*.* These vessels represented the first foray of the company into the field of transportation and seemed to represent a significant growth in the flexibility of the company towards overcoming market fluctuations and outside contract problems. Naturally, these major expenditures had a positive effect on the assets listed for the company, while the net profits dropped accordingly.

The year 1867 was one of celebration and controversy for the newly confederated Dominion of Canada. With the political union of the various separate colonies of New Brunswick, Prince Edward Island, Nova Scotia, Quebec, and Ontario, the entire structure of political decision making and economic markets was altered. For the company, this was a good opportunity to expand its market area, assuming that the new federal government maintained the current policies of protection for domestic industries. The man selected to fulfil the responsibility of Minister of Finance was John Rose, a director of the Bank of Montreal. Since holding these two positions could present a conflict of interest, Rose resigned from the board of the bank. Chosen to replace Mr. Rose on the bank's Board of Directors was Peter Redpath. Unfortunately, when he was appointed there was no one around from the family to congratulate him, as he had agreed to stay behind to run the company while almost everyone else connected with the business from both families had gone to England to celebrate the marriage of John James Redpath to Ada Maria Mills. The best man was the Reverend George Redpath, who it seems found his appropriate calling in life after leaving the sugar business. Following the wedding, the Drummonds toured Scotland and enjoyed the pleasures of the grouse shooting and fishing, while the Redpaths returned to Canada. This was to be the last time John Redpath would see the land of his birth, but as his son Peter later wrote, "he returned not merely to a colony but to a nation." The trip, however, took its toll on John's health, which had been poor for some time. John was now seventy-one years old and, since his arrival on the quayside at Quebec City, had worked almost continuously on various enterprises for fifty-two years. He decided it was now time to officially retire from business life, and he handed over the presidency, with the full agreement of the other partners, to his son Peter in January of 1868. John James Redpath likewise decided (following Peter's promotion) that he wanted to pursue his military interests and tendered his resignation from the partnership at this time.

*Overall, the two ship's measurements were similar and listed as: Extreme Length: 137 feet; Extreme Beam: 30 feet 9 inches; Extreme Depth in Hold: 17 feet 11 inches; Displacement Weight: 609 tons. Costs for the Helen Drummond were $30,862.81, while the Grace Redpath cost slightly more, at $31,438.92.

Under normal circumstances, the loss of half the partners from a business would cause considerable disruption of normal affairs, but such does not seem to be the case, as over the next few months things went on as normal, and it must be surmised that George and Peter had in fact been running the company for some time previous to John's retirement.

Meanwhile, two circumstances occurred elsewhere that were to have effects on the company's business in the future. One was the opening of the Molson's Sugar Refinery in direct competition with John Redpath & Son. The other was Finance Minister Rose's decision to adjust the import duties on a wide selection of goods, creating significantly higher costs of manufacturing for all the industries concerned. For the sugar industry, the result was even more disastrous as Mr. Rose dropped the differentials between refined and raw duties so much that, far from being protected, the refiners would make a loss of 10 cents for every 100 pounds of refined sugar produced, compared to the U.S. manufacturers and wholesale importers who would benefit immensely by this government action. The reaction of the company was obvious and swift. The production of the "hard" or loaf sugars was temporarily suspended, while the other grades of white and yellow sugars were cut back. Complaints and appeals to the government were ignored and in company with many other industries, John Redpath & Son publically registered complaints about the situation through letters to the editors of various newspapers. Some papers refused to print these letters as they contradicted government policies, which those papers supported. Other "opposition" papers happily published the letters as front page articles, with supporting editorials condemning the government in general and the Finance Minister in particular for their "betrayal of Canadian manufacturing interests." Throughout the months of April and May 1868, the issue continued to grow with the articles, letters, and insinuations reaching vitriolic proportions as the "free trade" and "protectionist" factions squared off against each other, making claims and charges that would make today's supermarket tabloids look conservative and moderate. One article in particular is worth quoting as it clearly shows how even in just a few years the tastes of the Canadian householder had changed. The article appeared in the *Evening Times*, published in Hamilton, Ontario, on Tuesday, March 24, 1868, and it argued that while other papers published articles quoting sources in "the Trade" as claiming that current duties protected and encouraged refiners and prevented importation of "superior" quantities of raw, the so-called "trade" was in fact wholesalers and importers, and in the opinion of the *Evening Times* the average retailer thought differently:

> *The refined sugar comes to them in 200 pound barrels, all clean and dry and of weight so full that every barrel will retail out to within a pound or two of its listed quantity. But the Raw West India Sugar comes to them in large hogsheads and on these there is generally a large margin of loss from leakage, wet and black looking sugar in the bottom of the hogshead and dirt. ... in the "good old times" when coarse wet and dark raw sugar was the rule and clean bright refined the exception ... refined sugar was a cash article, very frequently in short supply ... we feel safe in affirming that the public taste has now become habituated to the clear refined sugar at present supplied and will not tolerate going back to the filthy stuff that we used to see in the shops a few years ago. Customers will not again take*

in place of the pound of clean bright sugar, that they now get for ten cents [per pound] the same quantity or even a little more of dark, wet dirty raw sugar. The wholesale men will say "fix the duties as we want them and we will import for your use the prettiest cleanest brightest and strongest raw sugar that ever you laid your eyes on". We beg to ask, did they import such sugars in the days when they had the whole trade in their hands? No! ... If he was fortunate enough to secure a hogshead or two of this description there would be such a run on him for it that it would speedily be all gone and months might elapse before he could get any more of the same ... We make bold to say for the public that going back to the use of dark dirty wet raw sugar, unless upon the compulsion of poverty or necessity is now out of the question and need not be thought of.

Not surprisingly, the cut-backs in production at the refinery led to a significant drop in the year-end profits recorded in the company ledger. Ironically on the assets side of the ledger the figures finally broke the million-dollar barrier. Everyone at the refinery hoped that these problems would be short lived and that things would improve in the future. But in reality the worst for the business was yet to come.

Also in 1868, time finally caught up with John Redpath when he suffered a stroke in mid-April. For the remainder of this year and into 1869 he remained at his home of Terrace Bank, partially paralyzed, but in what his subsequent memorial referred to as "Little pain ... and [he] enjoyed a good degree of consciousness" until finally, on Friday the fifth of March, 1869, "John Redpath Esq. ... closed a long career of usefulness, by a peaceful death at the age of 73 in the midst of his family."

Many generous and effusive obituaries were printed in the various Montreal papers, and on the following Monday, on a cold spring day, with snow still on the ground, the funeral took place. It was described in the Montreal *Witness* as follows:

The Funeral of the late John Redpath took place on Monday afternoon from his residence, Terrace Bank, and was one of the largest which we have lately seen. In the procession, besides relations and personal friends, was a considerable number of our best known citizens amongst the mercantile and professional community. Also very many of the Protestant ministers of the City. The emplòyees in the sugar factory counting some hundreds, were also there, wearing crapes, and led by marshals with black wands, and after these came a large number of private sleighs.

The subsequent service took place at the Canada Presbyterian Church on Coté Street and the burial at Mount Royal Cemetery where he was laid to rest alongside his first wife Janet and four of his children who had previously died.

Peter Redpath in 1871.

Grace Redpath (née Wood) in 1870.

CHAPTER SIX

"The End Of An Era"

The government budget of 1869 brought nothing in the way of good news to the sugar refining interests of Canada. It continued to force a financial loss on the refiners if they tried to produce their best quality products in competition with the wholesale importers, who, in turn, were lobbying long and hard for the continuation and expansion of their advantage. As a result, the firm of John Redpath & Son cut its production even further. For Redpath's competitors, things were even more serious and both the Molson and Halifax refineries looked likely to close their doors before the end of the year. Ironically, in July of that year, John Redpath & Son received an offer from William Ince, a prosperous businessman in Toronto, to consider establishing a new refinery in Toronto as competition to one proposed for construction by another businessman, Mr. Aldwell. George Drummond responded on behalf of John Redpath & Son with the following synopsis of the industry at that time.

> *You will readily believe that we have given much careful consideration to the question of a refinery in Toronto, and were the trade in a good position we might not have hesitated. But such is not the case at this moment ... The total consumption of Canada required is ... 51 millions of pounds per year (including every kind of sugar). We can with ease turn out 3 millions of pounds a month and with very little change could make it 4 millions. Molsons we do not know exactly but it cannot be less than 20 millions per annum, Smith [Halifax Sugar Co.] must do ten millions per annum, for say a total production of refined at 66 millions of pounds. A full 50 per cent above the wants of the country [for refined sugar] ... The result is enforced idleness for a good portion of the year and excessive competition during the working season producing as might be anticipated very bare prices at this moment. There is not over 3 cents [per pound] difference between raw refining sugar and [refined] dry crushed, ... You will see how some of us must fare if Aldwell erects a business to add to the pressure to sell. If he has advantages over us we must stop, if not, he must find his hopes disappointed. I feel certain we know our business and have in that knowledge, and in facilities of every kind ... advantages he can scarcely be expected to offer.*
> *(July 22, 1869)*

Then in a statement reflecting the desperate state of the refining business and how far they were willing to go to be competitive, George continued:

> *We can for all practical purposes consider our works as valueless (for if we are driven out of the business they would be) and work rent free. We believe both wages and coal are from ten to twenty percent cheaper here than in Toronto. And the only advantage he would have would be in the carriage from here to Toronto ... Before the Messrs. Molson went into the business I pointed out exactly as I have now done the expected results, and one of them told me ... he repented not taking my advice having lost $150,000. A business dies hard.*
> *(July 22, 1869)*

For the ongoing partnership of Peter Redpath and George Drummond, although the death of John did not affect the running of the business, the legalities of the property ownership made it necessary to purchase the various plots listed to the estate of John. To this end, during the next two years, the various deeds were signed over by John's widow, Jane, to the accounts of Peter and George, consolidating the overall land rights in the hands of the active partners.

Towards the end of 1869, following a "proper" period of mourning, Peter Redpath began the first of a successive series of tours that were to repeatedly keep him away from the practical running of the company, leaving George Alexander Drummond, with his ordered business mind, to be the real power during the remainder of their partnership. The fact that Peter took to these frequent and often lengthy excursions following his father's death, coupled with the extensive series of letters from George to Peter, complaining of Peter's ongoing absences, suggests that like his brother George, Peter had only participated in the refinery out of a strong sense of duty to his father. Fortunately, these letters provide a very clear set of records of the ongoing difficulties the company was suffering at the hands of the government with its discriminating tariff, as well as documenting the continuing manipulations of the wholesale merchants, who had now gained the upper hand and intended to keep it, as can be seen in the following example from George to Peter, who was then in Cuba:

> *On the matter of the proposed tariffs ... to tell the truth my heart sank ... the prospect of another tariff squabble is sickening is it not? I fancy that the revenue of the Dominion is not sufficient for the expenses and the new Finance Minister is casting about for an opportunity of enhancing duties. Our danger is that he might yield more readily to any clamour against us than a man more firmly seated in his political position.*
> *(December 7, 1869)*

He also repeated these sentiments in a letter written on December 10, 1869, to the Honourable John Rose, M.P.

> *It has come to my knowledge that we are likely to have another fight over the sugar tariff, I know the effect of the existing duties have already been to deprive us of a very large percentage of our white sugar business ... the new Finance Minister has turned his attention to the sugar duties, no doubt being pressed for revenue, and we also suppose being influenced by the usual loose ascertains flying about with regard to government protection.*

In another letter to Peter on the thirteenth of December 1869, George wrote that sales were down and supplies of raw cane sugar were so hard to obtain that it might be advantageous to look at purchasing 1 million to 2.5 million pounds of beet sugar in Europe. By the twenty-seventh, sales had picked up somewhat as the tariff charges were not as bad as feared. However, recent problems with the captains of the *Grace Redpath* and *Helen Drummond*, coupled with the unexpectedly high costs of maintaining them in a seaworthy condition, made Peter propose the disposing of both ships, but George discounted it, replying:

> *I do not think there is the least use in attempting to sell our ships, wooden ships are every day less in favour, but I will institute enquiries. Some day or other one may be lost and we may realize on her that way.*
> *(December 27, 1869)*

In the new year, the increasing number of retail businesses going bankrupt began to worry George and he started to curb his sales agents, instructing them to be cautious in extending credit to customers. On January 11, 1870, he wrote to Peter:

> *Our refinery stopped on Saturday last ... business goes fairly ... not much selling, I hope to get to work again by February 1st but repairs and alterations as usual exceed anticipations.*

and in a follow-up letter of the twenty-fourth:

> *Most of our Western accounts are now reduced to very safe dimensions and I feel quite cosy about them ... sailing vessels of all kinds are extremely depressed in Europe. The Suez Canal apparently is going to cut them out of their last refuge, the China trade ... on the sugar house we are still repairing but hope to begin on Monday next ... our list of prices is reduced ... but will require to come down again as the New York market is lower and may sink.*

In an attempt to alert the government to the difficulties of the present situation for the refiners, George drafted a letter to various ministers of the Crown. The one to the Honourable George E. Cartier, the Minister of Militia, sums up the situation of the refiners quite succinctly.

> *We do not ask protection, but simply justice. We have no protection now and are in a very much worse position than almost any other class of manufacturers in the province ... woollen, cotton and tobacco manufacturers have a clear protection getting their raw materials in free of duty while our raw material actually has to pay a higher import duty than foreign refined sugar ... we consider that in the last tariff discussion we were victimized to appease the clamour of a few importers our position has been the subject of much misapprehension and we are obliged to say misrepresentation ... of course there are persons who cry out "Monopoly" and request a share of the trade. Now we lay this down as a fundamental principle that we cannot do a small business. Having machinery, skilled labour and capital, they must be fully employed or work at a loss ... the effect of the present tariff has been to cripple our trade in white sugar and to diminish the rest by more than twenty per cent as compared with the year before ... There are now four refineries in the Dominion and we think the interest has a right to the favourable consideration of the government as*

so many hundreds of families are now dependent on it for their daily bread.
(January 20, 1870)

Two days later, George again raised his concerns over business matters to Peter, but in a postscript he mentioned something more personal:

My baby [George Lawrence Patterson, their seventh child] is very much out of health, a very bad cold and cough and weak. I feel anxious about him.

By the first of February, matters of business were relegated to second place as news of the child took prominence.

My child is now worse today and yesterday we got a wet nurse in hopes of his sucking a little, he coughs so distressingly and cries all night.

After yet another week, the letter to Peter contained no business news at all.

We have had an anxious week at my house at least on two separate days we gave up our little baby, and with what courage we could muster, surrendered him to God. But the little thing rallied and this morning actually looks better. On Sunday evening at almost nine we all thought him slipping. Dr. Campbell for a time did so too and later I was called in to be beside him when he went. But on trying his pulse I felt sure he was not so low as he seemed and I said so ... Dr. Campbell has been scrupulous in his attention generally five times a day ... and this morning on leaving he said "well nothing has saved that child but indefatigable pluck and unflagging care" ... of course he is not yet safe but I think him hopeful, everyone has been so kind ... Helen is nearly knocked up ... to add to our trouble the wet nurse got hopelessly drunk at three a.m. yesterday, another was found ... before eight.
(February 7, 1870)

With the infant slowly recovering, George returned to the matters of business, which were increasingly serious as more retail houses, especially in Ontario, suffered economic setbacks, but the need to maintain long-term relationships required careful handling. Therefore, in a letter to their Toronto sales agent, Mr. Houghton, George stated:

We hear a very bad account of Smith Bros. of Toronto, they owe us $1,146.00 ... shall we get paid? very doubtful I think, a little diplomacy had better be exercised, we cannot afford to let them see that we distrust them ... we must be very careful next summer it is at present the manner of Toronto men to build up their City to have fine stores railways etc. and I look for dangerous times ahead.
(February 7, 1870)

Within the refinery, the time had again come to initiate more modernization and technical developments, and George used his contacts within the refining community of Greenock in Scotland to obtain advice on the best ways to proceed. Another situation requiring attention was the state of the two company barques, which were now in a serious state of disrepair and due for their regular inspection for insurance purposes.

In April 1870, Peter Redpath returned from Cuba only to go away again within a few weeks to the United States, leaving George to carry on alone once more. Throughout the summer of 1870, business fluctuated, but nothing succeeded in persuading the government to adjust the tariffs. Meanwhile, new installations of machinery within the refinery increased the capacity of the plant in the hopes of better days ahead.

With all these letters of "doom and gloom," it might be supposed that things for George could not have been worse, and yet once in a while in the volumes of letterbooks still existing, amongst the cramped handwriting and blurred ink, there appears a touch of the man instead of the businessman. The letters mentioned above referring to his child testify to his strong devotion to his family. In the following example we see that, like ourselves, George was not averse to a little contravention of the official rules of life when in August 1870 he requested a long time friend to do him a favour by bringing out a new sporting shotgun from England the next year. In the following lines, George refers to the custom duties for the piece.

> *Can it be smuggled out do you think?, or not. If so it would be well to take it out of its case and give the leather case a coat of dirt and a bespeckling of itinerary labels. (August 19, 1870)*

On a more serious note, the outbreak of war between Germany and France precipitated a sharp rise in the value of gold, causing a similar rise for the price of sugar. Certain that a long struggle would have serious implications for the French beet crop, George stated to Peter, "If the fighting lasts three months longer I look for higher prices," and he was not mistaken. As the year continued, so did the fighting, and raw sugar prices rose dramatically, thus increasing the company's costs of production. By year's end, the account books looked anything but healthy. Although the new machinery and improved technology had given the refinery a new lease on life and sales had been reasonable on certain grades of sugar, the combined negative effect of the duties on raw sugar and the financial losses on the two barques effectively wiped out the profits for the year, leaving the pitiful sum of $4,601.60 to be entered as a gross profit under the previous year's net sum of $145,047.87.

Records for the early months of 1871 unfortunately do not exist. However, subsequent papers indicate that early in January, George received serious news about the condition of the *Grace Redpath* and *Helen Drummond* and about the business activities of their captains. This news caused him to leave the business (with Peter still away) in the hands of Francis (Frank) Redpath who was working within the organization. George's crossing the Atlantic in the middle of winter indicates that the cause must have been grave indeed, and the fact that he returned a mere six weeks later shows clearly that this was no vacation. Upon his return, he immediately initiated actions to investigate the selling of the vessels, but he did not cancel the orders for continuing redevelopment of the refinery or the construction of the new buildings just underway, as it appears he took advantage of this trip to investigate establishing a production capability in the refinery for beet sugar. He also began to investigate the current insurance policies on the plant and associated facilities. In a letter to Peter in London dated June 23, 1871, George reported that:

Sales are pretty well off, I sent Houghton (the Company salesman) to Toronto and Hamilton last week and he cleared off all on hand at a good price indeed higher than I expected to get ... I have grave concerns on our insurances ... I have looked carefully over most of our policies and find we only have a partial coverage in the main building, the refining house and the charcoal 40, ... and worst of all I find the extension of the store shed south of St. Patrick Street has never been insured at all. At the moment we have $305,000.00 of sugar in the whole shed and we had only $105,000.00 insurance so I added $70,000.00 on the new portion ... at the new building we had three beams and columns up at the refinery when a rope broke and down they all were punched by a column then hoisting ... 3 beams broken and 1 column but no one hurt ... The "Helen Drummond" is discharging in New York I propose giving her a grain freight to Europe as no sugar is to be had ... The "Grace Redpath" is at sea Captain Botsford went to Egypt, did I tell you that the drafts [bills] on her are over $2,100.00 and the stealage of sugar is likely to be considerable ... The first lot of beet seems first rate.

Of the above mixture of information, one situation was to dominate George's attention over the next few months and this was the activities of the *Grace Redpath*. It seems the captain had been deliberately diverting the funds extended by the company for the upkeep of the vessels, and she was now in a dangerous state of disrepair. On June 24, George wrote to his brother Andrew stating that:

Botsford won't go to Canada in her (the "Grace Redpath") nor the crew ... I want the vessel sailed from Portland to Montreal we are in no hurry for the sugar ... a good deal depends on the state of the vessel and hope she is seaworthy for my sake do not let her be repaired in an American port.

Three days later in a letter to Mr. Hewlett (the company purchasing agent in New York), more details emerge:

The "Grace Redpath" came into Portland on Saturday, by letter so long ago as 8 April the Captain was ordered to fetch her on to Montreal direct, immediately on landing he went to our agent, handed her over and departed her (as he says) home. The whole affair is astonishing ... meanwhile after consulting her invoices of cargo we found much in the way of losses ... the obvious suspicion is that the whole is a case of plunder to which the Captain may be a party or again he may have only been a tool in the hands of great rogues ... we have appointed another man to her command. (June 27, 1871)

No records exist to show if the case was one of actual plunder or excessive losses, but the latter seems likely as no legal expenditures are found in the company accounts. At the refinery, the expansion program continued with an expenditure level reaching over $55,000 for the new buildings, including orders for a large steam boiler for the new power plant. Finally for this year, in a short letter to Hewlett in October 1871, George added a postscript that from the historical point of view represents a major milestone in the history of the "Sugar House":

With the new machinery in place we can now drop our old ways of making sugar.

This simple sentence referred to the decision that no longer would the company produce sugar loaves. Instead, the more modern centrifugal sugar, which had gradually displaced the loaves since 1863, would now rule supreme. The end of an era had come in the technology of sugar making and a link with the past, which reached back almost a thousand years, was now finally broken. What was once a standard symbol of quality was now relegated to a single line in the ledger under the heading "scrap - 4 tons of old Iron moulds $800.00." Fortunately, at the bottom of the page is another line showing that the company's financial fortunes were somewhat better than those of 1870.

Francis (Frank) Redpath.

CHAPTER SEVEN

"...A Devil Of A Time..."

Having been forced to, in effect, run the business on his own for the previous two years, and with the likely prospect that the situation would continue for the foreseeable future, George proposed to Peter that a revision of the partnership be undertaken and that Peter's younger brother Frank become a full partner instead of merely an employee. By this new agreement, George acquired 50% of the shares in the venture, Peter took 40%, while Frank was given the opportunity to buy in for 10%. This may not sound like much, but in monetary terms, it meant that Frank was required to pay $24,000 within ten days for the purchase of property and capital in the business, and he had to raise a further $26,000 for floating capital within three months. One interesting clause of the partnership agreement is that it was specifically stated that:

> *It is probable that Peter Redpath will be absent the greater part of the time.*

With the arrival of spring came the same round of problems that had plagued the company for the past few years, namely the upcoming tariffs, the number of business failures in the retail and wholesale trade (which left major amounts of money owing to the company), and the problems encountered with the *Grace Redpath* and *Helen Drummond*. On the first two issues, the normal round of complaints and deals needed to be struck, but on the matter of the vessels, George was determined to eliminate the problem. Unfortunately, he was just a little too late as the captain of the *Helen Drummond* was about to create an international incident.

According to the accounts recorded in various letters over the next few months, the circumstances appear to have been as follows: Captain Tregethin of the barque *Helen Drummond* had taken on a cargo of molasses in the Caribbean and shipped it to New Orleans, where, due to a lack of sugar business, he decided – without notifying the company – to take on a charter to ship tobacco to Naples, Italy. Upon arrival in Naples, he cabled George Drummond, notifying him that some minor repairs were required that would cost about $600. George cabled back that this sum was authorized; but when the account came in to the company, it amounted to $1,650 and the account was countersigned with Captain Tregethin's signature on behalf of John Redpath & Son. To put it mildly, George was furious. The vessels had long been a source of concern and expense, and this was the last straw. George sent a telegram to Peter in London notifying him of the situation and followed it with a letter in which he commented:

> *If Captain Tregethin signed that draft without noticing it to be for $1,650.00 he is a fool and deserves immediate dismissal. If he signed knowing the amount and concealing the amount from us he is a rogue ... the ship needs repair and should be sold in the United Kingdom ... and I must say I am sick of her.*
> *(April 19, 1872)*

On April 22, 1872, George notified Peter that there was:

> *No explanation of the money from the Captain. I have refused the debt ... can it be possible that Tregethin has cheated us? or is it just that he spent more money than he ought and is ashamed to admit it and cannot explain ... it may turn out we had better get rid of those horrid ships and a freight had better be got back to the U.K. and then let her be sold.*

Dealing with the sugar business at home, he continued:

> *Our business looks blue at present we are fairly driven out of the white sugar business ... New York dry crushed sugar is selling in Montreal and London sugar is coming in freely plus lots of Yellows ... our business is sinking like our ships.*

Finally, on the twenty-fifth, the explanation arrived from Tregethin that he had overspent, and George was obliged to pay the bill by sending money to agents in Naples. George hoped that this would finish the matter, but as we shall see, there was more yet to come. On the home front, things were not much better as the tariffs were due to be reviewed. Expecting the worst, George went to Ottawa to attempt a little personal lobbying to get an easing of the difficult position in which the Canadian government had placed the Canadian refiners (in fact, the Molson and Halifax refineries had already closed down.) In Ottawa, George learned that although the Canadian officials were sympathetic, they were not inclined to alter the status quo due to the upcoming general elections. The same could not be said for the U.S. authorities, who at this point dropped a very large bombshell into the situation by increasing the bounty to U.S. refiners for exporting their products, thus making the position of the Canadian refining interests even worse than before. The time had come for a frontal attack on the indifferent Canadian authorities, and George sent a series of letters to every member of the Cabinet as well as the leader of the Opposition.

His letter of May 8 to the Right Honourable A.G. Jones, M.P. for Halifax, states the desperate nature of the times.

> *The extra drawback given in the United States to assist their refiners is actually equivalent to 39¢ or 40¢ per 100 lbs ... we find it unprofitable under these circumstances to make refined sugar, and feeling under no obligations to loose money in supplying the trade we have warned most of our customers to look for their supplies elsewhere.*

This large change in circumstances would normally have caused the government to re-assess their duty levels, but the Macdonald Conservatives feared a loss to the Mackenzie Liberals in the August election and refused to take any action that would alienate those who were soon to vote. As a result, nothing was done to help the domestic industry. George recognized that the battle was lost and informed Peter (in London):

> *I have been at Ottawa "eating dirt" as my mother would call it, and beyond fair words did nothing to succeed in getting aid ... our dry [sugar] business is killed ... If you envy my position much pity, hurry back and share its pleasures ... to gain money I have sold off the Rockland Quarry for $32,000.00 ... we have paid the draft of Tregethin on us ... he is I now think not of calibre sufficient to do his ship's business. Confound those ships! We are not selling a great deal of sugar and lots of [imported refined] scotch daily expected by the spring fleet now arriving at Quebec. Our stock of raw is at the moment low, we are getting about 3,000 tons from Pernambuco.*
> (May 10, 1872)

On the same day, in a last-ditch effort to change the mind of the government, George addressed a letter to his friend Sir George Cartier, the Minister of Militia and Defense:

> *For years we have been worried by attempts to kill our business. Had we been poorer or less hard working, or less acquainted with our business, it would have been dead and buried long ago as Mr. Molson's and Mr. Smith's have been. Now one whole department of us has gone ... sugar refining demands an extensive and costly plant, we alone have expended over $400,000.00 in this country in this way and when we are threatened with extinction as an industry... we cannot secure more than a hearing ... I feel that the old prejudice against us is still at work by the importers ... would there be a chance to ask for a drawback on the export of refined sugar? ... by which means I could be occasionally as disagreeable to the American refiners as they are to me.*
> (May 10, 1872)

With the official declaration of the campaign for the general election, the various parties looked for candidates to fill the nominations. The Conservatives for Montreal West decided that the man for them was George Alexander Drummond; led by Sir George Cartier, they approached him to stand on their behalf. More than just a little disillusioned by his recent reception at Ottawa, George was not in a mood to take up politics. In addition, the current state of the business was absorbing his attention and so he replied on June 17:

> *In consequence of the absence of my partner Peter Redpath it will be quite impossible for me to leave the City or give attention to any other subject but my business at present, and as he (Mr. Redpath) contemplates an absence of about two years you will see that no other course is open to me but to deny myself the honour you have proposed to me.*

Seemingly, the nominating committee were not willing to take no for an answer, and over the next week a series of delegations to George's home persuaded him to reconsider. Still hoping to avoid the "honour," George made one condition for the holding of the nominating meeting.

> *That if this meeting is decided and united on myself (which I do not expect) I will push vigorously on, but if not, I shall feel compelled to decline the nomination.*

Much to George's surprise, the nominating committee was unanimous in its call for George to represent them and so he reluctantly accepted and went on the campaign trail. In a bitter and hard-fought campaign during which George was characterized by the opposition as a "tyrant" and "monopolist," he staunchly pressed the case of the Macdonald Conservatives even though those self-same men had virtually condemned his business by their actions. Perhaps he now felt, to paraphrase a well-known saying, "If you can't change them from the outside, join them and do it from the inside." When the election results were in, although Sir John A. Macdonald and his party had succeeded in holding onto a reduced majority, George Drummond in Montreal West and Sir George Cartier in Montreal East both lost.

Following his defeat, George felt that he needed a vacation and so he went to his property at Long Point in Ontario to do some hunting and in his diary he noted "bagging" thirty-seven quail, one woodcock, and a rabbit.

Upon his return to Montreal in October, he had to immediately return to Kingston where his elder brother Thomas was on his deathbed. Following this sad visit, he returned to the refinery only to hear reports of a major problem with the *Helen Drummond*, which was still in Naples and which was officially impounded by the Naples authorities. This time it seems that when the funds sent by Drummond to pay all the debts of the ship reached the appointed agents in Naples, they kept the money and handed over to the shipping repair company a bill of discount, which underpaid the repairers by a considerable margin. Demanding the remainder of their money, the repair yard served a writ on the ship's captain to impound the vessel until the supposed debt was paid in full. Initially complying with this writ, Tregethin cast off when the police and the shipping agents turned up with additional charges that Tregethin had been smuggling and were about to arrest him. Once out into the harbour, the captain assisted one police officer and two of the agents off the ship by throwing them overboard. He then sailed on to England leaving the authorities holding nothing but the impounding papers.

When read as an historic incident, this may seem amusing if not comical, but for George Drummond it was yet another problem he did not need. Certain of the rights of the issue, he contacted Peter once again, asking him to act on behalf of the company.

> *I fear the evidence is irresistible that the firm in Naples are swindlers ... the whole charge of smuggling has apparently been bumped up to serve someone ... there can be no question but you will absolutely require to go to Naples and settle it ... This has been a devil of a time for us. (November 25, 1872)*

The year concluded with the news that for the first time since its inception the company had made a financial *loss* amounting to $59,576.26. It was indeed "a devil of a time."

Despite the losses of 1872, there were a few positive developments at the beginning of 1873. The first was that Peter Redpath returned from Europe in early February and took up a stronger role in the running of the business. Admittedly, this was only after something of a "showdown by mail" between George and Peter. It would appear that Peter resented having to leave his activities in London to go to Naples, since he wrote to George complaining that:

I know that my credit has been of not a little use to the firm but I never received any consideration for it.

This shocked and angered George so that his letter of reply was, for this age of form and etiquette, extremely blunt:

Your credit I readily admit to have been of no little service to the firm, no one has ever more heartily or sincerely done justice to you on fitting occasions than I ... it is deeply to be regretted that you did not give expression to [your feelings] earlier ... as most assuredly I should never have agreed to take advantage of you for an hour and would have taken the earliest possible opportunity to relieve myself from a position in which ... escape from obligation to you was an impossibility ... I think you cannot deny that I have given to the firm ... an amount of time and thought which has been the next thing to slavish and much exceeding what you have bestowed on it. For even when here of late years, a large share of your attention has been given to other matters. I never grumbled nor even reminded you of this till you call it from me ... I never would have continued [in our partnership] had I known of its existence (that is your feelings) ... and I would rather terminate all arrangements than that it should exist.
(January 21, 1873)

Secondly, the Lachine Canal, which had remained at a depth of nine feet since its original construction, was now slated for an expansion. This would then allow vessels with a deeper draft to enter, permitting the company to buy larger quantities of sugar at one time for shipment to the refinery.

Thirdly, the company was approached by a group of Ontario businessmen led by L. Brunston of Mohawk, Ontario, to investigate the prospects of John Redpath & Son purchasing supplies of beet sugar if the Ontario group could establish a sufficient quantity of contracts with farmers. For George this was the answer to a prayer, as it would allow him to obtain supplies of sugar for his machinery without paying any import duties, and he could perhaps recover some of his lost business. He wrote immediately to Mr. Brunston stating his support for the idea.

Beet root sugar is excellent material for an ordinary sugar refinery, and several thousand tons have been used in the Canada Sugar Refinery originally made in France, Belgium and Germany ... we are prepared to buy all you can make at a fair price ... we have currently sugar now on the way from the interior of the continent of Europe via Antwerp and New York, which is a much greater distance than from Ontario.
(January 6, 1873)

Fourthly, an agent for the sale of the barques had been found in the person of Alfred Brown of Glasgow, who was appointed on the tenth of January with express instructions to sell the *Helen Drummond* as soon as possible and the *Grace Redpath* upon her arrival at Glasgow, which occurred at the end of February. By mid-March the *Helen Drummond* was sold and an offer was pending for the *Grace Redpath*. Although George did not consider it as high an offer as he had hoped, being extremely desirous of disposing of the vessels, he accepted without argument. Thus the first and only real attempt of John Redpath & Son to develop its own shipping interests ended in a relative failure.

On the negative side, the company learned that a vessel chartered to bring in the first shipment of raw sugars for the new season had foundered in the Gulf of St. Lawrence, and the insurance company was withholding payment on the policy. In Ottawa it was tariff time again, and George was certainly tiring of this yearly pilgrimage, as he revealed to the Honourable A.G. Jones:

> *I have no idea how the tariff will be treated in Ottawa this session, personally I am tired of having to go through a fruitless errand as all my last visits have been. Canada West [Ontario] is now regularly drawing her supplies of sugar from New York. We have been at a standstill for over two months, and though we recommenced work only about three weeks ago we have already been obliged to curtail our production and are now doing not quite half our capacity ... we are driven to use the lowest and cheapest raw material we can find and are now again boiling molasses which we have not done for years.*
> *(March 15, 1873)*

Shortly thereafter, a letter arrived from George G. Dustan, in which he asked advice from George on the best way to re-establish his bankrupt sugar company in Halifax. George was surprised at this proposal in view of the state of the economy, and said so in his reply of April 18.

> *One fact must be patent however to you and that is that there has not been a time of many years in which the business of sugar refining looked so blue. There can be no doubt that in the United States the refineries are too numerous and that no amelioration can be expected till a few of them fail and shut up. ... I think you are not aware that our own refinery has been entirely re-modelled since you saw it last. A new wing built and the whole now arranged and conducted on the Greenock plan, with the latest improvements. With the exception of new houses now building in Greenock and Liverpool we have a more complete establishment than any other. We have abandoned the making of loaves etc. and are fitted to do easily 100 tons per day. Nevertheless, we have been idle for several months and since we began again we have not been doing over 50 tons a day and not able to sell what we make even at loosing rates.*

Another problem at this time was the absence, yet again, of Peter Redpath, which left George to cope with the management of the company. Frank Redpath was taking on much of the daily administration and technical running of the plant, but the larger corporate policies were wholly for George to manage. Additionally, financial matters were not improving as the price of raw sugar was rising sharply, which in turn compounded the problems already experienced with the American refineries flooding the Canadian market. After the publication of the year's tariff rates, George wrote to the Honourable Frank Smith in the Senate to attempt to promote some action in the Upper House since the Lower one would not listen.

> *The Government you see has done nothing for us sugar refiners this session, which considering the precarious position they held for a time might be excusable, but I have never even had the smallest sign, of sympathy from them. Which after what I went through to save them last summer seems rather shabby treatment.*
> *(May 3, 1873)*

In early June, the Intercolonial Mine at Picton, Nova Scotia, suffered an underground explosion and fire that left sixty-two dead. As President of this company (through ownership by the refinery), George felt it was his personal responsibility to attend to the needs of the families of the dead and injured. He therefore dropped everything at the refinery and went to Picton where he authorized immediate payments from his own accounts to tide the people over. He reported this incident to Peter (who was now in Venice) and then returned to the subject of the status of the sugar business, which by this time was in extremely serious difficulties.

> *I find it totally out of my power to do more at present than keep daily business moving; a most unsatisfactory state of things due of course to your absence and the provisional condition of the cash and book keeping department ... I hear with some dismay that you propose ... to come back in October and leave in January. I had the anticipation that your present absence ... was to terminate about midsummer ... and that on your return you could relieve me for a fair time. You know that a visit such as you propose, can accomplish nothing as outside trips take up most of the time and attention you have to bestow. It is quite certain that the present state of things ought to end soon ... don't fancy that these remarks indicate any desire to terminate our partnership. I am just as willing to go out as stay in or to go on with a fair division of labour.*
> *(June 6, 1873)*

On a more technical note, the company was approached in June by a company from England, proposing the introduction of a paper bag to replace the heavier and more costly double cotton and jute bags that were then in use for the selling of the refined sugar. Always ready to look at new possibilities, George agreed to buy a thousand of them, measuring 27 inches by 40 inches and capable of holding 200 pounds of sugar each. Since similar paper bags were not properly introduced until the 1950s, it shows how far ahead of his time George was in this experiment. In fact, the bags did not work out as well as advertised by the manufacturer, and they were subsequently shown as part of a list of idle stores held by the company, while the innovation itself was abandoned.

Throughout the rest of the summer, the fortunes of the company continued to deteriorate. It was clear that no relief could be expected from the government as it was involved in a major problem of its own that became known as the Pacific Scandal, which eventually led to the resignation of the Macdonald government on November 5.

For the firm of John Redpath & Son, this prospective change in the government boded hard times ahead – if the Conservative government of Macdonald was apathetic towards the refiners' plight, the Liberal backers of Mackenzie were openly hostile. At the urgent demand of George Drummond, Peter Redpath returned to Canada. George then took this rare opportunity to briefly travel to his newly built country cottage at Cacouna near Rivière du Loup, and then went to the prairies, where he recorded in his diary the hunting of buffalo, antelope, and deer.

Upon his return from vacation, George had to deal with yet another approach from George Dustan in Halifax, who had ignored all the advice of George Drummond and had tried to re-establish his business. Now with the bottom dropping out of the market, Dustan desperately asked

George for advice and wanted George to take over his business. George agreed to meet Dustan in Portland, Maine, but he admitted he could do nothing to help, as the economy was, in his words, "foundering."

The national financial situation was now so bad that for the year as a whole, more than 994 commercial failures were recorded in Canada leaving outstanding debts of $12 million, of which more than $12,500 was outstanding to the Redpath company alone. These debts, coupled with the disastrous circumstances of the company's trading for the year, ended up showing a second consecutive loss in the corporate accounts. For George, the very future of the company was in doubt, and any and every economy now had to be put into place. Notices were placed through the various departments calling for cuts in the use of fuel and other supplies, with warnings that in the engine house:

> *I will consider it bad and wasteful management if the following happens:*
>
> *First – the boilers blowing off steam*
>
> *Second – the Fire doors being left open to keep steam down*
>
> *Third – too many boilers are fired up*
>
> *Fourth – keeping the back pressure of exhaust steam over 5 pounds pressure if it can be used in the pans or hot water tanks*

while within the plant proper, a notice written in both English and French read in part:

> *In consequence of the enormous breakage of window glass ... any breakage ... must be at once reported to the Foreman. If purely accidental we will replace it at our cost... any one breaking glass carelessly or wilfully, will be made to pay for it and will be liable to dismissal ... the cost of replacing all broken glass not above provided for, will be assessed monthly on the hands employed in the building where it is broken.*

George and Peter also began to make plans in the event of the Liberals winning the upcoming election.

Daughters of John Redpath: (from left to right) Emily Jane Bonar Redpath (married H.T. Bovey), Margaret Pringle Redpath (married Alexander Dennistoun) and Mary Redpath (married Thomas M. Taylor).

The children of George and Helen Drummond. Clockwise from the centre: Maurice, Huntly, Edgar, George, and Arthur.

CHAPTER EIGHT

"... *We Are At A Crisis Of Our Affairs...*"

Things were indeed looking bleak for the company and the events of the first few weeks of 1874 did not improve things. On the seventh of January, George Dustan once again pressed George Drummond to take over his refining operation to which Drummond replied:

> *For many reasons, not the least of which is that we do not see our way to make it pay we cannot accept your offer ... and most truly wish you a way out of any difficulty you may be in.*

Two weeks later, the company bookkeeper Falkiner disappeared. As he had been an employee for nearly ten years, this surprised George (Peter was once again travelling to England, ostensibly to collect his wife and bring her back to Canada following her extended stay with her relatives) and an investigation amongst the other employees revealed that Falkiner had been dabbling in stocks, had suffered losses in the previous year's general economic slump, and was taking to drink. George immediately ordered an examination of the account books and contacted their New York agents to keep a watch out for Falkiner. As George put it:

> *Our bookkeeper Falkiner has left, having been detected in a series of little peculations, the amount of which so far as we yet know, is not serious.*
> *(January 19, 1874)*

On the twenty-third, in another letter to Hewlett, he continued:

> *Falkiner has been seen in New York ... this matter is much exaggerated, his stock operations were small, and he owes very little in this city ... he had no power in our office to make a big thing even if he wanted ... there are plenty of applicants for his replacement.*

By the twenty-eighth, the tone of George's ongoing letters had changed:

> *Try to find Falkiner, he may be sailing from New York by the steamers "City of Brussels" or the "Greece" he may be with his mother and two daughters I will send photo and description.*

Finally the situation was resolved in his letter of January 31:

> *We hear Falkiner has sailed for England on the Greece...we*

got alarmed a little by a false entry in the books of September last amounting to $4,000.00, but it turned out to be in effect only a blunder, and is accountable by the supposition that he was muddled by drink when he made it ... as it is the matter assumes its original dimension and I don't think we will trouble him.

George now had to turn his attention to fact that the Liberals had indeed won the general election. Macdonald was out and the first Liberal government in confederated Canada's history was in power. Furthermore, the national economy was in a slump and reverberations of the Pacific Scandal still echoed within the business community. George felt strongly that there was a need to adjust the customs duties back to a more equitable level to enable the business to continue. He therefore undertook to discuss matters with the Honourable Isaac Burpee, the Minister of Customs, who was totally inexperienced in the intricacies of duties; in a series of letters from March 12 to April 6, 1874, George outlined the basic effects of the current and proposed tariffs to the effect that:

If the current ad valorem duty on sugar were simply abolished the first effect would unquestionably be to take away the inducement to import sugar from the places of its growth. This would diminish direct trade and make Canada more than now dependent on New York ... in addition the additional present specific grades of duty are unfair as they press too hardly on the lower grades and too lightly on the better sugars which has all but killed Canada's sugar refining industry.
(March 12, 1874)

We have an immense interest at stake this spring, having between five and six thousand tons of sugar now on its way to us from various quarters.
(March 25, 1874)

Loaf sugar refined in New York costs at present about 6¼ cents per pound ... and pays a duty in all equivalent to about 40% ad valorem ... vacuum pan Demerara costs 5½ cents per pound with a duty of 43% ad valorem ... these two classes are both refined sugar one white the other yellow and are fairly equivalent to what we produce from our refinery. On the other hand our raw material pays as follows:

Good refining sugar costs us about 4½ cents per pound and pays 47½ % ad valorem duty. From this class of sugar white refined is produced. While the darker Melado of average quality costs about 2½ cents per pound and pays equivalent to 50% ad valorem ... the higher classes of sugar evidently therefore do not contribute their fair share to the revenue or what is the same thing the lower qualities and the raw material of our manufacture are burdened with an excessive charge ... Besides stopping sugar refining in the Dominion. Our trade with the West Indies and our carriage trade are also sacrificed mainly for the benefit of New York ... We claim a remedy for this state of things as an act of Justice.
(April 6, 1874)

Surprisingly, these efforts actually seemed to have some effect as George learned that an alteration to the tariff would take place, which, if not giving them back their control of the trade, would at least reduce the disadvantage they were currently working under. But equally, George knew that any change favourable to the refiners would provoke a negative response from the wholesale importers, and he said so to the Honourable A.G. Jones, the Member of Parliament for Halifax.

> *I gathered from what took place on Saturday that there would be great difficulty in persuading them to do anything, and I believe that if any serious opposition be shewn, even after it is proposed, they may withdraw. Better therefore half a loaf than no bread. There will be no protection about it but the ruinous discrimination against refining will at least be modified ... but I have positively made up my mind that if the Government gives no relief and keep things at present I will stop my refinery as soon as I work off my present stock.*

Keeping Peter appraised of the situation, George wrote on April 11:

> *We have some hope of the tariff being changed to our advantage, I have been twice at Ottawa ... statistics on the refinery show a loss of $2,000.00 and over for* March. *Prices keep very low for refined in New York and we are lower in consequence ... I trust there is to be no question about your returning to your duties soon. I think you ought to be here now, and personally I cannot go on much longer in the provisional way of our present arrangements, having a great deal more than I ought to have to do, in consequence of your absence.*

At the beginning of April, the new tariff came in, and to George Drummond's surprise and pleasure it positively helped the refiners of Canada with a protection level of 25 cents. He felt he could now start planning the re-establishment of larger scale production and ordered his New York agents to begin buying the lower grade refining type sugars, which were cheaper under the new tariff than the more expensive types. He also recognized that there was the need to strengthen the hand of the refiners and so he contacted George Dustan on April 25.

> *I am just back from my third trip to Ottawa ... if this tariff passes into law and you care to renew your connection with me ... come and see me at once ... a scheme to sail you and put things in a working state we can at once mature, I will cable my partner to come out at once ... there is enormous opposition to it (the tariff) and it is a great pity you were not here as I feel they may listen to you better than I.*

George was not exaggerating when he said, "There is enormous opposition" to the tariff. The huge profits reaped by the importers (backed by the U.S. refineries) led them to initiate a press campaign using the many papers that were pro free trade. The members of the ousted government were also quick to condemn the Liberals and spotlight what they considered to be a contradiction in the supposed policies of the new government as can be seen from an article in the Montreal *Gazette* for April 18, 1874, by Sir Francis Hincks, the former Finance Minister.

> *The prevailing impression is that a professedly Free Trade Government has granted an enormous protection, at the cost of all the consumers of sugar, to a comparatively small*

> *refining interest ... In Canada [in 1868] after much discussion and controversy, a compromise was arrived at which did not satisfy the importers and which was loudly complained of by the planters ... the refiners were not dissatisfied until some recent legislation in the United States afforded an undue advantage in the shape of a bounty on exports to the United States refiners.*

Reading this article, George was put in the difficult position of either staying quiet and allowing something he knew to be false to go unchallenged or speaking out and being seen to criticize his own Conservative Party and defend the Liberals. He chose the latter and wrote to the editor of the *Gazette* rebutting Sir Francis's arguments on the refiners and the earlier tariff.

> *I beg permission to notice ... his mistake in supposing that the refiners ever accepted the tariff of 1868 as a satisfactory one It was not so. They opposed it to the last. But numbers and clamours prevailed ..."*
> *(April 22, 1874)*

Stung by this open contradiction, Sir Francis countered with another lengthy article justifying his position and condemning George Drummond. Sir Francis also attempted to justify his position by stating that, for the period 1870 - 73, imports of Melado type sugar for refining showed as:

1870	*20 million pounds*
1871	*14 million pounds*
1872	*3 million pounds*
1873	*2.5 million pounds*

for a total of 39.5 million pounds, which in his judgement proved that the refiners must have prospered to be able to bring in such a huge volume over the four years.

Unable to curb his anger, George again responded, systematically exposing the fallacies in Hincks's arguments with special reference to the aforementioned statistics. He thanked Sir Francis for supplying these figures as, in his opinion, they proved beyond doubt the case for the refiners. George suggested that instead of looking at the total volume, the clear downward trend that the figures showed as a whole was that of a total disaster caused by the imposition of the tariff on the Canadian refining industry, and he called upon Sir Francis to show otherwise. No further letters were printed from Sir Francis Hincks.

Desperate to gain support from his other senior partner, George wrote to Peter in London on April 27.

> *I have been at Ottawa for nine or ten days, neglecting everything else. The Finance Minister suddenly proposed the following Sugar Tariff:*
>
> - *Low grades as they were up to No. 13 Dutch Standard*
> - *Above No. 13 D.S. 1¼¢ per lb. plus 25% ad valorem*
> - *Above No. 16 D.S. 1½¢ per lb. plus 25% ad valorem*
>
> *You never saw such a storm, every wholesale grocer in the West either went to Ottawa or sent a deputy. Every retail grocer signed a petition against it. I worked night and day tabulating statements and had ... a long article printed ... ready for circulation. My impression is that the Finance Minister will either drop the 1½¢ rate or adopt 45% ad valorem on all qualities. In either case we will be better off, but we will have immediate opposition. The Halifax*

> *refinery will go on at once ... we have an opportunity of making money [from our refinery] for a year or two then we will have some competition. I feel like joint stocking the whole affair [of our refinery] at once. My information would be to have our property put in at $350,000.00 as a subscription of stock. We would offer to manage the affair for a commission of 2 or 2½% on the business ... and to retire altogether in three or five years. Now will you see the very unfortunate fact of your being absent may tell against your own wishes, views or even interests. Because while you are doing nothing I am driven to death and may decide wrongly. In short we are at a crisis of our affairs and at no time was the necessity for consultation so urgent. You had better return as speedily as possible, though it may now be too late to be before a decision is imperatively called for.*

As George feared, the new Finance Minister succumbed to the barrage of complaints from the wholesale grocers, but instead of adjusting the tariff openly, he waited until Parliament rose and used an Order-in-Council to revert the levels to those of 1868. The bad times were back again with a vengeance and George let his feelings be known in his letter to the Honourable A.G. Jones on May 4, 1874.

> *I was a good deal disgusted ... and I don't think I shall trouble them [the Government] again. I feel now perfectly released from any implied obligation to supply the trade and will work when I think there is a chance and stop when I please. I wish my ponderous and expensive works could be moved out the country.*

While the ongoing production of white sugar was an impossibility and yellow sugars brought in only a minimal level of profit, a major U.S. sugar refinery sought to acquire the rights to a process of removing low grade iron from the sugar (originally developed and patented by George Drummond.) The licensing of this process to the Portland factory gave some much needed income to the company accounts.

As the summer progressed, the refinery continued to work at a reduced level and further cut-backs were instituted to minimize costs. Many of the surviving letters of this period indicate repeated attempts to gain the government's ear through the co-operation of George Dustan since George could not hope to achieve success. Interspersed with these letters on purchases of cargoes, price levels, and daily business matters are occasional notes to various family members. Most of these are relatively minor or are not relevant to the history of the company, but there are a few pieces that almost cry out to be printed, and two of these are included below. They introduce a figure who would become a significant member of the company structure, and like earlier letters, reveal the man behind the businessman in George Drummond and his concern for the well-being of his children. In August, George decided that his son Maurice should continue his education abroad and he enrolled Maurice in Brighton College in England. In a letter of introduction to the headmaster, dated August 26, 1874, George described his son:

> *He has had measles but no other illness and is at present in good health. There can be little doubt that he will choose a mercantile career and therefore the modern department of*

your course would seem most suitable. I should like him to learn drawing, carpentry and music. He has had some elementary instruction in the last but so far displays no liking nor aptitude for it. Still I do not willingly abandon the hope of his being made acquainted with music. The only drawback being the possibility of its being taught in hours usually given to play. If this is the case I wish it to be omitted for the first year at least ... on the whole you will require to watch that he does not ... overwork his general health ... and against any repetition of which I earnestly desire your kind care.

In early September, Maurice was about to go to England on the S.S. *Peruvian* at the age of fourteen, *alone*. In today's society, when we must "street proof" our children in our own community, the idea of sending a child alone across the Atlantic to find his way through England to a new school seems incredible, but by the standards of the day, children were often seen as miniature adults and took on responsibilities at an age much earlier than those of later generations.

To guide his son on the intricacies of the journey, George included a letter in his belongings describing the route to follow.

My dear boy

Remember what I told you about your health on board ship, take as much exercise on deck as possible, and if not able to move about, take your rug and be on deck. On arrival at Liverpool go to the North Western Hotel take a room, have a warm bath, change your clothing and make yourself comfortable, telegraph as arranged to me, the Post Office and telegraph are always in one building in England. You will be one full day at least in Liverpool as you must go to London in a train leaving in the morning so as to arrive in London early in the day ... go to the Euston Square Hotel and take lunch or dinner and register your name in the hotel book. In case of difficulty or danger you can apply either by letter or telegraph or personally to my friends in Liverpool ... [to which he added a list of names and addresses] ... should you unfortunately lose your baggage, you must just get another outfit at Brighton. In railway travelling always see your baggage labelled with the address of the station to which you are going, and on arrival look after it promptly. Claim it and see that the cab man or railway porter takes it to the cab which you engage ...
Your affectionate Papa.

We are fortunate that a meticulously detailed notebook, maintained by Maurice throughout his life, still survives. In this, he recorded all his travels, listing not only the dates and destinations of his journeys, but also the mode of transport, distance travelled, and sights seen. For this particular journey he listed that he sailed from Quebec City via Belle Isle to Liverpool, taking eleven days to make the crossing. At Liverpool, he was actually met by an old friend of his father's, who came unasked and accompanied him to Brighton where Maurice started school.

Back on the business front, George Drummond had worked out a policy with George Dustan whereby Dustan would address the Liberal government on issues related to sugar since they would not listen to Drummond. Almost immediately, George regretted his decision because the proposals Dustan sent to the government were so detrimental to the interests of John Redpath & Son that George had to rush a letter to Dustan for him to amend things immediately.

> *In your communication to the Finance Minister re the sugar duties ... I perceive you have made ... a very great mistake by proposing moving the lowest grade mark up from No. 9 Dutch Standard to No. 13. The first effect will be to deprive us of at least one half of our business which consists in using cheap sugar below No. 9 and making low class yellows. Such a trade will hereafter be principally supplied by importations of muscovado and the lowest class of English and Scotch refined. In return of course we shall make more white but this will not keep us, still less, you going ... I conceive that the only way out of the difficulty is for you now to recommend (as having been omitted) a lower grade NOT above No. 9 D.S. at ½¢ per lb. plus 25% ...*
> *(December 15, 1874)*

Dustan immediately telegraphed the minister to cover his error, which allowed Drummond to follow up on the twenty-sixth with:

> *This appears very satisfactory. One thing pray keep in view if any change is now made, no half measures will do. It must be so liberal as to give home refiners command of the market. Your house will go on, there will be ours here and the Toronto project will probably resume ... the total consumption of Canada won't keep all going and we shall see a condition of things like that in New York ... where with a highly protective tariff the trade is gone to the dogs.*

To round out the year, George had another piece of good news as the accounts of the company showed that once again finances were in the black.

George Alexander Drummond in 1876

Helen Drummond (née Redpath) in 1876.

CHAPTER NINE

The Axe Falls

Early in 1875, George Dustan was invited to go to Ottawa and brief the government on the "sugar question." Dustan was in a panic and asked George Drummond what he should do. George replied:

> *Of course you must go up, if they won't talk to me, or listen for that matter then it must be you ... come here [Montreal] first and I will prepare your facts. (January 13, 1875)*

When Dustan did go up to Ottawa at the end of February, George made sure that in addition to any briefings given to Dustan there was also a written submission from John Redpath & Son to the Minister of Finance, the Honourable R. Cartwright:

> *Sir, We desire respectfully to make the following statement for the information of the Government,*
>
> *1. From an experience of six years under the present tariff we assert positively that it is impossible to conduct the business of refining sugar in this country without loss.*
>
> *2. That this loss is directly caused by the Tariff which overcharges low sugars as compared with refined.*
>
> *3. We have during the past five years remodelled our works and adopted at great expense every improvement known to us.*
>
> *4. Relying on the opinions expressed last session by yourself and other members of the Government we ... made preparations for continuing our business this season and in doing so have incurred still further outlay.*
>
> *5. To stop our works would cause great hardships to the large number of hands employed by us. Many of whom would require to seek work in another country and would scatter a trained body of men and surround with difficulties of the most serious character any future recommencement. Nevertheless this must be the result unless a change [in the Tariff] be made soon.*
>
> *we have the honour to be Sir,*
>
> *Your most obedient servant,*
>
> *John Redpath & Son*
>
> *(February 25, 1875)*

George hoped these combined efforts would result in some new initiative by the government, and he considered going to Ottawa himself at the end of March. The day before he was due to go, he learned that the United States government had altered its rate on the drawback to an unprecedented level of a dollar above the previous level. This instantly neutralized any move the Canadian government might have made to help the Canadian refiners and made Drummond's decision absolute.

He immediately cabled the government:

> *This U.S. change is instantly decisive as far as we are concerned ... the United States refiners have got all they asked ... this places Canada at their mercy ... and apparently the Government intends to do nothing in the way of remedying the crying injustice we are subjected to... if no consideration is to be granted to us ... if we are deliberately turned out of the country it will be felt by very many ... all through this session we have waited for the action promised and so far nothing has been done ... we see no hope of being able to continue refining, the necessity of stoppage is now beyond question.*
> *(March 30, 1875)*

To the two members of Parliament for Montreal, George sent a direct warning:

> *The new U.S. drawback is 48% as opposed to 35% and gives a profit of $2.00 per barrel to the U.S. refiners ... if no movement is made by our own Government at once, and of a sufficient character. We shall, as soon as we can, get rid of the raw materials now owned by us, shut up our works and as a necessary consequence throw all our hands out of employment. For ourselves it will be serious enough as we have in buildings and plant invested half a million of dollars, which will not only be unproductive but a source of expense. As a public work our industry is not insignificant. It gives employment to a large number of men - it feeds about a thousand mouths. It gives employment to ships and railways ... which will be supplanted by works ... in New York and Boston. Who will benefit by the ruin of our industry? not the consumer ultimately because as soon as we are closed the bounty can be withdrawn, and it is not so easy to re-open and collect a staff of skilled men who will in a short time be dispersed. Not the merchants of Montreal who have been so jealous of us. Because the only sugar business hereafter to be done by them will be local, as all Ontario will draw its supplies from the United States ... in closing us they have killed themselves also.*
> *(March 31, 1875)*

In a series of similar letters, most of the parliamentary members were warned of the severe consequences of the U.S. drawback, and Drummond called on Dustan to join in with:

> *You had better use all your influence with Nova Scotia members. The Government will not move unless pressure is brought to bear on them and if nothing is now done the matter is ended for all of us.*
> *(April 3, 1875)*

On April 6, George went again to see various members of Parliament and returned to Montreal despondent, as he stated to the New York purchasing agents in a letter dated April 10, 1875:

I have been over three days ... at Ottawa trying to draw water out of a well in a sieve or nearly so ... nothing so far about the matter has been done.

But on the eleventh, the government did take action, as even they saw that this drawback was deliberately designed to force open the Canadian market to U.S. sugar refining interests. George received the news the following day and cabled the Honourable Isaac Burpee:

We are today informed that the Government has ordered a reduction of the duties on raw sugars below No. 13 D.S. of 75¢ per 100 lbs. and will not allow U.S. refined to be entered for duty at the unnaturally reduced price produced by the excessive drawback now allowed by the U.S. Government. The reduction of duty on raw, is by itself, entirely inadequate but these two regulations combined will, we think, enable us to continue our business at least to the extent of working up our present stocks ...
(April 12, 1875)

For George, the past four months had proved almost too much for his health, so he decided to take a short break and visit New York. He contacted Hewlett to arrange for a meeting to discuss matters, adding:

My wife is coming with me. She sadly wants a change and a run among the shop windows and theatres will do her good.
(April 13, 1875)

Upon his return at the end of the month, George was certain that things were not going to mend in the near future. He informed Hewlett that, as their earlier discussions had suggested, it was impossible to continue and that John Redpath & Son would no longer buy any raw sugar until matters improved. As George put it:

Our business is killed for this season, all that remains to do is give it a decent burial.
(May 4, 1875)

During the summer, George had the pleasure of being with his family at their summer home at Cacouna. Even Maurice returned from England, aided by another letter of guidance from his father on the proper way to travel and what to watch out for.

My Dear Boy

You must take care at Liverpool, two or three steamers leave on the same day ... Mr. Paterson our agent in Liverpool says he will see you to the ship ... take care of your baggage at Liverpool as there is usually a lot of trouble and confusion and danger of losing it ... put two address tags on each piece ... I will meet you at Quebec and should I fail to do so, go to Russells Hotel ... and come down to Cacouna by first conveyance.

Your affectionate Papa

Maurice's notebook informs us that he sailed from Liverpool on board the S.S. *Peruvian* of the Allan Line on July 27 and arrived at Quebec on August12, returning to England on the S.S. *Moravian* (again of the Allan Line) between the seventeenth and twenty-eighth of September.

Returning to the refinery at the end of August, George Drummond received a disturbing note from Dustan, in which Dustan made all kinds of accusations and complaints against Drummond for making a fool of him with the government. Dustan further stated that he had been told that Drummond had been using him only to make a profit on him. George immediately responded with a long letter going over the many points of Dustan's letter, reminding him that at no time had he made any profit from Dustan's actions and concluding with:

> *I look on the past five years of my business life as entirely wasted and would now look back with something like gratitude on any event which would have stopped the business at that time and turned me out of the country.*
> *(August 18, 1875)*

As August turned into September and then October, George wrote to Peter wondering when "the other shoe would drop from Dustan," but on October 11 he received a completely different letter to the previous one from George Dustan.

> *On my return home the day before yesterday I received your very welcome letter ... for which I am much obliged and thank you cordially ... I never for a moment doubted you or your honour and your good intentions regarding myself ... I intend to be guided by you in all my propositions with the Government and beg you will keep me advised at all times how to act ... when I wrote you on the 13th August I was quite miserable - very poor in ready means, in fact unable to meet my family expenses ... I feared you had altogether forgotten me and as Mr. Peter Redpath had not replied to two important letters I thought I had unwittingly offended him ... The fight also seemed going against me ... this will account for the tone of my letter. You see ... I am every day writing and speaking on the subject. I even got the Toronto "Globe" to write an article for me ... all the Nova Scotia papers are with me and offer to write leaders on the subject. Would you write something on the question and I will get our chief papers to insert it without your name appearing.*
> (October 9, 1875)

The difference in tone and substance between the two letters convinced George Drummond that Dustan was not a stable person and could not be trusted as an ally. Never-the-less, it had been proved that Dustan's Liberal connections did get the refiners' message through to the government, where Drummond's Conservative contacts were temporarily powerless to act. He therefore maintained an arm's-length connection to Dustan over the next few years during the remainder of the issue; of the many articles subsequently published under the name of Dustan, one wonders how many were originally penned by George Drummond.

During October, the remaining stocks of raw sugar were used up and the employees were notified that the plant would stop altogether after cleaning up had finished. Once this happened, the government sent a letter of complaint to the company, criticizing them for causing "suffering" to further a political move. George rebutted this charge in a set of letters to all the government officials who had been involved in precipitating this event:

I learn today that it is asserted to the Government that we stopped our refinery solely as a political move and with a view to influencing the elections in this City against the Government ... It need scarcely be said by me that this is absolutely and wholly false, we have been engaged all summer in working up to a stoppage and only stopped when the last pound of our raw sugar was worked up, and you no doubt remember that this was the utmost we had hoped to be able to do ... but as we are exceedingly unwilling to let our hands scatter we have bought some sugar ... and on receipt will resume work on a small scale ... although the dull season is at hand with no prospect of much demand ... to keep our hands from starving.
(October 18, 1875)

For the remainder of the year, the refinery worked at its minimum levels of output and one section of the plant after another was closed down with no seeming hope for a start-up in the near future. Although the last stocks of sugar did not bring in much income, the lower costs of process materials and wages allowed the books to register a technical profit for the year, but the means by which it had been achieved and the sacrifices in labour and capital that were the result could not have been good news to George. The refinery worked through the normal Christmas break and into the new year, but eventually the last barrels of sugar were used up and the plant closed down completely. Certain in his mind that this final closure was the result of the years of apathy and then antipathy by the government, George made the closure of the refinery a very public issue. Starting with statements to the press, he followed up with an open letter to the Prime Minister.

Honourable Alexander MacKenzie,
Premier of the Dominion of Canada,
OTTAWA, Ontario.

Sir,
We beg leave respectfully to state for your information that since the adjustment of drawbacks on refined sugar by the United States, we find it impossible to compete with their refiners, and have consequently discontinued to manufacture.

American refined sugar has been sent in considerable quantities to Europe, paying freight and charges amounting to a half cent a pound, and has complete control of the Dominion market, as freights from New York and Boston to all important points in the Dominion are as low as from Montreal.

The rates of American drawbacks place their refiners on a better footing than before, for while hard sugars receive 15¢ per hundred pounds less drawbacks, soft whites and brown yellows are allowed 50¢ more, and these rates, being fixed as a result of an enquiry by experts, have an appearance of permanence which did not exist before.

We have therefore not felt it possible to do anything towards continuing the manufacture in this country, and though this is the crop season in the West Indies, and the time when active steps must be taken to secure supplies of all kinds, we have done nothing whatever in this direction, and unless a re-adjustment of duties is effected sufficient to meet the cost – either by reducing the charge on the raw material or by adding to that on refined sugar - we see no course open to us but to abandon our business.

(signed) JOHN REDPATH & SON

(February 29, 1876)

The effect of this decision to close for an indefinite period was quickly noted by the *Evening Star* of Montreal when it reported:

> *We were waited upon today by a deputation of operatives who have been employed in the sugar refining works of the Messrs. Redpath in this City, and who have been thrown completely out of employment by the paralysation of the industry by which they gained their bread ... By this ... three hundred hands are thrown out of employment ... a few experienced hands have been kept on ... and now the workers are on the street with no other recourse than to seek labour in the United States ... we understand that a public meeting is to be called to take this matter into consideration ... and it is to be hoped that when the meeting is held there will be formulated a calm, decisive expression of opinion such as will force the Government to pause and consider.* (February 28, 1876)

The subsequent public meeting was well attended, especially by members of the wholesale and retail grocers trade, who, recognizing the position their previous policies had now put them in, decided to try to reverse the trend through the following petition:

> *To the Honourable, the House of Commons of the Dominion of Canada, in Parliament assembled.*
>
> *We, the undersigned wholesale and retail Grocers, of the City of Montreal, having learned that the Canada Sugar Refinery of this city has been forced to close down, owing to late changes of the American "Draw-Back" on refined sugar, desire respectfully to represent that we look upon this event as a most unfortunate one to the trade of this city and province, as cutting off from us an important source of our supplies and rendering us entirely dependent on foreigners and as likely very speedily to result in enhanced prices to ourselves and the consumers of the article.*
>
> *We therefore pray that the Government will give the matter their serious attention and pass such changes of our Tariff this present session, as will enable our refiners to continue their business and supply us as heretofore with all grades of sugar as wanted.*

The government, of course, ignored this and all other protestations and appeals. Its course was now firmly set to a promotion of absolute free trade without regard to the costs to home manufacturers or their employees.

On the other hand, the general malaise within the economy had been deepening for the past two years and required some sort of investigation. Therefore a "Committee on the Depression of Trade" was established to report on aspects of the fall in trade throughout the lumber, coal mining, sugar refining, agricultural tool manufacturing, footwear, quarries, steam engines, cotton and woollen fabrics, and shipbuilding industries. Carefully screened and selected for the job, the members of this committee consisted of: David Mills (chairman), Messrs. Platt, Dymond, Sinclair, Burpee, McDougall and Workman. Each of these men was a staunch supporter of Mackenzie and, in the case of Mills and Workman, were rabid free traders. Throughout the term of their so-called investigation, they repeatedly refused to accept submissions from groups and individuals opposing their own version of free trade and packed the meetings with carefully chosen pro free trade advocates. If those who were examined showed any sign of criticism of free trade, they were subjected to an immediate barrage of condemnation and were listed as unreliable witnesses. As might be expected, the confrontation between these people on the committee and George Drummond (who had just lost his refinery) was something to behold. Even the newspapers recognized and commented on the differences between the attitude of George Drummond and the members of the committee.

In his first day of testimony on March 9, 1876, George recapitulated the status of his company, listing the physical capital of the plant at $600,000 with a capacity production of 224,000 pounds per day. For production, he stated it required $2 million in direct capital and $1.5 million in floating capital. He then went on to reveal that most of the raw sugar obtained for refining was of South American and Cuban origin, with figures of 41 million pounds of sugar being refined in 1874, paying over $600,000 in duty to the government. When asked what changes he had made in recent years, his answer was:

> *We are changing all the time. It is impossible to conduct such a business as ours without a large amount being expended in changes.*

To the question "What types of refined sugar do you make?" he responded:

> *All the sugars consumed in the country. But for the last four or five years we have produced none of the loaf or lump sugar, our principal product has been yellow and all hard sugar machinery has been totally idle since 1872. The Canadian demand has been supplied instead from New York and Boston.*

Then Mr. Mills asked "Why? ... Is it more profitable to manufacture other varieties instead of hard sugars?", to which George replied:

> *That was not the reason, The American tariff discriminated against the manufacturers of sugar and after informing the Government of the fact ... we were compelled to stand on what we had.*

Seeing that they could not get from George the answers they wanted, the committee started to press him to reveal specific costs, production levels, profits, wages, and a host of other figures that would have exposed the entire structure and business of John Redpath & Son. George naturally demurred from revealing such information to his competition, and when the committee demanded the figures, George refused. This was all the excuse Mr. Mills needed to label Drummond a hostile and untrustworthy witness. On the following day, the committee continued to hound George Drummond for his private company finances. When they could not get these, they changed tactics and Mr. Workman condemned the Redpath Company for adulterating and diluting its sugar with impurities. He claimed he had been reliably informed that Canadian sugar was not as "strong" as it was before Redpath's began. George rejected this outright and asked who was making these accusations. Mr. Workman would not reply, and when pressed by George to answer, finally stated that he "got it from his cook." George calmly replied that:

> *With all respect to that lady I would like to explain that she is mistaken entirely.*

Mr. Mills now took up the attack, by demanding to know why the Canada Sugar Refinery had closed down. George said:

> *My reason is because I cannot carry on the refinery at a profit ... we have been carrying on our refinery for a number of years at a disadvantage, but now the American bounty has settled the question conclusively we don't refine sugar because we cannot do it except at a loss.*

The committee obviously could not obtain anything acceptable to their pre-decided verdict and dismissed George. They then brought in a series of wholesale importers, all of whom were totally committed to maintaining their new monopoly on sugar and these importers provided numerous statistics for the committee to back their claims. The fact that these figures were provided for the importers by the U.S. refiners (and even the U.S. government had rejected the figures as totally worthless) was completely ignored, and the statistics were entered as a true reflection of the state of affairs, while George's figures were dismissed as lies.

The following day, a number of newspaper articles gave their views on the matter. In the Montreal *Gazette*, one reporter reviewed the case as follows:

> *The Depression Committee had a long sitting, Mr. Drummond being under examination for two hours and a half. The most remarkable feature of the examination was the zeal with which the Chairman ... attempted to prevent any evidence going in opposed to their pre-conceived notions that the Canadian refining interest is unduly protected. Every day makes it more apparent this Committee is not sitting to take evidence with a view to arriving at a conclusion, but with the object of sustaining a conclusion already arrived at. Mr. Drummond's evidence was exceedingly clear, and to every unprejudiced mind must be sufficient that refining in Canada has been rendered impossible by the policy of the American Government ... the [Canadian] Government and their friends ... seem to regard a manufacturer as a natural enemy of the country who it is [their] duty ... to suppress.*
> *(March 11, 1876)*

Even abroad, the obvious bias of the committee was recognized and an article printed some months later in a British trade journal under the title "*Sugar Cane*" stated that subsequent Canadian government statistics proved George's case beyond all question and that in his testimony:

> *Mr. Drummond appears simply to state that sugar from the United States receives a subsidy against which he is unable to compete, and he gives the very best proof of the truth of what he says by shutting up his refinery ... the tone of his interrogators would indeed lead one to suppose that he had, uttered some economical heresy ... and that the members of the Committee, all full of the enthusiasm of Free Trade, having converted their tribunal into an inquisition for the detection and punishment of Free Trade heresies were putting their victim through all the tortures of such a court, previous to his final excommunication and the casting of*

him into the outer darkness reserved for those who murmur against the sale of articles below cost price.
(October 1876)

Inevitably, when the committee released its report in April 1876, it took a staunch free trade viewpoint and denied that there was in fact any real depression and where there was an economic problem, the causes "are quite beyond legislative control in this country." On the matter of sugar they reported:

The Committee have examined several persons connected with the importation of sugar [N.B: they say importers not refiners]. They do not deem it necessary to consider whether it is to the public advantage that sugar refining should be carried on in this country or not. The number of men employed in proportion to the Capital invested is small, and the sugar market of Canada is so limited that the business of refining, if largely protected would be practically in the hands of very few persons ... The Committee have given careful consideration to complaints against the American bounty system and are of opinion that they are not well founded ... the Committee are of the opinion that a National Policy, founded on the greatest freedom of trade which the public credit will permit, is one most advantageous to this country.

This blatantly biased report for all the industries studied raised the ire of many sectors of the economy and even in Ontario, the bastion of free trade, one newspaper (the Toronto *Mail*) later printed an article on the committee and its results:

It would have been better named ... a Committee for devising ways and means for the extinction of Canadian manufactures and the promotion of American. From first to last its purpose appeared to be to obtain all the evidence possible that could be made against the former and in favour of the latter.
(October 14, 1876)

It then commented on the excessive attacks on witnesses by the chairman and others and questioned why the remaining members of the committee did not stand up to Mr. Mills.

But they knew that the Committee was part of the Government plan for throwing cold water on protection at all costs and hazards, and little as they might have thought of setting themselves against the Chairman they also knew that it was not really the little man at the head of the table with whom they had to reckon but a ... majority proud Premier who had the power of making things unpleasant, even for his friends ... the result is a report which will stand as a lasting disgrace ... as it is both in conception and execution a plea for the advancement of American industry and the suppression of our own.
(October 14, 1876)

For the workers of the refinery, of whom we unfortunately hear too little, all the reports in the world would not help their plight. For those unemployed in a period before the establishment of workers' compensation, and social security, the only means by which they could now survive was to either use up their life savings or move elsewhere to find work. In a desperate bid to salvage things, a number of the employees and local tradespeople drafted an appeal to the Prime Minister stressing their plight.

> *We your Memorialists humbly show that owing to the closing of the Canada Sugar Refinery many of us have been deprived of the labour upon which we have hitherto relied for our support and we all throughout the locality now feel the want of that prominent industry which has been in existence for twenty - one years...*
>
> *That most of us own property in the neighbourhood which forms a considerable portion of that suburb of the City of Montreal and which has all been built upon since the commencement of the Sugar Refinery and is daily depreciating in value as tenants, unable to pay their rents are leaving for the United States and other parts of the country from day to day...*
>
> *That our stores and shops, which have to a large extent been dependent on the wages paid to the employees of the Sugar Refinery are suffering from the loss of this trade...*
>
> *That many of us connected with other trades such as coopers, carpenters, bricklayers, millwrights, machinists, iron and brass founders, finishers, painters, glaziers, tinsmiths etc. feel the loss of business through the closing of that establishment...*
>
> *That we all regret the undue advantage given by our laws to the American Sugar Refiners ...*
>
> *That as the Canada Sugar Refinery is the first Canadian industry which has been blotted out of existence by unfair American competition we hope that it may be the first to be resuscitated by honest Canadian Legislation.*
> *(March 31, 1876)*

No reply was ever received and the doors of the company stayed shut.

In the immediate post-closure period, the importers and U.S. refiners now had total control of the market and implemented a series of price rises that were noted by the press; they also started to drop the quality of their sugar without reducing the price, thus cutting their costs of production and increasing their profit margins. In two separate articles in the Montreal *Gazette*, the situation was presented as follows:

> *To the Editor of the Gazette,*
>
> *It is now some four months since the Montreal Sugar Refinery has been forced to close down for want of support [by] the Government and the desire on the part of the Government to give a cheap article to people generally. This stands good in imagination only - facts do not bear it out ... certain grades of sugar having run out of stock at the refinery ... I find Sir an advance of 2 cents per pound ... and have actually seen a case where five cents per pound was paid over the refining quotation ... this Mr. Editor is only the beginning of what we shall be made to feel when our refinery is known to be finally closed down and the Americans have full control of our market. Then the "drawback" will be changed and New York prices, with all the additions ... will rule in Montreal.*
>
> *"TRADE"*
> *(March 20, 1876)*
>
> *To the Editor of the Gazette,*
>
> *The [Montreal] Witness denies that the prices of certain*

grades of refined sugars have advanced ... and gives as its authority "several leading grocers". Perhaps these leading grocers ... are importers of American and Scotch Sugars. But had the Witness reporter interviewed a few of the retailers ... he would find a contrary opinion ... I can safely say that neither the Scotch yellow nor the American white sugars can compare with the sugars supplied by Messr's Redpath ... The white sugar imported from the States to take the place of Redpath's ... is perfect trash while the price is higher ... sugars, like other goods are cheap just now because there is little trade but as soon as the demand gets brisk the prices will go up.

"HOME MANUFACTURE"
(March 21, 1876)

In a letter to the editor of the *Witness*, one long-time retail merchant, Alex McGibbon, submitted his opinion of how trade was suffering as the result of U.S. and "Scotch" domination. He also remembered how things were before Redpath started production:

I can refer to the time (thirty years ago) when the principal sugars sold in Canada were McFie's loaf sugar and "white bastards", these were the only refined sugars to be had, and for raw sugar we had Porto Rico, Barbados, Cuba etc. A part of a clerks duty at that time was to cut or break up this loaf sugar into pieces for table use, and when a housekeeper wanted a pound of fine sugar to frost a cake or to use with fruit it had to be pounded in a mortar, or rolled on a table as required ... Redpath's factory started about 1854 or 1855 and since then prices have kept very even and all kinds of sugar required in trade were furnished of the very best quality. We are now going back to the old times, but with this difference, the people will no longer use common raw sugar and instead of getting our supplies from the West Indies and other places of production, we shall have to depend entirely on the American and Scotch Refiners.
(April 6, 1876)

Even George Dustan entered the argument with an article in the Halifax *Morning Chronicle* warning of future price rises.

If it was certain that the American bounty would always exist, and that the American refiners would always supply us with refined sugar cheaper than we can manufacture it. Free Trade and common sense would say - sugar refining is not an industry that can flourish in Canada; let us rely on the Americans to supply us with cheap refined sugar and devote our attention to other branches of business. It is more reasonable to believe, however ... that the artificial state of affairs which exists under the influence of the American bounty cannot be relied on, but that, on the contrary, if the Americans get the monopoly of sugar refining ... they will act as all monopolists do and make us pay dearly for that which they now, for their own purposes sell cheaply.
(May 24, 1876)

As predicted, with competition out of the way, the U.S. refiners boosted prices. Even the subsequent drop in the drawback by the U.S. government did not stem the tide of foreign sugars entering Canada. Subsequently, trade journals in the United States revealed that the information used by the Depression Committee to justify its case (previously provided by the U.S. refiners to the American government in March) was totally false and designed to swindle that government and the American people out of millions of dollars in tariff revenues. Legal action soon followed in the U.S. but the Canadian government did not merely ignore this fact – they rejected it openly and maintained that the original data was true. This policy continued to be upheld even when a British Parliamentary Committee (researching the same situation in England) concluded that the U.S. refineries *had* manipulated the market to increase foreign sales. The fact remained that the Mackenzie government could not be seen to be wrong, so all subsequent information that contradicted the earlier statements of the committee had to be passed off as worthless. For his loyalty to the government's position, Mr. Mills was later made a Cabinet minister. In the face of this hypocrisy, George felt he could no longer stand to remain in Canada, and in late June he sailed with his family to England to take an extended vacation away from the circumstances of the last few years.

By the end of the year, the accounts showed a large financial loss for the company, while the official government statistics for prices and imports revealed that the predictions and warnings given by the refiners earlier in the year were being confirmed. The pro-government papers claimed these losses were irrelevant as they did not amount to "anything significant." The anti-government papers pressed the issue for all it was worth.

For George, this was time to forget his troubles and enjoy Europe with his family. As to Peter Redpath and other members of the family connected with the business, nothing is documented for this period. But it is safe to say that Peter is hardly likely to have remained around at this time when he had been scrupulously absent at the beginning of the year. The plant was closed and locked, with only a skeleton staff of maintenance workers keeping the machinery in working order, in hopes of a re-opening some time in the future. What they did not realize was that that day would not come until 1879, more than two years later!

Right: Sugar prices "out of sight," a commentary on the sugar situation by the Canadian Illustrated News, December 9, 1876.

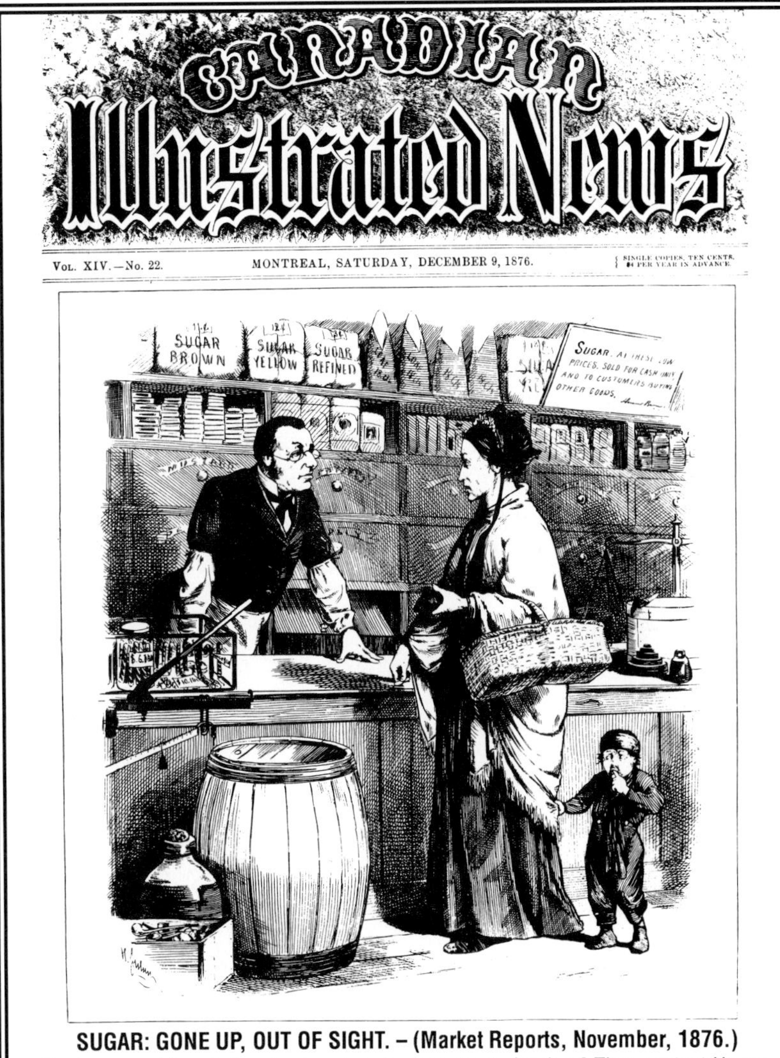

Canadian Illustrated News

Vol. XIV.—No. 22. MONTREAL, SATURDAY, DECEMBER 9, 1876. SINGLE COPIES, TEN CENTS. $4 PER YEAR IN ADVANCE.

SUGAR: GONE UP, OUT OF SIGHT. – (Market Reports, November, 1876.)

Customer: – Them's free-trade prices to consumers, be they? Then protect Home Manufacturers to death, sez I. I'd a'taken two pounds refined at the old Redpath price. Gi'me a quarter pound brown; that'll have to do for a week, *now.*

Grocer: – Very sorry, Ma'am, but we are positively losing money on sugar, even at these prices. (More's the pity. *Ed. Note.*)

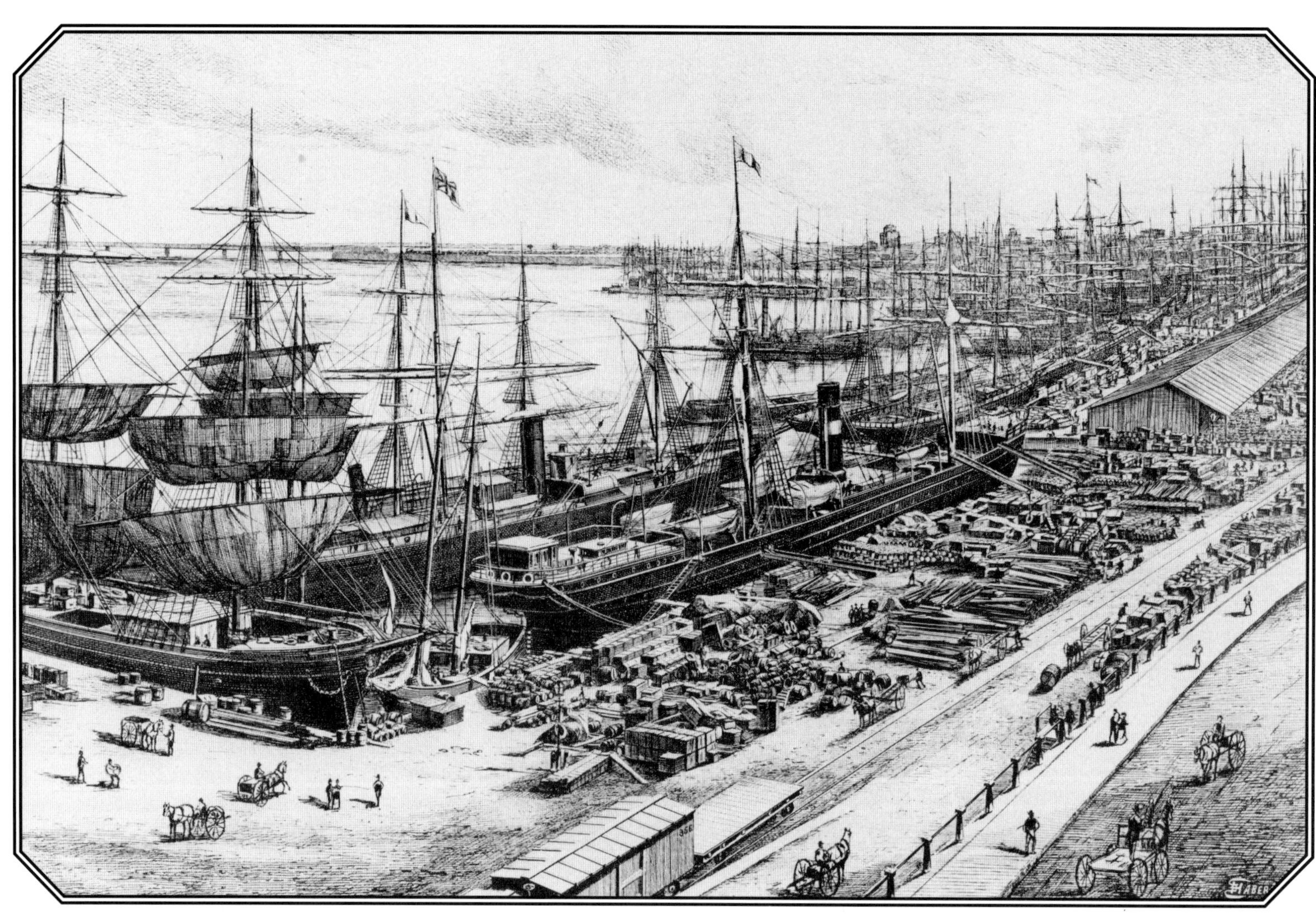

The Port of Montreal, 1875

CHAPTER TEN

Intermission

For the Drummond family, 1877 was far from a time of casual pastimes as George and his sons Huntly, Edgar, Arthur, and Maurice toured numerous refineries and factories throughout England, Scotland, and Europe, to study current business methods, technological advances, and production systems. Maurice's travel diary reveals that in August alone, they toured factories in Birmingham, Nottingham, Sheffield, and Manchester while in September they visited operations in Doncaster, Sheffield, Newcastle-upon-Tyne, Glasgow, and Greenock. At the start of October, the group moved over to the Continent visiting sugar beet factories at the Hague, Amsterdam, Cologne, and Brussels and then returned to the family on October 16, for a late season tour of the highlands, while of Peter and the other Redpath partners, we have no information.

In Canada, the free trade bonanza promised by Mackenzie failed to materialize as numerous businesses went into bankruptcy, and the various dubious methods used to press free trade came back to haunt both the Liberals and Mr. Mills in particular. The prices of sugar rose rapidly, as the American refiners found they had unimpeded control of the white sugar market, and British low-grade yellow sugars dominated the bottom end of the trade. Furthermore, the continuing number of articles criticizing the government's position, including the sugar cane article referred to earlier, goaded Mr. Mills into denouncing this specific article by charging it had been written by George Drummond. The editors replied publicly that he was totally mistaken and that the authorship belonged to a British source. This reply also referred to the increasing evidence emerging out of the United States of a deliberate fraud on the part of the U.S. refiners who were using the American drawback regulations and Canadian tariffs to extract an abnormal profit from their sugar dealings. These activities consisted of American refiners purchasing high-class raw sugars in the Caribbean from local planters, then colouring the sugar with an artificial syrup to make it look like the lower-grade sugars. This product was then imported to the United States under the low-grade tariff of that country, which allowed it to enter at highly advantageous rates. The coloured sugar was subsequently rinsed to remove the colouring, shipped to Canada, and listed as high-grade sugar, so that the maximum drawback could be claimed from the U.S. government, with savings to the refiners of up to $12,000 per cargo. According to the U.S. Customs Department, this practice defrauded the taxpayers of $3 million in 1876 alone. As a result, in September 1877 the drawbacks were substantially altered and legal action was initiated by the U.S. Department of Justice against the offending companies. Mr. Mills still refused to be convinced, however, and continued to publicly proclaim the committee's original position on the free trade question, but few were now willing to take his word for it.

In Quebec, the economic malaise had now become so serious that the Quebec Legislative Assembly decided to resurrect the concept of a domestic sugar beet industry as originally proposed by George Drummond in the mid-1860s, and on November 9, 1877, the *Journal of Commerce* published a report that:

> *Quebec is to have a beet sugar refinery ... The Quebec Legislature is to grant a large subsidy to encourage an enterprise.*

On the sixteenth, an article in the *Globe* newspaper noted that a long-standing bonus offered by the provincial government was being increased to $70,000 to be paid over a term of ten years, but no one took up this offer and the matter continued to languish for some years.

Confounded on all sides by the realities contradicting his assertions, Mr. Mills began to use personal attacks in early December to try to bolster his position. He also attempted to discredit the company of John Redpath & Son by publicly stating:

> *That refined sugars made from inferior grades of raw sugar are all of inferior quality and contain a much smaller percentage of sugar ... thus supplying the consumers through the refiners with the worst class of refined sugars. This is exactly what the Montreal refiners were doing; and in my opinion the country has lost nothing, but on the contrary has gained largely, when their establishment was closed. (December 12, 1877)*

Moved to respond to these accusations, Alex McGibbon, the Montreal retail merchant, defended the Redpath products with his own letter to the editor of the Montreal *Gazette*:

> *This is the most absurd statement which has yet appeared on this question and will certainly be news to the trade and customers generally. I have sold sugar for over thirty years and I can safely say that the trade was never during that time so well supplied with good pure sugars as when Redpath was in operation. Does Mr. Mills mean to say that the Scotch adulterated yellows and American whites are better sugar than what Redpath gave his customers? Consumers don't say so!, and if Mr. Mills was a short time in the business he would soon find overwhelming testimony to convince him of the fallacy of his opinion. The quality of the sugars is not only very inferior but the price is much higher ... than it was in Redpath's time.*

The final blow to Mills's argument came when the Montreal *Gazette* printed excerpts from the testimony of Mr. Gadesden, Chairman of the British Sugar Refiners Committee to the Royal Commission on Trade, during which he stated that the yellow Scotch Sugars:

> *Are a coarse material which the fastidious British consumer will not use and therefore it is sent abroad.*

This was followed by similar statements by Mr. Martinear, the secretary of that association:

> *That the exports [of yellows] in fact consisted of the refuse of the refinery which the British consumer will not take and are sent to Canada and other places where a low [quality] article found a market.*

Mr. Mills was now all but discredited, as was the Liberal party over its policy of free trade. During the period of their ministry, more than 7,200 businesses closed down, with financial losses amounting to more than $100 million. The time had come for Sir John A. Macdonald to re-establish his party under the banner of a new "National Policy," which advocated the repudiation of the free trade status (which had totally failed the nation) and the re-introduction of protective tariffs to assist domestic industries to get back on their feet. In support of the National Policy, the Conservative press and politicians made much of the destruction of the sugar industry under Mackenzie, and it became a rallying point for those against the government. Even in Toronto (the arch capital of free trade doctrine), the Toronto *National* newspaper re-printed Mr. Mills's December 1877 letter with its rebuttal by George Dustan of June 7, 1878, (although the suspiciously long gap between Mills's criticism of the Redpath Company and Dustan's reply could lead one to believe that Dustan had forwarded the criticism to George Drummond in Europe, who then drafted the reply subsequently credited to Dustan.) This rebuttal reads in part:

> *Most people will remember the famous – or shall we call it the notorious – Committee of Depression, and the manner of its dealing with dissatisfied manufacturers – among these were the refiners of sugar, who, by the way, did not appear voluntarily before the committee, but in obedience to its summons, submitted to be interviewed at considerable length, and the Chairman devoted his best abilities to prove from the mouth of the representative of that trade that his grievances were imaginary, his facts unfounded, and his complaints baseless ... The American refiners profiting by the discomfiture of our own manufacturers found an advocate in Mr. Mills who accepted with avidity and endorsed all their statements and applied them to justify the extinction of the industry at home ... Unfortunately the American Government awoke to the facts and a protracted and exhaustive enquiry – Proving that Mr. Mills and the American refiners were wrong and substantiating in a remarkable manner the facts, figures and arguments of our own refiners ... Under these circumstances, one would expect some contrition on the part of Mr. Mills ... but this we do not find ... Mr. Mills is still of opinion he was right ..." (June 7, 1878)*

In comparing the letters of Mr. Mills and Mr. Dustan, the Toronto *Mail* was even more blunt in its opinion of Mr. Mills:

> *Mr. Mills is shown at once to be ignorant of the subject, to have given immoral advice and to be determined to pursue an unpatriotic course ... utterly dishonest and incompetent, every friend of Canada will rejoice when he sinks again into that native obscurity from which he emerged in Canada's evil hour, apparently for the one sole purpose of*

depressing and ruining the industries of the Dominion.
(August 22, 1878)

Following an extremely bitter election campaign, the Conservatives were swept to power on September 17, winning 142 seats to the Liberals' 64. Within twenty-four hours, the *Morning Herald* newspaper printed the following notice:

We have to announce that by telegraph from Paris that Mr. Drummond, the eminent Montreal sugar Refiner, on hearing of the change in Canada, at once determined to start for Canada on the 21st.

Upon his arrival in Canada, George wasted no time in establishing his plans for the re-opening of the refinery and by the end of the year had purchased more than 4,000 tons of coal and quantities of charcoal as preparatory stock for the commencement of work. He also contacted many of the old employees still living in the city and invited them to re-apply for their positions, with guarantees that they would be given first chance at their old jobs. George also approached the government to try to learn what Macdonald's plans were for the assistance of the sugar industry. Finally, he met with George Dustan to review recent activities and to look for a future co-operation in re-establishing Dustan's refinery in Halifax.

The press was quick to pick up on the significance of this meeting and an initial article in the *Herald* on the development of the Halifax sugar refinery was supported by an editorial, while another newspaper, the *Reporter and Times*, went further and expounded on the intentions of both Dustan and Drummond.

The Policy decided upon both by Mr. Drummond and Mr. Dustan is to do nothing whatever until there is a law actually placed upon the Statute Book, by which law the Governor-in-Council will be empowered by an Order-in-Council at any time to impose upon any foreign products a surtax equivalent to the bounty given by Foreign Governments to the exported products of their country; thus giving Canadian refined sugar, as well as other products, a countervailing duty and a rapid mode of applying it to rapidly shifting circumstances ... Till such power is given by the Parliament and exercised by the Government it would manifestly be unwise and probably impossible for the sugar refinery interest to move a finger in the direction of immediate preparation ... we have no doubt whatever that the Government will ask for such power and will receive ... the authority required. If there was any one question more thoroughly canvassed and more powerful than another throughout Canada in the last election it was the Sugar Question.
(November 19, 1878)

By the end of the year the account books showed a general financial gain of $35,156.49 (there was no official profit as nothing was yet being produced). But it was still far better than the $26,475.98 recorded as losses for 1877.

The other significant matter that emerged at the end of 1878 and that carried on into 1879 was the future status of the various partners and the very nature of the structure of the company, for George was determined to see it re-established as a public joint-stock company.

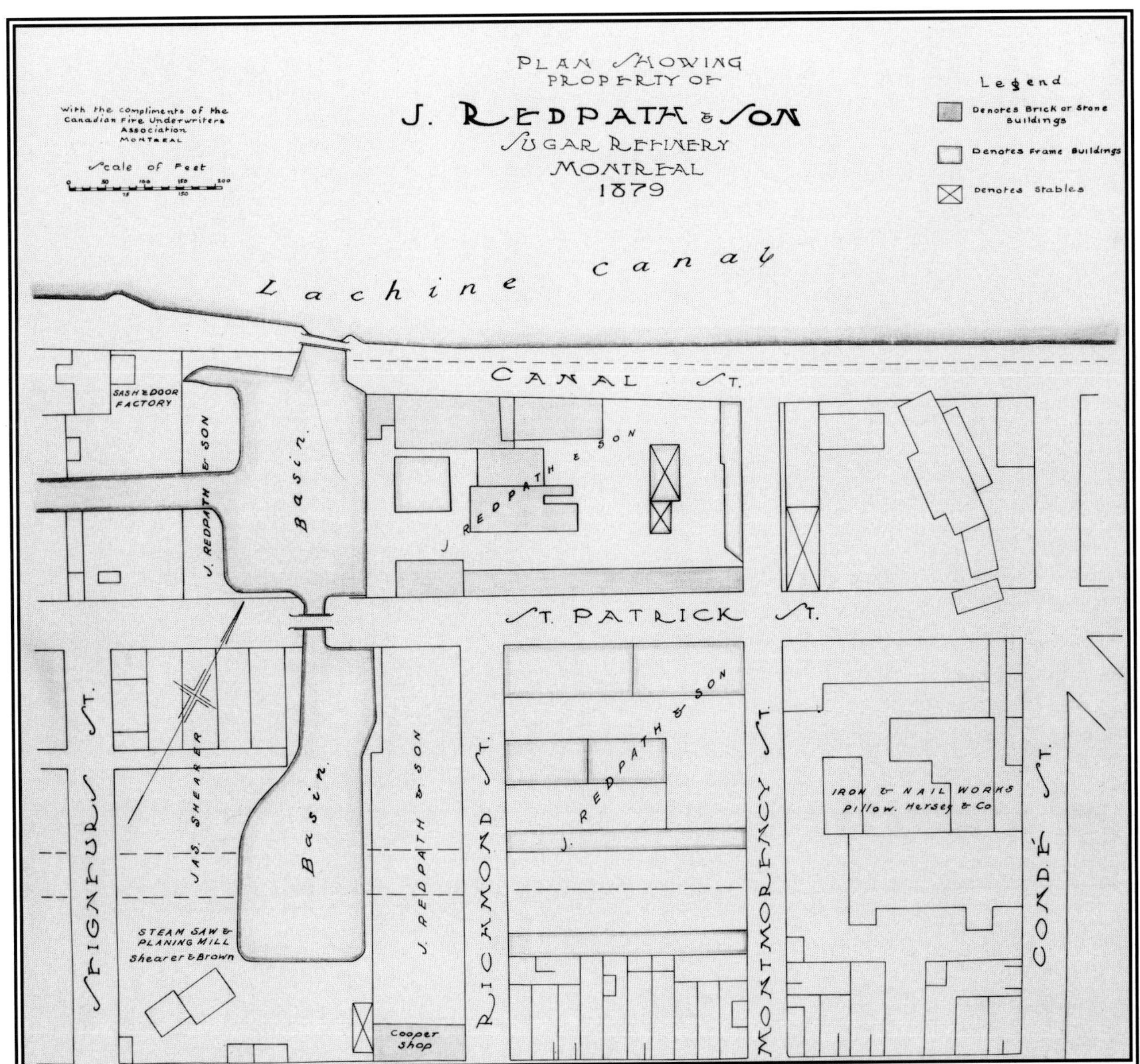

PLAN SHOWING
PROPERTY OF
J. REDPATH & SON
SUGAR REFINERY
MONTREAL
1879
With the compliments of the
Canadian Fire Underwriters
Association
MONTREAL
Scale of Feet
0 50 100 150 200
75 150
Legend
Denotes Brick or Stone Buildings
Denotes Frame Buildings
Denotes Stables
Lachine canal
CANAL ST.
SASH & DOOR FACTORY
J. REDPATH & SON
Basin
J. REDPATH & SON
ST. PATRICK ST.
JAS. SHEARER
Basin
J. REDPATH & SON
J. REDPATH & SON
IRON & NAIL WORKS
Pillow. Hersey & Co
STEAM SAW & PLANING MILL
Shearer & Brown
Cooper Shop
SEIGNEURS ST.
RICHMOND ST.
MONTMORENCY ST.
CONDÉ ST.

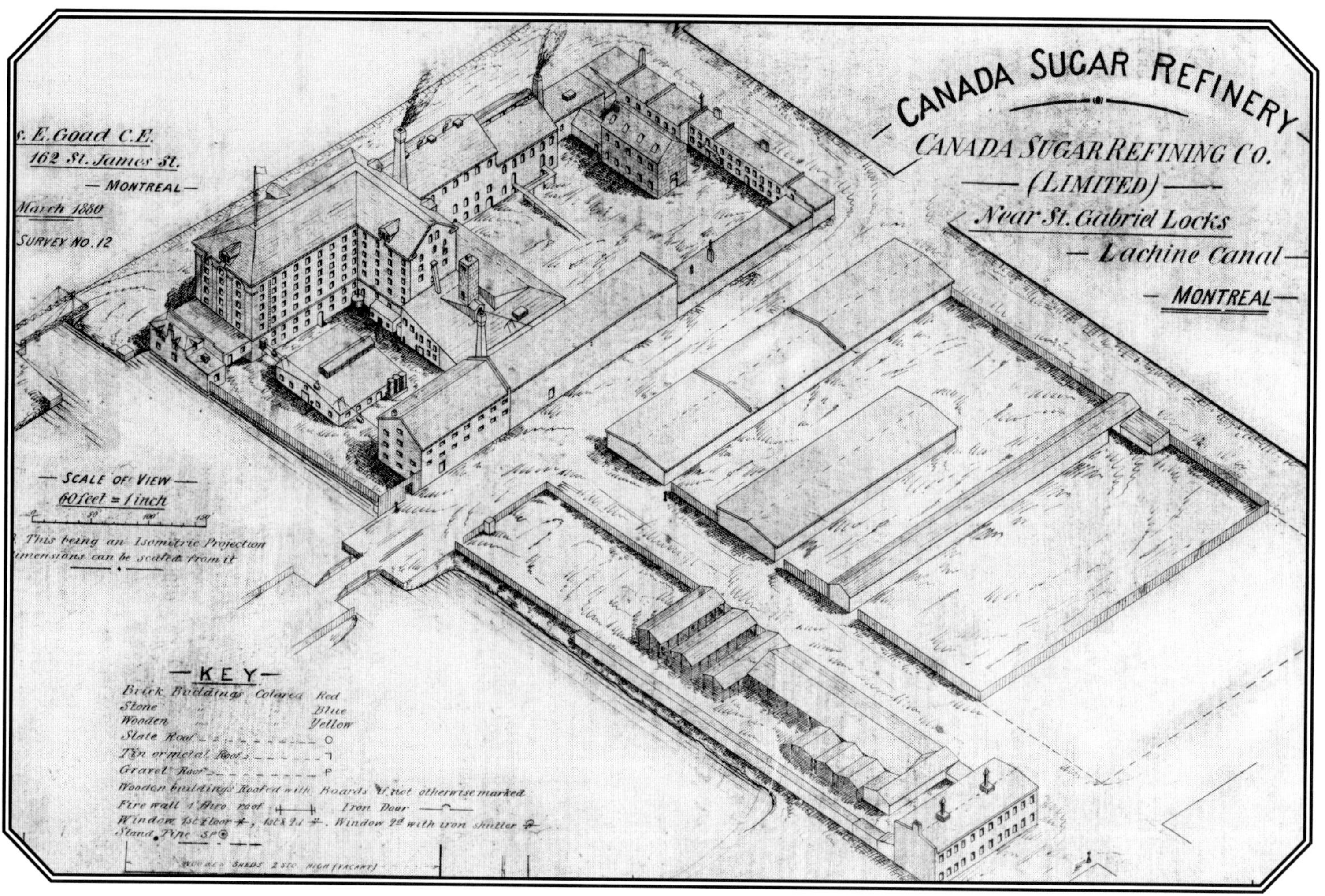
CANADA SUGAR REFINERY
CANADA SUGAR REFINING Co.
(LIMITED)
Near St. Gabriel Locks
Lachine Canal
MONTREAL
s. E. Goad C.E.
162 St. James St.
MONTREAL
March 1880
SURVEY NO. 12
SCALE OF VIEW
60 feet = 1 inch
0 50 100 150
This being an Isometric Projection
imensions can be scaled from it
KEY
Brick Buildings Colored Red
Stone " " Blue
Wooden " " Yellow
Slate Roof O
Tin or metal Roof
Gravel Roof P
Wooden buildings Roofed with Boards if not otherwise marked
Fire wall 1' thro roof
Iron Door
Stand Pipe SP
WOODEN SHEDS 2 STO HIGH (VACANT)

CHAPTER ELEVEN

"Another Opening"

During the first few weeks of 1879, George Drummond was repeatedly journeying between Ottawa and Montreal as he sought to achieve the double goals of obtaining support from the members of Parliament for better protection for the domestic Canadian sugar industry, and the preparation of the refinery to actually manufacture sugar once raw sugar supplies arrived.

On March 14, 1879, the new Finance Minister, Mr. Tilley, officially acknowledged the suffering of the sugar industry under the former regime.

> *We found that under the bounty system of some foreign countries, our sugar refining trade and other interests were materially affected. The Government has decided to ask this House to impose countervailing duties under such circumstances.*

When the new measures were passed, the various clauses added up to a protection of 24 cents per 100 pounds, which was more than even George had hoped for, and he accelerated preparation for work. There was also the matter of refinancing the company, and between them, Peter, George, and Francis agreed to incorporate the business and bring in other individuals as directors. An application was made for incorporation of the new Canada Sugar Refining Company Limited but due to certain application errors, the documents were returned. The submission then had to be redrawn, and it took until late June for the documents to be processed and passed by an Order-in-Council.

On the first of August, the refinery officially started production and on the eighth, the first meeting of the newly formed Canada Sugar Refining Company Limited was held in the offices of the firm of John Redpath & Son. The new directors included: Peter Redpath as President, George Alexander Drummond as Vice-President, and the Honourable John Hamilton, Gilbert Scott, and Francis Robert Redpath as directors.

Considering the poor record of attendance on the part of Peter Redpath during the earlier partnership, it is difficult to understand why Peter was made President of the new enterprise. Certainly George cannot have had any confidence unless some significant assurances were received from Peter. Perhaps it was the other directors who saw the son of the founder as the natural choice without looking too deeply at who actually did the work.

Since the property and refinery with all its machinery and stocks still technically belonged to the firm of John Redpath & Son, it was necessary to "buy" everything for the new company. Therefore, it was agreed that the purchase price would equal $400,000 for all of the real estate and plant, while the inventory of stock-in-trade and movables was valued at an additional $105,752.83, payable in the form of stock within the new company.

On the twenty-seventh, a further meeting of the directors resolved that 1% of the gross amount of sales of the company be allowed to the President and Vice-President as:

> *Remuneration for the management of the business, upon condition that out of such they provide for the payment of Mr. Francis Robert Redpath, who will attend personally at the sugar refinery as an assistant to the Vice-President in the technical management of the refining operations.*

Other clauses and stipulations for the new company included that a subscription book would be opened at the new offices for the company located on St. Francis Xavier Street in Montreal, on September 1, 1879. The sale of 1,710 shares of capital stock of the company would be closed September 30, or whenever the shares were sold. Each subscriber would be required to put up 25% cash, with subsequent payments due in October, November, and December. No individual would be eligible as a director unless he held at least 100 shares in the company. The President was to chair all meetings unless absent for business reasons, in which case the Vice-President was to assume the President's responsibilities. Finally, in order to maintain control of the company within the group, limits were placed on the sale or transfer of stocks held by the directors.

On the negative side, the paternalistic attitude of employer/employee relationships that had existed since the foundation of the company (and that had resulted in a record of no strikes in more than twenty-five years) was to change with the introduction of "outsiders" who pressed for a more stringent application of restrictions upon the rights of the employees. To this end, despite the objections of George and to a lesser extent Peter, the employees were subsequently required to sign the following waiver and indenture of employment, which virtually stripped them of any rights of redress against the company.

> *The undersigned employees of the Canada Sugar Refining Company (Limited) hereby severally agree with the said Company that it is an essential condition of their employment by it that the Company its officers and servants shall not be responsible except as hereinafter specified to such employees or to any other persons whomsoever for any injury or loss of life to any of said employees whether the cause arise from accident or the actual fault or negligence of fellow-servants or of the officers or servants of the Company or from defective or insufficient machinery, protection, plant or material or from any other cause whatsoever and in consideration of the foregoing out of the said employer's parties hereto severally exonerating the said Company its officers and servants from all risks and responsibility save as herein specified for any injury or loss of life that may occur while such employees are in the service of the Company as they hereby do the said Company hereby promises and agrees in the event of injury or death to any of said employees by accident or from any cause as aforesaid while properly and actually engaged in the work of the Company to pay to each employee so injured or to his widow or others interested in*

his life if killed the following sums namely: 100 dollars to the Estate or representatives of each unmarried man or widower in the event of his death as aforesaid who leaves no parents or children under fourteen dependent on him.

100 dollars in the event of the death as aforesaid of any such employee who leaves no widow but who leaves parents or children under fourteen or both dependent on him.

100 dollars in the event of the death as aforesaid of any such employee leaving a widow and 25 dollars additional for each child under fourteen dependent on him but not to exceed in all to widow and children the sum of 200 [dollars].

In the event of any injury as aforesaid, short of death to any such employee while properly and actually engaged in the work of the Company, the Company will pay to him such proportion of the foregoing sums as may be certified to, as just and reasonable by the Dean of the Faculty of Medicine of McGill University or by some Physician in good standing approved of by the Company.

It is expressly agreed that the foregoing indemnities shall not be for any reason or cause increased or decreased.

It is also incontrovertible admitted by said employees that their wages are in consideration of the foregoing agreement higher than they would otherwise be, and they severally guarantee the Company against all responsibility except as above stipulated.

Records for the early years of the Canada Sugar Refining Company Ltd. are unfortunately spartan in their information and show only that the annual dividends ran 15% for 1880, 12½% for 1881, and 10% for 1882. Fortunately a series of notes written in 1899 by Maurice Drummond describe the problems and technical failures of the previous twenty years and give us our best description of these early days. Maurice recorded that due to the financial losses incurred under the Mackenzie government, the new company had to pay out a significant amount in outstanding loans, which left the company with an initial deficit of $340,000. Furthermore, George Drummond's travels in Europe had convinced him that the operations of the refinery required significant changes to bring it to a peak of efficiency with up-to-date technology. Incorporating this new technology was not easy, and there were numerous problems before it was successfully put into operation.

For the Canadian economy, the effects of the National Policy seemed to be decisive as optimism returned to the marketplace, as illustrated on March 9, 1880, when Mr. Tilley rose in Parliament to congratulate himself and his government for the way the national economy was improving. He specifically referred to the positive way in which the sugar duties had turned out and the amount of employment that was being created. He declared that between 1878 and 1879, the effects of the tariffs could be easily seen as follows:

	1878	1879
Refined sugar from U.K. (pounds)	19,173,000	9,964,000
Refined sugar from U.S.A. (pounds)	38,000,00	11,500,000
West Indies raw sugar for refining by Canadian manufacturer (pounds)	4,728,000	37,800,000

At the same time, sugar beet companies were being incorporated in Quebec at Farnham, Berthier, and Coaticook, to establish a processing capability under the auspices of the provincial government, which was offering a new increased subsidy of $75,000.

For the Canada Sugar Refining Co. Ltd. (hereafter also referred to as the C.S.R. Co. Ltd.), the prospective competition of these beet operations did not have any immediate effect, and the daily production from the plant continued under the overall control of George Drummond. Once again Peter was absent from the company, being deeply involved as a Director of the Bank of Montreal in the ongoing political wrangling over the establishment of the Canadian Pacific Railway. By September, the situation was obviously not working out and, whether by choice or by request, Peter Redpath resigned as President and George Drummond was elected in his place. George's position as Vice-President was filled by Francis Redpath, who continued to run the daily technical operations of the refinery. Shortly afterwards, Peter Redpath and his wife Grace left Canada to live in England, where they purchased a magnificent house and grounds in Chislehurst, Kent, which had a history of occupation going back some 700 years. Here Peter spent the remainder of his life with only occasional visits to Canada. He also undertook a new career at sixty years of age by studying law and was subsequently called to the bar as a member of the Middle Temple in London. This shows that perhaps it was not that Peter did not care to work, as might be supposed from his travels following his father's death, but rather that he, like his brother George, merely needed to find his own place in life, free from the dominating influence of John Redpath.

George Drummond had now officially attained the position he had in effect held for the past eleven years, and he soon established his own style of presidency within the company. His concern for the workers led to the implementation of a subscription club among the employees for the purchase of Christmas gifts. He also implemented a system of annual bonuses for those workers whom he felt were contributing to the development of the company and he paid these bonuses out of his own private income as President, rather than, as might be expected, from general corporate funds. Unfortunately, despite these business successes, George's personal life took a turn for the worse when his wife Helen (the daughter of John Redpath) suffered a stroke while walking home from a visit to an old servant. The stroke resulted in a coma followed by an extensive period of Helen being an invalid and requiring constant medical care.

Meanwhile, in the Maritimes, a new enterprise, the Nova Scotia Refining Company, was being developed to compete with the C.S.R. Co. Ltd. The obvious assumption would be that this was the work of George Dustan, but in reality it was another group of investors who were working this plant up, and George Dustan was vigorously opposing it, as an article in the *Nova Scotian* explained on April 16, 1881.

> *The parties interested in the success of the scheme began to look into the causes of the delay and soon saw that there was a monopoly to be removed. Years before an Act had been passed by the Nova Scotia Legislative granting exemptions from taxation ... to a sugar refinery to be erected by a Gentleman [G. Dustan] ... who was not able to bring the scheme to a successful result ... It was determined ... to ask the Legislative for an act throwing open ... the*

Chislehurst Manor, Kent, England. The home of Peter and Grace Redpath.

> *advantages which this gentleman enjoyed ... The measure providing for [the new refinery] was passed ... The gentleman who had enjoyed the exemptions so long and failed to take advantage of them dropped out of the question ... The result was that capital was soon raised and operations commenced ... The refinery has a capacity for turning out 500 barrels of sugar per day.*

For the C.S.R. Co. Ltd., this represented the first real competition since the Molson Refinery had closed in 1871, and from this point onwards the competitive nature of the sugar refining business would only get stronger. In July, Maurice Drummond, at the age of twenty-two, came to work at the refinery, joining his father George. Maurice had just completed his education at Cambridge and was now destined to follow a mercantile career as his father had originally assumed in his letter to the school headmaster in 1874. Maurice proved to be an extremely valuable addition to the management team and received a salary of $25 per month for working six days a week, nine hours per day. In October, the final papers for the dissolution of the corporate entity of John Redpath & Son were signed and George Drummond was assigned to complete the liquidation of all remaining assets.

The following year of 1882 seems to have held few problems for the company, and George's plans for improvement continued to be implemented. In addition, new equipment invented by George Drummond for the reprocessing of the used charcoal was installed in the refinery, and additional patents for its use in the United States, Great Britain, France, and Germany, as well as Canada, were issued during the course of the year. In August, Peter Redpath returned briefly to Montreal to be present at the opening of the Peter Redpath Museum, which he had funded at McGill University and which remains today a classical example of a museum. Also at this time, Peter retired as a Director from the Bank of Montreal. In his place, George Drummond was elected to the post of Director.

To celebrate the New Year and to show George Drummond how grateful they were to be back at work in a successful enterprise, the workers of the refinery paid for the production of an illuminated address, which they gave to George upon his return from the Christmas-New Year break. In this age of self-reliance and lack of social services, it was obvious that George was considered a philanthropist of some note by his workers, helping them when they were ill or injured and providing an annual Christmas party for the workers and their families.

> *TO GEORGE ALEXANDER DRUMMOND ESQ.*
>
> *Respected and Dear Sir:*
>
> *We the employees of the Canada Sugar Refinery availing ourselves of the present auspicious season, beg most respectfully and sincerely to assure you of the very high esteem and affection which we entertain for you. We also desire to thank you, as we do from our hearts for innumerable personal favours which so many of us have received at your hands in times of sickness and trouble, favours which you Respected Sir in your large heartedness have deemed as of little moment, but which by us who needed them have been regarded as most timely and liberal.*
>
> *Nor would we forget the manner in which you have ever met our requests when pleasure has been our object, not*

only facilitating our efforts in every other way, but also making most generous provision for our enjoyment.

We therefore request your kind acceptance of this address at once a humble acknowledgement of these and many like favours and a heartfelt expression of the feelings entertained towards you by all of your many employees who trust and pray that you may long be spared to grace the post you now occupy at the head of this establishment. And not forgetting the amiable partner of your joys and sorrows we hope and pray that a benign providence may watch over and preserve her to be a blessing to you and your family.

Montreal, January 1, 1883.

In early April of 1883, there was a brief flurry of activity when the St. Lawrence River was once again blocked by ice and the water backed up in the Lachine Canal, forcing the entire workforce to stack the stocks of raw sugar on raised planks to prevent its spoiling. Following this event, on April 7, George decided to travel to New York for a vacation and took with him his wife Helen, his niece Agnes Drummond, and

The Peter Redpath Museum, McGill University, Montreal.

Miss Rommin, Helen's nurse and companion. In a letter written on May 3, George recounted the events that followed:

> *We reached New York safely ... We stayed at the Windsor Hotel and she [Helen] seemed to enjoy herself, and we left again on our return journey at 6:30 p.m. on Monday the 16th in excellent spirits indeed in extraordinary spirits. All went well, ... and we reached St. Albans, Vermont at 6 a.m. when she proposed to rise, stood up for an instant when the sharp and sudden blow of our part of the train against another with lightning rapidity, threw her backwards against the door of the little saloon, the door flew open and she stretched her length on the floor. Almost immediately unconsciousness ensued and so it lasted till we reached Montreal almost 2½ hours later ... On arrival at Montreal ... Maurice and I carried her out Dr. Craik being in attendance and we got her into the Victoria [carriage] and walked the horses home ... Several times on the way up she softly spoke ... On reaching home I, Maurice and Patrick Fairly the coachman carried her upstairs. The next few days are but indifferently remembered by me but the record of temperature taken by the thermometer indicates a development of fever [from the seventeenth to the twenty-third of April] ... Tuesday 24th and Wednesday 25th were pleasant and hopeful days she was bright and cheerful ... Thursday also was a good day ... Friday 27th opened badly, her eye was slow and heavy ... I went to the office at 9 a.m. but feeling uneasy returned at 1 p.m. and finding her ... worse ... sent off for the Doctor ... Meanwhile in answer to my enquiry she said she was "very well" but I was thoroughly alarmed. My opinion was combatted however by everyone. She spoke to me of "the dear boys*

In a pleasant moment of relaxation, George A. Drummond with Helen, shortly before her death.

they will all do well" ... later in the day when I asked if she knew me she answered twice "yes dear" ... her last words I heard her utter. From this time she steadily declined existing only in a state of sleepy stupor her pulse going up with the temperature ... Monday 30, midnight 106 F°, 1 a.m. 106⅗°, 2 a.m. 107⅕°, 2:30 ended the struggle ... with a prolonged sigh like inspiration she passed away in the presence of her sister Mary, of Agnes Drummond her niece, of Georgie, Huntly and Maurice and myself ... All the arrangements for the funeral were made for me by Thomas M. Taylor [husband of Mary Redpath Taylor] and took place on Wednesday, 2nd May from the house to Christ Church Cathedral and there to Mount Royal Cemetery.

Upon returning to work, George busied himself with the increasing need to have direct railway access to the refinery warehouse so that finished refined stocks could be more easily loaded onto railcars. To this end, he approached the Grand Trunk Railroad to run a spur line to the refinery. The Grand Trunk refused, as it was unwilling to apply for the right of way, and it was left to George to follow through. Naturally, the local inhabitants on the proposed route along the side of St. Patrick Street were strongly opposed to the running of a railway past their front doors. As a result, George was forced to consider petitioning the Montreal City Council and buying off opposition, or purchasing properties the C.S.R. Co. Ltd. did not really need, in order to get access for the line. The other issue that occupied George's efforts related back to the American Civil War, when the additional war premium insurances were charged on raw cargoes. In the United States, many companies had been applying for and obtaining rebates on these expenditures and so George likewise made application. The issue dragged on for five years until 1888 and resulted in a recovery of about 60% of the original outlay.

On June 26, 1883, Francis Redpath notified George that he no longer wished to continue as Vice-President of the company but rather he wished to hold the lesser responsibility of Director and oversee the daily production of sugar within the refinery. After some consultation with the other directors, George agreed and Gilbert Scott was selected to succeed Mr. Redpath. George also felt that Maurice's contribution to the operations required recognition; perhaps he even intended to propose Maurice as a future Director, for he gave Maurice 100 shares of the company, valued at $10,000, which yielded Maurice a dividend for that year alone of 10% (i.e., $1,000.) Production levels in the refinery averaged 2.05 million pounds weekly and in December a new type of product was introduced to the range of sugars produced by the company and its trademark for "Paris Lumps"* was registered in December 1883.

The next year, 1884, began badly for the company when an unexpected back-up of water in the canal flooded the entire refinery area with water levels recorded at 1 foot 8 inches in the "Y" shed and 11½ inches in "W" shed. Following the retreat of the water, all damaged sugars were immediately processed to try to recover as much as possible

* Paris Lumps were the predecessor to the more commonly known sugar cubes and were produced by taking slightly damp refined white sugar, compressing it into large flat trays, and then cooking the entire mass in an oven for up to three days. Once cooked, the slabs were cut with fine saws into lozenge or tablet shape pieces, that were then boxed and sold as a high-quality item; replacing the old-fashioned sugar lumps broken off the sugar loaf.

and the remainder of the stocks were once again raised on planks. Once spring arrived, work began in earnest to upgrade the refining operations and expenses for the new charcoal filtration building amounted to $53,500 including two secondhand boilers that were purchased from the defunct Coaticook Beet Refinery, which along with the Berthier and Farnham beet operations had closed down when the government funding had expired in 1883.

In Maurice's critical analysis, written some years later, some of these innovations were criticized as next to worthless as:

> *The Lignite filtering process had Taylor filters which were built into various corners and dark places and were always getting dirty.*

while his assessment on the economizers for the boilers showed they:

> *Were often dirty and neglected and only worked on the day shift, and then with only half the smoke thus loosing much of their value.*

Seeking to solve the problems of the refinery, George instructed Maurice to visit other facilities to study their methods. Before leaving, however, Maurice had another duty to perform for his father by acting as best man when his father re-married in late July. The lady George took as his second wife was a widow, Grace Julia Hamilton (née Parker.) Grace had been a long-time friend of the family and was well liked by the Drummond children. She was also a good match for George as she was a well-known local writer and womens activist and, in later years, held many positions of prestige and influence in her own right. Following the wedding, George and Grace travelled to Niagara Falls to enjoy a brief honeymoon while Maurice left on a visit to the Berthier beet factory, where he purchased some of their surplus machinery. In September, Maurice was in New York visiting the huge Havemeyer Refinery, following which he travelled to Great Britain and on to Leipzig where he initially studied the Lippman and then the Lach refinery (from which the filters had been originally purchased.) In January 1885, he continued his tour, seeing beet refineries in Dresden on the third and fourth of January, Lagnons' Refinery at Cologne on the seventh, and Von Raths' Amsterdam plant on the eighth, before returning to Great Britain on the tenth. While staying in London he saw the Duncan refinery on the eleventh, followed on the fourteenth with a tour of Abram Lyle and Sons at Plaistow wharf (on the Victoria Docks), which he described in his journal as "a rather dirty and depressing place." Travelling up to Scotland, he was in Greenock on the nineteenth and sailed for Canada on January 21 aboard the S.S. *Polynesia* of the Allan Line, arriving at Halifax on February 6. Here he took the time to assess the new Woodside refinery as future competition with the Canada Sugar Refining Co. Ltd.

Maurice returned to the refinery on February 10, 1885, and the following day he recorded in his diary:

> *Visit from Abraham Newlands Esq. Manager of James Duncan's Sugar refinery in London, Did not get any information out of him.*

Due to the previous year's flooding, preparations were

made for the anticipated April water rise. Sure enough, on April 24, water levels rose alarmingly as ice jams on the river backed up the canal. By 9 a.m., the water reached the top of the canal bank and breached the embankment within the Priests Basin. The water spread throughout the immediate vicinity and by 8 p.m. it was listed as being 13 inches deep in the "W" and "Y" buildings. Between the sheds, other stocks similarly raised were listed as being completely under water. As for the main buildings, 8 inches of water was measured in the boiler house. On the twenty-fifth and twenty-sixth, the floods abated slightly but on the twenty-seventh were higher than ever until the ice jams gave way and the water levels subsided within hours. The damage and losses were extensive and it took many weeks to clean the last of the mess created by the flood.

In Maurice's retrospective of the problems of this period, he recorded:

> *Prior to 1885 we never used belt conveyers or screws, but handled all the char and granulated sugar and yellow sugar in buggies with large squads of men at the machines in the char house, in addition the granulated was lifted out of the centrifugals ... We had no idea of the comparative worth to us of the different kinds of refined that we made, cost, hence we generally worked away 5 or 6 years behind the European refineries, keeping old kinds of machinery and processes.*

In hindsight, these comments are extremely revealing, but at the time, the opinion was that everything possible was being done to modernize the refinery. The time had come, however, when the economic upswing initiated by the return of the Macdonald government shifted to a downward trend, and sales began to slacken off. Within the refinery, stocks accumulated and the refined storehouse at the plant was supplemented by the use of additional leased facilities in the town. At the end of the year, George was approached by another sugar refiner, Alfred Brown of Glasgow, who had been of considerable help to George during the "intermission" of 1876-79. Mr. Brown proposed a joint venture for the construction of a ship to carry raw sugar for them both and any other refiners who would be interested in joining the scheme. George replied that he would be willing to go into the matter in the new year but cautioned that the current Canadian refining situation was not favourable and that much would depend upon the economics of the situation.

ALEX. McARTHU

CHAPTER TWELVE

"...A Hard And Anxious Time..."

Since 1879, the sugar tariffs had remained unchanged and the relative benefits of the protection granted had enabled the Canada Sugar Refining Co. Ltd. to establish itself in the market. It had also attracted competition from beet refineries to the north of Montreal. Due to poor business investments and careless farming methods, these plants had not succeeded and were closed once government subsidies had expired. The other competition came from the Nova Scotia Refinery at Halifax, which likewise was not financially able to maintain a constant output and was currently attempting to refinance its operations for a projected re-opening later in the year. But now, in 1886, a third and much closer competitor appeared in the form of the St. Lawrence Sugar Refining Co., which constructed a refining facility in Montreal with direct access to the St. Lawrence River, giving them the advantage of lower costs of unloading coal and sugar. George recognized that the market was not growing quickly enough to absorb all the projected output that could be delivered if St. Lawrence, Nova Scotia, and the Canada Sugar Refining Co. Ltd. were all in full production and he related his concern to Mr. Hewlett in New York. He also mentioned that the Nova Scotia Refinery was trying to manipulate the current tariff laws (which allowed sugar being imported directly for refining into Canada free of duty on the containers), by claiming that since the C.S.R. Co. Ltd. received its supplies in the winter via New York, it should be classed as an indirect shipment and therefore subject to additional tariffs.

> *I have had no end of a time here, Worry, Worry, Worry! Our Halifax friends, who are always on hand, having little else to do but to keep their neighbours (I mean us) right, sprang on us suddenly a new reading of the tariff viz that importation via N.Y. were liable to all charges from N.Y. to Montreal which leaves us in a position of paying 30% duties for Montreal while they only pay 27%. Our politicians are divided on the issue but see in it a good way to twist more money out of us. I feel we must appeal or loose much of what little business we have. ... The authorities in Ottawa said that they had always held this view of the tariff, so if it is won by them we will have to amend all our cargoes for three years back and pay up ... I must import soon via Halifax otherwise there will be an outcry ... We are doing some repairs at the Refinery and are silent but hope to begin again on Wednesday or Thursday. Sales keep very slow and stocks large.*
> *(January 4, 1886)*

Following an appeal on the interpretation of the tariff, the Minister of Justice ruled in favour of the C.S.R. Co. Ltd., which annoyed both the Finance Minister and the Customs officials, leading George to fear reprisals in the upcoming federal budget. In February, George again wrote to Hewlett about the market:

> *We are working nothing but Low [quality] stock at present as I can't go on boiling up granulated as it just won't sell.*
> *(February 16, 1886)*

Montreal floods.

By March, the warehouses were full and the fear of another flood, like that of previous years, led George to order all stocks to be raised to the upper floors of the buildings at the refinery. At their town warehouses, extra night watchmen were put on duty to raise the alarm in case of flooding. On April17, around noon, a huge ice jam blocked the river at Hochelaga and water levels rose rapidly. Initially, it was the city of Montreal that took the brunt of the flooding, and the warehousemen in the city storehouse had to move quickly. As George later reported in his diary, they got all the stocks to the upper floors:

> *Just in time, meanwhile we had raised the cooperage and filled the receivers in the refinery on the ground floor with water and all the sugars over 6 inches higher than last years flood and most 10 inches above.*

These precautions were unfortunately ineffective as this flood proved to be the worst in living memory. By 2 a.m., on April 18, the water was flowing over the Lachine Road, and the Priests Basin was completely filled and overflowing into the refinery yard. By 3 a.m., the water was lapping five inches over the raised sugar stocks in the "X," "W," and "Y" sheds. In the surrounding streets, flood levels were recorded as: 8 feet on Wellington Street at the corner of St. Patrick Street; 8 feet on Centre Street at the corner of Richmond Street; and 6 feet on St. Patrick Street at the corner of Montmorency Street.

The main floor of the refinery was under 4 feet 8 inches of water and this continued until about 9 p.m., when water levels began to drop slightly, but it was not until April 20 that the ice dam broke and the water fell back within its normal confines. Studies reveal that in comparison to a normal summer river depth of 17 feet, the estimated depth of the St. Lawrence River at the height of the flood was more than 48 feet 6 inches.

This event is recorded as one of the most severe floods in Montreal's history. Many people were stranded in their homes for days, and had to be supplied with food by boats that sailed along the streets. Most of the wooden sidewalks simply floated away, and thousands of businesses lost much of their stocks. Fortunately the C.S.R. Co. Ltd. did not lose all its sugar but it still incurred over $10,000 in damage and did not get back into production until May 5.

During the period of re-organization following the flood, the C.S.R. Co. Ltd. was approached by a consortium of British investors who were proposing to re-finance the Woodside

Sugar Refinery in Halifax and wished to establish an agreement with the C.S.R. Co. Ltd. and the St. Lawrence Refinery to limit production and fix prices within the Canadian market. When both Montreal companies refused, the matter seemed ended, but a week later George received a letter from Peter Redpath informing him that the consortium wanted Peter Redpath to join their group as a Director. Peter asked George for his opinion and George gave it in no uncertain terms, as well as recounting the state of affairs following the flooding.

> *It would obviously be of no service to the C.S. Refining Co. that you should take stock in their company and join their board. But it might be of great service to them. They could then raise money from people who would not know that no agreement had been effected [to limit production and fix prices] and would in this way do us positive harm ... My own opinion is that we in Montreal will certainly have to beat these Halifax people out of the field and can do it. My estimates are that we can certainly work cheaper than they can. As near as I can ... tell they have made no profit, but very much the contrary, they appear not to be able to buy sugar to go on with. I should now be vary chary of being associated with them myself ...*
>
> *The flood took us all by surprise, all our sugar had to be put 12 to 15 inches above the highest point the water reached last spring. Which was by far the highest in our experience at our place. But the water got into all the outside places, we had 5,000 barrels touched, most of them 4 or 5 inches deep, but as near as I can make out the loss is comparatively light and we think $5,000.00 to $6,000.00 will cover all the stock. At one time I feared it would be anything from $25,000.00 to $100,000.00. The worst thing is the uncertainty, the next flood may not come for another thirty years but it may come next winter and be 3 or 6 feet higher than last.*
> (May 7, 1886)

Thinking the matter over during the night, George followed up the next morning with another letter to Peter, stressing the dangers of the situation:

> *I am of opinion that your joining of the Halifax Co. board would be an entire mistake ... it would be of immense service to them, but what conceivable use it would be to us I would like to see but quite fail. It would reassure their stockholders and enable them to get more money, all based on the delusion that we have agreed to pool our production and that it could enable our Company to help them, when in reality it would only enable them to compete more strenuously with us. Let Fraser [the leader of the British consortium who made the initial approaches to Peter Redpath] put his proposals in writing and send them out here. In no other way can an agreement be arrived at. I could then judge of their value and advise you, but at present I can only repeat that in my opinion his proposals will not benefit either this Company or yourself.*
> (May 8, 1886)

Following receipt of the documents on the proposed Halifax offer, George saw no reason to change his opinion and notified Peter Redpath on the June 8,1886 that

> *So far as I can see the approaches made to you were an insidious attempt to save themselves without giving anything*

in return. I should speak rather severely of the attempt to rope you in to suit their own convenience. When Blackburn [the agent for the Halifax group in Canada] left me, it was practically decided that his company should buy up the Nova Scotia house and keep it shut. Evidently they were not in a position to do anything of the kind. The chance has been lost through their duplicity and now the Nova Scotia has been reorganized and starts again Hewlett in New York concurs with my judgement and says he knows Fraser in Liverpool, and has a very low opinion of his honesty ... therefore leave it well alone ... Business is bad as bad can be, granulated 6¼ with 2½ % off for wholesale and the new tariff adds at least 33¢ per 100 lbs. to the duty on raw ... our competition is serious, prices daily dropping and everything blue.

Also on that day, George had to deal with the financial problems encountered in his agreement with Mr. Brown of Glasgow to construct a sailing vessel for raw sugar transportation. George paid the money required but was forced to comment on the poor economic situation in Canada and Great Britain.

Here is my payment for the "Nile" ... I need scarcely say to you that the gloom and depression which continues to hang over everything makes me regret for your sake and my own that we have gone into this venture, and I would gladly learn that the ship could be sold, or my share in her anyway.

The next day George wrote to his sister Isabella on a sad note.

Death has once more visited my home and taken away the baby [Julian St. George - Born June 1885, the first child of George and Grace]. I feel it very much, he was a very fine boy. Edgar [George's third son by his first marriage] who has now lain in bed for eight months continues to hold his own and there are hopes of a recovery which could hardly have been said two months ago. His malady is an abscess at the base of the spine ... He is constantly attended by two of our best surgeons and has a trained nurse and you can fancy the conditions of my home last month when I tell you that I had on one day two nurses and five doctors in my home.
(June 9, 1886)

Shortly thereafter George's health failed and from July to October no letters are attributed to his hand, but under the control of Maurice Drummond the refinery continued with expenditures of $44,000 for various repairs, alterations, and installations of new equipment. Additionally, the accounts reveal that in order to obtain sugar, the company was purchasing raw supplies from such widespread sources as the Philippines, Brazil, Java, India, Cuba, and the West Indies for cane type raws and Germany, Belgium, and France for beet stocks.

Eventually, sugar prices began to rise early in the new year with Extra Granulated being sold wholesale at 6 cents per pound while the Medium Yellows were going at 5 cents per pound but this increase did not help the financial state of business. George was particularly sharp with their Toronto sales agent when three major orders were lost to the St. Lawrence Company due to the agent being unwilling to offer a discount to secure business. Business was now so unsatisfactory that George felt economies must be instituted in all departments and lay-offs were made across the work-force. In March 1887, George received a deputation from the other refineries now established within Canada. Obviously, the other refiners were hurting as much as the C.S.R. Co. Ltd. because they proposed a joint restriction on immediate production and an agreed quota system for further output. After some intense negotiations, the four main refineries signed an arrangement whereby, under George Drummond's chairmanship, each refinery would agree to hold a single vote, with George carrying the casting vote in case of a tie. Each plant would immediately cut back its output to 60% of the production recorded for the equivalent period the year before. Subsequent volumes would be determined by ongoing averages of sixty days' production for the previous year. This allowed the C.S.R. Co. Ltd. to produce 352,000 pounds per day in March, while in the following months production was limited to 60% of the total capacity of the refinery for April and May 1887, and 75% for June. Despite the agreement, it is obvious that George had reservations about at least one member of the coalition, as he revealed to Hewlett in a letter of March 30, 1887.

> *I think the agreement is pretty stiff to get out of ... three months notice is required ... both we and the St. Lawrence have the conviction that one of the Moncton men will try to cheat the deal. It will require him to perjure himself to cheat us but I do not think that will be much of a barrier. I daresay the rest will keep it all right.*

At home, the time had come once again to prepare for what had now become an almost annual inundation and this time George was taking no chances. All the stocks of refined sugar that could be removed were shipped to a rented ware-house in the west end of the city, while the raws required for production were piled on top of old syrup barrels. Every building was prepared with old bags filled with soil and sand (to block the water from the doors), and the refinery settled down to await the expected liquid assault. Sure enough, on April 22, water began to rise and for the next two days it continued to deepen. By the twenty-fifth it had risen enough to flood many parts of Pointe St. Charles but fortunately it did not reach the epic proportions of 1886. Following the subsidence of the water, George assessed the damage at around $2,000. This yearly "wetting" was now past a joke and as the President of the Montreal Board of Trade, he initiated a campaign to get a flood wall built along the river bank to prevent further flooding of low-lying areas of the city.

With the matter of sugar production fairly well settled for the near future, George turned his attention to his business connections with the Bank of Montreal because the unexpected death of the bank's President, Charles Smithers, had created a significant opening there. The official history of the Bank of Montreal states that Sir Donald A. Smith was made the next President on the basis of his

> *Knowledge of the northwest, rather than his indefatigable purpose or business acumen ... The Vice Presidency vacancy left by Smith's elevation was filled by George Drummond ... he had joined the Board of the Bank only five years previously on the retirement of Peter Redpath, and his elevation to the Vice Presidency in so short a time was a tribute to his character and astuteness.*[1]

But another viewpoint of this event is shown in a letter from George to Peter on June 13, 1887:

> *The affairs of the Bank of Montreal as you may imagine occupied a good deal of my attention ... some of the Board would have voted for me as President, but upon the whole, and as the best thing it was decided as you know. Sir Donald is popular and all the fears about the C.P.R. influence over him seem removed by me as Vice-President ... I expect Sir Donald will not keep the Presidency long, at least he says not ... and then (accidents excepted) I will be the President and Patterson or Murray Vice-President.*

In this last expectation, George was quite mistaken as Sir Donald A. Smith (later Baron Strathcona and Mount Royal) held onto the post for eighteen years until 1905. George continued his letter, showing the status of the company:

> *We are making splendid profits at the C.S.R. at the present moment but did no good for the first four months. I shall be disappointed if we don't make 125,000 - 150,000 dollars profit and we might pay a small dividend, and replace our losses gradually. We have the old place in an accomplished state of efficiency. Maurice is a splendid refiner and has every part under his thumb, and relieves me of all detail ... P.S. I have the conviction burned into me that the hard times of the C.P.R. are yet to come, and will come, and to keep the Bank of Montreal out of it will be my business.*

Nearly three weeks later, George was surprised to receive a notice from the St. Lawrence Sugar Company of their withdrawal from the agreed co-operative. He immediately contacted Mr. A. Smith of the Nova Scotia Refinery at Halifax.

> *Mr. Elmenhurst [of the St. Lawrence] hinted at such a step at the last meeting but I thought he might perhaps not take it. What his motives are I do not know but I am not in his confidence. I have no sympathy with him on the subject, and think the step most regrettable as I do not see how an entire break up of our combination is to be avoided and a return to ruinous competition is certain. I am writing to discuss the question with you and the Moncton confidentially. (July 3, 1887)*

On July 13, 1887, certain that cut-throat competition was about to erupt once again, George wrote to Hewlett to inform him that:

> *We are totally stocked up with all kinds of sugar needed and we are not likely to buy for some time once the combination collapses as prices are bound to tumble.*

Two days later, the refinery of the St. Lawrence Sugar Company burned to the ground due to a boiler explosion. There were rumours circulating at the time that the event was deliberate on either the part of St. Lawrence for the insurance, or by the other refiners in retaliation for leaving the group. But since St. Lawrence lost over $100,000 on uninsured stocks and machinery, and George had to rapidly cable Hewlett to revise his estimate on the future need to obtain sugar, the evidence seems to point to the fire being a simple accident.

For the remaining refiners, this sudden gap in production

was a godsend, and each company scrambled to increase its production to take up the slack in order to make a decent profit during the next few months.

At the end of August, George again wrote to Alison Smith of the Nova Scotia Refinery at Halifax.

> *Since my return [from vacation] I have not seen any of the St. Lawrence people but am informed that beyond question they are going to rebuild on a new site. As now at the busiest season of the year three refineries are more than sufficient for the business. The consequences for all from four or perhaps five going into operation may be imagined ... sales have been better these last few days but our stock of refined is not reducing ... I learn that the Woodside bond holders are trying to raise money to re-open.*
> *(August 30, 1877)*

During this period of expanded production, newspaper reports began to circulate of poorer quality sugar being sent out by some refiners. To counter this, George invited the Public Analyst for the District of Montreal, John B. Edwards, to randomly check their refined stocks. His report to the company was returned on September 9, and was immediately issued to the press to eliminate any suggestion that the supposed products came from the C.S.R. Co. Ltd.

> *Gentlemen*
>
> *I have personally taken samples from a large stock of your Granulated sugar "Redpath" Brand and carefully tested them by the Polariscope and I find these samples to be as near to purity as can be attained by any process of sugar refining. The test by the Polariscope showed in yesterdays yield 99.9 percent of pure cane sugar which may be considered commercially as absolutely pure sugar.*
>
> *John Baker Edwards*
> *Phd. D.Ch. F.C.S.*
> *September 9, 1887*

It is interesting to note that the average quality level for a similar grade today is around 99.98% pure cane sugar.

By the end of the summer, the annual slowdown in sales took hold and production levels were once again discussed among the three remaining companies. On October 24, George wrote to Alison Smith in Halifax about the disturbing news that the equivalent organization of sugar refiners in the United States had collapsed.

> *The sugar trust in the U.S. has burst this seems rather a "staggerer" and though on the face of it, it is certain that our risk of competition was from the United Kingdom, still a collapse of the much talked of trust will paralyse business here ... our business of late has been very dull indeed and our stock of refined has gone up to 15,000 barrels. I see nothing for it but to reduce our production to 75% on the 1st November.*

At the end of the year George gave his son Maurice fifty more shares of the company and a ticket to Havana as a Christmas present, for as George said in his New Year's letter of greeting to Peter Redpath:

> *Maurice left last Saturday for New York to go to Havana for his holidays. He had run himself down by hard work and I am pleased to let him go.*

CHAPTER THIRTEEN

"Too Many Cooks"

During the off-season of sales, the co-operative arrangement to restrict production pushed each of the companies – the C.S.R. Co. Ltd., the Nova Scotia Refinery, and the Moncton Sugar Refinery – into a position where they each made only 60% of their capacity output. This situation lasted until March when the agreement fell apart because the re-established Woodside Refinery in Halifax began to produce sugar and its President notified the group that his company had no intention of co-operating with the other refiners and intended to produce what he could in direct competition. On behalf of the group, George replied on March 17, 1888:

> *Of course this can have but one result to put an end to all concert between us on any matters and personally I am glad it came from your side of the country rather than mine.*

Almost immediately afterwards, George was called to appear before a government investigating committee established to study the restrictive production practices in various trades and industries. Following his presentation, his mind obviously jumped back to his previous experiences in 1875-76, and in a letter to Mr. Hewlett he recounted his ideas on the events.

> *It was perhaps better I went before the committee myself, it is distinctly hostile. The Chairman and principle man (conservative) being markedly so. Three of them tried hard to catch me and will twist my evidence if they can. The impression is they did not make much of me. I fear legislation, possibly it may take the shape of compelling us to sell for cash to all alike. If this is tried we shall have a nice time and some ingenuity must be exercised by us ... The Nova Scotia people withdrew from our production agreement ostensibly and perhaps really to meet the competition of the Woodside ... as a consequence sugar prices have gone down. Granulated 6⅞¢ per lb., yellows may be quoted ⅛¢ per lb. down sales keep light ... A general combination of refiners is hardly practicable at present or soon your [U.S.] trusts have made too much excitement for that. As to getting away, if I wait till I have nothing on hand it will be the day of Judgement, and hardly then for I fear I have lots to answer for then.*
> *(March 19, 1888)*

In April, George suffered the loss of his sister Agnes, leading him to write to another sister, Isabella, on April 2:

> *Poor Maggies death [November 1887] and then Agnes' so*

close together remind us of our advancing years ... My wife is well, the baby has been ailing but is now recovering ... we are planning to go south for a time to gain some sun.

In fact, George and his family were away until July and it was Maurice who took on most of the mantle of responsibility for the business.

Upon his return, George's attention was occupied until the end of the month with the problems of the Bank of Montreal. When he was once more able to deal with the issues of the C.S.R. Co. Ltd., he found that an opportunity had arisen for some export sales to Europe due to the major failure of the European beet harvest. George pressed Hewlett to investigate and see if a sale could be made by the C.S.R. Co. Ltd. This led, during the next quarter, to 25,000 tons of sugar being sold to the British and French markets, representing the first major exports to Europe by a Canadian sugar company. But within the domestic market, the fall in prices in the U.S. market spilled over into Canada, leaving sales at a standstill. In his regular communication with Hewlett, George commented:

Our sale room is as dull as Sunday, the drop in your market has apparently intensified the desire of the jobless to supply only actual wants, which will be light for at least two weeks.
(August 2, 1888)

Following the fire of the previous year, the St. Lawrence Sugar Co. had been rebuilding at its new location and George was anxious to know the level of competition he could expect once it opened. Following some investigations he informed Hewlett:

I now know pretty well the extent and arrangement of the new St. Lawrence house, and I am satisfied that E. [Mr. Elmenhurst] has had in his mind the desire to be able to say that he has as big a house as we have, and to propose that they and we should divide the business equally. If you remember our old per-centage were C.S.R. about 46% and St. Lawrence about 25%. Now I am certain that although he has put up a large building, and on some kinds of machinery has as much as we have. Still we could and can do more ... am I bound to respect this and surrender a share of my business? ... meanwhile we can not sell, both wholesale and retail men are holding off in expectation of a break in prices.

With the opening of the St. Lawrence house in September, prices fell and a month long price war ensued between the two Montreal refiners.

By the beginning of November, the stocks of better quality sugars for refining were running out and a ship with a cargo of 3.3 million pounds of beet sugar was significantly delayed; this news was communicated to Hewlett on November 8:

If the beet does not come in soon we shall be entirely out of good sugar, and the "St. George" is anxiously looked for. I wish our refined was going, but on the contrary we are piling up stock. I refuse no offers but simply reducing prices won't sell in this country, as it is the prices of yellow are down one cent since a month ago and granulated down 3/8¢, the latter is still too high.

This was followed on the nineteenth by:

Business very dull and we must close, if sales don't improve. Meanwhile we will keep prices low on the stocks already made.

On that same day, George received notice that, for his contribution to the development of Canadian business developments over the last thirty-four years, he was to be offered the rank of Senator and he commented on this to Hewlett.

PRIVATE, TO BE DESTROYED ... *I am today in receipt of a couple of letters, one from Sir J.A. MacDonald and the other from Sir Hector Langevin offering me a senatorship! My political ambition of this shape O, but my friends here, of whom I have only seen two, Maurice and Watson. Both are decidedly of the opinion that I could materially help the business by accepting. I doubt this counting for much ... I have not done anything to bring the offer my way ...*
(November 19, 1888)

George also replied to Sir Hector Langevin:

The offer of a senatorship which you and Sir John will propose for me is a great honour, and I appreciate the kindly feeling very highly. Perhaps you will let me have a day or two to review my present engagements and position and consult my friends. In the meantime I keep it private.
(November 19, 1888)

Two days later, after consultation with family members and friends, George notified Sir Hector of his acceptance. In his annual letter to Peter Redpath on current events, George stated:

As to my senatorship, well I did my best to keep out of it, not only negatively but positively, but when both Sir J.A. MacDonald and Sir Hector Langevin wrote me "hoping I would accept" and my friends were unanimous in so advising I could not well do otherwise.

Other points in this interesting letter include George's opinion of his status as Vice-President of the Bank of Montreal and mentions of his new home under construction on Sherbrooke Street.

I fully realize my own position in the Bank. G.S. [Gilbert Scott, Director] and Sir D.S. [Donald A. Smith] both would be pleased to see me out of it in view of the independence of my views, but I won't go and try hard to prevent myself from being put out ... My house has been, in an artistic point of view a great success, but has been much exaggerated in importance. I expect to finish for less than $80,000.00. It is much smaller than Angus' home or Abbott's and in short is not a bit too big for my present requirements.

In December, Maurice went for the second time that year to Europe to investigate new technology that could be incorporated within the refinery. Initially he toured the Tate plant at Silvertown in London's east end, followed two weeks later with a repeat visit to Lyle's plant a mile or so up river. Back in Canada, the C.S.R. Co. Ltd. shut down for the Christmas period on December 23. The books indicated that in spite of slow sales towards the end of the period and extensive expenditures, the company showed a moderate profit for the year and issued a 15% dividend on its stock.

At the start of January 1889, George began planning a major alteration at the refinery with the installation of new filter presses to remove the smaller particles of impurities from the sugar. He looked at those offered by Lyles in England, but chose instead the Casamajor Filter Company of New York, placing an order later that month.

> *Acting upon your strong recommendation and on the belief that your assurances that the sawdust process will prove an undoubted success. I have cabled my son to order six presses ... I have also ordered twelve circular sweetening off tanks 6 x 4 feet, of steel ... In short the whole work will be pressed on, and I put myself entirely in your hands and rely on you to make it a success.*
> (*January 11, 1889*)

The man sent by the Casamajor Filter Company to supervise the installation of the plant was B.J. Rogers, of whom Maurice commented in a note to his father on February 22, 1889:

> *I have seen Rogers making many notes and often appears in odd places around the refinery outside of the filter house.*

Meanwhile, George's ongoing concerns regarding the extreme competition his company faced led him to discuss the issue with Mr. A. Smith in Halifax:

> *Mr. Elmenhurst [St. Lawrence Sugar] has never evidenced ... any disposition to restrict production, and till he does I am quite of the opinion that prices will be unremunerative ... For years my company has been the mainstay of prices, and I have often held my stock back and allowed the St. Lawrence and others to sell, which could always be done at a fraction off ... this will not be our policy in future ... as you were aware I was willing to share with you all on an equitable basis but ... Mr. Elmenhurst ... wants more than he had, I see no reason to give it.*
> (*February 8, 1889*)

Also at this time, George made his maiden speech in the Senate and in later years he became the chairman of the Standing Committee on Banking and Commerce. As one biographer in the Montreal *Gazette* later recounted, when George Drummond spoke,

> *His opinions relating to matters of financial import were received without question ... and when Senator Drummond had spoken upon a question of this kind there was a consensus of opinion that little remained to be said.*

For much of the spring, George was occupied with the activities of the Bank of Montreal and, according to accounts, had to be virtually ordered to take a break. He therefore left with his family and "summered" at Cacouna, while Maurice ran things back in Montreal.

While George was away, production in the refinery remained steady. Sales of Yellow sugars were somewhat lower than 1888 and Extra Granulated only half that of the previous years. The Paris Lumps, on the other hand, were proving to be a very popular product line. Things continued in this fashion until the morning of July 21, when a large fire broke out at the refinery. Virtually the entire stock held in the "X" shed was destroyed and a subsequent internal inquiry judged that the event occurred due to spontaneous combustion of the "Java baskets" (the containers in which the cargoes from the East Indies arrived.) The initial losses were estimated at $91,000 but a subsequent negotiation with the government resulted in a refund on the import duties previously paid for the destroyed stocks, reducing the losses to $75,000. The company had to absorb this sum as it did not carry insurance on its storage buildings or the contents, a matter that was soon remedied upon George's return to work.

George's return to the refinery coincided with the completion of the Casamajor filter presses being installed and tested. Work on these presses continued until December 18, when George wrote to the Filter company in some irritation:

> *Enclosed is our first return shewing 11,871,580 lbs. of raw sugar treated by your filters in the six months from 17th June to the 16th December ... this is far below the minimum promised by Rogers. This is due to unexpected defects in our apparatus and methods, the which difficulties we have had to overcome to a considerable extent by experiment.*

Another and much more serious problem for the company was the collapse of a major European beet sugar syndicate, which resulted in a flood of beet sugar onto the market, reducing raw sugar prices within a week to only 50% of their previous values. As the C.S.R. Co. Ltd. had purchased large stocks of the better quality beet sugars while the prices were elevated, this unexpected drop in value represented a significant financial liability which, at the end of the year, became the major reason for the corporate profits being significantly reduced from $773,727.47 for 1888 to $105,740.66 in1889, although the $75,000 from the fire and $87,000 for a charcoal filter system also played their parts.

To finish this chapter on a happier note: On the morning of December 24, 1889, George issued the annual bonuses to the workers at the refinery. He then took the remainder of the day off to join his wife in supervising the moving of the final items of furniture into his new home at 874 Sherbrooke Street West. Built of red sandstone imported from Scotland, the house was described during its construction by an architect who published his account in the *Witness* of February 4, 1889.

> *The building which proves beyond question how great the advance in architecture as an art has been in Montreal is the house which is being erected at the corner of Sherbrooke and Metcalf Streets for Senator Drummond ... It is to be enriched by a wealth of carving and ornament ... The general design of the house is strong and good, the strong corner tower ... and the two gables rising steeply to the grotesque "beastes" ... produce a most admirable effect ... and not only are capital and panel to be richly carved, but these belts of carven ornament are to sweep about the house; and richly carved and ornamented porch ... window and balcony, add beauty and expansion to the whole.*[1]

Having moved into their house on Christmas Eve, George and Grace held a traditional Victorian Christmas

with their family. Some years later, an article credited George and Grace with establishing this large "Christmas present" as a home of quality.

> *George Drummond took a legitimate pride in his beautiful home on Sherbrooke Street West. He had reared the stately pile in his mind before a stone was put into place ... But to his gifted wife, [Mrs. Drummond], was due the home-likeness which marked this stately home of a noted, able and philanthropic citizen ... It was she who planned the rooms; the decorations; the arrangement of the priceless objects of virtu with which it was the delight of [Mr. Drummond] to surround himself ... when he could spare the leisure to enjoy his artistic leanings. This beautiful home ... housed many a notable guest. It ... echoed to soft laughter; to brilliant music; to the light step of youth and beauty, as, in the mazes of the dance, all that is most select in Montreal society gathered in the sumptuous drawing rooms.*[2]

(Left) The home of George Alexander Drummond. This house stood at the corner of Sherbrooke Street and Metcalfe Street, the location today of the offices of the Bank of Nova Scotia.(above)

CANADA SUGAR REFINERY.
PARIS LUMPS
JOHN REDPATH & SON
TRADE MARK
MONTREAL.
GEO. BISHOP & CO. STEAM - LITH.

CHAPTER FOURTEEN

"A Busy Year"

If the efforts and events of previous year's business activities had seemed extensive to George Drummond and the Canada Sugar Refining Company Limited, it was as nothing compared to the events of the next twelve months.

To begin the year, public criticism of banking practices led to a call for major reforms, including a minimum reserve of cash in the form of gold or silver against paper note issues. On January 11, 1890, representatives of all the chartered banks met in Montreal at a closed meeting and some two weeks later went to see the Hon. G.E. Foster, the Minister of Finance. As the country's leading bank, the Bank of Montreal objected strongly to the government's version of the proposed alterations, and George Drummond spent much time with his fellow bank directors in Ottawa, protesting in the strongest possible terms against the government plans and proposing its own recommendations. The ensuing negotiations and arguments continued until June when the Bank Act was implemented.

Meanwhile in the refinery, production was at a standstill and business was not good as George informed Hewlett on the fifth of February:

> *Our position is this, we are silent and have yet unsold 34,000 barrels of refined sugar, 14,000 of which is granulated. Out of the above we have 5,000 barrels of low yellows and the demand is running almost exclusively on these and granulated. To sell any sugar at all we have to meet the market ... our stocks of low yellow could be sold off in a day or two, but I won't sell it except with orders for granulated or high grade yellows ... We have in raws 6,800 tons which we do not need ... I never knew demand so bad, prices so disgusting and prospects generally so mixed up.*

Continuing the information on February 6, George wrote:

> *I do not believe anybody here is buying ... but we will ... have to pay a losing price for something. To pay $4.56 for 100 lbs. raw and sell refined at $4.62 both cash is a fine business. That little rascal Rogers of the Casamajor Filter Company is in Vancouver, British Columbia, trying to get up a refinery to produce 150 barrels a day. He left the Casamajor Co. a few weeks ago and says he is connected with the Havemeyer etc., whose money is it? The Woodside refinery and Dustan's at Halifax is about to re-open backed by Glasgow or Greenock people.*

The following week, after a substantial price rise for raw sugar, George ordered 4.5 million pounds of raw sugar as the refinery was low on these stocks. He expressed his regret at not knowing of the price rise earlier, which prevented him getting the stocks at the lower price, whereas the St. Lawrence had purchased extensively just before the prices rose due to their contacts in Hamburg and Berlin. (In the event, this early purchase did not benefit the St. Lawrence Sugar Co. as the ship bringing the sugar was lost at sea.)

Further troubles plagued the C.S.R. Co. Ltd. when on March 6, another fire occurred in the shed built in 1888 to dry the washed bags. No insurance had been acquired on the building and the whole thing was a write-off. George gave special bonuses to the men who had worked well in fighting the fire and specific instructions that in future bags were to be dried outside the plant either in small kilns on the other side of the basin or on top of the raw sugar sheds in sunny weather.

Shortly thereafter, George received a visit from a representative of the British American Investment Co. who indicated, in confidence, the intention of this group to invest significantly in the Canadian sugar refining industry by purchasing *every* refinery then in operation and placing them under a single control. George immediately initiated enquiries to check the validity of the enterprise. He found that the group was in fact bona-fide, with significant backing in British banking and United States and Canadian industrial circles. Some enterprises already floated by the group included the Denver United Breweries, the Baltimore Breweries, the Dominion Breweries (Toronto), the Bell Organ Co. (Guelph), the Massey Manufacturing Co. (Toronto), and the Harris Manufacturing Co. (Brantford).

To George this proposition obviously had possibilities, considering the problems he had been involved in within the last few years, and he agreed to discuss the matter further. In the meantime, he continued with the regular business of the company and discussed the upcoming tariff legislation pending in the United States Congress with Hewlett:

> *Surely with 800,000 tons of extra beet sugar likely to flood the market it is only a question of time till the tumble, comes ... it is beyond question to my mind that the present spurt is temporary and fictitious and that before we want the goods we shall be able to buy cheaper here.*
> *(March 25, 1890)*

Within three weeks, George was proved correct as prices fell.

In May, the Casamajor Filter Company notified George that Rogers in Vancouver wished to use the same system of filters currently leased exclusively to the C.S.R. Co. Ltd. Certain that Rogers had used his extra-curricular tours of the plant and the copious notes remarked on by Maurice to pave his way to establishing his own refinery without absorbing the costs of research, George decided to allow Rogers the process, at a price.

> *We shall be prepared to lease to the Vancouver house the sawdust process at a fair royalty ... of course we should expect a fair advance over the price paid by ourselves considering the large expense we have gone to in its introduction here.*

On May 16, there are further references to the proposed purchase by the syndicate, which offered to assess the value of the refinery based upon the previous three years' profits. George replied:

> *My own personal inclination would be to name $2,500,000.00 and if my fellow shareholders agreed to accept less by ¼ million I would not stop the way, below that there seems to me no use in considering the matter. I have not yet mentioned the subject to my directors, and am glad to know that others have been discreet as it has not got into the newspapers.*

George's hopes of maintaining confidentiality on the matter were soon lost, however, when on May 31, 1890, the *Acadian Recorder* newspaper reported:

> *An English syndicates agent is in Halifax for the purchase of the Nova Scotia and Dartmouth Refineries. The syndicate propose buying out the St. Lawrence and Canada Refineries in Montreal and also the Moncton House.*

Within days, a letter arrived from George Dustan complaining of his past failures and calling upon Drummond not to go into the syndicate as

> *I do not know the people who are moving in the matter but I suppose they are the men who wrecked my enterprise and cruelly stripped me of my property and concessions.*

Recognizing that Dustan would never accept responsibility for his own failure, George did not pursue the letter.

During the next few weeks, George had to split his time between the Bank of Montreal and the C.S.R. Co. Ltd. On the bank's side, the newly approved Bank Act dealing with financial reserves, bank failures, and securities had to be assimilated into the commercial structure. On the syndicate front, confidential negotiations continued until June 12, when George cabled the syndicate representative, Mr. Spencer:

> *In the event of a combination being formed incorporating the Canada Sugar Refining Co. Ltd. and the St. Lawrence Sugar Refining Co. Ltd. into a joint bureau. The present management of the Canada Sugar Refining Co. Ltd. would be willing to assume the sole management of the United Montreal refineries for a period of three years.*

Two days later, the initial agreement to sell the C.S.R. Co. Ltd. was reached with the syndicate for a price of $3 million for the property and plant. All stocks of raw sugar, coal, bones, cooperage materials, charcoal, horses and wagons, refined sugar in process or finished being deemed as extras.

A certain amount of excitement occurred three days later on June 17,1890, when a cargo barge packed with raw sugar hit a submerged object in the canal and sank. George notified Hewlett on the matter to the effect that:

> *The barge load of sugar which was stored up in the canal was saved by our prompt action, we started double gangs to pump and to discharge. In spite of the pumping she had 6½ inches of water over her deck skin. As the sugar came out it was put into the melter. There was some loss but we will make no claim for it as it was but a little.*

Other circumstances were also working against the best interests of the C.S.R. Co. Ltd. when the U.S. Sherman Silver Purchase Act, coupled with a revolution in Argentina, (which had caused major financial losses for investors when all properties were declared "nationalized") combined to create a massive downturn in the British and American economies. Stock market values fell sharply and sugar prices fluctuated widely. The United States was also now geared to follow a much more protectionist economic policy, which would have serious effects on the future capability of the Canadian sugar refineries to export to the United States.

Domestically, events took a turn for the worse, when the information about the proposed sale was leaked in the press. The employees of the C.S.R. Co. Ltd., fearing that the proposed new owners would not be as concerned about the welfare of the workforce as had George Drummond and the Redpaths before him, attempted to persuade George to repudiate the proposed sale. When George refused, they took stronger action and initiated the first recorded strike in the company's history. Shocked by this action, George sent a strong note to J.R. Cowans, the workers' representative.

> *It seems very hard that whether we shall work or remain idle, make ends meet or lose money. Should be dependant on the fancies or mischievous ends of our men. I suggest to you that if this wicked strike continues any longer we must make an effort to replace the hands and go on with our business. To wait patiently and do nothing, and suffer is very fine, but it is not business ... our business is to be scrupulously fair and after that to stand no nonsense.* (July 30, 1890)

No more is known about the results of the strike or how long it lasted but it seems to have ended fairly quickly as stocks and sales showed only a minor downward fluctuation and things continued towards a sales agreement, which was approved by the stockholders on August 1. Ironically, on the same day as George obtained approval to sell, he received a request from the syndicate representative for an extension on the purchase deadlines. This was due to problems in the syndicate over a previous purchase in the Chicago stock yards, and the economic nervousness of investors in Britain and the U.S. due to the revolution in Argentina.

After consultation with his co-directors, George agreed upon the following conditions:

- *That all payments be completed prior to December 31, 1890.*
- *That no publication of details of the syndicate be published until 50% of the purchase price was paid over, and in the event of the deal falling through* all *documents would be returned to the C.S.R. Co. Ltd.*

The syndicate agreed to the first condition but argued that the second would seriously impede possible investment and asked George to reconsider. Eventually George and the syndicate agreed that the sum of $200,000 would be issued to the C.S.R. Co. Ltd. as a non-refundable deposit on the eventual purchase.

In a private report made for the syndicate, the assessment of the Canadian sugar industry at this time reveals the following facts:

15th August - Analysis of the Canadian Sugar Refineries

There are five refineries in Canada, protected by high duties which prohibit competition from outside Canada ... the annual consumption of sugar in Canada is over 200,000,000 lbs.
... The purchase prices agreed are:

St. Lawrence Refinery (Montreal) $3,250,000.00 (includes all assets and stock)
Canada Sugar Refinery (Montreal) $3,000,000.00 (does not include stocks)
Nova Scotia Sugar Refinery (Halifax) $850,000.00 (includes all assets and stock)
Moncton Sugar Refinery (New Brunswick) $450,000.00 (includes all assets and stock)
Halifax Sugar Refinery - Not worked for many years - available for £40,000/-/-

The present managers of the St. Lawrence refinery and the Moncton refinery wish to go out entirely. The present managers of the Canada and N.S. refineries would remain at salaries to be arranged. George A. Drummond willing to act as Managing Director ... there could not be found a better man for the post ... In conclusion we may point out that the combination means the absolute control of this trade in Canada, and that without any increase in price to the consumer the combined concern would be able to increase the price to the wholesale houses sufficiently to show an immense return on the Capital invested. The business community appear ... to be watching the negotiations with interest ... and Canadian businessmen appear to have no doubt as to the success of the concern.

On August 27, 1890, George notified the syndicate of the final approval for the sale of "the whole real estate, plant, machinery and the goodwill of the business, ... stocks of cloth and bags and such like to be transferred at constant prices."

Meanwhile, the daily business of the refinery continued and the situation was such that some of the other refiners felt it would be necessary to re-establish the production quota system attempted in 1887-88. George was not immediately inclined to agree but later reconsidered and wrote to J.L Harris of the Moncton Sugar Refinery:

> *After the failure of the last scheme, which was mainly originated by me, I am not disposed to take much trouble about another. The only thing is that the present cut - throat prices may kill the syndicate operations.*
> *(August 21, 1890)*

Following discussions with the other refiners over the next three weeks, George was certain no positive agreement could be achieved and he anticipated very poor sales for the winter months if the syndicate deal did not relieve him of the company. In September, the U.S. government introduced the highly protectionist McKinley Tariff Act, which virtually prohibited imports to the United States while encouraging exports to Canada, undercutting the Canadian refiners.

George commented on this in his letter of September 27, to Hewlett.

> *I do not know what effect the alteration of the U.S. sugar duties will have on refining in Canada. I fear it will*

certainly give rise to much smuggling and much dissatisfaction in Canada. The Canadian duties will I think, or ought to be, altered too or there will be an outcry against the refiners that the Government will find it difficult to resist.

Three days later, George Drummond contacted the syndicate representative, Mr. Spencer, and referred to his letter of June 12, when he intimated that the management of the C.S.R. Co. Ltd. would be willing to assume the sole management of the Montreal refineries.

And I know that Mr. Watson, the secretary and Mr. M. Drummond, the manager of the C.S. Refinery would both be willing to continue their services, and I can say they are both exceedingly well qualified and competent. But as regards myself I may say that for a couple of years back, in consequence of my health, I have been desirous of less work and consequently of retiring from the Presidency of this Company. And I have, after mature consideration decided that I can not accept the position of G.[eneral] M[anager] or Managing Director of the proposed consolidation of the refineries. Though I should be bound to give the scheme my best aid at all times.

Nothing more is documented on the matter until an urgent cable to Mr. Spencer from George dated November 3, 1890, stated:

Please return all documents as soon as possible ... I am told that the Woodside concern is being floated on the knowledge of supposed large profits made by the other refineries. Whence does this false knowledge come?

The reason for the sudden end to the syndicate's plans came because of an announcement by Sir John Abbott that he and the government would consider the syndicate an illegal cartel and he prohibited its consummation. Why the government waited so long to issue the ruling is not known, but the fact that the Woodside refinery was being refloated and would have been outside the group, coupled with the knowledge that their directors were in Ottawa the week before the announcement, may have had something to do with the matter.

With the collapse of the proposed syndicate, it was back to business as usual and George and Maurice drew up plans for a major new expansion and improvement to the refinery operations. Trade mark registrations were made for new lines of packaged products including tins of Golden Syrup, Double Dried, Crown, Granulated Sugars, and Red Seal brands, while a new specialty Christmas product was produced for the first time. These Rainbow Lumps were coloured Paris Lumps and their recipe was described in Maurice's notebook as follows:

To make 300 - 25 lb. boxes ... Take 16 barrels of white sugar from the new building centrifugals at 250 lbs. each barrel. Spread out a barrel, add colouring matter dissolved in a quart of water and then rake and shovel over, press (dumping back the first few cakes), arrange in the stove in the order to be taken. After drying place each colour on a table and cut into 12 or 25 fingers according to the box, arrange with a finger of one colour then a white then another colour and so on.

The colours listed for inclusion suggest that a sugar dish filled with Rainbow Lumps would have been a colourful addition to a Christmas table and included dark blue, light blue, dark yellow, light yellow, dark red, light red, green and orange. There was also the pencilled note "Try to get purple."

At Christmas, bonuses totalling $1,160 were issued by George, despite the strike earlier in the year. A busy year had finally come to its close.

The docks at Montreal, showing the various cargoes, including sugar, being unloaded.

CHAPTER FIFTEEN

"When Fortune Turns The Wheel"

After the considerable number of events that occurred in 1890, 1891 seemed very quiet in comparison, although in themselves those events that did occur were serious enough. The Tariff Bill passed by the American Congress was eating deeply into the Canadian economy, and yet a number of people still advocated an open policy of free trade. One person attributed to hold these free trade opinions was W.C. Van Horne, the general manager of the C.P.R. This surprised George Drummond, for in their previous associations, Van Horne (who was financing the B.C. Sugar Co.) had definitely not followed such a line of reasoning. George wrote to Van Horne to discuss the matter and Van Horne replied with a letter that could easily have been written nearly a century later during the more recent debates on free trade.

> *I am not in favour of unrestricted Reciprocity or anything of the kind ... unrestricted Reciprocity would bring prostration or ruin ... No one can follow the proceedings in Congress at Washington and the utterances of the leading newspapers of the United States without being struck with the extraordinary jealousy that prevails there concerning Canada - jealousy growing out of the wonderful development of her trade and manufactures within the past twelve years. It was this jealousy that prompted the anti-Canadian features of the McKinley Bill. It was ... believed at Washington that the Canadian farmers largely depended upon the United States for a market ... and that it was only necessary to "put on the screws" to bring about a political upheaval in Canada ... as would inevitably lead to annexation ... If the result of the pending elections in Canada is what the authors of the McKinley Bill expected it would be, another turn of the screw will follow ... Putting aside all patriotic considerations and looking at the question ... from a strictly business standpoint, what, in the name of common sense, has Canada to gain by it at this time? ... We are infinitely better off in Canada ... and there is work for everybody who is willing to work ... Even if we were suffering from hard times we could gain nothing by unrestricted Reciprocity.* [1]

Since these attitudes reflected George's own ideas on the matter, George Drummond and Van Horne agreed privately to undertake to lobby for a Conservative victory in the upcoming election and they contributed extensively to the coffers of the Macdonald campaign. On March 5, 1891, the Conservatives did win the general election using as their slogan "The old man, the old flag, the old policy." This gave

George some hope that a suitably grateful government would look into the matter of the discrimination of the U.S. Tariff Bill and act accordingly. Eventually the government did respond by stipulating that all sugars imported for the purpose of refining below or equal to No. 14 Dutch Standard would be allowed in duty free while refined sugars listing above No. 14 D.S. would be charged 8/10 of a cent per pound. The overall effect of this measure was to take the previous 32 cents protection rate that had existed since 1886 and increase it to a healthy 43 cents per 100 pounds. This was good news for Canadian refiners as a whole but the excess production capacity within the country meant that continued cut-throat competition for the limited volume of sales within the Canadian market would continue and possibly worsen. On June 6, 1891, Sir John A. Macdonald died, and George travelled to Ottawa to attend the funeral and to participate in the debate over who should succeed Macdonald. The man selected was Sir John Joseph Caldwell Abbott, whom George considered a "neutral" on the issue of sugar duties and protection.

As the summer progressed, sales dropped considerably and George attempted to sell increased amounts of sugar by introducing new product lines, such as Golden Syrup in 2 pound and 8 pound tins, and granulated sugar in specially made 7 pound cotton bags measuring 8½ inches by 15½ inches. He also used the first known example of a cardboard carton package for sugar in 5 pound Paris Lump boxes. Economically, these were not a success but they show how clearly George was determined to take the technological lead in manufacturing sugar in Canada.

Besides slow sales, another problem for the refinery included a cargo of Cuban sugar aboard the *S.S. Kelvindale*.

This sugar was so poor in quality that it was virtually impossible to process, and when George complained to the grower he received no satisfaction whatsoever. The time had obviously come to switch the raw supplies from predominantly cane type sugar to beet type. On September 3, 1891, George contacted a London brokerage company to investigate future beet sugar purchases, stating:

> *So far as we see now beet sugars will be more useful to us now than ever before ... If ... it is a matter of some difficulty to supply such sugar on short notice we should require ... to place a standing order in your hands to buy for our account as parcels come into the market.*

Three weeks later, George received the sad news that his son, Edgar Lorne, had died in Bournemouth, England, following an operation for his illness. Nothing more is known for 1891 other than that at the end of the year, $1,540 was paid in bonuses to the workers, although for the first time it came from the official accounts of the C.S.R. Co. Ltd. as it was felt by the board that George had paid these bonuses out of his own pocket for long enough.

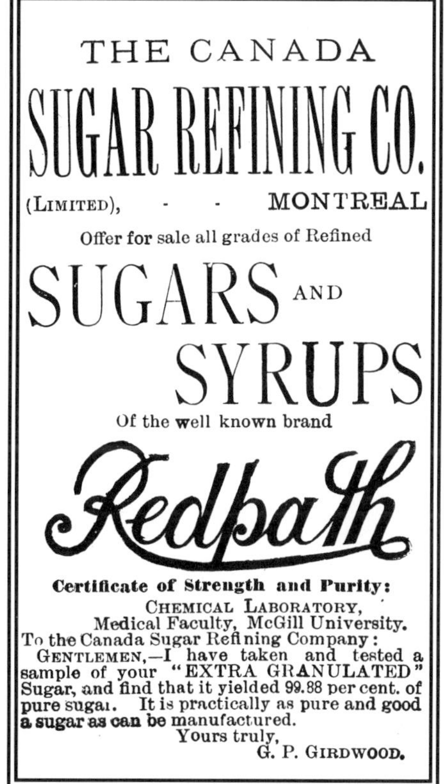

At the beginning of 1892, the plans for an entirely new style of manufacturing sugar were put into operation. Maurice left New York on the S.S. *Etruria* on January 26, and travelled via Liverpool, London, Dover, Calais, Paris, Munich, and Vienna to Aussig in Austria to sign the legal papers assigning the C.S.R. Co. Ltd. the rights to the Steffen Process of refining.* In Maurice's notes written some years later, he recollected the methods of refining used prior to this Steffen installation.

> *Up to 1890 our methods were simplicity itself compared to our [later] method of working, whatever raw was used it was simply melted straight and bag filtered, all on day shift. It was then put through one char only and the next day was boiled up with the granulated syrup as likely as not taken straight into the yellows, the only complication was the uncertain time taken settling the char and the blanks [the lowest grade of sugar] generally made from the last syrup of yellows. Compare this process to the [later] sawdust, double or treble char, refining granulated, yellow syrup ... and finally the Steffen Process.*

This process of refining required the facility of an

*This Steffen Process consisted of a set of box-shaped wagons with perforated floors. The raw sugar was placed in these wagons and washed initially with a series of warm molasses syrups and then with purer syrups as the refining continued. As these syrups already contained sugar, they melted the outer coating of molasses on the raw sugar but did not dissolve the white sugar crystal underneath. Instead, the crystals extracted additional sugar from the syrup and ended up larger in size than at the start of the process. After the set of rinsings, the wagons were wheeled to the rest of the process where the clean raw sugar was melted, filtered, and passed through the charcoal system to remove the colour. The pure liquor was then boiled in the vacuum pan to regrow the crystals and produce the refined sugar.

The interior of the raw sugar shed, 1892.

entirely new refinery, and the land on the east side of Montmorency Street immediately across from the original property was bought to house the construction. At the same time, it was recognized that the current storage sheds for the raw sugar would be inadequate to cope with the projected increase in production capacity that would hopefully result from the use of the Steffen Process, and in February similar plans were initiated for the construction of a new shed. The dimensions of the shed were quite large for its time, being 120 feet wide by 232 feet long, and so George contacted the Rosebank Iron Works in Edinburgh to design and produce the trusses to be used in the roof. Another innovation to be installed was a pair of overhead travelling electric cranes to lift the bags of raw sugar. As George explained in his letter to the Brown Crane Company also of Edinburgh on February 25,1892:

> *The height of the roof ranges from 25 feet to 33 feet therefore the cranes would never have to lift over 29 feet at most.*

In March when construction began, George reconsidered his original design and notified the Rosebank Company that, while the roof trusses were still to be made by them,

> *The installation of a double roof, as you propose, on a shed 120 feet wide is inadvisable in this climate as the valley between the two peaks would fill up with snow in winter and cause endless trouble. I have therefore caused another plan to be prepared of a single roof and sides making altogether 100 feet wide by 232 feet long ... we will also install only one crane at this time with the prospect of a second later if the first one works well.*

On March 18, Maurice returned with the official papers showing that the rights to the Steffen Process had been secured for $125,000. That same day, the excavations for the foundation of the new building began. Construction on this building moved quickly and by April the Steffen building was two storeys high, and the new raw sugar shed was nearly half completed. Suddenly everything ground to a halt on the raw sugar shed because the government announced plans to appropriate the site for a dock, and nothing could be done until the matter was resolved. The Steffen building continued, however, and George notified the Rosebank Iron Works that they were awarded the contract for fitting up the illumination for the facility.

A new vacuum pan in 1892, prior to installation within the refinery.

> *I now accept your offer to furnish an engine and dynamo attached for lighting of our new building, say about 200 lights of 16 candle power each. I do not understand such matters and would like it to be capable of running with any number of lights ... from 40 to 220, I presume it can be arranged ... The wiring necessary must also be provided. The building will be 150 feet long 70 feet wide and 5 storeys high, measuring 75 feet.*
> *(April 11, 1892)*

After some intense negotiations with the authorities, George persuaded them to drop the dock scheme and the construction of the raw sugar shed continued. In May, the Fawcett Preston Co. of Liverpool was contacted to supply a new 13 foot copper vacuum pan (to complement the triple effect evaporator already on its way); it was to be ready to ship by September 5. Fortunately, everything went according to schedule and in late July, Maurice travelled to England to inspect the machinery being prepared to complete the vacuum pan order. When he got there, an urgent cable was waiting for him from George:

> *We have completed the triple effect, so far we have completely failed to get it to work. It is highly eccentric in its action, anything like a systematic or continuous flow from one to the other has not so far been obtained and the loss from boiling over is enormous.*

Maurice discussed the problem with the production company, and in a series of telegrams back and forth across the Atlantic, a solution was worked out. After this, Maurice decided to take a short side trip to Paris. While there, he suffered a recurrence of an old problem he listed as malaria and he was confined to bed for two days. This illness required Maurice to stay abroad longer than he anticipated and he convalesced in Marseilles, finally returning to New York on the S.S. *Champagne* and then continuing by train to Montreal, just in time to see the roof put on the raw sugar shed. The Steffen building, however, was stalled due to the lack of delivery of the ordered wrought iron window frames. After much cajoling and arguing with the H. Rives Co., the window frames arrived and were quickly installed. The building was completed, the machinery connected, and test production commenced at the beginning of December. Almost immediately, several of the metal window frames showed signs of cracking. Upon examination, the frames were discovered to be cast iron instead of wrought iron and were breaking due to vibrations caused by the machinery. George notified the Rives Co. that he was demanding not only the immediate replacement of the frames with the correct article but also the payment of all costs of paint and glazing done on the original windows plus the same to the replacement units. During the remainder of this year, all beet sugar was stopped due to the excess prices current in Europe and the 91.5 million pounds melted was divided between cane centrifugals at 48.5 million pounds and lower grade Manila sugars at 43 million pounds.

From Maurice's notes on this period and the early months of 1893, we learn that there were several problems with the operation of the new machinery.

> *Due to a complete change in method, instead of getting beet 1st's we bought crystals and beet 2nd's largely to work by the Steffen Process ... we completely failed to work or at any rate to work profitably the Java sugars and only succeeded in making messes. The fine grain beet took a fortnight to work so that our Steffen building really did little ... the low raws eventually worked so well as did the Steffen that we built a second "cuite" pan ... from this point onward any sugars we could not work or which did not pay to work by the Steffen Process were run through the new centrifugals.*

One delay in starting proper production not mentioned in Maurice's notes was the extended duration of the annual letting out of the water from the canal, which held back operations for nearly three months. This was the first time in over twenty years that things had been stopped for this long.

In early February, word came from Ottawa that there were plans to drop the duty on refined sugar as well as on the raw. Recognizing that this would completely wipe out the Canadian sugar industry as it had in the 1875 period, George immediately wrote to numerous members of Parliament and ministers. Stressing the urgency of reconsideration in his letter to the Right Honourable J.F. Stairs, George stated:

> *Nobody with a grain of sense could object to the sugar refiners this year arguing and the abolition of the duty on refined sugar would at once deliver them into the hands of the American Trust. I calculate that the Canadian Sugar Refiners have this year already saved the country $800,000.00 by making and selling at the bare cost of production. During 1876, 1877 and 1878 (when we were forced to close and our competitors were driven out of business altogether) it was a fact that the price paid in Canada for refined sugar was ... the New York price plus 80¢ per 100 [lbs] ... This year it has averaged under N.Y. prices. Not one cent of extra cost has been incurred by the buyer in consequence of the duty as has been suggested by those who would steal our business ... the proposer of any notion to abolish the duty and the refiners at one swoop is a knave, a fool or a cad.*

Fortunately these efforts persuaded the government to leave well enough alone and business continued until April, when George Lawrence Patterson Drummond (George's fifth son, and a manager within the refinery) died after a short illness. Whereupon the plant closed for the funeral. By May, the Steffen Process, as mentioned in Maurice's notes above, was well into operation and George decided to purchase the second "Cuite" pan mentioned in his notes. He also ordered a second steam boiler from the Mirlees - Watson Company similar to the one purchased the previous year. According to the order, it was to be 16 feet by 7 feet 6 inches and was to be equipped "with all fittings complete."

June proved to be a disastrous month when the vessel *John E. Sayers* sank while bringing a cargo of raw cane sugar from Cuba, followed a few days later by another vessel, this time carrying beet sugar from Europe, running aground off the coast of Nova Scotia. By July, the refinery was running short of raw sugar as replacement cargoes had not been obtained, and when George received a letter from his Cuban contractors, J.M. Ceballes and Co. of Havana, asking to be excused from part of their contract, George's response through Mr. Hewlett was predictable and forceful.

> *We have entirely lost (as they know) one steamer cargo of their sugar. In addition we have lost a steamer cargo of beet sugar from which the salvage reduced the loss to something under 1,000 tons. We have lost probably over 2,000 tons of sugar and we hear of another cargo in distress. These unprecedented disasters on our importations obliges us to look out for supplies to fill our wants, and it comes to this. They have to lose money to fill their contract or we have to lose money to relieve them ... how can we say otherwise than that we expect them to fill their engagements.* (July 13, 1893)

As George feared, the third ship "in distress" was in trouble and it arrived at the end of July badly damaged by storms with nearly half its cargo ruined by sea water in the holds. For the latter two incidents, the insurance claims were paid reasonably promptly but on the loss of the *John E. Sayers* the insurance company refused to pay for reasons that are not specified. George was satisfied enough in the justice of his claim to initiate legal action against the Atlantic Mutual Insurance Co., which was eventually settled in 1895. The needed alternative supplies were eventually obtained in September and sufficient stocks were received to last through to the end of the year's production schedule, but only at the substantial cost of buying large quantities of European beet sugar while the prices were high (due to projected reports of a very poor year for beet sugar production.) In actuality the crops, when harvested, were far better than anticipated and prices fell dramatically, leaving the company to pay the higher purchase price previously agreed. George reflected ruefully in a letter dated October 9, to their sugar agents, C. Czarnikow Ltd. in London:

> *The prospects appear to be of our making a sound loss of money on our beet contracts both for October and November. So much for statistics of crops.*

Also at this time, George and the refinery were visited by Peter Redpath, who had returned to Canada with his wife to inaugurate the opening of the new library he had donated to McGill University. Peter was shown the new facilities and expressed much satisfaction with the way things had progressed at the refinery. He also asked George about the recent merger of the three Maritime refineries into a single entity called the Acadia Refining Co. Ltd. George informed Peter that, in his opinion, although their combined production would equal 1,400 barrels daily, he did not fear excessive competition as long as the government did not interfere with the duties at the same time. On October 31, 1893, George Drummond and his family joined many of the Redpath descendants at the formal opening of the library, which was located on the campus next to the Peter Redpath Museum. Other notables in attendance included J.H.R. Molson, the Governor General and Countess of Aberdeen, as well as many of the major industrialists of that time.

Many speeches were proffered, praising Peter for his ongoing generosity to the university and for the work he had done in the past, as well as complimenting him for the work he had put into overseeing the design and selection of all modern facilities for studying within the library. Mrs. Redpath also came in for some praise for the donation of two stained glass windows within the library. The day's festivities ended with a large dinner party hosted by George at his home, which was now a centrepiece of Montreal art circles, since it was filled with many exceptional paintings collected over the years from around the world.

Shortly afterwards, Peter and Grace returned to England to their home at Chislehurst. This was Peter's last visit to the land of his birth, for like his father before him, this long journey took its toll on Peter's health.

The Peter Redpath Library, McGill University, Montreal.

Peter and Grace Redpath in 1895, at their home at Chislehurst.

CHAPTER SIXTEEN

"What You Gain On The Roundabouts"

The Steffen Process was proving to be a good investment for the C.S.R. Co. Ltd. as production costs fell. The only difficulty was the byproduct of extensive stocks of low and mid-grade syrups which filled the warehouses. So much was produced that George instructed his staff to sell off as much as possible even at discounts that gave no profit. He also investigated the possibility of using the molasses syrups to generate a completely new product, liquor. He contacted the Booth Copper Co. of Toronto to provide him with a series of estimates on "the cost of the machinery for distilling molasses, the building size required to contain the machinery and the number of men required to run it."

At the other end of the transport system, George was continuing to have problems with obtaining raw sugars through the London agents Czarnikow, and he wrote on February 20, 1894, expressing his concerns.

> *I have bitter complaints in my office here of the way in which your business is managed. You fail to report shipments for marine insurance, and we only get the absolutely necessary information by repeated application to you by cable and otherwise. You fail to report details of all kinds, we daily expect arrivals at New York and Portland and we have no invoices, no marks, and no analysis. You ask us to claim certain sugars, what authority can we shew for doing so? No bills of lading, nothing! ... I wish you would put the correspondence part of your business into better shape and prevent the necessity for these repeated grumblings, which appear from my side only too well founded.*

Also in February came the unexpected and sad news that Peter Redpath had been suddenly taken ill and died on February 1, at his home at Chislehurst. This news was doubly distressing to George as it meant that of the original team who began the company in 1854, he was the only partner left alive (John James having died in 1884.) Feeling the weight of the passing years, George began to consider the option of retiring from business life.

In March, the Conservative government adjusted the Canadian sugar tariffs established in 1891, the major change being that the dividing line between raw sugar and refined sugar was moved up from No. 14 Dutch Standard to No. 16 D.S. The immediate result of this change was to cut the protection enjoyed by the Canadian refiners from 43 cents per 100 pounds to 27.5 cents per 100 pounds, but George was not altogether unhappy because it also allowed him to take greater advantage of the Steffen Process in competing with both his eastern and western rivals. As he said in a letter to Czarnikow on March 30, 1894,

> *The changes ... will facilitate our business in beet sugars and enable our purchases to be made with the same facilities as to the United States and at the same money also.*

Feeling in need of a rest, George waited until late April when Maurice returned from a two-month vacation in Europe before he in his turn crossed the Atlantic to study various European refineries (including the Lyle plant in London.) He also took the opportunity to establish personal contacts for beet sugar supplies, and to search the art showrooms of Europe for pieces he could purchase and bring back to his home on Sherbrooke Street. He returned in mid-July and was immediately visited by representatives of the St. Lawrence and Acadia refineries, who informed him that they were interested in establishing another trade restriction agreement. Since he knew that his extensive stocks of beet sugar would not arrive until the new year, he agreed to a short-term quota to be based upon the current July production levels of each refinery. As a result, the C.S.R. Co. Ltd. obtained a quota of 50% based upon the daily average production at that time of 411,836 pounds, which was maintained until the end of the year.

In October the C.S.R. Co. Ltd. was visited by Charles Lyle while on a tour of North America. This was a notable occasion because while members of both the Redpath and Drummond families had visited the Lyle and Tate refineries in Great Britain upon many occasions, this was the first recorded visit from a representative of either of these English companies to the Canadian operations and can be said to have opened the door to a relationship that has lasted to the present day.

By the end of the year, the beet stocks for the Steffen Process were expected to arrive, and George turned down the call from the Acadia and St. Lawrence sugar companies to extend the restrictive production agreement for another six months, since he felt that he would be in a better competitive position very soon and did not want to be hampered when spring arrived. In addition, he wanted to ensure that the quality of the sugar to be received in future was appropriate to the Steffen Process, and so he wrote to one of his German contacts, Mr. F. A. Neubamer of Hamburg, to specify the shipments he hoped to get.

> *In our contract for beet sugar we require 1st, 2nd and 3rd runnings in quantities of up to 1,000 tons ... The crystals must be large and free from any mixture of "smear" [very small crystals] ... the purpose being to get a sugar which will wash well and freely by the Steffen Process ... these sugars can be shipped from time to time from the present time till the end of February next, in quantities as they turn up ... you will engage freight for it ... to include inland carriage to Montreal from the port of discharge which may be Halifax, Boston or New York.*
> *(December 14, 1894)*

As a result of all these extra late-season expenditures, although the company did a moderate, if restricted, volume of 85 million pounds of melt, the additional costs changed a projected profit for the year of $93,000 to a loss of $12,000. Dividends to the stockholders were reduced to 5% and no bonuses were issued to the employees.

Unfortunately, the shipments of beet sugar did not arrive as scheduled and by January the stocks of refined sugar had dropped to 5.8 million pounds and only 600,000 pounds of raw sugar were available for processing. Obviously there was a need to secure further supplies, so George went to Belgium, France, and Germany to discuss matters and returned on March 20, confident that any future supplies would be regularly forthcoming. From March 30 to April 12, the Lachine Canal was emptied for its regular repairs and dredging. Once the water was let back in, George received a report from Maurice that there were problems with the area that ships would use for berthing to unload sugar. George therefore wrote to Mr. E. Marceau, the superintendent engineer for the Lachine Canal, appraising him of the projected problem:

> *The dredging in the canal above the Wellington Bridge is very narrow, and a pile of earth and rocks, some of them of enormous size is cast up on each side. Can you have these stones and boulders removed ... some of them could wreck any vessel which touched them if it got a little out of the centre of the canal. Also in my opinion the dredged portion of the channel ought to be, and might quite safely be made a good deal wider than it is.*
> *(April 22, 1895)*

A few days later, a spectacular fire broke out in one of the nearby factories on the canal. Concerned about the possibility of a similar catastrophe at his own facility, George decided it was time to beef up the fire-fighting capability at the refinery. He therefore sent a note to Francis Redpath (with a copy to Maurice Drummond) on April 30.

> *Dear Frank*
> *I place ... in your charge with full responsibility, all the apparatus and appliances provided against fire in and about the refinery. You will make a full and complete examination in the first days of each month, moving the taps and testing the hose. You will go over the watchmen's dock records and satisfy yourself of the duty being regularly done ... You will consider and review the provisions against fire, and if any fresh provision is in your opinion and examination required you will suggest it to me ... this duty is not to be deputed to anyone without my agreeing thereto ...*

In Ottawa, the government was again preparing to adjust the tariff levels. This time they recognized that allowing imports of raw sugar for refining free of duty meant they were forgoing a significant amount of revenue. To regain this revenue the government enacted new legislation that imposed a 50 cents per 100 pounds duty on raw sugars; additionally, in order to maintain the relative position for refined sugars, the duty was raised from 64 cents per 100 pounds to $1.14 per 100 pounds. Coupled with the U.S. drawback, this left the Canadian refiners with only an 11.75 cent protection per 100 pounds. As in the previous year, George was not too perturbed by this measure as he felt that by using the beet sugar he could fare better than his competitors. Just how confident he felt about his economic future can be judged from the fact that only five days after the new tariffs were announced, George completed the purchase of some 500 acres of farmland in the west end of the Island of Montreal, located in the present-day city of Beaconsfield and stretching from the edge of Lake St. Louis northwards to a point almost half a mile beyond the line of the present-day highway and railway tracks.

On May 10, 1895, George followed up on his earlier comments regarding fire precautions with some additional thoughts:

> *Judging from the newspaper reports at the inquest on the victims of the McDonald fire I infer that a change of Law has been made, and that employers are now required to drill their hands to some extent in the use of appliances, escapes etc. This we were in the habit of doing for our own satisfaction some years ago, but you will at once see it renewed and put in force ... my idea is that foremen and principal hands be enroled formally into a company. That the whole of them be instructed in the use of the hose, taps, pumps and fire escapes.*

In June, acting upon Maurice's advice, George ordered that all the machinery being used in conjunction with the Steffen Process and currently located in the old main refinery building was to be transferred and installed inside the Steffen building to increase output, cut costs, and reduce production wastage. Throughout the remainder of the year, work went on to complete the changeover and by the end of the year the estimated costs for the work done to that point were $20,000.

As the beet sugar stocks began to accumulate, most of the suppliers delivered according to their contracts. One exception was the Société pour l'exportation des Sucres, Antwerp, who quoted sugar at a set price. When it fell in value on the open market, they insisted on the original price being paid. George objected to this and claimed that market prices justified purchasing at the lower market price. When they refused to drop their prices, it forced George to correspond with the Société to the effect that:

> *It will be impossible to trust ourselves in direct dealings without the intervention of an agent to serve our interests unless we possess the confidence that in just such a case as this we get the advantage of any decline such as this ... and it has strained our relations ... with our regular correspondents to depart from our regular practice in order to have direct relationships with you.*
> *(June 10, 1895)*

After some negotiations, George obtained the desired reduction in price, and business continued unabated. During August, the company constructed a new storage shed, but due to the Dominion Bridge Company not delivering the iron roofing beams as ordered, wooden ones had to be used, much to George's disgust. Towards the end of October, George decided to investigate more fully the possibilities of distilling molasses and sought to order some boiling type molasses from Thomas Culwell in New York in a letter dated October 31, 1895.

> *To some extent it would be an experiment with us so far we have made no preparations for its use ... we have no wharf facilities for its discharge ... can you send us puncheons in the old style till we see the result of a seasons business?*

Previous pages: This 1896 panoramic view of Pointe St. Charles and the Lachine Canal shows the dominant position of the refinery within the area.

Throughout November and December 1895, the stocks of raw first-class beet sugar accumulated and by the end of the year had soared from the January figure of 600,000 pounds to 55.5 million pounds while refined stocks were more than 18 million pounds. To some extent, George had gone overboard in his purchasing and these excess stocks had to be assessed as expenses without recovered income, which pulled the projected profit down by $22,000, and which, when added to the other costs of the refinery, reduced a handsome gross profit of $328,500 to a still respectable $233,500, upon which the company issued a 15% dividend and employee bonuses totalling $2,000.

During the Christmas shut-down of 1895 and throughout the remainder of the winter into 1896, the balance of the beet-related machinery in "A" building was moved across the road into the new Steffen building. A list of some of the machinery involved indicates that this was a huge undertaking since power tools and fork-lift trucks did not exist at that time and everything had to be moved by hand.

Triple Effect Evaporator	*25 tons*
Iron Vacuum Pan	*15 tons*
Copper Condenser	*8 tons*
Granulator	*2.5 tons*
Statford Engine	*8 tons*
Water Pumps	*2 tons*
8 x 40 inch Western Centrifugals	*2 tons each*

Because the stocks of raw sugar filled every available space, two new sheds were erected to keep them out of the poorer weather, adding another $2,000 to the year's expenses. In order to clear some space, the company pressed vigorously into exporting its large stocks of syrup to Europe. Figures show that sales in France absorbed a proportion of the lowest grade syrups, while the Golden Syrup was exported to England in iron-bound oak barrels, to be sold in direct competition with Lyle's product of similar description. On the home front, attempts to increase sales were made by selling barrels of sugar to retailers and including a selection of paper bags into which the sugar could be readily measured. This "Star" brand granulated sugar was introduced in March 1896. According to the production lists, each barrel of 200 pounds of sugar contained five 10 pound bags, five 20 pound bags and ten 5 pound paper bags. By March, sufficient stocks of raw sugar had been accumulated so that additional orders for raws were postponed. In addition, as the forecasts for the remainder of the year indicated a general price rise, the company looked secure in its ability to make a good profit on the sugars already bought at the lower price levels. Regrettably, all the forecasts were wrong and in April 1896 the price levels for raw sugar tumbled and financial losses began to mount. By mid-May, the costs to the company from the combination of holding excess stocks and the price drop exceeded $20,000. One side effect of this price tumble was the final killing off of the Quebec beet refineries, which had been limping along with intermittent periods of production and numerous financial resurrections, followed by an equal number of collapses and failures. The Berthier Beet Co. recorded total losses of $50,000, so its machinery was dismantled and sold to a New Mexico Company for use there. The West Farnham factory equipment was sold off to a syndicate operating out of Rome, New York, and Coaticook was scheduled for stripping when it burned down at the end of the year.

June 1896 brought the general election and the Liberals

swept back into power under the leadership of the Right Honourable Sir Wilfrid Laurier ejecting Sir Charles Tupper and his Conservatives from an eighteen-year reign. George did not entirely welcome this news as it introduced another variable into the already complicated equation of doing business. Throughout August, sales were extremely slow and the stockpiles of raws mounted in the warehouse to a peak in September of 44 million pounds, while refined stocks were over 11.2 million pounds. The financial losses on the raw sugar price collapse had accumulated to $157,000 and excessive stocks added another $126,500 to the burden, making an accumulated loss of $283,500 up to October alone. Even the news that the competition, the Moncton Refinery, had burned down on September 20 did not help matters sufficiently. The time had come to initiate drastic cost-cutting measures and George notified Maurice of his thoughts on the matter:

> *Dear Sir*
> *I write this officially to put on record what I have said more fully at various times. It is of importance that extraneous expenses of all kinds at the refinery be stopped. New work which is not essential to the conduct of the manufacture must not be begun. A careful review should be made of the number of men in outside and stores, with a view of diminishing the number to the lowest point consistent with the work. As regards the store for refined sugar I am of the opinion that too many hands are employed and possibly the oversight of this department is inefficient (though I do not say this as of my knowledge.) In short economy must be rigidly enforced in every Department, particularly in the Engineer and Filter departments.*
> *Yours truly, George Alexander Drummond*
> *(October 14, 1896)*

Compounding these problems, the Customs bureau seized more than $150,000 worth of sugar, claiming it to be of a higher grade than specified in the duty returns, and demanded an additional $32,000 be paid over prior to its release. Obviously, George argued the case in the strongest possible terms but nothing moved the officials and so more money had to be paid out, compounding the financial woes. To cap everything else off and make the year end on just the right note of disaster, the Toronto sales representative, Mr. Murray, took a number of sizable orders from his friends and business acquaintances giving excessive discounts on the general and extremely low purchase prices. Because he did not include the appropriate freight rates to points of delivery beyond Toronto, they were charged directly to the C.S.R. Co. Ltd. by the railway company. In total, the company recorded a financial loss for the year of $290,000, of which $130,000 was attributed to extra expenses beyond normal accounts. At a time when stocks were normally at a low level, the C.S.R. Co. Ltd. had more than 14 million pounds more raw sugar than the combined comparable stocks for the Acadia Sugar Co. and St. Lawrence Sugar Co. It was, to put it mildly, not a good year for sugar.

Left: A view of the City of Montreal in 1896. Terrace Bank can be seen behind the tall spire of the church in the upper left quadrant of the photograph.

The Canada Sugar Refining Co. Ltd. in 1897, as photographed by Frank Redpath, upon the occasion of the delivery of the first shipment of sugar at the new wharf.

CHAPTER SEVENTEEN

"You Lose On The Swings"

While business had not been good for the C.S.R. Co. Ltd., their competitors had also been suffering losses from the various cut-backs in protection, and it was generally felt that the new Liberal government would not be inclined to look any more favourably on the sugar refiners now than they had in 1875. George began to draw the various elements of the industry together, as his letter to B.T. Rogers of the B.C. Sugar Co. reveals:

> *So far as I know, no representations have yet been made to the Government by the sugar refiners. No doubt the time may soon come to do so ... shall we all meet to discuss the matter?*
> *(January 6, 1897)*

There is no record that any meeting took place as a result of this communication, but the groundwork was certainly set for joint activities later in the year. Anticipating a major alteration in the duties by the government, George indulged in futures speculation by purchasing 17,600 tons of raw *above* the refinery's normal requirements. This was in addition to the huge stocks he had left over from the previous year. When the expected duty changes came in, although they were harsh, they were not as bad as had been feared, and so the company was "burned" yet again with excess stocks resulting in losses on this deal alone of $141,000.

In early April, the Customs' authorities decided to apply pressure on the C.S.R. Co. Ltd. to pay the disputed duties for the shipment seized in 1896, by refusing to allow any further shipments of sugar to be entered except as the higher-dutied refined. It was then the responsibility of the C.S.R. Co. Ltd. to *prove* that the stock received was below the No. 16 Dutch Standard level and claim a rebate. Furious at this prejudicial treatment, George wrote to Mr. R. White, the Collector of Customs for Montreal.

> *Such a rule is not, so far as my information goes, applied to any other commodity or company, and I think it oppressive and exacting. However I have not the power to contest your demand and tender the full amount of refined duty for the last cargo ... AND DEMAND IMMEDIATE FREE ENTRY OF SAID GOODS.*
> *(April 3, 1897)*

Outside the refinery on the canal bank, the annual repairs were supplemented in 1897 by the construction of a new wharf. Once the work was completed, it was noticed that the contractors had left a few items behind and George notified Mr. Marceau of the Canal Department.

> *I beg to direct your attention to a large quantity of cubic lumps of stone now lying in the Canal opposite the new wharf ... between the Wellington Bridge and St. Gabriel locks. These stones are certainly a great peril to the navigation and absolutely prevent the use of the above wharf to vessels of the draft of the improved depth of the Canal, and I trust they can be taken out during the time the water is still out.*
> *(April 14, 1897)*

On the twenty-second, the Honourable W.S. Fielding, the Finance Minister, introduced his new tariff system, which extensively changed the pattern of official Canadian business thinking. The free-trade mentality was once again back in power and as a concession to pressures from Canadian refined sugar importers, and as a retaliatory measure against the U.S. high protectionist tariffs, he completely re-vamped the system of duties. On raw sugar, the earlier duties were maintained at 50 cents per 100 pounds but the refined duty dropped from $1.14 per 100 pounds to $1.00, making it much more profitable to import refined sugar than previously. This forced George to write in haste to the Ministry of Justice on April 23, 1897.

> *The tariff is now out and we know the worst and that is bad enough ... As regards sugar the cutting down of the rate ... is just carrying out the current idea of taking from the manufacturer "a little of the too good a thing he has hitherto enjoyed from his political friends the Conservatives". But as the Conservatives had previously acted on the same principle before this change ... we were already near the point at which the manufacturer had nothing to part with ... we are perilously near the point ... at which we can be snuffed out by the Americans or Germans. I am not going to make any more representations, but as a manufacturer must just consider myself as under notice to quit.*

Following consultations with the other sugar companies, George drafted a letter on their behalf to the Minister of Finance:

> *They [your Memorialists] are convinced that under the proposed rates, it will be impossible to conduct their business so as to exclude foreign refined sugar. More especially under the existing conditions created by enhanced drawbacks recently granted by Continental [European] Governments.*
> *The difference between the raw and refined duties, which has been in force for two years, was far from satisfactory to the refiners, and was the subject of protests from them to the late Government, and they may say that any difference heretofore allowed never did anything beyond limiting the importations of foreign sugar ...*
> *Under existing circumstances they therefore protest against the reduction and apply for a restoration of at least the former rate of difference. Failing which they seriously apprehend a condition of things which will react in an adverse manner on every one concerned with and dependant on the trade ...*
> *8th May, 1897*

George Alexander Drummond on behalf of
Canada Sugar Refining Co. Ltd.
St. Lawrence Sugar Co. Ltd.
Acadia Sugar Co. Ltd.

After numerous letters and even some personal representations, it was obvious that the government was not inclined to change its position and so the refiners decided that the only way to protect themselves was to segment the Canadian market and allocate portions to each refiner, thus eliminating normal competitive conditions. By this agreement, the Canada Sugar Refining Co. Ltd. was allocated 39% of Eastern Canada's wants; the St.Lawrence got 36%; and Acadia, with two refineries, received the remaining 25% of the Eastern Canadian market. In Vancouver, the British Columbia Sugar Company gained all Canadian wants west of Winnipeg.

The initial agreement was scheduled to last five years and each company agreed to put up $50,000 as a security of good faith. To raise some of this money, the C.S.R. Co. Ltd. sold off an area of its coal-storage land to K.W. Blackwell, President of the Canada Switch & Spring Co. for $30,000 and the money was deposited in a holding account with the Bank of Montreal. The agreement was formally signed on July 8 and was scheduled to take effect on the fifteenth.

This agreement gave George a perfect opportunity to break away from the continual harassment of daily business decision making and within two days he had left on a trip to Europe from which he eventually returned in late November. In the meantime, he left instructions for the construction of a new home on his property in Beaconsfield, and while in Europe he purchased furniture, paintings, and artwork to be brought back to Canada. During his absence, the first ship to use the newly constructed wharf alongside the new buildings of the refinery arrived and Frank Redpath, being an amateur photographer, recorded the event with some excellent shots of the canal, the vessels, and the refinery.

Upon George's return he found several situations required his attention. One was an offer from a Mr. C.C. Robertson inviting the C.S.R. Co. Ltd. to participate in a joint venture to establish a beet sugar plant in the United States, at a location to be selected by George. George's reply on November 24 was:

> *The production of sugar from beets is a very different thing from sugar refining, which is the business of this Company. Besides the Charter under which we operate does not allow of our operating outside of Canada.*

Another situation was the settlement of the outstanding Customs claim from 1896. Having repeatedly argued without success, George finally gave up and paid $32,937.19, with the comment of his frustration appearing in his notebook.

> *I will yield place to no man in my inability to understand Lawyers and Ministers of the Crown and the present circumstance is no exception to the rule.*
> *(November 29, 1897)*

And to prove the old saying that problems come in threes, the Grand Trunk Railway seized a shipment of sugar, claiming it had not been paid for by the company. George argued that responsibility for the payment lay with the

The Canada Sugar Refining Co. Ltd. in 1897, as photographed by Frank Redpath, upon the occasion of the delivery of the first shipment of sugar at the new wharf.

senders of the goods and refused to pay. When the G.T.R. equally refused to release the goods, George instituted legal proceedings that eventually resulted in a judgement in favour of the C.S.R. Co. Ltd. The G.T.R. initially refused to comply but then reversed their decision and ordered the C.S.R. Co. Ltd. to remove the sugar from their yards immediately or face being charged storage fees from the original date of its seizure.

At the end of the year, Maurice commented in his notes on the results of the work within the refinery and it gives us a good picture of the refinery at that time.

> *With the finalisation of the removal of the machinery from the A1 and A2 buildings no more sugar was worked inside either building. The top two floors of A2 were inspected and found to be very shaky and were pulled down in 1897. A new roof was then added ... In A1 building [the original building of the 1854 refinery] there remained 2 small copper pans and 1 small iron pan, a granulator for whites, a disintegrator and packer for yellows, and 16 centrifugals capable of putting through 300,000 lbs. in 24 hours ... there also remain pots for blanking, all rigs for barrelling and Tin syrups, Paris Lump rigs, a mill for powdered and Ex Ground ... 2 boiler pumps and a beam Engine in A2 ... Thus we did odd things such as Paris Lumps, Powdered, Extra Ground Sugar and Syrups in 1897 ... The total cost of the removal exceeded $55,000.00 but Fire Insurance was reduced by $7,000.00 and the number of Foremen and Labour were decidedly reduced.*

The cut-backs, alterations, and various savings produced their needed results and by the end of the year a total of 85 million pounds was recorded as melted, of which at least 95% was beet type sugars. The corporate dividend was issued at 12% on a net profit of $231,000 and the employees shared in the better financial circumstances with bonuses totalling $2,125.

For some time during 1896 and 1897, arguments had been developing within the industry over the use of the Dutch Standard as a system for grading sugar. Many other countries had switched to the more scientific use of the polariscope. The disadvantage for the C.S.R. Co. Ltd. in this change was that the testing of sugar by the polariscope method discriminated more against beet type sugars. In January of 1898, the government announced its intention to switch the method of testing for the estimation of duties to the polariscope system. George had no doubt that the source of this proposal were the Maritime refineries, who were highly cane-oriented, and who would stand to gain a significant advantage in the event of its acceptance.

After raising the question with the government, and receiving no satisfactory reply, George purchased 28 million pounds of beet sugar prior to the expected introduction of the tariff with a loss value effect of $76,800 on the books. During March, most of George's time was spent in Ottawa trying to amend the proposals to use the polariscope system; upon those occasions that he was in Montreal, he stayed at his new country home in Beaconsfield attending to the purchase and breeding requirements of his special stock of sheep and cattle. He also made plans to visit his third son, Arthur, who was living in the southwestern United States while recovering from tuberculosis. This illness had forced Arthur and his family to move each winter from the colder weather of Montreal to the warmer and drier climate of Colorado. Although we have little information about Arthur in his early years, we do know that he had, since his graduation as an engineer, worked alongside his elder brothers Maurice and Huntly on the management staff of the refinery. Many of the technical details of the extensive improvements undertaken during the earlier years were directly supervised by Arthur. This forced exile for Arthur left the family "team" incomplete and required Maurice and Huntly to keep him informed on current events by letter. Fortunately, some of these letters have been preserved and their intricate detail provides much in the way of revealing the business thinking of the Drummonds during this time.

On April 5, 1898, the new tariff system came into effect, so that all sugars were now tested and assessed by degrees of polarization for the quantity of sugar found within the crystals. This significantly altered the financial benefits the C.S.R. Co. Ltd. had enjoyed in the past and started serious discussions within the company on the plans for the future. All purchasing agents were notified that on any future orders, preference was to be given to sugars of low polarization to take advantage of the tariff provisions. Arthur was informed of these matters and a number of others in a revealing letter written by Maurice dated May 14, 1898.

Dear Arthur:

The Tariff at Ottawa is still unsettled like most other affairs there, such as a railway to the Klondyke; but there is not the slightest interest taken in gold discoveries now that a war is going on [The Spanish American War]. Skaife has just returned from Cuba - he says Spain won't put up much of a fight as their fortifications, guns and ships are in a terribly bad state ... We have erected a small old engine in the 6th floor loft of the old building to tackle the main hoist and then we will not need to be always running the old beam engine and breaking down the line of shafting all the time somewhere or other. In the new building we changed the yellow "porcupine fliers drive" ... by a parallel line of shafting and can stop the fliers without stopping the engine as before ... we put an overhead conveyer to carry the coarse grain which comes over the end of the riddles straight back to the rollers ... instead of the old worn out wooden floor we put a tile floor at the presses. Instead of the slate, which was always going to pieces and with the lengthened ventilator (skylight) the presses look well. We are pulling out more of the wood floors in the Char house and have got every one of the char bins lined with galvanised iron ... we will tackle a good deal more of the wood here and in the old buildings as it wears out ... We built a new lump drying stove with coil which was at the end of the old double drying granulator system and a plain window fan and our Lumps now dry in 8 hours instead of 3 days and 25% more at a time if we want ... We are putting up a grinder for the lime, to reduce it to powder before adding water to make the cream of lime. Other places which have done this claim a large saving in lime and better Liquors etc. I think I told you the improvement in the "cuite" we finish the pan with beet, not cane, molasses and finish the wagons with 5 or 6 good beet syrups and get now a sugar dry of 99.5% purity. We continue to make the "Austrian Granulated, made in Canada" as the brand on the barrels say ... The City has put up two immense boards supported on 6 or 7 big posts on each side of the Canal near the new building of ours, which the initiated believe are going to be inscribed with 3 foot letters a notice to boats to be careful and not drag up the City water pipes with their anchors as the dredge did further up the Canal last summer and nearly caused a water famine - the public believe that the notice will be Canada Sugar Refining Co. and one of our men had the cheek to insinuate that we were going to put on "Austrian Granulated Made in Canada"! The new Seigneurs Street Bridge is nearly completed otherwise very few improvements in Montreal this year.

Yours Affectionately
M. Drummond

This last sentence actually was more important than its passing inclusion might make it appear, since with the construction of a large bridge immediately next to the refinery, access to the city was considerably improved and the long detours that heavier vehicles were forced to make to other bridges was eliminated.

At the refinery, modernizing and alterations continued, as detailed in Maurice's letter. But on June 23, one of the workers, Mr. A. Harrison, was killed by electrocution while doing paintwork on various pieces of equipment. In a letter to the company lawyers, George stressed his certainty that the "deplorable" accident had been the fault of the electrical system installed by the electrical company and was attributable to the city by virtue of its failure to locate the fault in its inspections. As George put it:

Can we get at the Lachine Hydraulic Co. some way, either directly or as representing the widow or can we get at the City ... I would like to get some damages from one or the other for Mrs. Harrison ... we are paying the widow $2,500.00 in conformity with a private arrangement with our employees.
(June 25, 1898)

Unfortunately, no additional material has come to light as to whether they were successful in obtaining damages for the widow. Little else is recorded for the remainder of the year, except for the establishment of a preferential status for British goods in the tariffs on August 1 and for November, when Maurice left to go on an extended vacation in Europe. While passing through London, he again visited the Lyle Refinery and once on the continent he toured several prominent beet factories. Fortunately, many of the letters he sent back to his parents have survived, showing that on this tour he visited Paris, Dieppe, Rouen, Zurich, Basle, Vienna, Budapest, Belgrade, Sophia, Constantinople, Athens, Naples, Rome, Pisa, and Genoa, describing as he went the various sights and events that he witnessed. Finally for 1898 and, outside the confines of the company, George's position as Vice-President of the Bank of Montreal was enhanced when the President, Donald A. Smith (now elevated to the peerage as Baron Strathcona and Mount Royal), was appointed the High Commissioner for Canada in London. This left George acting as the de-facto President of the bank, a position he had been waiting to hold for nearly twelve years.

Early in 1899, George decided to enhance his Beaconsfield property and indulge his passion for golf by installing a full-size nine-hole golf course on the land next to the house. On a more serious note, however, the rumours from Ottawa indicated another change in the tariffs with the British preferential rate being raised from 25% to 33½%, which would significantly increase the likelihood of large quantities of British-made sugar entering Canada. These changes were being roundly denigrated by the Conservative opposition, provoking counterclaims that these criticisms smacked of disloyalty to the country and lack of respect to the Crown. As a staunch Conservative, George Drummond felt it was his duty to caution his party on the political repercussions that could ensue within the business community if these criticisms continued. He therefore wrote to the Honourable Sir Charles Tupper, the Conservative opposition party leader and former Prime Minister.

Mr. Foster [the ex-Finance Minister] made many of our business friends lukewarm for the Conservative Party by his pinching of the Tariff, but that was to a considerable extent countervailed by the fear that the Liberals would do worse. Now that it has been shown that they are not so

bad as was feared and the Conservative speakers and press make it their business to twist them [the Liberals] with it [the new British Preferential Tariff] so continuously, the manufacturers are getting convinced that their policy is to be either neutral or Liberal. I cannot conceive a stupider course for the Conservatives to follow, but then I am not a politician. [1]
(March 24, 1899)

Obviously this letter and other representations made to the Conservatives by prominent individuals from across the country had an effect since the rhetoric quickly diminished and the new tariff was implemented with little real opposition.

At the refinery, problems were encountered in the springtime with the ongoing dredging of the canal. This dredging was significantly increasing the levels of mud and solids being found in the water, and many of the machines, which used canal water as a coolant or for steam, were found to be clogged with the mud. As a result, the company was forced to install water filters and when this did not work, to arrange for alternative sources of water from April 9 to May 1 when the drained canal was refilled.

During the summer months, it became clear that the U.S. government was planning to increase its drawbacks to U.S. sugar refiners in order to allow them to compete in Canada against the British preferential products. George foresaw a new trade war in Canada, with the Canadian refiners trapped between the larger European and U.S. refining industries. He therefore wrote to Finance Minister William Fielding, expressing his concerns.

The current world production of sugar is estimated to be 5,000,000 tons per annum of beet and 2,500,000 tons per annum of cane with beet sugar increasing and cane remaining static ... British Free Trade policies have ruined her own refineries since all the Continental Governments have not reciprocated but rather have maintained a highly protective attitude and merely flooded Britain with their sugars to the ruination of the British interests ... In the United States they consume 2,160,000 tons of imported sugar per annum as well as growing their own cane in Louisiana and beet sugars in their Mid West ... by extensive lobbying their beet interests have pressed for protection and European beet sugar is discouraged and practically non existent there, except in an emergency ... the U.S. has mainly bought cane and their high demand which grows at a rate of 250,000 - 300,000 tonnes per annum makes prices higher than would be otherwise ... For ourselves we buy mainly beet sugar as it remains cheaper than the cane due to the U.S. demand for the cane and our Canadian Tariff favours the high class sugars ... I do not hesitate to say that in the past the consumers have benefited by these facts, the refiners have had a good deal of competition, the grocers who distributed the goods say they have done so without profit. In addition to this the reduction of the relative duties between raw sugar and refined ... has permitted of considerable importation of foreign refined sugar which is on the increase today. The importation takes the form of white from Germany and Holland and of yellow sugar from England. The German white sugar is granulated mostly from raw beet juice without the elaborate and costly filtration of the refiner and therefore much inferior to the Canadian refined ... The English yellow sugar

is a drug on their own market where in most cases it is a by-product and consequently cheap ... If we are to fight this competition we must have cheap access to our raw material ... if anything is done to impede the importation of suitable raw material or to enhance its cost without at the same time impeding the importation of the competing foreign refined, sugar refining in Canada will speedily come to an end.
(June 16, 1899)

For the remainder of the calendar year, little is known of the activities within the refinery. There does, however, seem to have been an effort on Maurice's part to examine and review the various activities of the company since its establishment in 1879 as the Canada Sugar Refining Co. Ltd. These records, statistics, and comparative analyses still exist in two large volumes, and such is the depth of information held within these two pieces that only a small portion has been used in this text. The example following, for instance, gives an indication of the international connections achieved by the C.S.R. Co. Ltd. at this, the end of the century.

GOODS AND EQUIPMENT SUPPLIED TO THE C.S.R. CO. LTD. - 1890 - 1899

Varnish for granulator - McCaskill, Dougall Co., Zanzibar
Boiled linseed oil - Robert Ingham Clark & Co., Westham, England
Vermilion brand paint - H. Beck Co., London, England
Valcan cement - Charlton Bros., Elswick, Newcastle-upon-Tyne, England
Rubber hose - Boston Belting Co., Boston, U.S.A.
Reducing valves - Best Manufacturing Co., Pittsburgh, U.S.A.
Canvas conveyors - G. Cradock & Sons, Wakefield, England
Steel rope - Dominion Wire Rope Co., Montreal, Canada
Coal conveyers - Link Belt Machinery Co., Chicago, U.S.A.
Wire rope - Buremant & Co., London, England
Sacks and bags - Timewell Sack Filling & Sewing Co., Chicago, U.S.A.
Sacks and bags - Morris Meyers & Co., Liverpool, England
Sacks and bags - E. Walcher, Brussels, Belgium
Perforated copper cloth - Fontaine & Co., Aix-La-Chappelle, France
Perforated copper cloth - H. Patsch Co., Hagen, Germany
Perforated copper cloth - North British Wire Manufacturing Co., Glasgow, Scotland
Tarpauline bags - W. & D. Watson, Dundee, Scotland

Senator George Alexander Drummond.

CHAPTER EIGHTEEN

"The New Way"

With the advent of the year 1900, a new century was celebrated, and optimism for the future seemed to be dominant across the country. The population of Canada was growing by leaps and bounds and would continue to do so for the next decade, especially in the west of the country, as shown below.

	1900	*1911*
Montreal	328,172	490,504
Toronto	209,892	381,833
Calgary	4,392	43,511
Edmonton	4,176	31,064
Regina	2,249	30,213
Saskatoon	113	12,004

This growth led many businessmen, including George Drummond, to speculate that the time was right for expansion and diversification of production. Maurice was instructed to develop plans for a major reconstruction of the entire site, to bring it entirely up to date, and to standardize the requirements of the company during any normal stoppage. Maurice quickly fulfilled his duty, and his notes indicate that it took seven days to stop the entire process in a proper manner, and four days to restart, during which time the higher grade sugars could not be made. Additionally, the list of the standard stock to be maintained for sale at times of shut-down gives a very good indication of the variety of products available to the Canadian consumer.

1200 *barrels of coarse grain sugar to make about -*

1,600	*50 pound boxes of Extra Granulated*
1,500	*25 pound boxes of Extra Granulated*
10	*200 pound lots of Fine Grain*
10	*50 pound lots of Cream Yellows*
10	*100 pound lots of Extra Fine Yellows*
2,000	*barrels of Crown brand*
250	*barrels of Powdered*
500	*boxes of Powdered*
50	*half barrels of Ordinary brand*
700	*large boxes of Paris Lumps*
1,200	*small boxes of Paris Lumps*
20	*barrels of Paris Lumps*
15	*half barrels of Paris Lumps*
20,000	*bags of Granulated*
1,600	*bags of Yellows*

Maurice also went once again to Europe between March 10 and May 14, 1900, to obtain the latest information on technological improvements.

Outside the refinery, Canada was involved in the Boer War, which had started the previous October. Already two detachments of troops had been sent and seen action in the Cape at the Battle of Paardeburg, suffering over 130 casualties. Feeling it to be his patriotic duty, George became involved in collecting funds to acquire food and household goods for the dependants of the soldiers. He also acted in a similar capacity to raise relief funds when on April 26 a major fire occurred in Ottawa – Hull, which killed seven people and caused $10 million damage. As part of this latter effort, when he received a cheque from his Belgium suppliers, "La Société pour L' exportation des Sucres," he responded, thanking them for their donation of £100 "towards Ottawa sufferers" but indicated that the fund had already been well subscribed and no more money was needed. He then proceeded to suggest an alternative use for the money as well as revealing his opinion on the Boer War and the current opinions being expressed in Belgium.

> *Your cheque therefore will not be applied to any purpose till your wishes are known. At the same time, there is the "Patriotic Fund" destined for the support of the dependents of the soldiers now in South Africa. A gift from you to this would be very useful and much appreciated, and would do something as an offset to the stupid Pro-Boer sympathies of Belgium.*
> *(May 12, 1900)*

No record exists as to whether the cheque was cashed or cancelled, but it certainly proves that George did not pull punches when it came to matters he felt impugned the honour of his country. During the remainder of the year, much of George's attention was taken up by the worrying signs that Maurice was suffering from some form of illness that was affecting his nervous system, for he was plagued by severe bouts of dizziness, stiffness in the muscles of the leg and arm, and a periodic "neuralgia" in his right eye.

In January 1901, George and his son Huntly took two days off from the business to travel up to Toronto to hear Winston Churchill speak on the war in South Africa and to invite him to dine at George's home in Montreal, which he did a week later. Later in the month, it was announced that Queen Victoria had died. George immediately ordered black armbands for the staff and black draperies for the main door of the refinery. Across the nation, deepest mourning was put into place and most public events were cancelled. The Victorian era was now officially ended and under its new King, Canadians, including George Drummond, looked to the future with a sense of optimism and were ready to adopt the new conveniences of the age. It might be thought that at the age of seventy-two, George would have been conservative in his activities. Instead, following a visit to New York, he wrote to a Mr. Kidder enquiring on the purchase of an "Auto-mobile."

I see from your pamphlet that your Labours have reached something tangible and that the Kidder Motor is on the market. I am interested in this matter, more or less, though our Canadian roads are not the best for such vehicles. The objection I have to all your class of machines is the danger of gasoline. At my farm I have two English engines ... burning ordinary oil. That seems to me ideal if it were practicable. America runs upon Gasoline even for stationary engines but I certainly would not use on in or about my farm ... A few days ago I visited the show in Madison Square Gardens and looked over the motors, they ranged in price from $600.00 to $750.00 dollars or thereby. Why should yours be $1,000.00. Let me know your very best price for a light runabout delivered to me, here, duty paid in the end of April. Let me know if you have considered and see any chance of running a plain illuminating oil explosion engine. Has your machine the objectionable trait of escaping steam while in motion?[1]
(January 29, 1901)

Three months later, having received the appropriate information, George ordered his first car from Mr. Kidder.

After thinking over the matter, the very bad roads which we have here, being the cause of my hesitation. I have decided on having one of your auto-mobile vehicles at the price and of the character described by you. My son suggests the following specific features:

1st A seat behind to carry a man to be taking charge of the vehicle when at home and starting. This seat to be back to back with my own.

2nd The gasoline tank to be a little larger (desirable but not critical).

3rd A catch or brake lever so as to leave it on when standing (this seems most necessary).

4th Gun-metal cylinders.

5th Heavy Pneumatic tyres.

6th An injector to fill the water tank.

... the price to be $1,000.00 dollars complete ...[2]

(April 3, 1901)

On March 13, 1901, a small fire broke out at the refinery in the bag-drying kiln. It was soon extinguished but it brought back the recognition that fire precautions had lapsed and needed improvement, and George instructed Maurice to attend to the matter.

I request you to take steps at once to re-organize the Fire brigade out of the staff at the Refinery. You will of course take the employees according to their aptitude and availability. Each man to be educated to use and apply the fire apparatus.
(March 16, 1901)

In April, the water levels in the St. Lawrence River and the canal began to rise, causing fears that the refinery area would be flooded. As in the past, every available man was put on the job of stacking the sugar on top of planks, raising it a full 20 inches over the 1886 flood mark. The river did rise substantially but not sufficiently to cause any flooding, and the danger passed without incident. During the end of April and throughout May, the company followed up on its previous experimental plans for the establishment of a means of distilling molasses, by designating an area of the plant as the location for the future development of a distillery. There was also an investigation of prospects for a molasses-based cattle-food additive that would use up the large stocks of molasses produced under the Steffen Process. In this, the C.S.R. Co. Ltd. was copying the Tate sugar company in Great Britain, who were making a substance called "Molassine" as a food for livestock.

As well as overseeing the business of refining sugar, the Bank of Montreal, and several other companies of which he was either President or a Director, George became the chairman of the committee organizing the preparations for a visit by the Duke and Duchess of Cornwall (later to become King George V and Queen Mary) to Montreal. From May until September, George was increasingly involved in every aspect of the planning of the celebrations. One item particularly took up George's attention and this was the commemorative medal to be struck and issued at the time of the visit. George participated in the design of the medal and wrote to Lord Strathcona, another member of the committee, on the design of the medal.

> *I would like to get on the reverse with figures of our volunteers the words "South Africa 1899 - 1900" because what I think we want to celebrate is the great fact I never expected to see, that Canada has fought for the Crown and Empire on foreign soil.*[3]
> *(July 2, 1901)*

Just prior to the regal visit, George received a letter from Lord Minto (the Governor General) offering George the honour of Companion of the Order of St. Michael and St. George or C.M.G. George's response was, on the surface, surprising.

> *The communication was so entirely unexpected and the time so unsuited for any explanation, that I did not attempt to make any. I now take the earliest possible moment to ask leave, respectfully, to decline the honour you purpose for me. As your Lordship may perhaps remember I have never directly or otherwise indicated any expectation or desire for honours.*[4]
> *(September 5, 1901)*

At first sight this refusal may seem odd but, as will be seen later, there was a reason.

In Ottawa, pressure was brought to bear by several business and political groups on the federal government to establish a domestic sugar beet industry. As a result, the government removed all duties on beet processing machinery that would be imported prior to June 1904. At the provincial level, following a series of growing experiments carried out by the Ontario Agricultural College, the Ontario government joined in by initiating a major financial promotion in the form of grants and loans to companies that wished to establish beet sugar processing facilities. Several communities within the province took advantage of this bounty by offering tax concessions and land grants to attract investment. Four centres of production were subsequently founded at Dresden, Wiarton, Wallaceburg, and Berlin (now renamed Kitchener), bringing the total number of sugar companies in Canada to eight and the number of plants to ten. Furthermore, extra duties were placed upon foreign sugars of all classes by the federal government, thus increasing the costs of production to those sugar refineries already established and who relied upon imported sugar for their supplies. Despite these problems, George was more concerned about the continuing medical problems of Maurice, who since April had shown signs of severe stiffness in the muscles of his right leg. Maurice was continuing to work daily at the refinery but George felt it was important to get some expert advice on the matter; he ordered Maurice to go to Europe to see medical specialists on the subject. Maurice left for New York on October 26 to catch the German liner *Kronprinz Wilhelm*, and over the next three months he visited most of the health spas and clinics across Northern Europe, undergoing various treatments of massage and "baths." According to his diary, these treatments were of little actual benefit to his condition and he returned on the Norddeutscher Lloyd's *Kaiser Wilhelm der Grosse* in early January. In his usual business-like manner, Maurice did not return empty handed, for he had used some of his time to study new refining techniques at various European factories and brought back plans that he would use in the refinery during the coming years.

As the war in the Cape continued through 1902 and into 1903, questions were raised about the need for Canada to support the Empire not only with land forces but also at sea. The only problem was that Canada had no navy of its own and relied upon the British navy for protection. But due to the growing arms race between Britain and Germany towards building bigger, faster, and better armed warships, Britain was already fully occupied. This left an increased awareness within the Canadian government that although Britain "ruled the waves," the coastal waters of North America were dominated by a United States that was once again becoming more aggressive in its attitudes towards Canada. To counter this, George Drummond joined with other prominent Canadians who felt that the Dominion needed her own navy, to form the Navy League which was to act as a pressure group over the next few years and help to found the Canadian Navy.

At the refinery, all the plans for changes were now in place, and alterations to the northwest corner of the refinery were begun in order to build a distillery. To men of the religious background of the Drummonds and the surviving members of the Redpath family who were stockholders, the concept of adding a facility for the production of intoxicating liquor presented something of a moral dilemma. On the other hand, business conditions dictated that some use of the molasses be made, so it was decided to establish a separate company that would be known as Montreal Products Co. Ltd. and be a wholly owned subsidiary of the C.S.R. Co. Ltd.

At the start of June 1902, news reached Canada that the Boer War was ended and throughout the country, banners and flags were hung to celebrate the victory. George ordered food and drink for his workers. Tables made of planks and barrels were set up in the yard and a festive lunch was provided for one and all.

Shortly afterwards, George decided to build a larger home for himself on his Beaconsfield property and hired A.T. Taylor as the contractor for "Huntlywood," named after the place of birth of George's father and grandfather in Scotland. When completed, it was an impressive structure of thirty-two rooms, with a huge circular staircase in the centre of the building and a decorative cupola on the roof. The building was painted yellow and white and became a distinct landmark for travellers coming to Montreal from the west, as it was clearly visible from the main railway track to the south of the building. Surrounding the house, to complement his nine-hole golf course, an additional area for a putting green was established on the front lawn, with a rose garden and fountain completing the effect of being a residence suitable for a man of substance.

During the summer, as the pilot plant for the new distillery was installed, George and Maurice heard that a major sugar company in the United States was contemplating expanding into Canada by constructing a refinery at a not yet disclosed location. Extremely concerned at this potential development, Maurice was sent by George to discuss matters with the Federal Sugar Co. in Yonkers, New York, on July 28. The exact nature of the discussions are not known but Maurice returned to Montreal the next day, and one month later, both George and Maurice travelled down, spending two days in closed meetings with the President and chief executives of the Federal Sugar Co. Again the substance of the meetings is not known but in a letter to Mr. Lee of Hewlett and Lee in New York, George made these comments.

> *The Federal Co. does not, I presume, desire to come here to make money, that is impossible. There are five refineries here now and work for only three of them. We ourselves could double our production in a days notice. Four beet factories (new) just about ready to start and to add to the delightful prospect, the possibility of our being prevented by fresh legislation from importing beet sugar for our use.*[5] *(September 29, 1902)*

In September, the completed distillery pilot plant began operations and seemed to be running smoothly. As

The Drummond home of Huntlywood in Beaconsfield, at the west end of the island of Montreal.

might be expected, there have been numerous tales about the workers secretly fitting taps to siphon off alcohol for personal consumption. The authenticity of these rumors could not be confirmed by company sources but one union representative has stated that in later years he knew for certain these tapping lines existed, hidden inside the tunnels used to transfer the hard liquor between buildings; since there is no reason to doubt that the ingenuity of the workers who installed the machinery in the first place was any less than that of those who came later, we must assume that these taps existed from the very beginning. Unfortunately, the Montreal Products Co. maintained separate business records, which were not retained during subsequent moves and clearances of old papers, unlike those of the Canada Sugar Refining Co. Ltd.; therefore, apart from some minor references and changes recorded in letters and various notes, there is little to record about the activities of this part of the company history.

May Drummond with her two dogs at Huntlywood.

As the year drew to a close, there was a disturbing revelation that money was missing from the company cash box. A subsequent investigation could not determine whether it was deliberate theft or poor bookkeeping that was to blame, but George was determined to avoid the problem in the future and wrote to the company secretary, Mr. W. Watson, and then to Frank Redpath as follows:

From statements shown to me today I fear that the "shortage" of the cashier at the refinery will reach $1,300.00 to $1,400.00 possibly more. In my opinion too much ready money is circulating at the refinery. With the exception of cash payments of bonuses and the wages I see no reason for any money being kept there. In any case I do not wish a subordinate employee to be a cash keeper. If money is kept for say bonus Frank Redpath ought to handle it and no one else - and if he deputes his cash to anyone he would be responsible. I want you to go into this subject and sketch out a scheme of action embodying the foregoing hints as far as possible.[6]
(December 29, 1902)

Watson is now preparing a scheme with a view of preventing any repetition of the deplorable experience we are now going through. If these can be effected it will be for the benefit of yourself, for you must be responsible for all monies sent to the refinery. In this connection let me ask what we can do about the money now missing. I am prepared to admit on my own account a general responsibility and am prepared to, bear the consequences for this time. But there must be an improvement.[7]
(December 30, 1902)

During the 1904 Anniversary celebrations: Speeches to the employees.

CHAPTER NINETEEN

Cheers And Tears, Ginger Ale And Champagne

Following an extended winter period shut-down at the beginning of 1903, refinery operations began in February and continued until March, when a further stoppage was caused by the emptying of the Lachine Canal to allow repairs to the lock gates. Upon re-starting three days later, large ice jams were reported to be developing on the St. Lawrence River, and water began to rise in the canal in an alarming manner. Once again production had to stop while every available man was turned out to stack the bags, and although the water came perilously close to spilling over the canal bank, no actual flooding took place. Following the subsidence of the water levels, it was decided that this annual threat must not be repeated and the plans for the proposed new raw sugar shed were altered to make the shed floor a full 3 feet higher than the highest recorded flood level of 1886. Construction of this new shed began with the spring thaw and was a massive undertaking, dwarfing almost every other building on the site. Its shape likewise was totally unlike any other building in the complex. Instead of the traditional flat or sloped roof, it had a curved vaulted roof covered with corrugated metal sheeting. Its size of 232 feet 6 inches long, 100 feet wide, and 72 feet high at the centre, gave it a capacity of 26.8 million pounds, more than double that of the entire previous set of raw sugar sheds. Furthermore, it was connected to the refinery by an impressive overhead cable system to move the bags.

The new raw sugar shed and bag conveyor system, built in 1903.

In April, the Canadian government instituted a specific rise in tariffs on all goods originating in Germany as a retaliation for a similar earlier move by Germany on products from Canada, Britain, and the U.S.A. As a result, George had to rapidly revise his shipping schedules, for at least 25% of his raw beet sugar came from or through German sources.

Another problem for George and the company was the

loss of his main supplier of barrel staves. This company was located in Wallaceburg and was now supplying the beet sugar refineries that had opened in that province, forcing the C.S.R. Co. Ltd. to seek alternative sources. No company in Quebec was willing to quote at the prices and quantities required by the refinery, and so a U.S. company was engaged to produce the staves. However, when the first shipment arrived, its quality was so bad that the staves were unusable, and a strongly worded letter of complaint was despatched to the manufacturer, Church and Bar, in New York.

> *In all my experience I never saw such trash offered, and I think the matter very serious. Obviously the stuff cannot be used for barrel making and to us it is only good enough for firewood ... we insist that you replace this stock and guarantee to provide proper quality material in future or we will have no hesitation in cancelling our business and instituting legal action to recover any money we had spent. (April 1, 1903)*

Further problems for the C.S.R. Co. Ltd. developed when, in addition to the four established beet refineries in Ontario, a fifth was planned for Peterborough. Similarly, in Raymond, Alberta, the Mormon industrialist, Jesse Knight, was founding his own Knight Sugar Co. to take away the business of that area from the C.S.R. Co. Ltd. as well as the B.C. Sugar Co.

May brought no better news in the refinery as a sudden water loss in the Lachine Canal, due to defective locks, caused a major problem in obtaining coolant water for the machines, resulting in some damage before the machines were stopped. The distillery was likewise forced to stop production, but this provided the opportunity to enlarge the capacity of the liquor plant, since good prices were being obtained for the alcohol.

Problems seemed to follow George in June as he was forced to vacate the Union building in the city, where the head office was located, due to a small fire in a neighbouring office. George contacted the owners of the building, notifying them that until the state of the building was improved, he would relocate and the entire staff moved into rapidly established offices within the refinery. On July 4, the revamped distillery re-opened and rapidly began to use up the stockpiled quantities of molasses until by August 15 all the reserve was used up and liquor production had to be cut back. On a personal level, George was once again worried about the health of Maurice, who had suffered three relapses during the year. Despite objections from his son, who argued that he was quite capable of continuing to work, George insisted on Maurice taking an extended vacation, and so on November 14 Maurice left on what would turn out to be his last major tour. Perhaps he recognized the fact he would not regain his health because his itinerary certainly covered many of the sights of the world. True to his nature, however, he started his holiday in England by arranging a tour of the improved London facility of the Lyle company, " where Charles Lyle and a principal hand shewed me through."

Despite his obvious difficulties in health, Maurice's description of the Lyle plant in his notebook is impressive in its thoroughness and is a credit to his determination to take the opportunity to benefit the company whenever and wherever possible. A week later he was in Paris, making similar reports on the Say refinery. Here he received a telegram from

from his father, complaining that word had reached George of Maurice's work activities and insisting that he relax. Obeying his father, Maurice did make the effort to put aside business and act like a tourist, apart from one minor exception. Some idea of the scope of his travels can be seen in the extract below of Maurice's itinerary, as recorded in his notebook, and it remains as a tribute to this well-travelled gentleman.

November 1903

14-15	*New York (from Windsor Station) (via Utica N.Y.)*	*470 miles*
17-23	*London (Paddington) (via Plymouth landed & Bristol)*	*3,722 miles*
27	*Lyles Refinery and return*	*40 miles*
29	*Paris (Gare du Nord) from Victoria (via Dover & Calais)*	*287 miles*
30	*Say's Refinery in Paris*	–

December 1903

4-5	*Nice (via Dijon, Lyon, Arles & Marseilles)*	*675 miles*
7	*Monte Carlo and return*	*30 miles*
11-12	*Rome (via Genoa & Pisa)*	*467 miles*
15	*Albinio, Lake Nemi and return*	*45 miles*
17	*Tivoli, Hadrians Villa and return*	*40 miles*
18-23	*Cairo (via Naples & Alexandria)*	*1,446 miles*
25	*Pyramids of Gizeh and return*	*16 miles*
30-31	*Assuan [Aswan] (via Luxor)*	*550 miles*

January 1904

2	*Philae & Nile dam*	*25 miles*
5	*Luxor ("Thebes")*	*133 miles*
5-10	*Karnak, Tombs of the Kings etc*	*50 miles*
10-11	*Cairo*	*418 miles*
13	*Hawandich Refinery*	*30 miles*
18	*Sakkarah (Memphis)*	*50 miles*
28	*Port Said (via Ismaitieh)*	*145 miles*
29 - Feb 2	*Naples direct*	*260 miles*

February 1904

3	*Pompeii and return*	*35 miles*
4	*Vesuvius and return*	*32 miles*
5	*Montreal (via Gibraltar & New York by Saratoga N.Y.)*	*5,256 miles*

Total Mileage for this journey *14,222 miles*

Following Maurice's departure, George had to attend to another personal matter, for he had once more been offered a C.M.G. by Lord Minto. When he again politely declined to accept the honour, it prompted a rather tart letter from Lord Minto that such an offer would not likely be made again. George therefore took the opportunity to explain to the Governor General the history of his refusals.

> *I should not have minded the rebuff if it had not been that the nomination by the Government got out, and for the third time excited talk. People are good enough to express curiosity as to the serious hidden reasons which occasion refusal. My explanation is thus: Years ago under Sir J.A. MacDonald it was proposed to me the honour but I made no move. Later Sir Charles Tupper (without my knowledge) sent my name to Mr. Chamberlain and then told me what had been done, and was confident that all was settled. Mr. Chamberlain's reply was to express regret that it*

> *had come too late as all the honours at his disposal were allocated. Sir Charles then was confident that it was only a question of a few months; this was for a K.C.M.G. [Knight Commander of the Order of the Cross of St. Michael and St. George i.e. a knighthood]. Of course after this the subsequent offer of a C.M.G. was absurd to say the least of it ... Again Lord Strathcona told me that Mr. Chamberlain had informed him of his intention to give me the K.C.M.G. this was a year and a half ago ... I trust this will explain to your excellency my reason for demurring once again.*[1]
> *(November 14, 1903)*

When Maurice returned in February 1904, George was encouraged to see that his son appeared much improved, but chastised him for "working" while on a supposed vacation. They then jointly prepared for the year's operations.

One area that required immediate attention was the system of wooden plank roads throughout the refinery yards, which were showing serious signs of wear. Further installation of this type of surface would last for two or three years before requiring replacement at a cost of 80 cents per square yard. So an alternative, using slag from blast furnaces, bonded by a compound of tar and sand, was suggested by Maurice, based upon what he had seen at the Lyle plant the previous November. Although this would cost $1.10 per square yard, it would last considerably longer than the plank system and would have the additional benefit of raising the yard level, thereby reducing the problem of flooding. Little more is known of this period of the company history until August of that year, when the fiftieth anniversary of the company was celebrated. George Drummond, too, had a cause to celebrate as he had just been notified of his award of K.C.M.G. On August 12, the official celebrations to commemorate the founding of the company were held in the main yard of the plant. A newspaper review of the event reads as a tribute to the work of the past half-century.

> *A jubilee was celebrated at the Canada Sugar Refinery yesterday when the occasion was observed by presentations and congratulatory addresses ... The jubilee was marked by a large gathering of the employees whose address to the head of the Company was as follows:*
>
> *To the Honourable Sir George Drummond K.C.M.G.*
> *Sir on this occasion ... we your employees deem it a fitting and proper time to give expression to the high regard and esteem we entertain towards you, and to congratulate you upon the high honour conferred on you ... We wish also to return our grateful thanks for the generosity and sympathy which you have always shown towards your employees and their families in time of trouble and distress.*
>
> *On behalf of the employees*
> *Alexander Bower ...*
>
> *There was also a very pleasant function in advance of the main feature of the celebration ... on this occasion Sir George presented to Mr. & Mrs. McMenamin, Mr. & Mrs. John Bennett, Mr. & Mrs. Alex Bowen ... Silver Tea Sets. He also presented loving cups to Mr. McMenamin and Mr. Bower ... [these four men had been employed with the company since 1854]*
> *(August 13, 1904)*

The dignitaries, guests, and members of the employees' committee. Sir George is on the balcony to the right of the central flag display; Maurice Drummond is second to the left of the flag.

Another and more personal account of the day's festivities is found in a letter from Maurice to his brother Arthur in Colorado.

I should have written you sooner about our Jubilee, which was most successful. The weather was beautiful and we have been having generally this month cold rainy weather. The offices were all cleaned, curtains at last put in the windows and mantel pieces actually put on all the fireplaces, also a formal painting and flags all over the inside and outside. At 4 p.m., August 12th. Proceedings started in the lower inside office ... Father presented a tray and tea set

The official photograph of the employees of the Canada Sugar Refining Co. Ltd., 1904.

(from Birks) to McMenamin, Bower and Bennett ... The employees had presented a silver headed cane to John Bennett, (N.B. McMenamin came to work in the refinery on August 12th, 1854), the Company gave (privately) cheques as follows Mr. McM. $2,000, Bower $1,250, Bennett $1,250, Mrs. McM $250, Mrs. Bower $250, Mrs. Bennett $250 ... the speeches made were short and good.

At 4:30 p.m. In the yard at back of the office facing the balcony - Upper seats on the slip going to Char House. All employees were there as the refinery was closed for three or four hours ... Ladies and Gents on balcony, photo by Notman - then photo of men, presentation of illuminated address to father ... from employees ... then band, music, conjuring tricks provided by Company. Also singing and

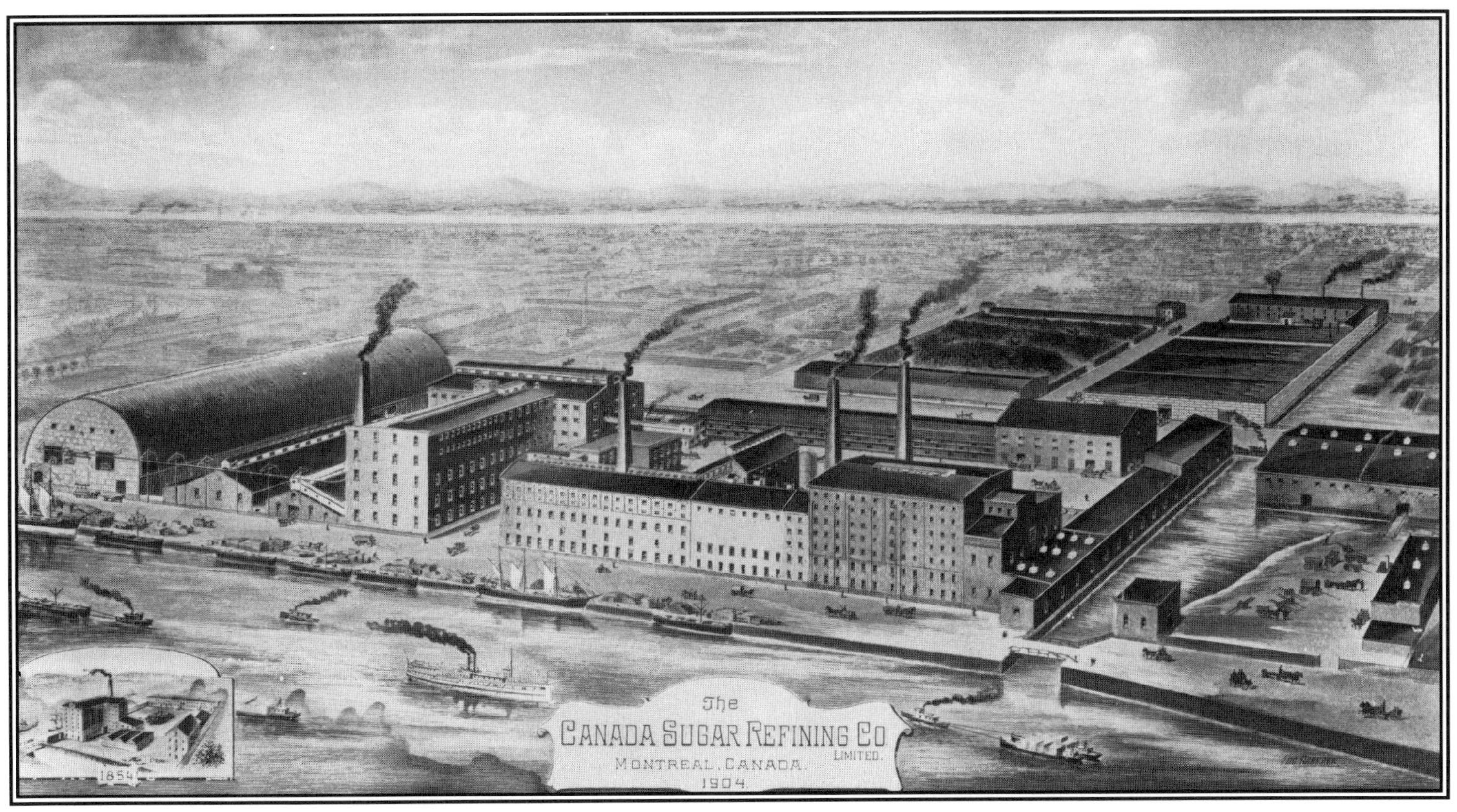

The Canada Sugar Refining Co. Ltd. 1904.

dancing by talented members of the refinery and they were really good. Meanwhile the mens dressing room had been laid out for refreshments given by Company ... and all the men had a good tuck out, meat sandwiches, coke, ice cream, fruit, ginger ale, coffee etc. There was plenty. I hear quite a little was taken home. All was over by 6:30 or so and the mens time was paid by the Company. We are also getting up 1,000 framed coloured pictures of the refinery to be ready in about a month. Everything was quite orderly. Father, Huntly, Frank, Bessie etc. went away early but I stayed until 6:30.
(August 20, 1904)

A further piece of relatively good news for the C.S.R.

Co. Ltd. was that, for their competitors, the attempts at establishing a beet industry in Ontario were not going well. In Dresden, after two years of moderate production, the local government decided to recoup some of its investment by raising assessments on the local plant. That company's response was to close the factory, dismantle the plant, and ship it out by barge to the U.S. Wiarton's attempt likewise ended in total failure due to incompetent management and production staff. This plant also closed in 1904 with the assets going to the United States. The Peterborough plant was never completed, and the Berlin factory was in grave difficulties as the farmers were suspicious of growing beets. Of the entire group, only the Wallaceburg Sugar Co. was developing into a stable industrial concern by purchasing cane raw sugar to supplement the beet sugar and increase the working span of the refinery season.

In October, the regional allocation agreement between the major sugar refiners signed in 1897 was finally ended (after two sets of extensions) and open competition was again the norm due to the increasing pressure of the Wallaceburg Sugar Co., who were outside the scope of the agreement. To end this year on a pleasant note, on the evening of November 7, George Alexander Drummond was invested as Sir George Drummond by the Governor General of Canada, in a glittering social occasion reported in some detail by the Montreal *Star*.

> *Special to The Montreal Star;*
>
> *Ottawa, November 8, - The State ball, given by His Excellency the Governor-General last night, at Government House, was one of the most brilliant affairs of its kind ever given in Canada. Over two thousand invitations had been issued, not only to residents of Ottawa, but also to society people in Montreal, Toronto, London, Quebec and other cities, and about one-half the invitations were accepted.*
>
> *The ball-room was banked with greenery and flowers, and the white walls made an excellent background for the gorgeous uniforms of the Cabinet Ministers, Consuls-General officers, and the beautiful and multi-coloured gowns of the ladies present.*
>
> *After removing their wraps in the dressing rooms, the guests made their way to the ante-room, where Capt. Bell, A.D.C., received them. Passing thence into the ball-room, they lined up on either side of a wide aisle formed by crimson cords held by six guardsmen.*
>
> *At half-past nine o'clock Their Excellencies entered the ball-room preceded by four honourary aides de camps Col. Lessard, Col. Neilson, Col. H. Smith and Col. Irwin. Following them came Ladies Eileen and Ruby; Elliot, Major Maude and Mr. Guise.*
>
> *Passing up the aisle, Lord and Lady Minto took up their position on the dais at the far end of the room, Sir Wilfrid and Lady Laurier standing on the left of the dais.*
>
> *Capt. Bell, A.D.C., then advanced, bearing a crimson velvet cushion upon which lay the order of Knighthood to be formally conferred on Sir George A. Drummond.*
>
> *Immediately behind him came Sir George A. Drummond, the central figure of the investiture, supported on either side by Mr. Collingwood Schreiber and Sir Jas. Grant, both wearing their orders on their breasts.*
>
> *They advanced up the aisle, making three bows as they proceeded until they came to the dais.*

Major Maude, Military Secretary, then read the King's Warrant, Sir Wilfrid Laurier read the admonition. His Excellency placed a ribbon around Sir George Drummond's neck and fastened the order to it. Sir George knelt, and his Excellency dubbed him a knight, tapping him first on the right shoulder and then on the left with a sword, saying: "Arise Sir George".

The party then walked slowly backwards to the door bowing as they retired ...

... Sir George Drummond wore full court dress [suit] of black velvet and diamond buttons. Lady Drummond had on a lovely costume of white sequined net over accordion pleated ruffles of burnt orange chiffon. The corsage trimmed with orange coloured flowers, and diamond and pearl ornaments. Supper was served at twelve o'clock in the Racquet Court. Where numerous tables had been placed, decorated with pink and white chrysanthemums.

Sir George Alexander Drummond, K.C.M.G., in official court dress for his investiture.

The article concluded with two full columns of descriptions of the guests in attendance and the gowns worn by the ladies.

George had now reached the top rung of the Montreal social ladder, but there is a saying that for some people, whenever they succeed or achieve a victory, fate steps up and slaps them down. And to George it certainly must have seemed as if he were destined to be treated by fate in that way, for shortly after his investiture, he obtained reports from specialists engaged to review the health of his son Arthur. Their results were not encouraging as they reported his tuberculosis would continue to keep him away from the cold and damp atmosphere of Montreal for a minimum of two to three years. Arthur was extremely upset by this as he felt he was responsible for Maurice's illness by not taking on his share of the business responsibilities. George wrote Arthur a long letter stressing that no blame or fault lay in anyone's hand and offering to extend an annual income to Arthur to be used for speeding up his recovery.

On the other hand, without Arthur and with Maurice once again showing signs of weakness and re-occurrence of his illness, George Drummond, at the age of seventy-five, began to seriously consider who would take over his place as head of the company. The obvious choice was his robustly healthy son Huntly.

On March 3, 1905, Maurice's illness took its long expected toll when he suffered a severe stroke that completely paralyzed his right side, preventing him from walking or even writing. With this event not only did George lose his "right-hand man" at the refinery and the person most likely to have succeeded him as President, but we as well have lost our primary source of information about the daily events in the company. During the next couple of years, either no one seriously took up the job of recording the information as Maurice had done, or these later papers have not survived the ravages of time. We are therefore forced to rely upon occasional newspaper articles, unattributed notes, and some production figures to determine the course of the company until the materials surviving become sufficient to allow for the story to continue with more certainty.

One activity George Drummond was involved in during 1905 was the establishment of the Canadian Preference League magazine, *Canada First*, which was a patriotic journal in the true imperial style. The sentiments expressed in the editorial of the first issue give clear indication of the level of George's feelings towards *his* country.

> *Canada First was founded for the purpose of strengthening members of the Canadian Preference League in their determination to give practical preference to Canadian goods and Canadian Institutions, to foster the growth of Canadian sentiment and to educate public opinion in this direction in every legitimate way. We stand for Canada, first, last and all the time.*[2]

Records show that George was a stockholder in the enterprise and his nephew H.A. Drummond was the secretary and business manager for the journal.

Sometime during the summer, a fire broke out at George's Beaconsfield farm, and one of the animal barns was completely burned to the ground. Fortunately, many of the horses and prize cattle were being exhibited elsewhere and so the main losses were in the structure itself. In late November, having recovered a little from his stroke, Maurice travelled to Colorado to winter with Arthur; leaving everyone in the refinery hoping that he would recover sufficiently to take up his place with the company once again.

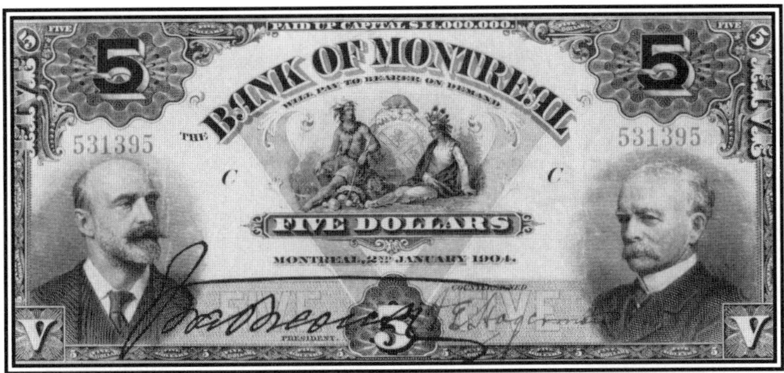

In the days before the central bank monopolized the issue of currency, the major banks produced their own bills. This five-dollar bill shows Sir George on the right and E.S. Clouston on the left.

Outside the company, George Drummond had been occupied throughout the year with various activities on behalf of the Bank of Montreal. In March, he had participated in the takeover of the Peoples Bank of Halifax, which added twenty-six branches to the Bank of Montreal system. In April, discussions were initiated with the Peoples Bank of New Brunswick for another takeover that was successfully concluded in 1906. Abroad, the Bank of Montreal was aggressively seeking to "cash in" on the lucrative speculation market of South America, and George was involved in negotiations for the establishment of a branch of the bank in Mexico City. In fact, things went so far that the bank invested heavily in a company called the Mexican Light, Heat and Power Co. and George was at one point listed as its President. His main activity for the bank in 1905 was, however, very much closer to home when he oversaw the completion of the new corporate headquarters for the Bank of Montreal at the corner of Craig and St. James streets. Fittingly enough, on December 4, 1905, at the first annual meeting to be held in the new headquarters, George Drummond was elected the thirteenth President of the Bank of Montreal.

Also in December, the first accounts of Huntly Redpath Drummond appear in the company books signing various daily documents as he began to take over Maurice's responsibilities. Huntly was born in Montreal in 1864, the second son of George and Helen. He was educated at Montreal High School and at Rugby School in England. For several years, he had worked in the Bank of Montreal as a clerk and then as a secretary at his father's mines in Nova Scotia before coming to the refinery as a supervisor. As a keen sportsman, Huntly had been a member of the Montreal Football Club, scoring the winning try (touchdown) for the team in the 1886 Canadian Championships. He was also Honorary President of the Montreal Ski Club, having won the ski club's first jumping competition in December 1905 at the age of forty-one with a jump of 75 feet.

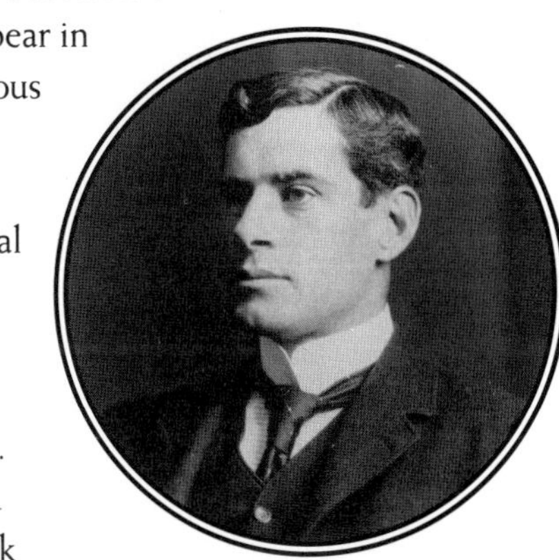

Huntly Redpath Drummond

Following a quiet Christmas, 1906 began sadly for the Drummonds when on January 15, Maurice died in Colorado. Arthur accompanied the body back to Montreal where Maurice was buried in the Drummond family vault opposite the Redpath family plot in the Mount Royal Cemetery. Not including this final trip from Colorado back to his native

Huntly Redpath Drummond achieving his winning ski jump in 1905.

home, Maurice had accumulated a total travelled mileage of 241,528 miles, including crossing the Atlantic thirty-two times, the Mediterranean seven times, and the English Channel twenty-nine times (not including ocean passages direct to Europe), a feat that would be considered impressive even by the modern standard of international travel let alone the standards of the Victorian and Edwardian eras.

In business matters likewise, things did not begin well for the company in 1906 as the federal government increased the tariff levels on both raw and refined sugar imports to a uniform 30%. This placed the refiners at a significant disadvantage relative to the importers because the refiners were paying duty on 108 pounds of raw sugar in order to obtain 100 pounds of finished product for sale, whereas the importers paid duty only on the 100 pounds of refined sugar actually imported by them, without having to add in any of the refiners' costs of production. When these matters were raised as concerns by the sugar refiners, the Tariff Commission agreed to hear the argument of the sugar importers but *not* the sugar refiners! During his testimony, one of the importers, Robert Anderson, accused the refiners of robbing the Canadian public under the fixed pricing agreements established between the refiners and the Wholesale Grocers Guild. Under this agreement the refiners would sell refined sugar at a lower price to members of the wholesalers' guild, who in turn agreed to purchase their stocks exclusively from the Canadian refineries and maintain a set margin of profit. According to Mr. Anderson, this was a deliberate robbery of the Canadian public for the financial gain of the refiners and Wholesale Grocers Guild members. What it really meant was that he and his fellow importers were effectively excluded from selling into that lucrative market and he wanted legislative action to force the "door" open. Unable to speak before the commission, George was forced to go to the newspapers to get his point across. In an article printed in the March 20 edition of the Montreal *Gazette*, George stated that Mr. Anderson's forty-two page report to the commission on behalf of Messrs. Robert Crooks & Co.

> *may be summed up as an unreserved indictment of the Canadian duties on sugar, under which Mr. A. asserts the refiners here have a complete monopoly of the Canadian market, and amass enormous profits at the expense of the Canadian consumer ... the reply we now make is an endeavour to show ... that Mr. Anderson is not a reliable authority on this matter and to give his conclusions an emphatic denial and contradiction as inconsistent with the facts ... we do not hesitate to affirm that the information he*

offers the Government is inaccurate and unreliable, and his conclusions absurd. His proposed Tariff changes would certainly answer his purpose and transfer to the importers the entire business of the supply of refined sugar to this country and deprive the West Indies of the traffic and preference they now enjoy.

This was answered by a series of vitriolic and personal attacks upon George in newspapers and trade journals by Mr. Anderson and the Crooks company but George's stature as a man of business held him in good stead, and the tariffs were modified in the next budget.

Huntly Redpath Drummond (seated on the bench in front of the door) as part of the championship football club in 1884.

A quiet moment at Huntlywood (from left to right) Mrs. Arthur Drummond, Sir George Drummond, Sir Frederick W. Taylor, and Miss Agnes Drummond, circa 1905.

CHAPTER TWENTY

The Building Of A "New" Sugar House

As well as being the start of a new year, January 1907 was the start of a complete reconstruction of the refinery, which would dominate the corporate operations and finances for the next several years. The numerous plans and designs drawn up by Maurice Drummond were now to be implemented by Huntly and his brother Arthur, who had returned to Montreal determined to work in Maurice's place despite his own illness. On January 7, the first stage of the work began with the removal of the original 1854 refinery building, which for several years had been used only for storage and the occasional production of sugar when the main refinery was closed down for repairs. According to most accounts, the entire building was demolished for a cost of $5,500 in preparation for the new construction. However, visits to the site and the comparison of photographs taken before and after the work tell a different tale. It seems that although the upper brickwork floors were certainly removed, the first two storeys of solid stone masonry, so meticulously detailed by John Redpath in the 1853 contracts, were still so structurally sound that they were able to be retained and used in the new construction. In 1991, this section was still visible from the bank of the Lachine Canal, although in a sadly abandoned state.

By a strange twist of fate, at the same time as the original refinery was being torn down, the last direct family link to the Redpath family was broken with the passing away of Peter Redpath's widow, Grace, at Chislehurst on January 29 and George's sister Jane Redpath at the family home of Terrace Bank on January 30. Since John Redpath's death in 1869, in accordance with his will, the home had been maintained for Jane by the executors of the estate. Now the house was finally empty and the various pieces of furniture and heirlooms were divided among the family members or sold off. The property itself was also sold and the grounds were subdivided. Today various houses, apartments, and offices stand within the original grounds of the

The Soviet Consulate on the site occupied by Terrace Bank.

house bounded by Sherbrooke Street on the south, Mount Royal Park to the north, Mountain Street to the east, and Redpath Street to the west. The great house was demolished and another road, Doctor Penfield, was pushed through from east to west almost exactly on the location of the front steps. Today the property previously occupied by Terrace Bank is technically part of the Soviet Union as it is located within the boundary fence of the Soviet Consulate.

As a result of the growth in the trade between Canada and Great Britain under the Preferential Tariff established in 1906, the Canadian government initiated a system to restrict trade with other countries by stipulating that trade deals must be conducted with the other countries only through agents located in Canada. For the C.S.R. Co. Ltd., this threatened the business and personal relationship with Hewlett and Lee of New York that had existed for more than thirty years. In a private letter, Mr. Lee suggested avoiding the new legislation by establishing a "dummy" corporation and agency in Montreal under the supervision of George Drummond. Recognizing that, as economically attractive as this scheme might appear, it would provide perfect ammunition for his political and business enemies, George replied very quickly and definitely.

> *I am exceedingly desirous of your doing nothing to raise international trouble between your country and mine and while you must (if no change is made by Parliament) accept the situation and only work through Canadian posts for our business. Still I want you to be able to say if challenged hereafter that you did not a thing to raise any feeling or reprisal.*[1]
> (February 15, 1907)

The next day George received a letter from Mr. Lee on the matter of an earlier conversation; despite the confirmation of his sentiments expressed above, George felt it vital to place the matter in no doubt.

> *You mistake my real wishes about the Tariff. You cannot do anything whatever such as you have in view in your private lines without compromising me, and I cannot say more than this. That I specifically desire you not to do anything beyond simply obey the law leaving the dissension to others.*[2]
> (February 16, 1907)

Mr. Lee obviously got the point and dropped the matter. Unfortunately, this government policy did play havoc with the schedules for purchases as well as the costs of buying the raw sugar, forcing the company to limit its orders for sugar in hopes of future changes that would improve matters – which is why on March 2, George had to write to Mr. Lee:

> *Of course you understand I had to withdraw from the market as soon as I had secured enough sugar for the meantime.* Strictly for yourself. *We have stored enough to last us up to the emptying of the Canal, about April 6th... Our sales of refined have been very heavy, say 20,000 barrels for the week ... We will notify you as soon as any changes occur at our end or in Ottawa.*[3]

Shortly thereafter, tariffs and duties once again pressed to the fore when the sugar trading duties with British Empire members were enhanced, giving significant advantages to those countries over the general rates for other countries by allowing sugar into Canada at much lower rates of duty.

This measure was also coupled with a special provision for the beet sugar factories who were allowed to import two pounds of foreign raw sugar for every pound of refined sugar derived from domestic beet root at the lower preferential rate instead of the general rate. Despite vehement protests by George and the other sugar companies, this policy was continued until 1911. News also came that Mr. F.C. Durant of Philadelphia had been given the rights to develop a sugar refinery at Saint John, New Brunswick. This brought back echoes to George of his younger days when G. Dustan had also tried his hand from this location, and George's opinion was that this enterprise would probably go the same way as Dustan's.

Back in the temporary facilities of the head office at the refinery, the demolition of the old refinery was causing some logistical problems for the President and his staff. George wanted to return to the Union building that had been earlier vacated, but the rate of renovation was not progressing as quickly as expected. To speed things up, George contacted the owners of the building indicating that he was willing to purchase the entire structure, if he could be guaranteed occupancy by May 1. On May 5, George and his staff moved into the renamed Drummond Building, leaving the refinery to continue with the preparation of the site for reconstruction.

To complement the refinery reconstruction during the summer, the C.S.R. Co. Ltd. reached an agreement with the Department of Railways and Canals for the leasing of a stretch of land on the bank of the canal. On this land, the company constructed two large cranes and conveyor systems to assist in the quicker unloading of vessels carrying both the raw sugar and the huge amounts of coal required to fire the many boilers within the plant. They also purchased two small towing barges to help in the transfer of raw sugar stocks from the larger vessels that were beginning to bring in the sugar and that were too deep in draft to enter the Lachine Canal. Named the *Madge* and the *Edith*, they were a far cry from the more elegant barques of the nineteenth century but equally were to prove far less costly (at a price of only $4,500 each) and far more effective in their humble duties than either of the other two ships had been.

No other documents have survived the passage of time from 1907, except a list showing the variety of products available for sale. It is perhaps appropriate to look at these figures at this time when the plant was taking on a new appearance and to reflect on the significant number of changes that had occurred in the fifty-three years since production first started with the "bastard" sugar from iron loaf moulds.

	BRANDS	AVERAGE NET WEIGHT
BARRELS	*Granulated*	*300 pounds*
	Crown Granulated	*300 pounds*
	Yellow - Medium	*319 pounds*
	Yellow - Golden	*329 pounds*
	Powdered	*286 pounds*
	Extra Ground	*236 pounds*
	Paris Lumps	*211 pounds*
HALF BARRELS	*Granulated*	*156 pounds*
	Powdered	*286 pounds*
	Extra Ground	*286 pounds*
	Paris Lumps	*100 pounds** *(discontinued in 1907)*
KEGS	*Paris Lumps*	*50 pounds** *(Special order for Hudson's Bay Co.)*
BAGS	*Granulated*	*100 pounds - Jute with Cotton bag lining*
		50 pounds - Jute with Cotton bag lining
		20 pounds - Jute with Cotton bag lining
	Imperial Granulated	*100 pounds - Jute bag with paper lining*

From the historical perspective, if 1905 to 1907 were spartan in their sources of information, 1908 and 1909 are almost nonexistent; the only documentation available relates to costs of the reconstruction and the annual figures of production. That is not to say, though, that things were not busy at the refinery, for in the early months of 1908 the rebuilding of the A1 building on the lower stonework of the 1854 plant began in earnest, and much of the machinery required for the fitting out of this area as a spare refinery was installed in the late summer. In addition, various other areas of the refinery were overhauled and revamped or had new machinery installed at considerable cost. Some of these included the remodelling the original refined sugar warehouse for use as a Paris Lump mill and the installation of four new charcoal filtration kilns within the kiln house. Across the road, in the production area of the refinery, further additions included two new filter presses, a sand filter press, a complete coal-handling system, and a new electrical generating plant, completing the year's efforts for a total cost of $220,750.

In a similar fashion, the alterations dominate the few surviving documents from 1909. They show that the completed A1 building received more of its required machinery, including sugar shaking screens with conveyors, charcoal tank heater systems, vacuum pumps, and a triple effect, while outside in the yard the slag road system laid in 1904 was covered by proper paving.

In February 1909, the shareholders of the company authorized the establishment of a committee to, in their words, "inquire into and determine the remuneration for services due to the President."

The report they returned later in the year contained several conclusions and give light on the activities of George as President:

> 1st *That it is understood that the annual salary allowed to the President ... is not equal in amount to that enjoyed by the Chief Managers of less important Refineries ...*

> 2nd *That Sir George has incurred considerable expenses on behalf of the Company that have not been recouped ...*
>
> 3rd *That for a whole year, during which the Company's operations in consequence of adverse markets shewed unfavourable results he served gratuitously - thus relinquishing the salary to which he was entitled ...*
>
> 4th *That by his able and zealous administration he has raised the Refinery to a very high state of efficiency and has so prosperously conducted the business as to warrant the distribution of ample dividends and to accumulate the large surplus profits now on hand...*
>
> *The Committee therefore recommends that the Annual Salary of thirty thousand dollars be continued ... and that in view of the very special circumstances above stated he be requested to accept a bonus of ... $150,000.00 as compensation for all services and outlays to this date.*

Sir George subsequently thanked the committee for its kind statements but declined to accept the bonus.

Elsewhere in the sugar industry, the beet sugar industry of Ontario, now consisting of the fairly stable Wallaceburg Sugar Co. and its less prosperous rival the Ontario Sugar Co., merged in June to become the Dominion Sugar Co. Ltd., a name that would loom large in the future fortunes of the Canada Sugar Refining Co. Ltd.

April 1909 brought another set of alterations in the tariffs as the British and General Tariffs were equalized, thus allowing greater amounts of sugar from sources outside the Empire to be brought in. Despite this, the previous year's

Sir George enjoying a game of golf on his own nine-hole course.

preferential tariffs had persuaded George that unless some significant changes took place, the days of the imported sugar beet as a primary supply were numbered. Another source of concern for George and the other sugar refiners in Quebec and the Maritimes was the continuation of the importation benefits granted to the beet refiners in 1906 - 1907. This one-sided benefit in favour of the Dominion Sugar Co. caused considerable resentment among the other refiners in Canada.

To counter this, the Acadia, St. Lawrence, and C.S.R. Co. Ltd. came to an agreement in the summer of 1909 whereby they would purchase raw sugar jointly in large quantities thus gaining better discounts. This sugar would then be divided among the parties according to a schedule and all costs would be shared. As a result, from this agreement deliveries to the refinery of cane sugars for the period of August to December amounted to a total of 175,000 barrels.

Finally, as 1909 was drawing to a close, George was occupied by company business on two fronts. The first was the ongoing privilege granted to the Dominion Sugar Company that was severely hampering sales for the C.S.R. Co. Ltd. in central and northern Ontario as well as out west. To counter this, George initiated private talks with several prominent politicians from the Quebec and Maritime areas, outlining the difficulties this preferential treatment was having on the sugar industries based in the lower provinces. His tactics obviously worked, for although the preferential legislation was not removed, an allowance was made for the other refiners to select 20% of their imports for the year to be charged under the Preferential Rate instead of the General Rate of duty. This concession precipitated the

second situation with which George had to contend, because the St. Lawrence Sugar Co. decided that with the 20% allowance, it no longer needed to co-operate with the other refiners and notified them of its decision to leave the group purchase plan. After consultation, the C.S.R. Co. Ltd. and Acadia agreed to continue their part of the bargain and take up the sugar initially ordered for the St. Lawrence.

At the same time, George received the new estimates for the work planned for 1910 within the refinery complex. Considering the work that had already gone on for three years, it represented an impressive list of proposed development at an equally impressive cost of $62,359.

Left: In a rare moment, Sir George relaxes with some of his family, including his sons Arthur (above) and Huntly (with pipe). The ladies are Mrs. Arthur Drummond and Miss Agnes Drummond (right).

A photograph taken during the annual spring shut-down caused by the draining of the canal, note the lack of smoke.

CHAPTER TWENTY-ONE

"*A New Captain*"

As the programme of development for the refinery was being implemented during the mid-winter shutdown in January 1910, George made arrangements to travel to Ottawa. He was planning to investigate rumours that free trade was once again rearing its ugly head in the corridors of power. Tragically, in the midst of these preparations, he suffered a major heart attack and was confined to bed. Telegrams were immediately sent to Arthur in Colorado (who had returned there as his health was showing signs of repeated weakness) and Guy (George and Grace's second son, who was then on holiday in Paris.) Both returned to Montreal immediately. Three weeks later on February 2, 1910, George Alexander Drummond died at the age of eighty-one. At his bedside were Lady Drummond, Arthur, Guy, Huntly and his wife Mary Ellen, and George's niece, Agnes Drummond. Because of his significant influence on numerous aspects of political, business, and social life, his funeral was more than merely well attended as recorded in the Montreal *Gazette*:

> *Fitting tribute to the man who for many years past had been regarded as Montreal's leading citizen was paid yesterday afternoon when an almost unprecedented gathering of representatives of the business interests and citizens of the metropolis met to show their respect for the late Sir George A. Drummond by attending his funeral. Although at the strongly expressed desire of the deceased the funeral ceremonies were particularly unostentatious, this could not detract from the general evidence that the people of the city realized that the community had suffered a decided loss. Practically every important business and corporate interest in the City was represented at the obsequities, while the leaders in the financial professional and business world were mixed with many less prominent citizens representing the many institutions in which the deceased had taken a prominent part. It had been the wish of Sir George that there should be no undue ostentation in connection with his funeral and his wishes were carried out to the letter. But this could not prevent the citizens of Montreal from showing their sorrow at his loss, and their appreciation of the worthy citizen who had been taken away. A more impressive tribute could not be imagined than that paid yesterday afternoon, the force of general regret being more apparent by the absence of any effort to give it formal utterance. Early in the afternoon a large crowd gathered around the Drummond residence on Sherbrooke Street where a private service was held which was attended by the immediate relatives and friends of the deceased. At the same time the*

> *Church of St. John the Evangelist, where the public service was held was opened and the edifice was soon filled. When the cortege set out from the residence to the church a procession on foot was formed behind the hearse preceded by the official representatives and mourners while in the long line that followed probably two thousand people silently proceeded to the church. Space in the body of the church had been reserved for the mourners and other representatives but the majority of those in the funeral cortege were unable to enter all the space already being occupied. At the church door the remains were received by the Rev. Arthur French and were carried to the steps of the chancel where the casket was deposited on a catafalque. The service then proceeded in the simple and impressive liturgy of the English Church. The service was fully choral … there was no elaboration and only an hour after the casket was carried into the church the … cortege set out on its final journey … for the Mount Royal Crematorium.*

The gap left by the death of George Drummond was great in all those enterprises that he had captained, but none was greater than the void in the Canada Sugar Refining Co. Ltd. Maurice was gone, Arthur was not well enough to take on the responsibility, and none of the other directors of the company felt able to fill the shoes of the dynamic man who had guided the company for more than fifty years. Instead, the directors felt the natural person to succeed George Drummond was his son Huntly Redpath Drummond, who had worked quietly as technical manager of the plant for many years. Huntly was not one to be demonstrative or expressive in his feelings, preferring rather to take a more low-key but none the less determined approach to his business dealings. Almost immediately, Huntly had to make the appointment of a manager for the refinery to replace himself as he took up the president's role. Although there were several possible candidates, one individual did appear most qualified and this was William Redpath, or "Willie" as he was commonly known, the grandson of John Redpath and the son of Francis Redpath. One point stood against Willie, however, and that was a tendency to drink during business hours. Huntly was uncertain on this choice and sought the advice of Mr. Lee as a long-time friend and business colleague. In his reply dated February 7, 1910, Mr. Lee expressed his feelings on the matter:

> *The more I think it over the more disposed I am to believe that should the position of responsibility be given him, he will quickly realize how vital to his own interest, let alone the interests of others entrusted to him, it will be to keep straight … That he can keep himself straight has certainly been demonstrated during my last two visits to Montreal and it was also I think for a time after your father spoke to him. It will not be as easy to persuade him to drop the use of liquor altogether as to do so during business hours … He is very bright, has had the unusual advantage of a splendid business schooling under your father and knows the Company's business well. I believe that being thrown on his own resources he will quickly develop into a good Manager and be equal to any changes or emergencies in the business which may arise later on … He must know that unless he is prepared to keep straight he would have no chance of retaining such a position.*

After discussions among the directors, Willie was not

given the position but was put in charge of general operations without the title and appeared to sober up to his new responsibility. In the meantime, Huntly had to deal with the situation of the quantities of sugar arriving under the agreement with Acadia and to establish a programme for future purchases. On February 16, 1910, he wrote to Hewlett & Lee, picking up where George had left off only a few weeks previously.

> *I note that your estimate of the conditions of the market is that it will certainly have an upward tendency ... Luckily we have this escape from the high price of crystals, with our new facilities we are able to use ... up to 40% of the total purchase of Muscovado Sugars [by the agreement]. This would make about 16,000 tons ... I have not yet gone fully in to the question of the 20% allotment but expect to have that tomorrow, and will be able to figure out how much of these sugars we will be able to get in that way.*[1]

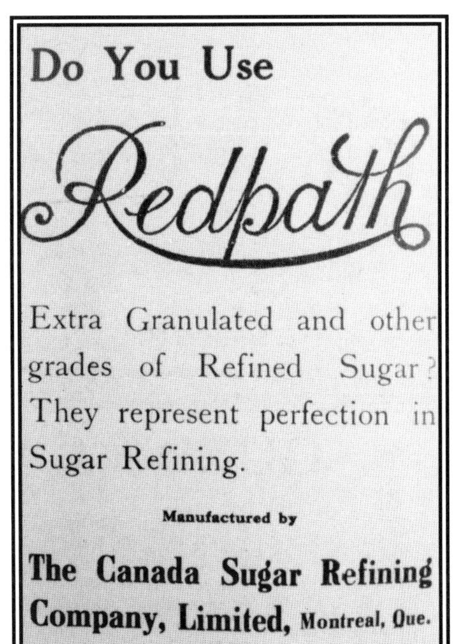

Huntly also sought to come to grips with the long-term direction of the plant re-vitalization by ordering a report on the cost estimates for any new work to be done over the next three years. This list was impressive, if not a little alarming in its size, since it revealed that work already on order would cost $43,210; work needed to be done through 1910-11 amounted to $30,250; and additional work advisable in the future totalled $106,375, for a grand total in the refinery of $179,835, on top of which was an estimate for work to be done in the distillery that added a further $64,150 to the reckoning.

Elsewhere, events were taking place that would have serious implications on the company when the Canadian Finance Minister W.S. Fielding met secretly with President Taft in Washington to discuss plans for reciprocity between the two countries. The unusual thing about this meeting was that this time the initiative for reciprocity had come from the United States. Prime Minister Laurier and his government were initially caught off guard by the American overture, and as a result the Liberals at first hesitated and then began to discuss the issue with the American representatives. Once the fact of the meeting was revealed, Canadian reaction seemed positive, especially in the prairies. In addition, veiled threats from the U.S. delegates to impose heavier duties on Canadian goods if talks failed added inducement to complete a deal.

For Huntly, this issue was an impediment to the long-term viability of the sugar interests and needed to be fought. He began to organize members of the Montreal Board of Trade into a lobby group to press for caution. He also began to purchase large amounts of sugar in the expectation that a major change could occur if reciprocity went into effect. At the same time, he had to deal with the fact that in Saint John, New Brunswick, a proposed new sugar company formed by the merger of the Woodside,

Halifax and Moncton refineries into the Atlantic Sugar Refineries was issuing large quantities of stock. To obtain more details, he contacted Mr. Lee.

> *Kindly let me know if you have heard anything more about the Atlantic Sugar Refining Co. I should like to see their prospectus if that were possible. I have some memorandum regarding it and they seem to be piling the stock issue on the basis that will preclude any profit whatever.*[2]
> *(August 8, 1910)*

Even with all his efforts, Huntly was not altogether sure that he was able to completely "fill the shoes" of his father and he said so to Arthur in Colorado. Certain business interests obviously thought so too, and they approached the C.S.R. Co. Ltd., proposing a merger with the Dominion Sugar Company. Having only just begun to become accustomed to the reins of power, Huntly was incensed at the thought of them being taken away so soon and he rebuffed the offer. In his letter to Arthur describing the incident, he commented on the proposal and wondered if there was some way to eliminate the increasing competition of the Dominion Sugar Co., to which Arthur replied:

> *You certainly are having your hands full of business these days and you are handling things admirably in my opinion, ... The truth is of course that these financial men are always looking for some method of getting a good rake off out of mergers, combinations, re-organizations etc. ... I am mighty glad you are feeling yourself competent: I knew you were myself or else I would not have urged you to take the position and now you think so yourself all is rights. My feeling is to stand out of any merger, as yours is. As I have said before, you are going to be a big man in Montreal and while the opinions of older men are always to be listened to respectfully half of them are really old women and when a man knows he is right, allowing other men to persuade him to do differently is simply weakness. As to Wallaceburg you can not kill them off now they are too strong and the time passed four or five years ago ... as to our trading agreement with them the cardinal weakness is allowing Wallaceburg to increase and take the extra consumption of Canada while we keep about the same output. This has got to be changed in favour of the C.S.R. Co. Ltd. somehow. As to the Wallaceburg's new process for refining cane at a nominal price; why I don't believe it. They simply have got to melt it, regrain it whiten it in some way and handle it, all of which they may do cheaper than we do but it certainly costs money and they turn out an inferior product.*
> *(December 12, 1910)*

About a week later, in response to another letter from Huntly, Arthur commented on various individuals within the "family" group in the refinery, referring to the salaries they were getting.

> *I laughed when I read about Frank, Willie and you. Frank R.[edpath] always used to strike the Governor as often as he could pluck up courage, (about once a year) for a rise in pay. When he couldn't get that he used to work him on the bonus, a perfect scandal ... Willie if you gave him a definite status, would simply sit down on that and do less work instead of more. Personally I would*

rather see George at the head. I would know then that absolutely nothing would be neglected or let slide. However these little things are part of your job and you did just right under the circumstances ... You have got to tackle the bonus system of the refinery soon. My advice is to eliminate it as it stands and only give it for conspicuous hard work or brains or necessity and raise the salaries of the men you don't want to lose.

Huntly took his brother's advice and stopped the payment of bonuses in 1910, implementing instead a pension scheme for the older workers that paid out $3,016 to those who had retired that year.

The proposals for reciprocity that Finance Minister Fielding revealed in January 1911 provided for free trade in most natural products and for reciprocal tariff reductions on several manufactured items, including sugar. This, in Huntly's judgement, would open the floodgates as they had in 1875. Most Liberals were jubilant over what looked to be a major coup, while the Conservatives were despondent, as they feared that the agreement would appeal to the voters and provide Laurier with another election victory. Much of the organized opposition to the agreement came from the business, financial, and manufacturing companies in Toronto and Montreal. Prominent in this group was Huntly who made a rousing speech to the Montreal Board of Trade and then proposed a motion for the Board of Trade to renounce the reciprocity agreement as a detriment to Canada. Some people even argued that the movement to free trade was merely the thin end of the wedge that would eventually "crack" Canada and lead to annexation by the United States.

Canadian anxieties over reciprocity were further increased because of statements by various prominent individuals in the U.S. government, including the Speaker of the House of Representatives, who remarked:

I am for the bill ... because I hope to see the day when the American flag will fly over every square foot of the British North American possessions clear to the North Pole.

As a result, the opposition to reciprocity grew steadily, especially among the business community.

Within the refinery, the alterations continued, resulting in a detailed series of letters between Arthur and Huntly.

I was very glad to hear that the C.S.R. Co. Ltd. had a good year as this has been worrying me a lot on your account, but all is well. I think that the immediate installation of the central conveyer from the crystal shed should be started at once. It will pay for itself in two or three years in Labour alone ... I think, now that labour is getting so expensive that we should put in everything that cuts down the number of men employed and I think everything we have done and propose doing is all right on that scene ... (Arthur to Huntly, January 26, 1911)

The St. Lawrence have been talking to us about Wallaceburg ... and wished to adopt a great many radical ideas in order to check them; among others, turning out 50% of Imperial [grade sugar] and selling it at a cut rate, specially to meet the Wallaceburg competition ... I do not think we need be so excited or take any such radical steps ... altogether while our [profit] margin may have been on the large side and might probably be reduced. I think we

are bound to recognize that these people are a factor and have come to stay, and after twenty years we can hardly complain if we do not occupy the whole of the field ... we do not own the whole market, and we had ... better not do anything that might savour of procuration against this man.
(Huntly to Arthur, January 26, 1911)

About the St. Lawrence and Wallaceburg, I think with you the elimination of the latter is an impossibility, perhaps politically not even desirable. As for making enormous quantities of the 2nd grade granulated to fight them the whole idea is childish; ... if you must fight them lower the cost of our best sugar and that reduces their price automatically ... Now about salaries and bonuses I am glad you had the courage to hold off last year, as I have said before I think the bonus system is a vicious one and should be done away with entirely except as a very special thing. It is all right when a man has earned it by some special hard work but is rotten when spread all over the refinery, being given to men simply because they had it the year before ... If you decide to give bonuses I think a short note to each recipient stating that the year has been a good one financially for the Company and consequently you are enabled to pay a bonus might possibly bring to their minds some idea that the bonus system is not necessarily permanent.
(Arthur to Huntly, February 1, 1911)

I agree exactly with what you say about the St. Lawrence, meanwhile ... I am certainly not going to lower our quality but I feel there must be something behind their desire to get us to do this ... I note what you say on the bonuses ... I have got this in advisement. I do not think I will make very much change this year in this matter as with the last cut it caused much comment among the men, although I have revised some of the items and brought in pensions for the older men.
(Huntly to Arthur, February 14, 1911)

With the advent of summer, Huntly was placed in a difficult position as Willie's tendancy to drink resurfaced to such an extent that it severely interfered with the running of the refinery. As a result, Huntly was forced to relieve Willie of his duties and instructed him to obtain treatment. On July 17, 1911, Huntly penned a personal note to Willie.

I trust that you are already getting some benefit from your trip and gaining in health to help you in the struggle on which your future hangs. Doctors can give you a start but you must work out your own salvation. When I had to say to you that your continuing in the refinery was conditional on total abstinence on your part from liquor of any kind, it was solely due to the fact that this was the only way of saving one whom I genuinely like apart from business considerations.[3]

By August it appears that Willie had obtained treatment and was looking to return to work, to which Huntly replied:

Before you go to the Refinery you must come and see me. As a condition of your employment I must have a pledge from you of total abstinence from alcohol in every form. In

my position I cannot have a repetition of the old condition that prevailed before you left, but I am willing to give you a fair chance.[4]
(August 18, 1911)

Willie did in fact return to work and seems to have overcome his problem, as no further communications on this matter are recorded and Willie continued in the employment of the company for the next several years.

While dealing with this personal problem within the refinery, Huntly was increasingly occupied with organizing opposition to the free trade agreement by supporting the Conservative party in the run-up to the general election scheduled for September. As part of this support, he made a speech to his workers within the plant on the upcoming election and the effects of free trade on their jobs. Whether this action was appropriate for a man in Huntly's position, the Liberal media, led by the Toronto *Globe*, did not think so, and it attacked Huntly in an editorial of poisonous tones. Incredibly, through an amazing degree of incompetence, they identified Huntly not as President of the C.S.R. Co. Ltd. but as head of his main competition, the St. Lawrence Sugar Co., which considerably undermined the authority of their accusations.

PRESIDENT OF ST. LAWRENCE SUGAR REFINERY AGAINST RECIPROCITY

Montreal September 6 … Mr. Huntly Drummond, son of the late Sir George Drummond and President of the St. Lawrence Sugar Refinery, is using his position as head of the company to get his employees to vote against reciprocity. Yesterday he ordered his workmen to cease work and listen to addresses by Mess'rs Doherty and Godewe Conservative candidates. Mr. Drummond also spoke, and urged his men to defeat the measure. Hitherto, explained President Drummond the company had remained neutral in election matters, but in the present instance the issues at stake were of such a far reaching nature that it behooved the company to assert itself. By reciprocity the interests of the concern were being affected, and it was well that all the employees connected with the company should be made aware of the fact, as their interests were wrapped up, as it were, in the interests of the company. Mr. Drummond then declared that the company was unequivocally opposed to reciprocity, and intended to fight the government in the present campaign.

Eventually the outcry caused by Huntly's action reached such a pitch that Huntly felt obliged to defend himself in a speech during a political debate on the issue.

Gentlemen,

The other day I had the pleasure of speaking to the employees of the Refinery on the subject of the present election. My reason for doing that, was that I consider this election the most important that have ever been held in Canada, and the question at issue so closely affects every man, that I felt it only right to let everyone know where I stood and how I feared it would hurt them. For so doing, I have been pilloried in the Liberal Press, and by the Liberal candidates: The Toronto Globe, the chief organ of the party in Ontario, said that I should be put in jail for coercion, and Mr. Rivet here stated on the platform, that I was intimidating my men.

Gentlemen, I wrote to the Globe and said that I had too much respect for my men and for myself to try and do anything so foolish as attempt to coerce any man, no one believes more firmly than I do in the sacredness on the ballot. We ask no man his religion or his politics in the Canada Sugar Refinery and to Mr. Rivet, through the Star, I said "Come on, address my men yourself if you want, you are free to do so". Did he come? No, and I will tell you why, it was because he was afraid, because he thought there was more profit in lying about my attitude than in doing as he did, and fairly and squarely defining where he stood and why.

Gentlemen, the Liberal party say it is time to make a change, and I agree with them, only we want different changes; they want to change the trade policy of this country, under which it has prospered and grown rich, as you know, and I want to change the government of the country, a government of men who have lost touch with the people, who think that they and not the people are masters, and that they can do anything they want, change the whole idea of our policy, turn us away from England and towards the United States, without even asking our leave, saying, "Hear take this, open your mouths and shut your eyes, and see what a nice surprise I'll give you". They gave us the surprise all right, and I think we'll give them another on the 21st.

Gentlemen, we are not children, or fools, we are men, and able to think for ourselves, and we want proof, not appeals to pass a rotten policy on account of our white hairs (others have white hairs, and are getting more every day, thinking of this iniquitous pact). Now in these last days of the campaign, don't let yourselves be drawn away from the two main issues; does this Reciprocity Pact threaten Protection (without which we could not exist) and what is more important still, does it threaten the life of Canada, as a Nation; I say it does.

If it goes through (and I do not believe it will) what will be the situation in this country; the farmer will have free trade in everything he produces, and he will pay duties on everything he consumes; does anyone outside a lunatic asylum think he will be satisfied; consider what has happened already; the farmers of the North West came down in a big delegation to Ottawa, they scared Sir Wilfrid so much that he promptly gave them all they wanted, now if they come again (and they will come) does anyone think that Sir Wilfrid won't give them what they want next time. I for one, fear he will; The present cabinet remind me of a row of nine pins, all standing up very straight and fine, but what happens, along comes the ball, and you see them lying round in every direction, hunting for cover; politicians look fine and imposing, that is their business, but you'll find these ones hollow when you try them out.

About annexation. Now let me say to start with, that I don't believe there are any Canadians consciously annexationists, but the point is what are the Americans thinking (mind you they are ninety millions to nine) what is Taft thinking, what has he said, what is a bigger man than Taft, and that is Hill, thinking, and what has he said; what has Champ Clark said; what have dozens of the leading papers in the U.S. said; why Gentlemen, they have all openly preached, let this thing, Reciprocity, go through, and it is the first step to the adoption of Canada; and if they are talking it openly, what are hundreds and thousands of other Americans thinking. You have had a taste of it already, I have seen, and it makes me sick to see it, American newsboys on St. James Street, selling American papers, to try and influence free born Canadians in this election; whose papers, you ask, why the meanest, lowest, most contemptible of the lot, Hearst.

Gentlemen, I believe that Canada is big enough, and strong enough, and Has good enough men to run her own affairs, without interference from the yellow dogs of any country, and I hope, and I believe that on the 21st on this Month, you, by your votes, will show that you believe in Canada, that you believe in the finest and grandest country on earth, and that you will say. "We will hand down this grand heritage that has been left to us in trust to our children not impaired, or mutilated, but bigger and better than when we got it.
(September 18, 1911)

On September 21, 1911, the country rendered its verdict and Sir Wilfrid Laurier was swept out of power by the Conservatives under Robert Borden by 134 seats to 87. All Huntly's efforts of the past months seemed justified, and he could now get back to the business at hand of running the company as the free trade deal was dropped. But within weeks he was again having to direct his attention towards the government as it was made known that there were plans to develop stronger trade arrangements with the British West Indies and other parts of the Empire. Taking a leaf out of his father's book, Huntly contacted the new Minister of Customs, the Honourable John D. Reid, offering his expertise on the matter of sugar duties.

I gather ... that it is possible the new Government may be doing something to favour trade within the Empire, and more especially ... the British West Indies ... At present the imports into Canada from there are mainly sugar ... As the subject of sugar duties is a very intricate one, may I ask you before any changes are made that you will allow the Refiners the privilege of stating their case before you and their claim to a strictly reasonable protection of their industry.
(November 2, 1911)

Following negotiations with the ministers, Huntly produced a report for them on the current situation. In his covering letter, he outlined the refiners' position.

I would like to emphasize the point, that in submitting this memorandum I have endeavoured to avoid putting any obstacle in the way of the trade policy of the Government, or that might in any way embarrass it ... The vital point is that there should be a fair margin of protection to the refiner ... I do not approve, nor would I ask for excessive protection.
(December 7, 1911)

The Canada Sugar Refining Co. Ltd. in September 1912. Note the difference of visibility caused by the smoke of the industries along the canal.

CHAPTER TWENTY-TWO

"Redpath Must Be Everywhere"

As 1911 drew to a close, Huntly began to make preparations for one of the most dramatic changes in the history of the company. With the installation of the new machinery for making individual cartons of sugar, a decision about who should run these machines had to be made. In the past, all packaging had been done by the men or by boys, but now Huntly decided to staff his new packaging building with women. This news shocked many of the older workers at the refinery and there was even talk of a strike to prevent the women being employed, but by direct negotiations, Huntly persuaded the workers' representative that this change was in the best interests of the company. In return, the company had to agree to pay the women a lower wage, equivalent to the boys in the refinery. Once agreement had been achieved, Huntly ordered the installation of a new ladies' dressing room, complete with lavatories, fixtures, and lockers. He later wrote to Arthur telling him of the results of this change. He also dealt with other business matters, which are referred to in Arthur's response on January 14, 1912.

> *You must be feeling pretty fine about the C.S.R. Co. Ltd.'s shewing it certainly is fine. However I suppose we will have lean years soon. Would not a little circular to the stockholders help ... saying you anticipate decreased dividends as soon as the new refinery starts ... As to cars to carry sugar in bulk, of course there is nothing in it to an individual manufacturer but the question occurred to me that perhaps if we built some special cars, we could get sufficiently low rates from the railway to make it worth while to send up consignments to Port Arthur or Winnipeg in them. This is the trick that the Chicago Packers work to get cheap rates ... and maybe sugar would come under a lower classification if loaded in bulk.*

In fact, the use of bulk railcars along these lines did not come into operation for nearly fifty years, which shows how dynamically Huntly and Arthur were thinking on the future prospects for the company. Arthur then continued:

> *As to boilers, the present Lancashire battery is giving more steam than they ... should and new stokers might give us more but they certainly would waste coal in doing it so I think that new stokers are not the solution of our difficulty ... As soon as the new packing house is running we can move the shop into the old "E" store and get ready the place where the present shop lies for a new range of boilers. There is no rest for the wicked ... As to the new boiler breaking down occasionally as it has done it is just what I expected. By the spring when the men know all about it, there will be*

no trouble. We had a devil of a time with the Vickers stokers when we first installed them a fact which is all forgotten now, as is the way in the refinery.
(January 4, 1912)

A week later, Huntly notified Arthur of the start-up of the Atlantic Sugar Refinery, to which Arthur replied:

What an incredible fool to put that refinery in St. John. Now what you are nervous about is whether he really can turn out cheaper than we can. He can't unless labour is cheaper. You ought to feel more anxious about the Acadia with its new plant, but we have always done better than they have. By next spring we will practically have as perfect a plant as you could build new and in some ways better than the typical American plant ... I don't see that after next spring we will have any big expenses for two or three years ... so we will be on even terms with them as far as operating expenses are concerned and probably miles better in our Capital. Meanwhile I would like to see our cartons and the new ten pound package pushed even at a loss. "Redpath" must be everywhere. Advertise more in Ontario with "quality" emphasized.
(January 21, 1912)

Shortly thereafter, the issue of the government's proposed trading arrangements caused concerns among the Canadian sugar refiners, for it seemed the 20% quota would be restricted or even abolished. Mr. Daviss of the Acadia Sugar Refining Co. wrote to Huntly looking for support in his effort to persuade the government to change its mind. Huntly was certain that at this time nothing could be done but encouraged Daviss to do what he could:

I have your second telegram in regard to going to Ottawa to get the privilege of importing non preferential sugar increased. I think it would not possibly do any harm ... to press for this privilege. At the same time ... I do not see how the Government can grant this request to increase the privilege without putting a serious bar in the object they have in view which is the increasing of trade with the British West Indies. I quite agree that the present is a very difficult year: the supply of preferential sugars is to be specially limited ... and practically we have to go and buy non preferential sugars.
(January 29, 1912)

On February 17, Huntly was informed by Mr. Daviss that nothing had been achieved by his trip to Ottawa and in addition, due to technical difficulties at the Acadia refinery, they would be unable to take the sugar originally agreed to under the sharing arrangement that had been in effect for the previous year. This forced Huntly into the position of either reneging on the contractual obligation with the suppliers and suffering the consequent problems of legal action and political censure, or taking the entire volume of sugar in the hope of selling it off. Huntly chose the latter course and so notified Mr. Daviss. Compounding things at this time was another issue concerning the Wholesalers Guild, who were in a trade war with a group of retail tradesmen styling themselves as the Canada Brokerage Co. Both sides were attempting to undercut the other and steal business for themselves. Furthermore, both attempted to pressure the sugar companies to boycott sales to the other group. Huntly tried unsuccessfully to get the protagonists to reconcile their differences, but the open hostility with which the two groups faced each other made this impossible, and Huntly stated his resolve not to be biased towards either side. This annoyed certain individuals in the Wholesalers Guild who then proceeded to send anonymous letters to the members of the wholesale trade, attacking the C.S.R. Co. Ltd. for its stand. This action forced Huntly to write in defence of his own position to Mr. Beckett of the Guild.

> *In the matter of the Canada Brokerage Co. ... our resolution to deal fairly with everybody, and not grant concessions to individuals, has had a great deal to do with the disfavour with which some people regard us ... I note what you say about the Canada Brokerage Co. being a combination of retailers ... their claim and excuse is that the cutting of prices is widespread among the other dealers in Toronto, and that they are doing only as others do ... I would recommend you adopt my proposal of selling to them direct and put them in a position where we can keep a strong search light on their business to see they keep straight.*[1]
> (March 18, 1912)

Within the refinery, production continued until the end of the month when a number of shipments of raw sugar failed to arrive as scheduled, which forced an early closure in preparation for the regular spring draining of the canal. Huntly contacted Mr. Lee immediately:

> *The sugar from the "Korona" Cargo is coming in so slowly, that we have run out and are shutting down earlier than anticipated ... You will kindly route any sugars that we have coming, if possible, by some other line, and you may inform the New York Central that their disgraceful handling of this cargo, has converted me into an advocate for direct shipment to Canadian ports, the result will be an absolute loss of all sugar freight to them.*[2]
> (March 28, 1912)

Meanwhile, continuing pressure was being brought to bear upon the company in the Wholesalers Guild matter, and a group of Northern Ontario merchants wrote to Huntly calling upon him to extend a larger discount on the face price of sugar to their organization to allow them to compete with the undercutting prices of the Canada Brokerage Co. Huntly replied on April 24, 1912.

> *I note what you say in reference to the cost of your wholesale houses of doing business ... but it is impossible for the refiners to make any advance in the rate of discount. The competition of Wallaceburg is extremely keen and any additions to the cost of distribution would simply mean the curtailing of our business for their benefit ... As to your contention that the Wallaceburg is selling well at a profit ... that one refinery should have sold its stock at a profit is hardly an argument that all the refiners are making money ... The margin of profit in refining is not large at any time and depends for its existence very much on the fluctuation of the sugar market.*[3]

By May of 1912, preparations for the introduction of women into the workforce were complete and the initial group of women consisting of forty "girls" was supervised by

The Gables, the country house of Huntly Redpath Drummond. Located on part of the Beaconsfield property of G.A. Drummond.

its own forelady and under-forelady. Although under the agreement with the men, the women were paid at the boys' rates, Huntly established the women in the "special" labour category for wages instead of the lower "common" labour category used for some of the yard labour. This gave the women wage rates ranging from 80 cents per hour to $1.10 per hour; the under-forelady received $1.40 and the forelady, Miss Kennedy, received $1.85 per hour. Some elements of the male workforce were resentful, especially those receiving less than the women, but Huntly allowed these grumbles to slowly die away.

Meanwhile, outside of the company, since George's death in 1910, the Beaconsfield property of Huntlywood had been left empty. As the executor of the Drummond estate, Huntly obtained agreement with the other members of the family to sell off the bulk of the property. To this end the house, farm, and grounds north of the railway tracks were sold to Sir Hugh M. Allan for $200,000, while much of the land below the tracks and extending down to the lake front was disposed of in June to the Island Land Co. for $23,021.

In May, estimates for the work underway at the refinery and proposed for the balance of 1912 were received by Huntly. They added up to $172,125 and were split between the refinery, the char house, and boilers for the power house. Plans were also drawn up for the long-term development of the refinery once the current year's installations were complete. The upward trend in the population and the concurrent growth in per capita consumption indicated that an extended programme of construction and expansion would pay handsome dividends in the long term. Following discussions, Huntly and the board approved a set of expansions to be implemented over the next eight years that dwarfed everything done so far. Starting with a 10% increase in capacity of output for the plant during the balance of 1912 at an estimated cost of $88,100, the expansion would continue with a 15% increase for 1913 ($195,825), a 50% increase for 1914 ($215,000), a 25% increase for 1915-17 ($560,500), and conclude with a 50% increase for 1918-20 costing $360,000 for a total increase in output capacity of 150%, and a total cost of $1,429,425.

Towards the end of summer, the new packaging plant was in full operation and alongside the regular listing of bags, barrels, and half barrels, a new selection of boxes and cartons were added including:

Powdered Sugar in 50 pound & 25 pound wooden boxes
Extra Ground in 50 pound & 25 pound wooden boxes
Ordinary Paris Lumps in 100 pound, 50 pound & 25 pound wooden boxes
Extra Hard Paris Lumps in 100 pound, 50 pound & 25 pound wooden boxes
Red Seal Paris Lumps in 5 pound cardboard cartons
Granulated Sugar in 5 pound and 2 pound cardboard cartons

Sales of two of the lines, Red Seal Paris Lumps and Granulated Sugar in cartons, were soon growing so rapidly that production was diverted from the barrelling system into additional output in cardboard cartons. The products were being sold from the Maritimes to the Yukon and Redpath was indeed everywhere. That autumn, the company took out a large stand to display its new products at the Canadian National Exhibition held in Toronto. This exhibit was favourably reviewed in the *Canadian Grocer* magazine.

REDPATH SUGAR EXHIBIT

One of the entirely new features of the National Exhibition this year was the striking exhibit of the famous "Redpath" Sugar, made by the Canada Sugar Refining Co., Limited, of Montreal.

It was only to be expected that this company should be the first to exhibit at the Fair, as they have been the pioneers of the sugar business in Canada from the beginning. Their's was the first granulated sugar produced in the Dominion, and last year introduced the latest improvement, the two pound and five pound sealed cartons.

These attractive looking cartons were much in evidence in their exhibit, and made a fine showing. The big sign over the booth flashing forth "Redpath Sugar – The Canadian Standard since 1854," the striking photograph of the big Redpath Refinery in Montreal, and the samples of different sugars on exhibition made the Redpath Booth exceedingly interesting to every man, and more particularly to every woman.

The demonstrator made very clear the superiority of "Redpath" sugars, illustrating it with samples. The pure crystal whiteness of Redpath, when compared with ordinary white sugar, must have been an eye-opener to those who had been in the habit of accepting the ordinary kind.

The two pound and five pound cartons naturally attracted a great deal of attention, and the comments made must have been gratifying to those in charge. One could not help seeing the great advantage in buying sugar, as one buys tea, spices, breakfast foods and so many other groceries, in sealed cartons, which protect it from contamination of any kind. The cartons are very convenient, too, for keeping the sugar in the pantry.

The unanimous approval expressed by the thousands of visitors to the booth promised a demand for "Redpath" Package Sugar much greater even than at present, which means a great deal, for the cartons have sprung into popular demand almost overnight.

When Canada's finest sugar is thus put up in the most attractive way, and vigorously advertised, it simply cannot fail to be a splendid success. Grocers who feature "Redpath" Sugar are enjoying a most satisfactory trade, and those who have not previously paid much attention to "Redpath" are waking up to its possibilities.[4]

Despite this success, by the year's end a review of the general figures revealed that expenses for plant, maintenance, and renewal were considerably higher than anticipated for a total of $1,306,269.76. Even so, the optimism for future profits was so strong that no reduction was made in the next year's plans for expansion, which estimated a further $261,000 being invested in the plant, $45,000 of which was to be for an additional carton packaging system. Even Arthur voiced his surprise at the extent of the plans proposed and raised particular questions on the development of the distillery.

Don't Miss the Exhibit of
Redpath Sugar
At the Toronto Exhibition
REDPATH Sugar is to the front again with a most interesting exhibit
Manufacturers' Building Annex, under the Grand Stand at the big Fair.
Here are shown samples of sugar in the different stages of refining,
sugar to the pure white crystals of REDPATH Extra Granulated, and the
Paris Lumps. The Exhibit shows very clearly the great difference between
and second grade sugars.
REDPATH was the first sugar refined in Canada—the first shown at the
Exhibition—the first Canadian Sugar marketed in 2 and 5 Pound Sealed
for over half a century it has stood first in the estimation of both the Trade and the
The Canada Sugar Refining Co., Limited,

> *I confess you surprise me when you talk of enlarging the distillery as well as the plant ... If you think it necessary however I think that putting new apparatus in our present building as you say is the proper thing. George is crazy about a new building for the distillery. I myself can't see any sense in it. Our present building is good enough and moving everything would cost a small fortune.*
> (February 12, 1913)

Shortly afterwards, Huntly succeeded to the position of President of the Montreal Board of Trade and was elected as a director within the Bank of Montreal. Arthur's prophesy of Huntly becoming a "big man" was definitely coming true.

With the coming of spring, sales began to steadily increase, despite the general economic conditions of the Canadian market. Having taken the initiative to develop the new product lines, the company was well in charge of the market and used its advantage without hesitation. On the supply side, due to the previous year's problems with overland shipments of sugar, volumes coming via Saint John,

Halifax, and New York fell by half, while direct shipments increased proportionately. Furthermore, the growth in the preferential rate of tariff made purchases from the British West Indies more economic than imports of beet sugar from Europe, so in May the last orders of the beet type sugars were received and processed, leaving only cane type sugar to be refined in future through the plant. In June, a sudden jump in the price of raw cane sugar made Huntly think of reversing his decision but its equally rapid fall by the end of the month calmed his concerns. The other sugar refiners were not so sure, however, and Mr. Daviss of the Acadia Sugar Co. wrote to Huntly stating that he had been approached by St. Lawrence wanting to re-enter the co-operative purchase scheme. Huntly saw this as pure cheek on the part of St. Lawrence and so informed Daviss.

> *Four years ago it is true these [supplies] were divided among the three refineries: after that the St. Lawrence declined to continue taking their share, and for another year you and we each took a half. Later you were unable to continue, and we then took up the whole of the production of these sugars at considerable cost to ourselves when they failed to arrive as required ... I cannot see why the St. Lawrence should now be able to come in and ask for part of these sugars, seeing that for the last few years we have taken the risk of taking them all. Having done so this year and made all the arrangements accordingly for our own needs. I do not see why we should now have to upset them.*[5]
> *(June 30, 1913)*

During August and September, Huntly took his family on a tour of Great Britain, while the company set up another display at the C.N.E., which included one of its new packaging machines. Many visitors were reported to have spent up to an hour watching the new method of making sugar for Canada's kitchens. Returning from Europe in early October, Huntly found that the Grand Trunk Railway was planning to extend the siding running along St. Patrick Street without consulting the company. Since it was the C.S.R. Co. Ltd. who originally had to obtain the right of way at its own cost, Huntly considered this spur private property and notified the general manager of the Grand Trunk Railway of his disapproval on November 26, 1913.

I notice that you are proceeding with the construction of a switch and siding on the south side of St. Patrick Street at the end of the Canada Sugar Refining Company's siding. You are ... aware that when this siding was projected ... the most determined opposition was made to it by the inhabitants and proprietors of the street ... Now apparently you propose to allocate the use of the siding and the benefit of all our trouble and expenditures to other parties without consulting us. Evidently the alteration of this siding ... may make a serious difference in the value to us of the siding. We must, therefore protest against the alteration of the siding and hold the Grand Trunk Railway responsible for any consequences adverse to the interests of this Company which may result there from, also against the appropriation of rights which this Company has acquired at considerable expense.

Following negotiations that dragged on into the following year, a deal was concluded with the Grand Trunk Railway and the right of way was signed over in exchange for a cash settlement.

Within the refinery proper, the construction of the new packing building was falling behind schedule and, with the weather beginning to deteriorate, Huntly pressed the contractors to speed up their rate of progress to ensure completion before the winter set in. In a letter dated December 1, 1913, Huntly reported to Arthur on the progress of construction.

Dear Arthur,

I went over the building today and this is the position of affairs.

The steel is up to the eighth storey with most of the uprights of the ninth and tenth finished. They expect to have the erection of all the steel complete in say three days ... The rivetting is complete up to the sixth storey. They were working on the seventh and eighth this morning. They should be very nearly done by the end of this week ... Four floors of terra cotta are complete, and the fifth will be done probably by tonight. They can do about two floors per week, provided the riveters keep ahead of them ... The walls, stone and brick, are complete up to the fourth storey and they are now working on the fifth ... Some of the partitions on the second storey are done and some forms in on the third storey ... I enclose you a copy of the estimate they have given me which will show you what they expect to do up to the time when they should have caught up with the original schedule they made us ... They are not out of the wood yet but the progress made in the last three weeks is remarkable ... If we have two weeks more of open weather we should be almost out of the woods, but I am afraid it is a great deal to hope for...

Early in January 1914, Huntly was pressed by several local groups to stand for the position of mayor of the city; he politely declined as his full attention was already being given to solving an urgent problem caused by city plans to replace an existing power house on the Lachine Canal with a larger one. In order to lay the foundations for the building, the canal was to be emptied for several weeks. Due to the extremely short notice of this plan, the various industrial factories would have to make drastic changes in their plans. Huntly organized a meeting at his offices and the results of the meeting were reported in the *Gazette*.

The announcement ... that the Canal would be unwatered on Monday next ... has caused much perturbation among mill owners and manufacturers who operate large plants on the Canal banks ... It was hoped by the Government ... that this would cause less inconvenience than at the usual period, which is just before the commencement of navigation, in the early spring. This was not the view of the case taken at a meeting of manufacturers ... held yesterday ... and the meeting, did not adjourn until after a strongly worded protest had been drawn up and adopted for forwarding to the Department of Railways and Canals at Ottawa. The adoption of the protest was moved by Mr. Huntly Drummond who maintained that the draining of the Canal at this time of the year would not only seriously affect industrial conditions in some of the largest Montreal factories, but would have the effect of throwing thousands of men out of employment ... it would be impossible for many of the plants which depend on the Canal for water power to obtain auxiliary steam power at such short notice, and that, if the Canal is unwatered on Monday some of the factories will have to close down, and that ruinous losses are certain to result.

Despite these arguments, the canal was emptied and the refinery was forced to cut back production to about 60% until mid-March. During the next few months, Huntly was busy with various organizations and petitions, including one to the government on behalf of the Board of Trade over the proposed ratifying of the reciprocity agreement with the West Indies; a state dinner for the improvement of trade with Belgium; the establishment of the Housing and Planning Association for Greater Montreal; and meetings of the boards of directors at both the Bank of Montreal and Royal Victoria Hospital. The refinery seems to have reached a satisfactory level of efficiency, sales maintained a steady monthly average throughout the long hot summer, and the workers were given a 3% pay raise.

The month of August arrived, and with it came news of the outbreak of war in Europe. As a result Huntly was kept busy dealing with its effects on production and assuring the public that war would not cause a sugar shortage, as will be seen in the next chapter, but he did take a day off from his round of engagements to participate in a small celebration at the refinery on August 12. The report in the Montreal *Gazette* of this event is a pleasant note upon which to end this chapter and this period of history for the company, for the reality of war was about to intrude.

Sixty years is a long time to serve one Company, but such is the splendid record of Mr. James McMenamin, who has been Superintendent of the Canada Sugar Refining Co. Ltd. formerly the Redpath Sugar Refinery, since its foundation in 1854, the late Sir George Drummond having brought him as a young man from Greenock Scotland ... Associated with Mr. McMenamin as Mechanical Superintendent is Mr. Alexander Bower who has been in the same employ since 1859 ... thinking that some recognition on the part of the Company was in order Mr. Huntly Drummond, the President and his brother Mr. Arthur L. Drummond, yesterday presented these two faithful and able employees with gold sovereign and cheques on behalf of the Company which they have served so faithfully and well for so many long years.
(August 12, 1914)

Shipping out part of the 10-million pound contract for the United Kingdom in June 1916.

CHAPTER TWENTY-THREE

"A Patriotic Stand"

With the outbreak of war in August 1914, the patriotic fever that swept the English-speaking portion of the country in support of the motherland was reflected within the refinery. Several of the younger men immediately joined up, including Huntly's younger brother Guy (who, as well as being a major shareholder in the company, was a familiar and well-liked figure around the plant as he acted in the role of intermediary between his brother, the President, and the men on the shop floor.) Such was Guy's fervour to "be in it" that despite the fact that he had previously resigned his commission in the Canadian Army to pursue a career in business, and that he had returned from his honeymoon only two weeks earlier, he at once returned to the colours, taking with him at least four of the workforce into his own regiment. Everyone was confident that "it would all be over by Christmas" and things would return to normal. In the meantime, business events were beginning to develop at an alarming degree of momentum. The British government started purchasing as much raw sugar as was available for immediate delivery and placed huge orders for the next three months, thereby depleting the normal outstanding world reserves of raw sugar and driving up the prices for raw on the United States market. Coupled with this was the natural domestic instinct of the Canadian consumer to ensure supplies by buying up extra sugar "just-in-case." This precipitated a shortage of sugar in Canadian grocery stores, causing the retailers to order increased volumes from the wholesalers, who in turn demanded immediate additional supplies from the refiners. Unfortunately, the refiners could not instantly respond to this sudden multiplication of demand with increased output and were thus placed in the unenviable position of being accused of deliberately hoarding sugar in order to drive up prices and make a quick war profit. In reality, nothing could have been further from the truth, as can be seen in a letter from Huntly to the Honourable Robert Rogers in Ottawa when he stated:

> *My idea is that the Government should, as it can, guarantee Great Britain a supply of food at cost price, and if there is any deficiency pay it itself: It would be a patriotic stand, and I feel sure it would be the greatest help we could give them now, and one that would be endorsed by the whole people.*

To further this principle, Huntly Redpath Drummond wrote a series of letters to the presidents of the other Canadian sugar companies, urging them to withhold price rises, even to the extent of taking a short-term loss in order to serve the national war effort; he added that under no circumstances should sugar be sold to speculators, but only to their regular lists of wholesale and retail distributors. The other refiners, however, were less than enthusiastic about holding back, and they soon increased their prices in the Canadian market to match the higher prices being obtained in the United States. Disappointed in this "less than patriotic" attitude, Huntly issued a statement on August 11 to his wholesale customers:

> *Our Montreal competitors have advanced their price half a cent per pound to five cents per pound on one-hundred pound bags ... while our price remains unchanged at four and a half cents per pound ... advise all customers ... that Redpath sugar must be sold on our basis ... present conditions ... will undoubtedly bring a rush of orders to ourselves, so we will, in self protection, place certain restrictions on all future business ... No order entered (accepted) from any firm already having supplies on the books ... customers must declare their willingness to sell on our basis and to discourage all speculative buying ... All customers will be given supplies in the proportion that they have been in the habit of taking during the corresponding months of 1913.*

In another letter to his brother Guy, Huntly stated:

> *We are selling sugar at 4½ cents (per pound); the American price is 7½ cents per pound ... under these circumstances ... the temptation to export sugar from Canada and take advantage of this unprecedented difference in price might prove too strong for some people here. This would immediately nullify any good that we are doing by keeping down the price for the benefit of Canadians. The only thing to do would be for the government to put an embargo on the export of sugar.*

This co-operative attitude on the part of Huntly Drummond was not lost on the government, and Sir George Foster, the Minister for Trade and Commerce, approached Drummond to assist the ministry in developing policies on sugar pricing. Huntly took this work to heart and rapidly contacted the other refiners. Through some intense negotiating, he persuaded them all to agree to a common policy on restraining prices and voluntarily suspending exports.

At the same time, there was a reported shortage of sugar in central Canada. This led to an outcry by Manitoba retailers to the federal government, who then passed on these complaints to Huntly Drummond asking him to provide sugar from the C.S.R. Co. Ltd. to the western provinces. To which Huntly could only respond:

> *In the present month we have already exceeded the total shipments of last August ... we are working day and night and turning out every pound of sugar possible ... with the war ... a number of consumers have been trying to hoard sugar. This foolish and unpatriotic attitude ... is responsible for any complaint of a scarcity of sugar ... Our aim has been not to increase the burden of the consumer at this time, no matter at what loss of profit to ourselves.*

By early September, the situation had not improved and although every pound of sugar was immediately sold, the company could not keep up to the excessive demand, nor could Huntly's appeals to patriotic self-control curb the fact that retailers were making excess profits at the refiners' expense. Finally, Huntly had to write in strong terms to Sir George Foster that

> *the sacrifice which we are making for the benefit of the consumer is being absorbed by the retailer ... This is ... an intolerable condition for us after all the sacrifices we have made.*

However, the government was not itself immune to the revenue opportunities of this price rise and slapped a new duty on imported raw sugar, which had to be paid by the refiner. This action was the final straw for Huntly and on September 4, C.S.R. Co. Ltd. prices were raised to cover the cost of the new duty.

By this time the efforts of the government to establish a common pricing policy for goods were proving to be singularly inept. Therefore Huntly was personally requested by the minister to work on the government's behalf to obtain an equilibrium price agreement among the refiners, to recommend future pricing policies, and to act as an intermediary between the refiners and the various government departments.

The last known picture of the Drummond brothers together, prior to Guy's departure for the Western front in September 1914. From left to right: Huntly, Guy, and Arthur.

On September 14, 1914, the St. Lawrence and Acadia Sugar Companies once again raised their prices, drawing a sharp rebuke from the minister. To prevent excessive demand upon the C.S.R. Co. Ltd., Foster specifically instructed Huntly to raise his prices to match the competition. By the twenty-fifth, the higher United States raw sugar prices had collapsed, leaving many of the refiners with high-priced raw sugar coming in but refined prices falling, which reduced or even eliminated any profit margin. Huntly commented in his letters to Guy that their own company was fortunate in holding little in the way of high-priced stocks,

> *as this would have been patently dangerous in view of the ridiculous high price of raws ... and not at all sensible business practice.*

The government now decided that a conference of the refiners and ministry representatives was needed to discuss future wartime measures. At that conference Huntly was able to warn the Canadian authorities of the attempts by the German and Austrian governments to obtain money for their war effort by confiscating and selling the beet sugar produced in occupied Belgium, then forcing the people of Belgium to buy German sugar directly from the occupying military authorities. The immediate distribution of this information and an implementation of a ban on the Belgian product prevented an estimated $50 million reaching the German war coffers.

As the war continued into 1915, the intensive demands of wartime production, combined with the increasing difficulties of obtaining raw sugar, led to more emphasis being placed upon immediate output. Thus the pre-war plans for the reorganization of the refinery were steadily cut back or postponed and only essential repair work was done to keep the plant going. On a personal level, Huntly suffered the loss of his brother Guy on April 22, 1915, during the first German gas attack on the Ypres Front. According to all reports, Guy was in the second line of trenches when the frontline French Colonial troops panicked and fled in the face of the totally unexpected poison gas. Guy attempted to rally the colonial troops but was hit in the neck by shrapnel. He soon died in the arms of one of the men from the refinery who had enlisted with Guy in 1914. Subsequently, his men were compelled to leave his body behind as they too were forced from their trenches by the gas; his body was never recovered. The news of Guy's death came as a shock to everyone and Huntly was devastated by this loss. A memorial service was held in London (where his wife, although several months pregnant, was doing fundraising and war work with her mother-in-law, Lady Drummond) and another service was held simultaneously in Montreal that many of the major political, business, and social figures of the day attended. In addition, the entire refinery workforce came of their own volition and submitted numerous personal letters of condolence expressing their affection for Guy.

Guy Drummond in regimental uniform.

Upon his return to business in May, Huntly is reported to have maintained a much more determined attitude towards the need for an Allied victory. In addition to previous donations given for the purchase and maintenance of a fleet of ambulances to be used at the Front, Huntly was one of a group of businessmen who each donated a minimum of $100,000 to purchase and equip Canadian troops with additional machine guns and some early armoured cars.

Through the remainder of 1915, domestic sales maintained a steady average of about 13.4 million pounds per month as consumption stabilized within Canada. Through some astute purchasing of raw supplies from the British West Indies, stocks of sugar were kept reasonably secure until the end of the year when a sudden shortage of ships to transport further raws led to the depletion of all the accumulated reserve. This forced the closure of the plant until sufficient supplies could be obtained to allow re-starting and continuing production for an extended period of time. Unfortunately, this lack of shipping capacity forced the company into a period of increased costs as the only alternative to bringing raw sugar directly to the refinery in ships was to trans-ship the material by rail from Maritime ports or through New York, thus placing the company at a direct cost disadvantage relative to their Maritime competitors.

For the world at large, the war that was supposed to have been over by Christmas 1914 was now into its eighteenth month, with no end in sight. Huntly was deeply involved in the promotion of the first Canadian war bond issue for $50 million in November 1915 (it actually raised over $100 million within a single week.) But behind the continued support for the war effort was an increased awareness of the impact the war was having on the daily life of Canadians at home. More and more products were either in short supply or completely unavailable as industries were converted into war production centres, and the government exercised controls through legislation such as the War Measures Act. For the Drummond family, May 1916 was a sad month when Arthur died of typhoid contracted while on vacation in Florida, which left Huntly as the only surviving child of George Alexander Drummond. On a happier note, a government-approved export order was secured in May for 10 million pounds of refined sugar to the United Kingdom. This order was approximately twice the equivalent volume of domestic sales for the same period and such was the efficiency of the processing of the order and its rapid dispatch that the British government soon put in another order for 2.24 million pounds in August. This earned $730,000 of additional income for the company and to reward the employees for their extra efforts, Huntly ordered a pay raise of 8% across the board. For the remainder of the year, however, things were not as positive, because the increasing level of government controls on purchasing raw sugar, coupled with the difficulties of obtaining suitable shipping, left the company with wildly fluctuating levels of stock and a production rate of only two-thirds that of the pre-war period.

With the coming of 1917, two issues dominated the thinking of Canadians. First was the question of conscription, which was supported by most of Canada and the English-speaking population in the province of Quebec. On the other side was the French-speaking population of Quebec. This issue was reflected in miniature within the refinery between the predominantly English-speaking management and the French-

speaking workforce. Relations between the two sides slowly deteriorated and hardened into fixed viewpoints that would have long-term implications for the future. The second issue concerned the huge jump in the cost of living (18% in three months.) To solve this problem, the Conservative government of Robert Borden decided to take control of all aspects of the acquisition, distribution, and pricing of foodstuffs, fuel, etc., and W. J. Hanna, the former head of Imperial Oil, was appointed "Food Controller of Canada." Hanna's immediate actions as Food Controller were not what most of the public expected, or wanted, in the face of the higher costs and prices. Instead of rolling back prices to lower levels, as was generally expected, Hanna initiated a publicity campaign exhorting people to eat less and to change their tastes to more readily available (if less popular) food products. His Food Board deluged grocers and restaurant owners with regulations and restrictions on food preparation and even portion sizes, while food manufacturers were immediately banned from exporting any of their production. For the C.S.R. Co. Ltd., this represented a major revenue loss as in the previous three months of 1917, exports to Great Britain had totalled 32.4 million pounds, which had earned $2 million for the company coffers. Furthermore, Hanna ordered the sugar refiners to set up an official committee to co-ordinate purchases of raw sugar and threatened total price controls if they did not comply.

During the next few weeks, Hanna continued to extend his controls over all aspects of food and implemented regulations left, right, and centre. Then, without taking the time to study the actual stocks of sugar available or taking into account the availability of domestically grown beet sugar, he speculated publicly that the availability of sugar in the near future was so limited that he might have to ban completely the production of chocolate, preserves, and candies. This naturally set off a round of panic buying by consumers and forced Huntly Drummond into trying to stem the panic by issuing public statements of his own (on behalf of the refiners) in direct contradiction of Mr. Hanna. This obviously did not sit well with the gentleman and perhaps set the tone for future dealings with the sugar refiners in general and Huntly Drummond and his Canada Sugar Refining Company Ltd. in particular.

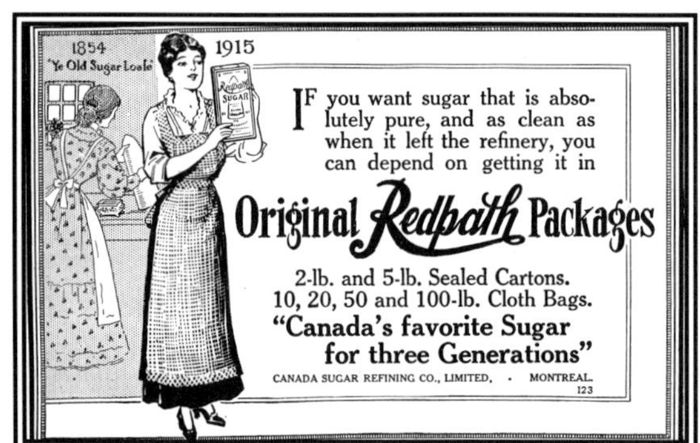

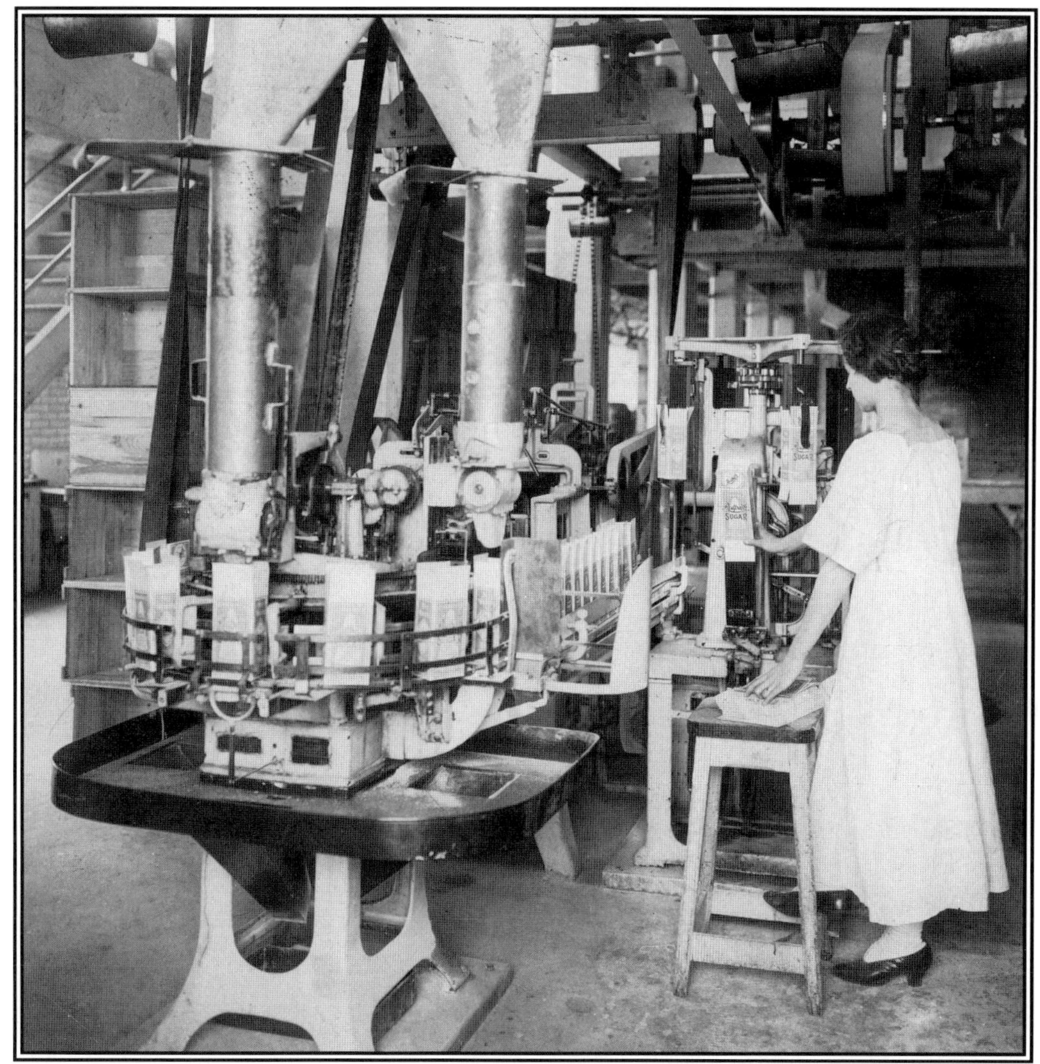

Filling 2-pound cartons on the automated packing machine.

Wrapping and packing Redpath tea cubes.

CHAPTER TWENTY-FOUR

"Big Brother"

From August 1917 to the end of the war and beyond into 1920, the control of the government over virtually every aspect of the sugar business gave Huntly Drummond and his company almost no freedom to react to market forces. All their years of expertise and economic rationale were eclipsed by the politically motivated decision making emanating from Ottawa, and from the very beginning of government control, things did not go well for the refiners. The first example of this came on September 25, 1917, when the committee of Canadian sugar refiners met in the offices of the Canada Sugar Refining Company Ltd. Their aim was to co-ordinate a policy of obtaining raw sugar and curb their output to the market in order to retain supplies for future needs in case of a shortage (which in fact did not exist.) One of the refining companies (the Atlantic Sugar Company) wanted to raise overall prices in order to provide a financial cushion in case of future cuts in sales by government decree. The other refiners, led by Huntly Drummond, disagreed and argued that in the face of the threats by Mr. Hanna to place the refiners in the hands of government officials it would be a disastrous public relations move. The Atlantic Sugar Co. reluctantly agreed and the prices remained stable. On October 5, another meeting was held to discuss a directive from Mr. Hanna to completely stop buying raw sugar (this directive was the result of intense pressure on the Canadian Government from Herbert Hoover, the United States Trade Secretary who was attempting to corner all sugar supplies possible for the U.S. sugar refiners, to the detriment of everyone else in the market.) Following intense discussions, all the Canadian refiners agreed to cease purchasing raw sugar for the time being.

At the next meeting of the committee on the fifteenth of the month, a complaint letter from Hanna was read. It stated that in direct contravention to Hanna's directive of the fourth, raw sugar had been bought, and in his view the refiners were not doing their duty to the country. This shocked the group and led by Huntly Drummond, each company in turn claimed that it had not gone back on the earlier agreement – that is, until Mr. O'Grady of Atlantic admitted that his company had accepted delivery of raw sugar after the fourth but that since negotiations on the contract had been started before that date, it could not be counted as contravening the agreement.

As this gave Atlantic a significant margin of additional supplies compared to everyone else, the other refiners felt this was "twisting the rules" and objected strongly. Subsequent investigations by Huntly and the other refiners revealed that in reality the deal was completed after the deadline on the fourth but the contract was backdated to the third of October to circumvent the ban. Later in the meeting, the subject arose of the need for a Canadian representative on the International Sugar Committee (which had been established in New York by the United States and British governments to oversee purchases, pricing, and allocations of sugar between the Allies.) After some heated debate, consideration of candidates fell to a choice of two sugar traders already in New York, but when no agreement could be reached the Atlantic representatives (backed by the British Columbia Sugar Company) demanded that their nominee be selected or else they would quit the committee. With the meeting in a state of uproar, Huntly Drummond, as the chairman, adjourned the meeting until later in the afternoon, using the time to persuade the other sugar companies that in the interest of co-operation the Atlantic nominee be accepted. Upon re-convening, before Huntly could announce the acquiescence of the committee to the Atlantic demand, the Atlantic representative notified the group that he had telephoned Mr. Hanna during the intermission to notify him that the committee refused to accept the Atlantic nominee and that Hanna must impose a choice on the group. Obviously no agreement could now be reached and the meeting terminated without result.

The vacuum pans within the refinery, insulated with wood stripping.

Following the meeting, Huntly Drummond tried once again to gain a consensus and even went so far as to travel to New York to interview the Atlantic nominee and brief him on the current state of affairs in the Canadian industry. Imagine, then, Huntly's surprise when he met the gentleman and was informed that not only was the man not willing to act as a representative for the refiners, but that he had never wished to and had informed Atlantic of that fact some time previously.

Returning to Montreal in something less than a good mood, Huntly informed the other refiners, who were equally annoyed. At the request of the other refiners, Huntly returned once again to New York to try and settle the matter once and for all. Following interviews with a number of candidates, Huntly recommended a Mr. H.S. Connell to the group on October 29. The majority of the refiners readily agreed, except Atlantic, who demanded to know why they

A battery of centrifugal machines.

had not been given prior notification of this new recommendation, as they had their own replacement choice. Huntly's answer was that significant pressure was being made by the British and United States representatives of the International Sugar Committee for Canada to stop procrastinating and appoint a delegate. Thus the action of proposing Mr. Connell (who was recommended by both the British and U.S. teams) was the quickest way to resolve the issue. The response of the Atlantic representatives was to refuse to accept Connell and they repeated that only their choice would be acceptable. This time the other refiners were in no mood to placate Atlantic and voted overwhelmingly (including the B.C. Sugar Company) for Connell, at which point the Atlantic representatives stated that they quit and left the meeting. The refiners' group now decided to write to Mr. Hanna on the events of the day, notify him of the majority recommendation, and request his confirmation of their decision.

Nothing more was heard on the matter until November 12 when a curt note from Hanna to the committee informed them that a Mr. J.R. Bruce (an individual no one had nominated) was appointed as of the fifth, upon the grounds that he (Hanna) had been informed by Atlantic that no choice had been made by the committee and that only he could solve the issue.

Huntly's immediate reaction was to write a very strongly worded protest to Hanna, in which he asked if this attitude on the part of the government by overruling the majority of the industry in favour of one company was to be the standard for future dealings. If it was, he concluded that the committee should disband. As might be expected, from this point onwards and for the rest of the war, there was absolutely no co-operation from Atlantic on the joint decisions of the remainder of the sugar refiners led by Huntly Drummond. Meanwhile, on the matter of the appointment to the International Sugar Committee, Huntly felt it was more important to secure supplies of sugar than to create an incident between the refiners and the government, so he went once again to New York to meet Mr. Bruce and impress upon him the need to obtain secure supplies of raw sugar for Canada, and during the next few years the two men developed a strong business relationship and personal friendship.

Upon his return to Montreal, Huntly reported to the refiners' committee that he was impressed by Mr. Bruce, but he also revealed some alarming information that is found in a letter to the President of the Acadia Sugar Company on November 26, and which brought into question Hanna's objectivity towards the situation of the refiners' committee and their dissenting ex-member.

> *In my opinion the Food Controller [Hanna] did everything possible to help the Atlantic getting sugars, even to the extent of sending Bruce a telegram ... [instructing him] ... to prevent me from seeing the information that they had.*

Filling 100-pound bags.

From the international point of view, the year ended on an equally unpleasant tone with the growth in power of the International Sugar Committee, which unfortunately was dominated by the American sugar companies, who saw the legislative powers of the International Sugar Committee as an ideal method of squeezing out the Canadian sugar companies from the North American market. Initially the American refiners used their representatives on the I.S.C. to try to establish a ban on Canadian sugar entering the United States. When this failed, they switched tactics and pressed for all Canadian sugar purchases to be grouped under the British quota as they were part of the British Empire. This would then have excluded Mr. Bruce from representation on the I.S.C. and would have ensured that sugar would enter Canada only once Britain had obtained all its needs.

On December 1, Huntly appealed to Hanna for immediate support for Mr. Bruce but received no reply. It was obvious that little or nothing could be expected in the way of support from the Food Controller and so Huntly initiated a mailing campaign to various ministry officials, members of Parliament, and Cabinet members, stressing the seriousness of the situation (the Canada Sugar Refining Company had less than a week's worth of raw sugar left in reserve.) Amazingly, this tactic seemed to have an effect, for on December 6, Hanna issued a statement indicating that the Canadian government would not tolerate the biased International Sugar Committee acting to isolate Canada from its fair proportion of sugar supplies or its representa-

Cutting (left) and packing (centre) Paris Lumps. The cooking ovens are behind the pillars (right).

tion on the committee itself. Huntly Drummond was not content with Hanna's posturing and implemented his own brand of insurance for the Canadian refiners by negotiating directly with the British Royal Commission to appoint the Canadian representative as their representative also, thus ensuring his participation at all meetings. To this proposal the British readily agreed, thus cutting off the manoeuvring of the American sugar interests and securing Canada an equal say in future sugar purchases alongside Great Britain and the United States.

On the home front, the need to retain able-bodied men for work within the refinery instead of losing them to the more lucrative munitions factories was temporarily solved by the spectacular expedient of two pay raises in four months, the first in April 1917 of 10% with a further 9% in July. With the introduction of conscription in August, the likelihood of losing more men to serve in the war led to a major extension of past corporate policy, and more women were introduced into the refinery workforce to almost completely take over the packaging functions, while the actual refining process remained the bastion of the men (now dominated by older employees, retirees brought back to fill the gap, and young boys.) Despite these problems, the extent to which Huntly Drummond continued to care for the needs of his workers during this time can be seen in two examples. First, for the men of the workforce who were likely to be called up, Huntly wrote to the union representatives as follows:

I have much pleasure in saying as follows ... any man ... who takes a bond of $50.00 or $100.00, should he be called to the colours at any time during the year of payment, whatever he has paid will be accepted by the company as payment in full, the balance due will be paid by the company, and the bond presented to the man called out. These men will be performing a patriotic duty in serving their country and the Canada Sugar Refining Company would like to take this means of expressing its appreciation of what they will do.

Second, for the new batch of female employees, Huntly's concern that the earlier facilities for changing clothes, washrooms, and new packaging machines were of an appropriate standard for an enlarged female workforce led him to hire his own nieces for a week or two to test out the new equipment prior to its general use. Years later one of the nieces recalled, "You had to be careful folding up the cardboard packages for the granulated sugar because if you did not put the box [into the machine] correctly, the sugar would burst the seam and spill onto the floor."[1] On the packing and setting tables for the production of Paris Lumps things were even more dramatic. "We had to release a valve to let the damp sugar flow onto the trays before being put into the ovens to bake, and if we didn't shut off the valve quickly enough we got a lap full of very warm wet sugar."[2] One advantage the nieces had was the generous allowance of one hour for lunch (as opposed to thirty minutes for the ordinary workers) and since the girls' mother was obviously unsure of their getting a proper meal at the plant, the family chauffeur was sent to collect the girls, take them home for luncheon, and then return them to the refinery for the afternoon session.

By the beginning of 1918, the war in Europe was a constant and seemingly never-ending nightmare, draining both the cream of the manpower and the bulk of the production of the nation. The newly established unionist government under Robert Borden and his mixed bag of Liberals, Conservatives, and Independents was in the process of establishing even more restrictive legislation over the acquisition, processing, and distribution of food supplies. Canadians were restricted to 1½ pounds of sugar per person per month and the retail price had risen to 10 cents per pound from a pre-war level of 4 cents per pound. The winter was particularly severe and there were extensive fuel and food shortages throughout the country. Hanna responded with a typical disregard for the realities of the situation by demanding an increase in sugar production, to which Huntly Drummond replied:

> *Our own refinery has been shut since the middle of December when it totally ran out of raw sugar, but I hope to start up next week. Although it will be on a basis so small that it will probably cost me double the margin in refining until we can get some supplies; however the need is so great here we cannot consider these things at the moment.*

Obviously not satisfied with this answer, Hanna decided to take matters into his own hands and started allocating raw sugar supplies in direct contravention of the previous rotation system developed by his own appointee, Mr. Bruce. Curiously, most of Hanna's allocations were to the Atlantic Sugar Company, who had consistently refused to co-operate with Mr. Bruce and who had previously boasted in their advertisements of their successes in obtaining sugar outside the official system but who were now caught short of raw sugar due to the loss of two ships to enemy submarine attack. As a result of this loss, they besieged Mr. Bruce to allocate them sugar beyond their official quota. He quite properly refused and subsequently complained to Mr. Hanna of the demanding attitude of the Atlantic Sugar Company. Huntly Drummond found this new action of Hanna's intolerable, after having repeatedly worked to governmental directions, even to his own detriment; to see deliberate favouritism being displayed to a competitor who had openly flouted government legislation was just too much. In a series of powerful letters direct to Hanna, Huntly

Drummond condemned Hanna for not supporting Bruce in his efforts to provide a balanced supply for the industry as a whole. He also stated quite boldly,

> *This company alone [Atlantic] has been responsible for any and every trouble that has occurred since the beginning in this sugar control*

and he condemned the tactics of intimidation reportedly used against Mr. Bruce by the Atlantic agents who claimed that if he (Bruce) failed to supply them with sugar they would get Hanna to over-rule Bruce and give them sugar directly. As might be expected, Hanna did not reply to Drummond's statement.

Meanwhile, a new situation arose in the United States where the International Sugar Committee raised the price of sugar bought from the British West Indies for Canada to the higher priced level of the Cuban sugar generally bought for the United States. The impact of this was to immediately raise the costs of production for the Canadian refiners and eliminate any profit that might be gained from exporting sugar into the States or abroad, which would in turn allow the United States refiners to dominate international sales and impose a virtual monopoly price on any future sales to the Allies. Huntly Drummond now had to divert his attention to this problem and it took a considerable amount of his time and effort to get the decision overturned. Failing in yet another attempt to damage their Canadian competitors, the United States refiners changed tactics by using the United States government and its concerns over the overburdened ports and railway system of the eastern seaboard to precipitate a total ban of sugar to Canada.

To understand the context of this situation, one must look back to 1914 when the majority of sugar for the eastern refineries of Canada (especially the Canada Sugar Refining Company Ltd.) came in ships directly up the St. Lawrence River. From 1915 onwards, the use of ships for transatlantic war work forced the company to use the old routing whereby cargoes were off-loaded at New York, transferred to railcars, and brought up to Montreal by train. This of course represented an increased cost of production as well as extra tariffs, but as Huntly stated, "Better an expensive something, than a cheap nothing." For two years supplies had been coming by this alternative system, but now the Port of New York and the regional railway were complaining that the outward-bound war cargoes had to take priority over inbound through cargoes and with no warning they imposed an embargo of all sugar bound for Canada, thus entirely cutting off the inland refiners from their supplies. This produced a situation akin to panic among the Canadian refiners and Huntly Drummond sent several desperate telegrams to both Bruce and Hanna imploring the Canadian government to take an immediate and strong stand on the matter. As Huntly wrote to Hanna:

> *I regard this embargo as another direct blow at Canada. If it is strictly enforced then Canada will get no sugar whatever; and we shall see a [sugar] famine here ... I understand the English members of the commission are doing all they can for us ... but unless you bring pressure to bear, through our government, on the American interests. I am afraid the results will be either a famine or a very large increase in costs.*

Hanna's response on January 22 was less than helpful:

> *"Unfortunately we cannot handle United States Department."*

Faced with the certain continued closure of his refinery for an indefinite period, Huntly appealed directly to higher circles of government and was heartened to hear two days later that Mr. Hanna had been replaced by Mr. H.D. Thomson as Food Controller. Within days, the situation began to improve as strong and repeated representations by Mr. Thomson and G.E. Foster (the newly appointed chairman of the Canadian War Board) persuaded the United States government, the Port Authority for New York, and the railway companies supplying that area to release the stranglehold imposed by the embargo. It must be admitted, however, that for many months afterwards there were varying degrees of embargo re-imposed as circumstances changed and New York became a much more difficult port through which to bring raw sugar. At the same time, the British government withdrew three of its four mail steamships from their normal American routes, drastically cutting the available cargo space in vessels for the shipment of sugar when it did become available. By February 26, Huntly wrote to J.R. Bruce:

> *The difficulty of getting sugar through New York is so that for the Montreal refiners Boston delivery would be far better ... Philadelphia would be out of the question for us on account of the freight rate ... since December 1st, 1917, our refinery has been closed for 36 days and operated for 52 days at about one-half of its capacity ... in the meantime, one of our competitors has been ... running full. You can perhaps realize what a tremendous disadvantage we are working under.*

Despite his best efforts, however, the situation for Huntly Drummond and the company continued to deteriorate as the various governments bickered over the supply of vessels for North American coastal trade. In fact, the British shipping ministry went so far as to accuse Canada of failing to support the war effort.

> *American owners are giving up their entire fleets for war service, we do not think it is proper that Canada should sit back and do nothing to help their own sugar situation.*

Finally at the end of March, the refinery was totally without stocks of raw sugar and the plant had to be shut down and the workers laid off. Incessant ministry demands for production were met by Huntly with initially polite and later terse replies that the company would dearly like to supply anyone with sugar if they could only obtain it. But since the government had failed to assist them in getting sugar, there was simply none available to refine.

As spring arrived, so did the new crop of Canadian Food Board edicts, which included the stipulations that no individual was to have more sugar than would last for fifteen days of ordinary consumption; making candy at home was prohibited; manufacturers were limited to forty-five days of raw sugar supplies; any person or institution with quantities greater than the limits was required to return it to the dealer from whom it was purchased for a refund; and any unreturned excess could be seized by and forfeited to the Crown with various fines and penalties being levied.

Within the food processing industry, which was now the largest section of the company's market, limits were introduced on the use of sugar in ice cream, baking, and candy. Licences for making chocolates, beer, soft drinks, marshmallow products, soda fountain syrups, and desserts were given only to those manufacturers producing prior to March 1918. Retail grocers were forbidden to sell any sugar to a food manufacturer unless a special government permit was obtained; canning using sugar was restricted to the processing of fruit and fruit juices.

These edicts were yet another blow to the company's already restricted output, and Huntly Drummond is reported to have laughed at the stipulation of an upper limit of forty-five days of sugar supply, for as he put it:

> *If we could get more than three or four days worth of raw sugar saved for future use I for one would be grateful ... we are now only working at half our normal capacity which eliminates all hope of a profit on current production.*

Furthermore, the continued drain on manpower through conscription made the maintenance of a core workforce impossible and the obtaining of replacement workers increasingly difficult. To counter this, the company instituted two separate pay raises of 8% in May, followed in October by a further 7% (making a total for the year of 25%.)

By July, the refinery had once again run out of sugar since the allocations of raw through governmental departments failed to match the demand for refined sugar. Huntly attempted to obtain stocks and had almost succeeded when the International Sugar Committee decreed that based upon statistics (supplied by the American sugar refiners), Canada had received all the raw sugar it was entitled to under their quota system, and consequently no more sugar would be allowed into Canada until 1919.

Evidence suggests that by this point Huntly Drummond felt the strain of being constantly beset by disasters and was probably wondering why he was bothering to continue fighting for the Canadian sugar industry in the face of such determined opposition abroad, apathetic support from his own government, and the obvious evidence that his Maritime competitors were openly receiving sugar by flouting the official allocation system. J.R. Bruce did press the case for Canada, stating that Canadian refiners were being unfairly discriminated against. Unfortunately, the International Sugar Committee turned down Bruce's submission and insisted that if Canada wanted additional sugar, it should import it from Great Britain, who in turn stressed that they could not spare any. Thus it was two months before any significant amounts of sugar reached the Canada Sugar Refining Company Ltd. while their Maritime competitors continued to obtain supplies of sugar almost unhindered.

In September, Huntly was on vacation at his family home at Cacouna near Rivière-du-Loup when he was recalled to Montreal to hear of the latest threat to the company; this time the situation seemed to be serious, as the "attacks" were coming simultaneously from the Atlantic Sugar Company and the International Sugar Committee.

In short, the latest proposal by Atlantic was that all shipments of raw sugar for Canada should be restricted to the ports of Saint John, New Brunswick, and Halifax, Nova Scotia, which were of course the local ports for the Maritime refiners.

Huntly Drummond immediately contacted C.C.

Ballantyne, the Minister of Marine and Fisheries, who replied that "the government is very much opposed to the suggestion," which satisfied Huntly, but not Atlantic, who then embarked upon a campaign of submissions to various departments of both the Canadian and United States governments.

In a letter of September 26, 1918, Huntly wrote to their sugar brokers in New York:

> *Mr. Bruce's office has unearthed another plot on the part of the Atlantic to ignore the other refiners. Briefly it is this; to have all the sugar which is used in Canada imported through Canadian ports, which has a patriotic look to Canadians and appeals to Americans as a view of relieving the congestion of New York ... this is merely another instance of the constant plots that are going on, but it shows how wide awake we have got to be with these people.*

Despite Huntly's strongest efforts, the measure gained support from the United States government due to encouragement from the U.S. refiners, who saw opportunities for themselves in the situation. J.R. Bruce pressed his view of the folly of such a decision in a letter of October 28 in which he stated that such a policy decision would:

> *Interfere with Canadian distribution to the extent of causing famine ... Take three times as long to move [the sugar] from the sea board to refinery ... Consume Canadian coal for its transportation by locomotives and steam vessels ... Increase the price of sugar by 20¢ per one hundred pounds.*

Even Lloyd Harris of the Canadian War Mission in Washington raised his doubts of the value of this suggestion and offered his judgement that for the American interests this measure would have two main advantages:

> *To force the Canadian Government to find its own tonnage to carry Canada's Sugar ... and to relieve ... the congestion at railway terminals and piers in New York Harbour.*

He further stated that any suggestion of diverting Canadian ships from their current use in war shipping would only create shortages elsewhere; he continued with the following observation:

> *It is unfortunate that in this matter the recommendations ... are supported by the interests of the Atlantic Sugar Refineries ... I am informed that representatives of this refinery have approached officials at Washington representing their campaign as being on behalf of the Canadian people ... in spite of protests of the Canadian Food Board.*

Finally, saner heads prevailed and Huntly was probably relieved to receive the following letter on October 17, from C.C. Ballantyne:

> *The Government is very much opposed to the suggestion that all sugar for Canada should come in by the Canadian Maritime ports, and I am quite sure the representations that have already been made by the government will entirely prevent this being done ... as for sugar for the Montreal refineries, it is the intention of the Government to use their influence to have it routed in the usual way, and you can depend upon my entire support in this matter.*

Another crisis had passed and Huntly returned to his interrupted vacation but maintained a steady eye on further attempts by Atlantic Sugar during the next month to revive the debate. Fortunately, it never passed into legislation and world events soon made its implementation obsolete. With the signing of the Armistice in November 1918, the horror of the past four years of war was finally over. To celebrate the victory, Huntly ordered a major celebration to be organized at the Union Hotel, which the company would pay for. One retiree of the company who participated in the celebration recalled that following a night of intense partying, a number of the men decided to continue the party at the home of the President (who had left earlier in the evening.) "Rowdy and pie-eyed," they knocked but "weren't let in" so they contented themselves by singing songs under the nearby gas street lamp, but in the morning, amongst the hangovers and the continuing cheers and tears of victory, there were more sober thoughts on what the future might hold.

NING Co. LIMITED
LET
Redpath
SWEETEN IT
Nº3 CANADA SUGAR REFINING Co

CHAPTER TWENTY-FIVE

"An Unfortunate State Of Affairs"

In the immediate post-war period, the shock of being at peace was buoyed by a renewed optimism that within a short period of time the country would be back to normal and that consumer goods would once again start to flow freely to the store shelves. Unfortunately, the devastation in Belgium and France and the virtual bankruptcy of all the European economies meant that it would be some time before things would return to normal "over there." Even in Canada, the dislocation of agriculture and industrial production (because of the needs of the war and, more importantly, government interference) led the Canadian government to decide to retain its wartime restrictive measures for the foreseeable future.

For the Canada Sugar Refining Company Ltd., this continued interference in business was now beyond a joke and was significantly harming the long-term interests of the company. Huntly Drummond wrote to J.R. Bruce in November, informing him that the refinery was closed down on October 30, 1918, and would not re-open until enough sugar was stockpiled to allow for an extended run of production, which would be probably in the new year. To underline this desperation for sugar supplies, Huntly reminded Bruce that, unlike some of his competitors, the C.S.R. Co. Ltd. had consistently put the needs of the country first and had never received all the sugar allocated them for 1918 (having obtained only 110 million pounds of an allocation of 140 million pounds.) His final words of the letter were prophetic, considering the events that were about to engulf the sugar industry.

> *It certainly appears that continuing the Government control of the sugar industry is likely to involve the trade in a fearful mess.*

During the months of December 1918 and January 1919, as war-torn Europe slowly emerged from its heavy restrictions and rationing, housewives went on a buying and stockpiling bonanza that rivalled the events of 1914. The result was an immediate shortage of many of the goods (including sugar) that were amply available under normal buying conditions. This led to a retail price rise, which once again was blamed by the media on the refiners. For the refiners, the continuation of the wartime restrictions on price rises under the Canadian Trade Commission made a

Left: A Federal 3-ton model X delivery truck.

growth of sales within Canada profitless, and the only markets that offered any hope of a profit to cover the losses incurred through the war were overseas. Therefore, Huntly Drummond approached the Trade Commission for approval to tender for a major order of sugar to the United Kingdom. After much bureaucratic delay, the Canadian government approved and although the British Royal Commission rejected a proposal for 40 million pounds at the moderate post-war price of 73 cents per 100 pounds, an agreement was signed in March for the Canada Sugar Refining Company Limited and its fellow refinery in Montreal (the St. Lawrence Sugar Company) to refine 60 million pounds of raw sugar that would be supplied by the Royal Commission on a toll basis, whereby the only hope for a profit would be by processing the sugar quickly and efficiently – a hope that would be cruelly dashed by the events that followed.

At first, things went extremely well and the pre-war investment in improved machinery proved itself invaluable as production for the order reached 134,000, 100 pound bags in March alone, but now disaster struck. Within Montreal, the union of carters, who dominated the activity of shipping goods by wagons and carts, went on strike across the city. By March 22, Huntly was notifying the Royal Commission that the striking carters were attempting to blockade all local factories and that all his supplies of coal were cut off, but that he hoped to be able to cover his agreement to deliver as per contract. By March 25, Huntly had to admit defeat:

> *The Carters' Strike here was carried to such an extent that they absolutely prevented all receipt or despatch of sugar, and finally prevented us from getting any coal to run the plant, compelling us to shut down. Our workmen were perfectly satisfied up to this time, but were terrorized by mobs of striking carters outside who threatened them, and finally, they went out [on strike] themselves. Naturally in going out they put in a claim for increased wages of fifty percent [having already received a cumulative increase of 53% over the war period] to give some colour to their desertion of their employment while a great deal of sugar was in process ... we have had to shut down the best way we could ... and we have decided to make certain repairs and leave the plant closed until matters clarify themselves ... it might be a week or two before we could even make a start and it will then take some time for us to be producing fully ... I do not anticipate ... difficulty filling the second lot ... but it looks like a delay of something like a month in our shipment of refined at the present moment ... As you know we took this order to give steady employment to our men, as we do not think there is very much [profit] in it for us at the price, and it is a very great pity that we have not been able to carry out our good intentions in this respect ... but you will understand that these outside circumstances were too strong for us.*

On March 29, Huntly again wrote to the Commission Agent, Mr. O'Neill.

> *I am sorry to say that matters here are very unsettled indeed: The carters strike, after being apparently settled on Saturday has broken out again worse than ever. Like most strikes they depend entirely on terrorizing employers into meeting their demands, and nobody here in this city is allowed to do any shipping whatever ... Our own men we*

are leaving alone ... and there does not seem very much chance at present of an early resumption of work.

It was not until May 25 that Huntly was able to report that they had returned to work and some 9 million pounds of sugar were ready to be shipped for the Commission order; however this was not without cost, as Huntly said:

We have only been able to do this by cutting our domestic trade shut, and scraping every bin in our stores bare. Had I not been anxious to help out the unpleasant situation ... I should not have attempted to do this, and it has certainly injured our domestic business.

The company was now in a position of not having any sugar available for current production and they were forced to refuse new orders until the Royal Commission contract was filled. During the next month, the refinery used over 2.8 million pounds of its own stocks of raw sugar in order to try to comply with the schedule originally set in the contract.

In the meantime, the shortage of raw sugar supplies on the world market, coupled with the intense buying of available stocks by the British and United States sugar interests, left the Canadian sugar companies scrambling to obtain supplies for themselves. Inevitably, raw sugar prices rose, and when the sugar companies hesitated to buy at the higher prices (fearing a backlash from the consumer when the increased costs were passed on), the government stepped in and insisted that the refiners buy sugar at the higher price due to a reported shortage of sugar in the prairie provinces. After some investigation, Huntly informed the authorities that there was, in his judgement, no significant shortage and that the wholesalers and food processors in the west were simply trying to avoid paying their own western suppliers by crying wolf to the government, hoping the authorities would do exactly what was being done (i.e., requiring the eastern refiners to ship west and suffer a financial loss on every shipment.) Despite this revelation, due to the continued and vocal pressure from the Manitoba and Saskatchewan Wholesale Grocers Association and the Western Canada Fruit Jobbers Association, the government preferred to garner political points than to look at the economic realities of the situation, and the refinery was ordered to stop selling to its eastern wholesalers and to ship railcars of sugar to Winnipeg, Swift Current, Regina, Saskatoon, Calgary, Edmonton, Red Deer, and Lethbridge.

Bowing to this government demand, the company immediately shipped west over 100 railcars of sugar during the following three weeks. They also agreed to send additional loads in the future, subject to the simple condition that first they would have to obtain additional supplies of moderately priced raw sugar. For as Huntly notified the government:

Conditions change so rapidly in the sugar market that at present it is really highly important that no avenue of supply should be shut off to us. The demand for export sugar has been so great that the United States appear to be alarmed that there will not be enough sugar to go round and ... it is impossible to get a single ton of sugar at the present moment from any source.

In response, instead of helping the company obtain more raw sugar, the government chose its own solution and on August 25, 1919, all outstanding export licences were cancelled and directives were made to ship all available sugar west. By the beginning of September, this westward flow provoked a strong reaction from the Fruit Growers of Ontario, whose chairman telegraphed the Minister of Trade and Commerce:

> *Thousands of tons fruit decaying. We have no sugar and have been in this condition for sometime ... Ontario's needs are greater than the Northwest and are surprised such a preference would be given to that district when Western Ontario is the most important in the whole Dominion.*

For this the government had another simple solution: it ordered the Canada Sugar Refining Company Ltd. to ship more sugar to Ontario, while still continuing to supply the western provinces. Stretched beyond all reasonable production capabilities, the refinery ground to a halt when its raw materials did not arrive in sufficient quantity to match its output. As Huntly put it:

> *We have had no choice but to ship out all the sugar we have been making ... and we have not one pound in stock today.*

By October, the British Royal Commission noticed it was not receiving its contracted supplies of sugar and complained to the Canadian government about the "poor business methods" of the C.S.R. Co. Ltd. in not fulfilling their contractual obligations to the United Kingdom. The government responded by forwarding a copy of the complaint to Huntly Drummond with a postscript that he was "not helping Canada's image" by not complying with his contract. Huntly was, to put it mildly, stunned and replied to the government in what can only be termed as sarcastic tones that he could hardly be expected to send all his sugar to the United Kingdom while the government had banned exports, or were they instructing him to break their own laws. Within twenty-four hours, a Ministry telegram lifting the embargo stipulation for this contract was on Huntly's desk, with the incredible end statement that the refinery must continue to send shipments to the western provinces and Ontario as well.

By the end of the month, the refinery had only two weeks of raw sugar in stock. Output was running at 3,000 barrels a day and the outlook for further supplies was virtually nonexistent except at exorbitantly high prices. Inevitably, supplies ran out and the refinery was forced to shut down once again, making a total of five shut-downs so far for the year. On top of this, two separate pay raises of 6½% in May and 6% in June had pushed the costs of production far beyond any hope of making a profit for the year's efforts while the Government of Canada continued to call for sugar to be shipped everywhere at once. Finally in November, Huntly stated flatly that they could do no more and that conditions were impossible to resolve. Among his list of adverse circumstances for the year 1919 were the following:

- *The influenza epidemic sweeping the world had lost him over thirty workers, who were severely ill for a number of weeks, and at least ten were either dead or were not expected to pull through.*
- *The refinery was being worked far in excess of safe levels of output, and maintenance was being neglected to*

maintain maximum output to meet the government demands.

- *The shipping season was almost over and there was no hope of achieving a stockpile of raw sugar for the winter or despatching any more refined sugar to cover the Royal Commission contract (who were now threatening legal action and a total ban on future Canadian purchases if the supplies were not forthcoming).*

- *Domestically the supplies of the company were being dispersed from Prince Edward Island to Alberta with incessant demands from all quarters for increased supplies and the only way to satisfy one customer was to deny others.*

The government now began to recognize that things were seriously wrong and on January 8, 1920, they took strong action by fixing the price of sugar at a retail limit of 16 cents per pound. This reduced the refiners' wholesale price to 14½ cents per pound without regard to the inclusion of any freight costs, which meant that the company would make a loss of 93 cents on every 100 pounds of sugar shipped to Winnipeg or beyond. All complaints from Huntly to the administration were ignored, and the dictates still streamed from the bureaucrats to purchase the expensive raw sugar, process it, and ship it countrywide regardless of cost or losses. This time, however, Huntly was not so compliant as he previously had been and the refinery was temporarily shut down while overhauls and safety repairs were completed to curb the rising levels of industrial accidents that were occurring in order to meet the government's demands. In order to end the ongoing conflict with the Royal Sugar Commission over the amount of sugar still owing, Huntly used his own funds to purchase refined sugar in the United States, paid the exchange duties, and passed it on to the Commission, thus completing the contract and hopefully ending the conflict. Overall he was estimated to have spent about $15,000 of his own money and the company lost over $38,000 on the contract at large.

At this point, Huntly Drummond began to record in his journal his increasing concerns with the unilateral policies of the government towards raw sugar purchases, domestic supplies, and exports, of which the best example was the Canadian Trade Commission directive that in pursuance of "powers granted with the object of ensuring a sufficient supply of sugar to the people of Canada," each refinery was specifically assigned a quota to be produced every month for the next year, irrespective of any problem and that any shortfall was to be made up by increased production at the end of the year. Within the refinery itself, things were not smooth either as the workforce militated for wage raises. On May 19, 1920, Huntly wrote to Sir George Foster, the Minister of Trade and Commerce, on the current situation:

> *Dear Sir George: Knowing of your interest in anything ... which affects the cost of living I am writing to you to inform you of an unfortunate state of affairs ... This year knowing the cost of living had advanced some 12% over last year we voluntarily raised the rate of wages for our men by 17½% ... This year's increase means 130% over the rate paid in 1913 ... the rate of wages now paid is the highest current rate at any manufactury in our neighbourhood. In answer to our offer ... we were presented with demands ... of approximately 60% which would have amounted to over $400,000.00 extra in wages for this*

year, besides a great many other onerous conditions ... we could not accept, so our men have declared a strike ... I have consistently, since the beginning of the War endeavoured to keep the prices ... at the lowest possible point, sacrificing ... very large profits which others considered legitimate ... I know positively that a large number of our men were surprised and pleased at the increase, but the majority being in a union (with foreign leaders) are not allowed to go on working. With the present cost of sugar making a thousand tons [of raw sugar] is worth $440,000.00 compared with the pre-war price of $40,000.00 ... it is impossible for any company to hold large quantities of raw material without turning it over [into refined sugar] immediately ... we may be compelled to re-sell some of the raw sugars we have bought to prevent financial losses ... We do not ask for interference ... It is time we began to work on principle instead of expediency in this country.

Sir George replied on May 20, in somewhat intimidating tones:

It is singularly unfortunate that at the present time ... that the refinery should be shut down or that Canadian refiners should sell a single pound of the raw material which they have contracted for ... sugar we must have if we can possibly get it ... I do want to bring to your attention most forcibly and most seriously the situation which will develop if either or both of the above contingencies happen.

Concurring for once with the official government position, Huntly wrote back the next day:

It is true as you say that a shutdown under present conditions is very unfortunate. It is worse than that : A shut down deliberately caused by the action of alien labour leaders from a foreign country ... is in my opinion a crime. Naturally I shall sell no sugar unless the obstinacy of the strike leaders should make the taste of financing my purchases heavier than I can bear ... I have hopes that our trouble will not be of long duration ... some of our men actually wept when they were ordered out by the union.

But it was not until four weeks later, in June, that Huntly was able to report to Foster:

Our strike has come to a satisfactory conclusion and that the men have accepted the terms which were offered them before they went out ... and apparently see that they made a fatal error in listening to agitators.

Once again production commenced and in order to re-establish a more cordial relationship between management and workforce, Huntly established a committee from both sides to organize the first corporate picnic in the company's history, to take place later in the year.

Unloading coal from a barge for use in the refinery boilers.

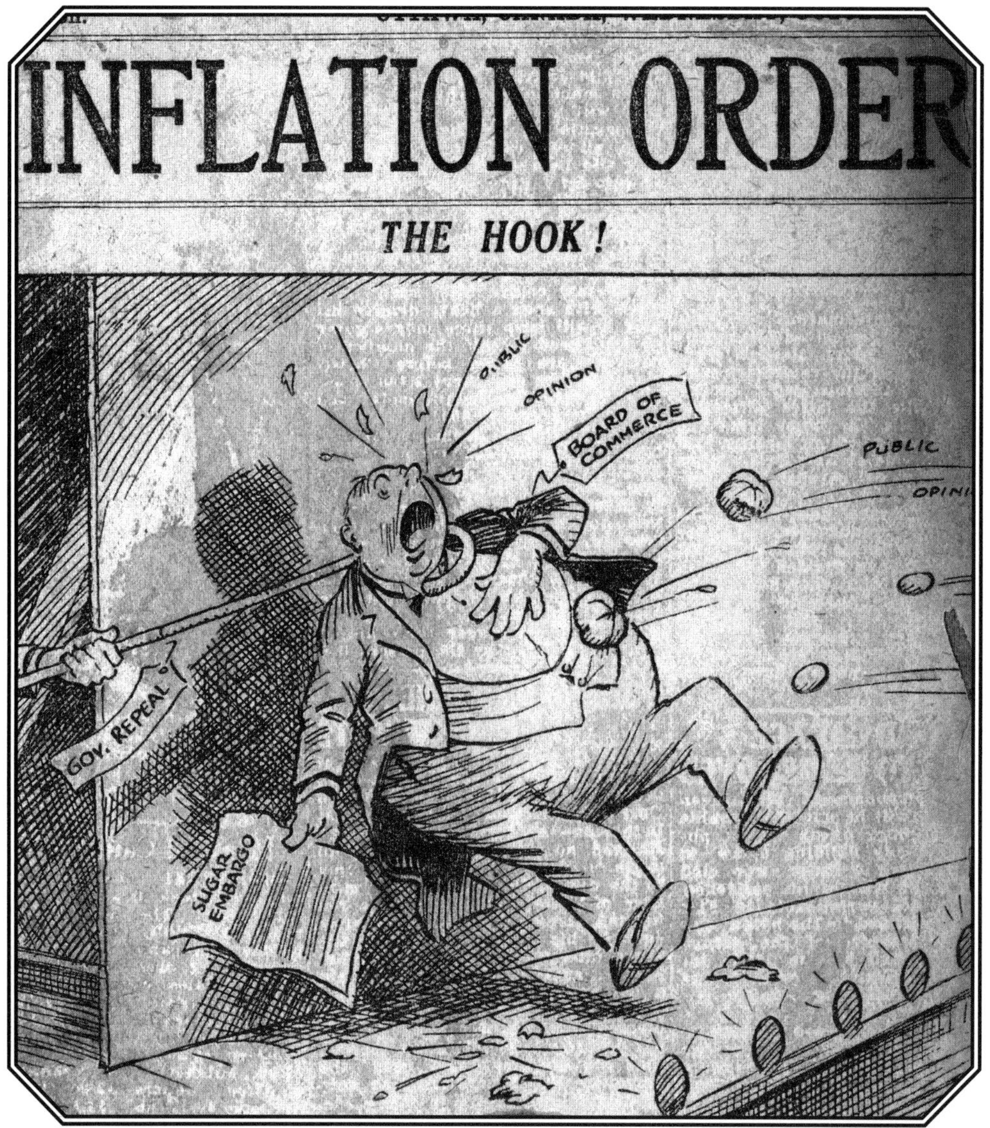

A cartoonist's view of the government reaction to the Board of Commerce embargo decision.

CHAPTER TWENTY-SIX

Dance Of The Millions

For Canadians at large, the summer of 1920 represented the beginning of a new period of economic growth that would last for almost a decade and become known as the Roaring Twenties. Within the sugar industry likewise, financial trends indicated a strong and prosperous future for sugar in a free market system. However, the reality was that the market was anything but free or open and as a result the events that were about to follow led to a disaster that would threaten the very existence of Canada's sugar industry and change forever the nature of the C.S.R. Co. Ltd. The foundation of this future disaster was based upon three major factors. First, the government controlled the refiners and were demanding that two years' supply of raw sugar be purchased, in anticipation of a world sugar shortage. Naturally the refiners expressed grave doubts on the wisdom of this policy, due to the current high prices of raw sugar, and the inevitable financial losses if the price collapsed while they still had excessive stocks of the high priced raws, but the government refused to listen and *ordered* the refiners to continue buying. Second, the government controlled the prices of refined sugar and chose the customers to whom the refiners were allowed to sell. Third, all exports of sugar to the United States were banned. In fact, the government's position on sugar was made abundantly clear in a ruling of the Board of Commerce of Canada on June 11, 1920, when, in an investigation of prices and profits in the sugar industry, they stipulated:

> *The Board will not recognize prices based upon replacement values on a rising market. It will be its duty in good time, as it hopes to as carefully protect the trader on a falling market by permitting him to average his costs down as it must now carefully protect the consumer in compelling the trader to average his cost up ... It will prohibit all others than refiners from selling to wholesalers. It will prohibit wholesalers from buying from others than refiners. It will prohibit speculators from buying or selling at all. It will define the legitimate profits of refiner, wholesaler and retailer respectively ... Furthermore ... as a warning ... the board proposes to recommend the prosecution criminally of every firm and trader whose profits seem to the Board to be unfair or whose prices seem to it to be unjust and unreasonable ... This Board is entitled as a court, to declare its own jurisdiction, subject to reversal by the Supreme Court ... to which court only, an appeal lies from this Board upon a matter of jurisdiction be made.*

On July 1, 1920, Parliament was prorogued and the

controls on the exporting of sugar lapsed. This provided a heaven-sent opportunity to the refiners of Canada to recoup some money on the high prices they were paying for raw sugar by exporting to the United States where prices were, on average, almost 5 cents per pound higher than Canada and were likely to rise even higher. However, the Department of Trade and Commerce poured cold water on their hopes with a somewhat sinister letter on the fifth when they stipulated:

> *It is extremely desirable however that there should be no change in actual practice looking to the provision of sufficient supply of refined sugars for Canadian consumption ... provide first for home consumption before using the privilege of export ... The Government has still in reserve some powers which might if necessary be exercised to bring about the result desired.*

Huntly Drummond immediately wrote to Foster explaining the refiners' position and asked if the government realized the sacrifice being made by the refiners by not exporting to recoup their increased costs, incurred not as a result of normal business decisions but as a direct result of governmental directives on purchasing raw sugar. During the following week, prices of governmentally controlled refined sugar rose and at one point reached 17 cents per pound, while in the United States it was 24 cents per pound. However, the raw price the refiners were forced to pay to acquire stocks as per governmental directives was 20 cents per pound. Thus the refiners lost 3 cents on every pound they sold. Desperate to solve this problem, Huntly pressed the authorities to either allow unlimited exports to the United States or allow Canadian prices to rise to natural levels. The Canadian government did neither and the losses went on.

In the midst of this time of corporate difficulties, one of the few lighter moments came on August 21, 1920, with the holding of the "First Annual Picnic of the employees of the Canada Sugar Refining Company Limited" at Otterburn Park (St. Hilaire.) In a specially chartered train, employees were picked up at Bonaventure Station, St. Henri, Pointe St. Charles, and St. Lambert to be transported to the picnic site. Once there, the day's activities consisted of a series of sporting events with various prizes for each category.*

To complete the day's events, a dance was held with the popular steps of the day, (the foxtrot, Spanish Boston, one-step, and two-step) being blended with the more traditional waltz, gavotte, lancers, and cotillion. The day ended with refreshments being served on the train back to Montreal. According to the numerous letters of appreciation from employees to Huntly and the members of the organizing committee, the objectives of re-establishing a good relationship between employer and employee were successfully achieved.

On the business front, however, things were not as cheerful, as throughout August matters worsened. Raw prices continued to rise while refined prices were frozen, and the refiners were not only forbidden to make a profit but were not even allowed to minimize their losses. Eventually the "bubble" burst when, attracted by the abnormally high prices

* For details of the sporting events see Appendix 3.

of sugar in the United States, sugar from Holland, Germany, Czechoslovakia, and other European sources suddenly poured onto the U.S. market, panicking the Cuban growers who had previously held back their sugar to force up prices. The Cubans reacted by slashing their prices and pushing even more sugar onto the U.S. market. World raw prices tumbled and in some cases United States banking interests were forced to draw in their extensive credits to American refiners and a number of sugar refiners were forced into liquidation. This shock wave of a glut of sugar in the American market had a major spill-over effect for the Canadian industry; once again Huntly Drummond wrote to Sir George Foster:

> *I wrote to you last on the 6th of July in regard to the sugar situation, since that date the situation has developed normally, as I knew it would, and the position of the refining industry in Canada is today a serious one. While prices were going up, the Board of Commerce did not allow the refiners to sell their sugars at replacement values ... at the same time, the Government prohibited the export of sugars from Canada. Since then the price of raw sugar has declined from 22¢ a pound to less that 10¢ a pound ... unless the Government implements the promise made by the Board of Commerce to protect the refiners when prices did decline the consequences will be disastrous to the interests of Canada.*
> *(September 30, 1920)*

As prices continued to fall in the United States, the American refiners dumped more and more sugar into Canada where prices were higher. The media began to editorialize on the question of why U.S. sugar was retailing at 11 cents a pound while Canadian made sugar was wholesaling at 19.7 cents a pound. Huntly attempted to answer the question in an open letter to the papers:

> *The Board of Commerce, a while ago, when sugar was scarce ... compelled the Canadian refiners to stock up with raws in order that a constant supply might be assured. The Boards order required refiners to lay in sufficient to carry them through till January 1921. This they did and only three weeks ago there was $63,000,000.00 worth of raw sugar on hand in Canada, which is about enough to last till the New Year. Most of this had to be purchased at peak prices ranging from 19 to 21 cents a pound. It is being sold now refined at an actual loss ... But I think that I can say that as soon as present stocks of sugar are used up the price will drop. It may even go as low as 7¢ a pound.*

As an example of the losses faced by the Canada Sugar Refining Company Ltd. alone during this period, the figures for October 10, 1920, showed that the refinery had in stock 74,089,668 pounds of raw sugar, nearly 20% of the total Canadian supplies, and for every 1 cent that the future price of sugar dropped, another $740,897 would be lost. Despite these figures being made public and that over the previous two-week period the C.S.R. Co. Ltd. had lost $2.5 million, the newspapers exploded with a series of articles on the iniquities of the sugar "barons" for denying the Canadian consumer its "divine right" to low prices. The sacrifices of the previous seven years when Huntly had, almost single-handedly, persuaded the Canadian refiners to forgo profits in favour of the consumer were totally ignored or forgotten;

instead, the only thing that most reports stressed was that Canadian sugar prices were higher than those of the United States. At governmental levels, the Board of Commerce reviewed the situation and determined that sugar from the United States was being dumped into the Canadian market thus unfairly competing with the Canadian refiners, and in compliance with its promise of June 1920, it ordered the termination of U.S. imports for the next two and a half months in order to allow the Canadian refiners to work off their high-priced stocks and at least minimize their losses (there being no illusion within the industry that any kind of profit could be made; in fact by this time, the C.S.R. Co. Ltd. had lost nearly $5 million.)

This decree of exclusion produced a backlash of indignation across the nation, which consisted of complaints in every newspaper in the country, "instant" protest rallies at government offices, and telegram campaigns to M.P.s in Ottawa, all of which were carefully co-ordinated by the wholesale and industrial food manufacturers who were expecting this decree and who wanted the cheaper U.S. sugar. So vehement were these methods that the government was overwhelmed at the so-called "public" outcry against the Board's decision. Recognizing that his newly formed Conservative/Liberal government stood to lose heavily in the polls over this issue, the Prime Minister, the Right Honourable Arthur Meighen, and his Cabinet issued an Order-in-Council only forty-eight hours later, suspending the Board edict on the grounds that the Board had no authority to make such a decision. Caught completely off guard by this reversal of governmental commitments, the C.S.R. Co. Ltd. and every other refinery in Canada immediately shut down and the nation's entire sugar-refining workforce of over 2,500 workers was laid off.

Even the members of the Board of Commerce who had issued the original ruling were shocked by this Cabinet decree (which was in direct violation of the expressly stated legal jurisdiction of the Board given June 11) and some members of the Board wrote to the newspapers on the issue to persuade the public of the honest need of the refiners at this time. Additionally, Rhys D. Fairburn, the Sugar Controller for Canada, stated in an article published in the Toronto *Daily Star* on October 15, that much had not been revealed in the widespread campaign of anti-refiners' articles that would have justified the refiners' case; specifically, that it was directly due to governmental controls and directives that the refiners had purchased sugar at a time when they had strongly argued against just such purchases; that throughout the period the refiners had saved the Canadian consumers millions of dollars by selling sugar in Canada at 18½ cents per pound while exports to the United States would have fetched 27 cents per pound; and that they were entitled to sell off their sugar and break even, which would regrettably mean temporarily higher prices for Canadian consumers in order to ensure the future existence of the industry as a whole.

Inevitably, this appeal was swamped by a tide of counter-articles demanding that nothing must come before cheaper prices and that the disaster was "just too bad" for the refiners. To this latter contention the Cabinet eventually took heed, issuing an Order-In-Council on October 21, 1920, permanently cancelling the edict of the Board of Commerce with the justification that,

> *The decree exceeded the authority of the Board and ran counter to the purpose and intent of the legislation from which the Board derives its power.*

In other words, the powers of the Board were biased from the beginning. For as long as raw sugar prices rose, the Board had absolute power to suppress market prices, ban exports, and dictate purchasing policies in favour of the consumer, but once raw prices fell, the Board was expressly forbidden to cushion the losses of the refiners by temporarily maintaining a higher price against the consumer. To make matters even more insulting, in the same statement it was admitted that the sugar industry, by following governmental decrees, had saved the Canadian consumer over $20 million at the refiners' expense.

The refiners were now faced with the imminent collapse and destruction of the entire Canadian sugar industry. Losses were mounting by the hour, and without some form of assistance, the industry was almost certainly doomed. Backed by letters of support from the other refiners, the Board of Trade, and some major industries, Huntly Drummond pressed the government for short-term loans, and while the government admitted in private that the industry was entitled to assistance, publicly they merely convened a Cabinet meeting to discuss the issue and permitted Huntly to attend in order to state the refiners' position. At this meeting, Huntly made the following statement:

> *Our contention is that the conditions which have brought about our present situation, and which the present order of the Board of Commerce was designed to relieve were not of our making ... We willingly admit that the Government, in establishing control of our business was acting in the best of faith and for the public welfare. Our claim is that the Government created these bodies to protect the consumer in a rising market ... that they promised to protect the trader on a falling market and that they have tried to fulfil that promise. We appeal to that sense of Justice which should find a resting place in the breast of every honest man for such a promise to be fulfilled. As it is now stated [by the Cabinet] that there was not a warrant-in-law for the action of the Board we do not press for the order to be confirmed, but leave our claims for redress in the hands of the people and the Government of Canada with complete confidence that justice will be done.*

In retrospect, it is hard to understand why the refiners did not question the government Order-in-Council, when by the Board of Commerce's own ruling it had clearly stated:

> *This Board is entitled as a court to declare its own jurisdiction subject to repeal by the Supreme Court ... to which Court only can appeals from this Board upon a matter of jurisdiction be made.*

Whether there was a desire to avoid a national crisis that this issue could have precipitated between the jurisdiction of the government and the Courts, whether the refiners wanted to rely upon a quick solution by obtaining governmental funds in exchange for not challenging the Order-in-Council, or whether Huntly really believed that an appeal to honest justice, fair play, and the relative merits of the case would work, we cannot know. The fact remains, however, that the unsteady political situation and the need to carry votes weighed more than "honest justice," therefore the Prime Minister immediately leaped upon the opening left by Drummond by asking, "Do I understand that you do not challenge the government's position that the order of the Board of Commerce was without warrant-in-law?"

Huntly carefully replied, "We do not challenge the governments' claim, but."

"Then there is no further need of continuing this hearing," interrupted the Prime Minister. "The object of this meeting was to give you an opportunity of showing why, in your judgement the government's order suspending the order of the Board of Commerce should not be final. As you do not take issue with the government's case, there is no need to go on." Then, without allowing Huntly to finish his sentence, or giving anyone else the opportunity to speak, the Prime Minister adjourned the meeting and left the room, closely followed by his Cabinet colleagues, leaving Huntly alone and speechless. The whole meeting had lasted approximately sixteen minutes and the Canadian sugar refining industry was left to its own devices to save itself; a few days later the members of the Board of Commerce quietly resigned.

The repercussions of this disaster on the Canadian sugar industry were immense. The debt burden was so great that it exceeded the face value of the stocks of sugar, machinery, and properties of all the Canadian sugar refineries, amounting to over $25 million. Huntly Drummond stated that the debt for the C.S.R. Co. Ltd. alone, amounted to the average profit for thirty-seven years' work. To shore up the company in the immediate term, Huntly emptied his savings accounts (lending $40,000 to the company) and mortgaged his home along with other properties he owned. He sold off almost 90% of his outside stock holdings and worked for the next eight years without pay. However, this betrayal by the government was a deep blow to Huntly after all his years of loyal commitment to the best interests of Canada. For some time, his health failed and he was even rumoured to have died. Fortunately, he recovered his strength and resumed his business dealings once again, although not with the same vigour that he had exhibited in previous years.

This abandonment of the sugar industry by the government, despite its earlier repeated pledges of support, resulted in a major crisis of confidence within the Canadian business community. This was especially true within those industries holding large inventories by governmental directive, and some elements argued for a review of the matter, as seen by an article in the *Financial Times* of October 23, 1920.

> *WHAT ABOUT THE MORAL ISSUE IN THE SUGAR SITUATION? NOW CLEARLY UP TO THE GOVERNMENT*
>
> *Are the people of Canada essentially honest?*
>
> *Is the Government of Canada an honest Government?*
>
> *These seem to be the issues that are apparently overlooked by the newspapers who, with practically one accord, are condemning the efforts of the Sugar Refiners of Canada to get the Government of Canada to live up to the agreement made with them on the Government's behalf by the Board of Commerce.*
>
> *The situation, briefly, is that the refiners, under Government control, were forced into doing business at a potential loss on a guarantee that they would be protected*

on a falling market to the same extent that the consumers had been protected on a rising market.

The people benefited by this arrangement to the extent of at least thirty million dollars at the expense of the refiners.

Now the refiners are threatened with additional losses which may run into twenty or thirty millions more, and the people, as represented by the Government and the newspapers are welching on their bargain.

Like Germany, which found excuses for declaring a treaty a mere scrap of paper when it profited her to do so, Canadians, in this instance, are being made to appear as violators of an agreement fairly made in their behalf and fairly carried out by the refiners.

And the astonishing thing about it is, that so far as The Financial Times is aware, not a newspaper commentator and no minister of the Government, has given a single thought to the moral aspect of the case. All they are concerned about, apparently, is to save the sugar consumers three cents a pound on their sugar for the rest of the year by taking that amount out of the pockets of the refiners, where it rightfully belongs.

Granting that the Board of Commerce is without legal power to apply to the situation the remedy of its making, what about the equity of the case?

Is the Government so powerless as to be unable to carry out a contract, made in its name and in its behalf, after it, or the people it represents, have enjoyed all the advantages of the undertaking, merely because to do so involves some financial sacrifice?

What will be the effect upon future efforts of the Government to regulate business in Canada if it leaves the sugar industry in the predicament which it is now in, admittedly as a result solely of Government interference?

There are plenty of ways of keeping faith with the refiners without necessarily inflicting injury upon the consumers.

If the Government is honest and square it will find without delay the means to help them out.

The Financial Times refuses to believe that, in this matter, the Government and the newspapers reflect the real spirit of the Canadian people.

It believes that the Canadian people are essentially honest and square, and that they do not desire to go back on a bargain merely because it will profit them to do so.

Despite this, the government remained unmoved and the industry was left to fend for itself.

The raw sugar shed and coal crane dwarf the boys scavenging in the mud bank of the drained Lachine Canal in this April 1927 photograph.

CHAPTER TWENTY-SEVEN

Picking Up The Pieces

In the immediate aftermath of the government's abandonment of the sugar industry, it became a case of "every man for himself," as the companies scrambled to unload their immense holdings of sugar. Prices collapsed as the quantity of sugar being supplied far exceeded the amount demanded by the market. By the fifth of November 1920, the price per pound for sugar had dropped from 19½ cents to 14 cents. Additionally, the Dominion Sugar Co. aggravated the situation even further by using its advantage as a domestic grower to offer its sugar at 13 cents. By the twelfth, wholesale prices were down to 11 cents per pound and still dropping. The losses involved were estimated at $150 million and sugar company stocks were next to worthless. Finally in an attempt to take a pause from its precipitous fall, the industry as a whole closed down in mid-November. In a report of November 14, 1920, the Toronto *Sunday Morning* quoted:

> *This is the gloomiest day in Montreal's financial history that ever came to it; and everyone is in dread of what Monday will bring forth. At least one hundred and fifty million dollars has been lost in buying raw sugar at over 20 cents a pound - now worth less than 10 cents. The five Canadian refineries are all in it and nothing but liquidation is ahead of every one of them, save the one in Western Ontario which has a beetroot outfit in its organization. But there was an immense loss made independent of refining companies. And the loss of over ten millions in buying Atlantic Refining Co. shares has also to be included in the slump ... there are more ruined men and families in Canada ... than ever before at any time.*

Throughout the next few months of 1921, the prime principle upon which the C.S.R. Co. Ltd. worked was survival, and every cost reduction possible was implemented. Prices continued to fluctuate wildly on the wholesale market, and rumours were rife on the subject of closures or business failures. In October, the President of the Atlantic Sugar Co. resigned and that company had to undergo a complete financial restructuring. Within the refinery, in September, all temporary or extra labour was dismissed. Outside warehouses were vacated, and estimates of the minimum staff required to carry on the work of filling bags and shipping were made.

In addition, the method of bringing in raw sugar via railcars was now deemed as unnecessarily expensive and was reversed in favour of the direct shipment of stocks by boat to the refinery. By the end of 1921, matters were so uneconomic for sales within Canada that many of the refiners stopped selling sugar and turned their attention to exports into the markets of Europe.

At the beginning of 1922, the growth in the Canadian economy created a demand from the sugar industry for the removal of many of the wartime restrictions and a drastic cut in freight rates. The Maritime refiners claimed that the current rates of shipment effectively cut them off from supplying the west of Canada and demanded a special allowance to permit their competing in that area. Because of this, Huntly was forced to appear before the Railway Board to argue for the maintenance of the status quo, based on the argument that under the current economic problems within the sugar industry, everyone wished to expand their market area, including the C.S.R. Co. Ltd., and that preferential treatment of one particular group of refiners would damage the business of the rest.

Despite contradictory claims by other refining representatives, Huntly's argument won out and the rates remained the same. Unfortunately, this precipitated a retaliation from the Maritime interests in the form of a price war across Canada throughout April and May. Shortly afterwards, opportunities became available for sales to Germany, France, and Great Britain due to poor harvests of their beet sugar crops. The Atlantic and St. Lawrence sugar companies once again ceased selling sugar in Canada and concentrated exclusively on Europe, while the C.S.R. Co. Ltd. maintained its position of selling to Canadians first, thus maintaining a competition with the Dominion Sugar Co.

By the close of the year, although prices were still relatively low compared to 1919/1920 and the huge losses incurred at that time were still being worked off, the industry as a whole had stabilized and government statistics showed an expansion of the industry in 1922. The long journey to recovery seemed to have begun.

As a step towards the much-needed recovery of the industry, the refiners agreed to change the basis upon which sales had, up till that point, been made. This change was reported in an article in the Montreal *Gazette* on January 20, 1923.

> *A feature of the wholesale grocery trade is the new term on refined sugar sales. Heretofore, buyers could place an order at a certain price, getting deliveries as they required them, if the price declined they got the benefit of it; if the price advanced they got delivery at the prices they ordered; consequently buyers were operating at the refiners expense. This has all been changed during the past week or two ... All sales in future will be in car load lots, with terms cash, fourteen days less five per cent. So that buyers in future who wish to speculate in refined sugars will have to do so with their own money.*

Throughout the following spring, prices fluctuated in the Canadian market, reflecting in miniature the wild price swings of the U.S. market, where the huge post-war growth of stock speculation led it to become the economic centre for trading sugar as well as many other products. In another article in the *Gazette* on March 13, 1923, the current situation was examined and showed how powerless the individual refiners had become as stock market trading had swallowed up their past influence.

> *New York has become the world's sugar centre ... Before the War, Hamburg's Continental beet sugar made world prices*

but the fulcrum of the sugar trade is now located here owing to the volume of trading having been more than tripled on the local exchange during the past year ... Transactions recently have been running from 75,000 to 100,000 tons daily ... It is estimated that sugar brokers commissions amount to as high as $60,000.00 a day. The market has been so active that many refiners are deploring the speculation that has arisen.

Rumours of mergers and take-overs between U.S. refiners were constantly being floated and then denied. Eventually even the U.S. government began to take note that extraordinary events were taking place, and they launched an investigation to study the situation. For once the Canadian papers did not attack the local sugar refiners as it was recognized that to obtain sugar on the world market, the Canadian businesses had to pay the going price for the product. By April, the sugar that had been $8.15 for 100 pounds on January 1, 1923, was fetching $11 on the Montreal market. On April 19, the U.S. federal government instituted an injunction completely shutting off trading in sugar futures unless backed by actual ownership or control of the commodity. It also considered criminal proceedings against various officials of the New York Coffee and Sugar Clearing House Association, while across the United States groups of women banded together calling for cuts in sugar prices and boycotts of the refiners. In the Canadian market, things were not as wild as New York but the increased prices did cause rumours about the sugar "barons" to circulate once again, and a Special Committee of the House of Commons summoned the heads of the sugar companies to Ottawa to see if there was a "sugar trust" to artificially raise the price of sugar.

Just before the committee sat, the Finance Minister introduced his new budget and took particular stock of the sugar price situation, as he stated on May 12.

Taxation on sugar is a burden on the whole people and a reduction of the duty on sugar is one of the most direct means of lending relief. During the War sugar advanced to very high prices. After the War there was for some time a reduction until prices have become somewhat normal. Quite recently however we seemed to be returning to War time conditions with respect to the cost of sugar ... In some quarters it is alleged that speculation in the United States ... is the cause of the rapid increase of prices ... In the United States ... householders in many places are organizing boycott campaigns ... nothing of the kind has yet occurred with us but the consumer is everywhere feeling keenly the burden of high cost.

Mr. Fielding then instituted duty reductions consisting of 50 cents per 100 pounds on both raw and refined sugars. He also set a limit for the implementation of the dumping clause to a price in the market of 8 cents per pound so that below a market price of 8 cents per pound no dumping legislation would apply but above 8¢ per pound it would apply.

This created an immediate problem for the refiners since a uniform drop of 50 cents per 100 pounds on both raw and refined imports represented a reduction on refined sugar of 50% of the duty but only 40% on the raw sugar, thus weakening the domestic protection. In addition the on-again off-again dumping clause based upon an arbitrary price gave no security to the refiners. With this in mind, the refiners went into the meeting of the Special Committee determined to show that they were due for some consideration instead of criticism. Testifying before the committee, Huntly pressed the refiners' viewpoint as reported by the Ottawa *Citizen* on May 15, 1923.

> *That advances in the price of sugar were due to the increased price of the raw product and that the Canadian Sugar Refiners were to be thanked for adsorbing a portion of this increase rather than to be blamed for increases, was the claim of H.R. Drummond ... who declared that raw sugar had risen $3.25 per hundred pounds since January last while the price charged by the Canadian refiners had been advanced only $2.64 ... The witness referred to the clause in the budget which removes the dumping duty after sugar is increased over eight cents a pound as "a staggering blow to the refiners" ... with this clause removed sugar purchased cheaply on the New York market might be dumped into Canada at a lower price than [Canadian] refiners could obtain their raw material ... "Your view is that you and the public are victims of circumstances over which you have no control?" asked Chairman McMaster "Absolutely, and the refiners are hit worst" replied the witness ... Mr. Drummond strongly objected to submitting figures on the cost of production by his Company. It would give United States competitors an unfair advantage he argued.*

The following day, similar objections to revealing cost figures were put forward by J.W. McConnell, President of the St. Lawrence Sugar Refinery, and W.A. Hobbins of the Atlantic Sugar Refineries. The committee eventually agreed to hear these details in a closed session but also reserved the right to issue a statement concerning costs if such a statement were deemed necessary. At the same time, news came from New York that the injunction taken out on trading had been struck down by the courts and speculative trading was once more to begin.

In the following days, representatives of farmers in the Ontario beet growing industry were called to testify and took the opportunity to criticize the Dominion Sugar Co. for its handling of the farmers, which was mistakenly taken by an uninformed section of the press as applying to the industry as a whole. In the end, the committee came to the conclusion that the refiners were as subject to the outside influences of the market as was claimed and cleared them of all possible wrongdoing.

For the remainder of the year, prices continued to fluctuate as speculative buying again predominated in the United States following the failure of the injunction. The C.S.R. Co. Ltd. continued its programme of shifting towards direct shipments, with the year-end total being divided 75% direct and 25% by rail. Also at the end of the year came news that the Berlin (now renamed Kitchener) sugar beet plant of the Dominion Sugar Co. was to be disposed of, as it had not operated for two years.

Early in 1924, a memorandum was put together by the Atlantic and St. Lawrence companies with the proposition that all the sugar companies unite in the purchasing of the raw sugar through a single agent. Their argument was that in doing so several advantages could be gained, including economies of operation by the reduction of commissions to agents; efficiency of operation by purchasing jointly; greater confidence amongst members on the actions of their competitors; and lessening the individual workload for each company by joint action.

It also concluded that no significant opposition would be expected from the government or the public and the plan should be implemented as soon as possible.

Huntly viewed this memorandum with interest but his instincts told him that the repercussions from such an association would be far greater than the others estimated. He expressed his caution on the matter in a response dated February 26, 1924.

> *In reference to memorandum to hand this morning, the scheme as a whole appeals to me. I think the idea is a feasible one and a considerable saving would be made by putting in force such a scheme. The detail of working it out would be more difficult on account of our geographical situation but I am inclined to think that even this difficulty might be overcome.*
>
> *The political aspect of the case, I consider, is a most serious one at the present time. I feel that we would get an immediate re-action from Ottawa on this scheme becoming known to the public as it would very quickly. Individually, members of the Cabinet would undoubtedly agree that we were quite within our rights, but collectively, as a Government, I do not consider that they have the backbone of a jelly fish. We would probably make enemies of the B.W.I. producers, and in all likelihood would lose what little sympathy we may have at present from the consuming public.*
>
> *If it were known that we were buying collectively, as it very quickly would be known, it would naturally be thought that we were also selling collectively as sure as two and two makes four ... Under the present conditions I feel that we would make a serious political blunder if we made any move along the lines suggested, and I would suggest that this matter be left in abeyance until we see what happens at Ottawa this Spring.*

After considering Huntly's reply, the memorandum was withdrawn and business continued as usual.

On May 26, all production ceased at the C.S.R. Co. Ltd. for just over half an hour as the workers and directors gathered together to witness the presentation of a gold watch and a purse of money by H.R. Drummond to William Hurst, a boiler stoker in the plant. According to the newspaper accounts, this award was for:

> *The deed of bravery ... performed on Sunday, May 11, when Mr. Hurst rescued from drowning, James Lawrence, son of a War widow residing in Pointe St. Charles. While at his work in the boiler room, he heard cries from the bank of the Canal ... and found that a small lad was struggling in the water ... Mr. Hurst who had been working in the intense heat of the boilers was covered with perspiration. He showed no hesitation but jumped into the icy water fully dressed, and brought the boy to the side of the Canal where he was helped out ... Three cheers were given for the hero who received his honours bashfully.*

Later that summer, news came of the establishment of a new sugar beet operation in Manitoba with a projected capacity of 18,000 tons per year, followed in November by the announcement of plans for yet another in Raymond, Alberta. The Canadian sugar industry was becoming positively crowded. As might be expected, the proposition of this extra capacity coming on the market the following year pressed the current refiners to sell additional sugar now, which caused a drop in the overall price of sugar through till the end of the year.

With the coming of 1925, Huntly ordered the installation of a new set of boilers and turbines to produce power for the refinery, effectively establishing the refinery as self-sufficient in energy requirements. In addition, any excess steam produced was adopted for use throughout the refinery in the melting, boiling of the sugar, and heating of the refinery buildings in winter. Plans were also drawn up for the continuation of the alterations interrupted by the Great War. Much of the machinery involved was now long past its working prime and costs of repairs were mounting. Especially vulnerable in this regard was the Steffen Process, which by this time was becoming an outdated and expensive method of processing raw sugar. It was decided that in the upcoming year, this entire system would be removed, subject to market conditions existing at that time, and the bringing in of raw stocks by direct shipment would be increased from their current level of 83% to 90%.

Elsewhere in the Canadian sugar industry, construction of the Raymond, Alberta, beet refinery was continuing with over 6,000 acres of sugar beet being contracted for delivery that year. In addition, two other plants were projected for development in 1926 if the Raymond plant succeeded. In the Maritimes, Acadia Sugar was recovering its financial stability after a number of poor years, and in December 1925, the Atlantic Sugar Co. announced a major refinancing scheme to vastly increase its base capital. Huntly was in no doubt that unless they moved to improve and modernize, the C.S.R. Co. Ltd. would soon be left behind by the competition.

Throughout 1926 and into 1927, the entire efforts of the company were centred on the overhauling of the machinery. Unfortunately, for reasons that will be explained below, no documents or statements remain from 1926 to detail this major undertaking. We are, however, fortunate that a detailed series of photographs were taken and survive to show us in graphic detail the final removal of the old Steffen Process and the redevelopment of the plant. The year 1927 likewise is undocumented on this matter except for a set of three pencilled pages of notes dated July 1, 1927, which give a list of the costs of the renovations to that date.

Upon completion of the bulk of the project in July 1927, Huntly decided the time had come to give the workers a reward, and he instructed the re-convening of the Picnic Committee. As in 1920, the event took place in August at Otterburn Park, St. Hilaire, with a special train picking up the employees at various points in the outlying districts of the city. The various games and contests were almost unchanged, with only the prizes being noticeably different, showing the changes that had occurred in people's tastes in only seven years.*

Huntly contributed the cost of refreshments during the day as well as a coupon redeemable for a one-dollar bill for spending as the employee wished. The day was, as in the previous event, rounded off with a dance containing most of the same types of dances but with the special addition of a Prize Waltz, for which the winning couple each received a $10 gold piece donated by Huntly.

* For details of the sporting events see Appendix 3.

First wagon floor in the "W" or Steffen Process building, January 1926.

Sawdust washer floor, "W" building, January 1926.

Vacuum pan floor, "W" building, April 1926.

Demolition of the old powerhouse, August 1926.

Demolishing the old chimney, September 1926.

Centrifugal floor, "W" building, March 1927.

The value of such events to the employees of the company can be seen in the warm letters of thanks received by Huntly, one of which in particular deserves repeating as it came from one of the employees on the Dance Committee for the Picnic.

> *Enclosed herewith is a letter from the Picnic Committee which speaks for itself, but I feel that I cannot let another occasion pass without telling you how much your kindness and generosity is appreciated by all your employees. Being in a position to hear the opinion and comments of the men down here at the Refinery, I am sure you will forgive me writing to you, when I say that it is only to pass on the fact that in my opinion there is not a better loved or more popular President of any firm that I know of ... You just seem to know how to spread kindness around without any effort and in just the way that is most appreciated by the men you employ. Of course this is confidential as nobody knows that I have taken this liberty - but I believe that "the deeds of good men should live with them" not after.*
>
> *Yours sincerely,*
>
> *Gretta Wainwright*

Construction of the new powerhouse, October 1926.

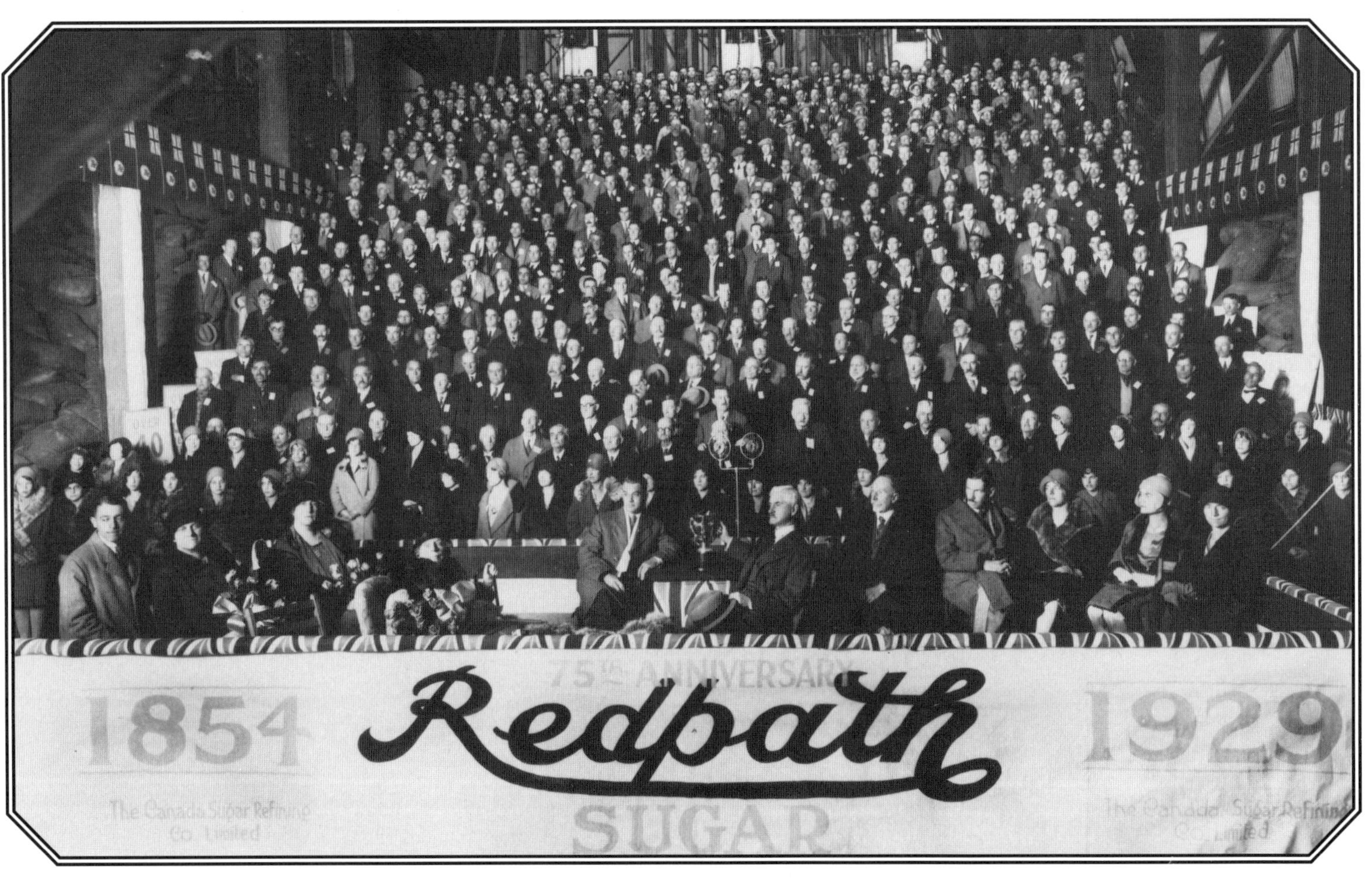

The official employee photograph, in the raw sugar shed, for the seventy-fifth Anniversary celebrations.

CHAPTER TWENTY-EIGHT

The Final Straws

"A state of uncertainty exists in the Canadian Sugar Industry." These were the leading words of an article in the February 10, 1928, edition of the *Financial Post* and they referred to a condition that had begun the previous November. At that time, the Canada Sugar Refining Co. Ltd. had completed its renovations and was well prepared for a successful competitive season in 1928. But at the end of the month, news broke of a major shift in the method of selling sugar by Cuba. Previously, all trade was carried on by free agents but now the Cuban government took control into its own hands, restricting production and sales from a past high of 6 million tons per year to 4 million tons, of which 3.05 million tons were to be sold to the United States and another 150,000 retained for domestic consumption. The remainder was offered on the government-controlled market and was immediately bought up by European refiners at prices well above the normal margin. This left the Canadian refiners totally wanting in their supplies for either domestic or export sales and forced a panic scramble to secure raw sugar for the spring start-up at greatly increased prices.

This was not a good way to start the year and it got worse in April with the news of the new tariff schedule, which proposed to substantially increase the rate on raw cane sugar to assist the beet sugar industry to a position where it could supply 50% of the Canadian sugar consumed. By this measure, production levels for the cane refiners would be slashed by over 80% from their capacity output making any production totally uneconomic for everyone except the beet industry. While immediate protests and memorials to the government did achieve a degree of relief, the attitudes displayed by the government indicated clearly that matters were not likely to improve. Soon, rumours began to circulate of secret negotiations among the cane refiners for the consolidation of some of the businesses, but no one openly stated that such things were occurring.

No detailed records of how these situations affected the C.S.R. Co. Ltd. exist, but since 35 workers were laid off in November, 55,200 square feet of property was sold to the Northern Electric Co. Ltd., and the last horses in the stables were sold, we can assume that the remainder of 1928 was not a good year for the company.

Despite these bad indications for the company, Huntly's concern for his workers obviously did not diminish, for in January 1929 the entire refinery was closed for a day while the workforce and all heads of departments were addressed by Arthur Gaboury, Secretary General of the Province of Quebec Safety League. According to the newspaper review of the address:

> *Mr. Gaboury reminded the men that prevention of accidents in industrial plants was not a matter for the employers only ... the duty of the men remained ... and they must accept the responsibility of adopting the safety methods introduced for their benefits ... under the provisions of the Workmens Compensation Act.*

From March to August 1929, Huntly was in Europe on a mixture of business for the Bank of Montreal and personal sightseeing. It also perhaps gave him an opportunity to reflect upon his own future and that of the sugar company for which he had worked for most of his adult life. Upon his return, in a pleasant change from other times, he came back, not to a problem but to a celebration of the seventy-fifth anniversary of the founding of the original company under John Redpath and the corresponding fiftieth anniversary of the establishment of the Canada Sugar Refining Co. Ltd. by George Alexander Drummond. Over 600 employees were gathered in the large raw sugar shed and ranked according to years of service. On the platform, members of the Drummond family led by Huntly accepted the proposals of congratulation from the workers. In addition, a large silver loving cup was presented to Huntly by the company representative, Mr. A.H. Thompson. In his acceptance of this gift, Huntly said:

The loving cup presented to Huntly Redpath Drummond at the seventy-fifth Anniversary celebration in 1929.

> *I am profoundly moved by this demonstration ... the occasion appeals to me especially because I believe that the feelings permeating this ceremony is genuine. I have friends in the various walks of life, but no friend I esteem so highly as my fellow workers of the Canada Sugar Refining Company ... the main thing in this Company that distinguishes it from many others is that we have here a united spirit of co-operation.*

Despite all these glowing statements and praiseworthy gifts, world overproduction of sugar made prospects for a recovery seem weak, but even these poor prospects were eliminated with the Wall Street crash in October, which reverberated around the world and precipitated similar panics in other international stock markets. The boom of the twenties was definitely over and as the economy of Canada slid, with that of the rest of the world, into the massive depression that was to follow, the death knell for the C.S.R. Co. Ltd. had begun to ring.

During the next few months, reports of sugar prices collapsing, uncertainty about Canadian tariffs, U.S. protectionism for its own industry, and the determined preferences towards Canadian beet sugar interests led Huntly to decide the time had come to leave the company as its President. Negotiations were opened for a merger with a competitor although the name was kept secret, as the report from the Montreal *Star* of December 18,1930, shows:

Huntly Redpath Drummond, President of the Canada Sugar Refining Co. Ltd. has sent a circular letter to shareholders which suggests that the Company may sell out to another company ... The head offices of three of the largest sugar companies in Canada are in Montreal. These are St. Lawrence, Atlantic and Canada ... Whether any of the local companies are interested in acquiring Canada Sugar is not known, but the possibility of a merger of such companies has often been gossiped about in the financial district ... Another company which might be in the market is the Dominion Sugar Company which is a beet sugar producer and has a plant in Wallaceburg, Ontario ... This company might, it is suggested, be seeking a steadier production status by going into cane production. It is not expected that any details of the proposed sale will be divulged until they are submitted at the meeting which has been called for Saturday morning December 27 at 10 o'clock at the head office of the Company in Montreal.

According to the letter the meeting is a special one "especially for the purpose of considering and if thought fit approving the sale and transfer of a portion of the company's undertaking, consisting of its sugar business to a new company for the considerations, and upon the terms and conditions set out in an agreement which will be submitted to the meeting".

It is also announced that the meeting will also be special "for the purpose of considering and if thought fit approving, ratifying, sanctioning and confirming a by-law which will be submitted to the meeting authorizing the division of the assets of the company ratably among its shareholders after the completion of the said proposed sale of its sugar business and to authorize the directors after completion of such division to take such action as may be necessary or convenient to enable the company to surrender its charter or in the alternative to cause the company to be wound up under the winding - up act ... As there is but a small distribution of the shares of the C.S.R. Co. Ltd. Most of them in the hands of the Drummond family, it is considered a foregone conclusion in the street that the deal will go through.

Nothing whatsoever remains of any official documentation of this last period. However, discussions with retired executives of the company indicate that the initial approach was made by the Dominion Sugar Company President, C.H. Houson, following a failed attempt by Dominion to acquire the St. Lawrence facility. It was they who took the lead in all subsequent negotiations, so that the Canada Sugar Refining Co. Ltd. ceased to exist at the end of December 1930, as it was taken over by the Dominion Sugar Co. to create a new entity entitled the Canada and Dominion Sugar Co. Ltd. C.H. Houson became President of the new concern, but Huntly remained on the Board as Vice-President until 1957, when he died at the age of ninety-three. It is also asserted that to placate the feelings of a "crusty old gentleman," the take-over was always referred to as a "merger" when in the hearing of Huntly Redpath Drummond.

The question remains, however, why records on such a vital part of the company history should be missing when other minor information from earlier years survived. The answer is quite simple. Following the merger and the installation of Dominion Sugar executives in the Montreal offices, a disgruntled employee of the Canada Sugar Refining Co. Ltd. deliberately burned all the company books and records in his charge, covering the last ten years of the company history, which is why we know so little about the change of this proud company into its new form as a division of a larger corporation.

What we can deduce and what is known is that shareholders of the Dominion Sugar Company received 300,000 shares of the new Canada and Dominion Sugar Co. Ltd. while the Canada Sugar Refining Co. Ltd. shareholders obtained 200,000. Nothing was left to chance in showing which side of the business was in charge.

The story of the Redpath and Drummond "Sugar House" had ended, and success in the future was to rest on the making of an industrial leader that could compete in both the national and international markets.

Huntly Redpath Drummond

CHAPTER TWENTY-NINE

Postscript

It might be supposed that following his surrendering control of the C.S.R. Co. Ltd., Huntly Drummond at the age of sixty-six would have taken a well-earned retirement. In fact, nothing could be further from the truth, for like John Redpath, Peter Redpath and George Alexander Drummond before him, Huntly Redpath Drummond continued to advance in business circles. During the next quarter of a century, he was involved extensively in many commercial and social projects both in Canada and abroad. He was especially active in the Bank of Montreal, becoming President from 1939 to 1942, then Chairman of the Board from 1942 to 1946, whereupon he retired from active business in the bank; but he retained the title of Honorary President until his death in December 1957.[1] It is also recorded that he turned down the offer of a senatorship, being only the second person to that point in history to do so.

Within the company proper, the various elements of the "Canada" were assumed within the Dominion group. But it is not the place of this book to tell that part of the story. That will be left to the second part of this work, which will document the establishment and growth of the sugar beet industry in Ontario, followed by the continuing history of the company after the merger in 1930 up to the present day.

Appendix 1

"ESSAY ON SUGAR and GENERAL TREATISE ON SUGAR REFINING"
by R. Niccol
published in 1864 by A. Mackenzie & Co.

The process of sugar refining, as conducted on the Venetian system, may be divided into two distinct branches, that of separating the earthy and other impurities, and that of expelling the molasses or liquid portion of the sugar. The former is effected in what is termed the 'primary' operation, by bullocks' blood and lime water; and the latter by claying ... or liquoring ... .

To refine sugar under this liquoring system, it is first boiled in pans with about six quarts of bullocks' blood and quantity of lime water; the scum and impurities produced by the successive additions of blood being continually removed till the sugar casts up only a clear milky froth, which indicates the removal of the sugar, a little of the finest indigo is added. The heat of the fire is applied direct to the pans containing the sugar. The next process is that of evaporating the purified saccharine solution or liquor, which is effected in open shallow pans by a moderate fire; the boiling being continued till the sugar has acquired the proper degree of viscidity, which is easily ascertained by what is called the proof-rod or proof-stick, which is simply a piece of wood in the form of a small oar. When the evaporation is completed, the hot sugar liquor is removed from the evaporating pans into coolers, in which it is stirred or agitated by men with oars, to prevent the formation of a crust. It is then granulated with an oar, the violent motion of which, continued for some time during the cooling process, destroys the viscousness of the sugar and completes the granulation, the beauty of the refined product depends in a great measure on the perfection of this process. The next step is to fill the moulds, which are earthen or metal vessels like inverted cones, the apex or tip of which is placed downwards ... .

At the extremity of each mould is a hole for the escape of the syrup or liquid portion of the sugar. However, before the moulds are filled with the sugar from the heater ... they are washed in a cistern, the hole or aperture in the tip of each mould being thereafter temporarily closed with a plug or piece of old filter-cloth, to prevent, in the meantime, the escape of the syrup or liquid portion of the sugar, on the moulds being filled. This done, the moulds are arranged in rows, with their points downwards on the ground-floor of the sugar house, where they are filled; which apartment is known as the fill-house; the moulds being supported by small cast-iron cones, called stools, which are placed between them for this purpose ... .

The filling of the moulds with the clarified and concentrated sugar is effected by men with scoops or basins, as they are called; and in order to prevent adhesion of the more solid portion of the sugar to the moulds, and to lay the grain of the mass evenly and regularly throughout, the sugar at the surface of each mould is detached from the sides, when the mass is allowed to remain at rest till it has acquired some degree of firmness. The sugar in the moulds is then stirred around three or four times, and the first part of the refining process is finished. The moulds with their contents are next day hoisted to an upper floor of the refinery, where they are placed upon stoneware or earthen jars or pots, the stoppers or plugs at the tip of each mould being previously drawn out, and an iron bolt, called a pin, thrust up the aperture in the tip. This causes to exude a quantity of syrup or liquid sugar, which, at the end of about 24 hours, is removed, and the pots, after being emptied of their charge, replaced under the moulds as before ... .

The process of liquoring then commences, by pouring upon the surface of the sugar in the moulds a portion of the liquor above removed, which, passing through the sugar, carries off the coloration and leaves the goods proportionately whiter as each successive time it is applied: the syrup or drainage being of course done by the pots beneath, which are emptied and replaced frequently ...

The various kinds of syrup thus produced are used for future operations: these are known as second syrups, third syrups, etc., respectively, as the case may be. By this means the brown syrup is expelled, and the sugar is in due course found to reach the proper degree of whiteness, which is ascertained by tipping the loaf out of the mould. The proper degree of whiteness now having been attained, the liquoring process is discontinued, the loaves are left to dry for some time: the last "brushing-off" of the loaves is then made. The brushing-off process consists in scraping the surface of the sugar in the moulds with a small iron blade, the soft or clay sugar being thus removed from the face base of the loaves, and collected in a wooden box ... .

Each mould, after the loaf has undergone brushing-off is simply knocked against a small wood block, or against the inside of the brush-off box, for the purpose of slacking the loaf in the mould which is then replaced upon the pot, and so on throughout the whole process ... .

This being accomplished, the next operation is the "turning-off". This consists in placing the tip of the loaf between three cutting knives fixed in a conical frame, the latter being made to revolve at a comparatively quick motion, by turning a handle connected to the gearing: the motion, however, may be achieved by machinery. This operation is performed in a few seconds in the case of each loaf, and removes the coloured sugar from the tip which is thus finely dressed off and finished. The apparatus used is termed a turning-off or turning-down machine, the loaf is then placed in a wooden frame ... and left to stand till the following morning when they are each wrapped in lining or white paper, and placed on racks in an extra-heated apartment of the refinery, containing an arrangement of heating steampipes, and termed the stove, with the views to their being rendered perfectly hard and dry. The loaves, when stove-dried (which is accomplished in about four days), are then rolled up in outside or blue-coloured paper, fastened with twine; after which they are piled up in rows against the pillars or columns of the sugarhouse, or other supports and tip pointing in opposite directions alternately. The loaves so treated are now ready for the market ... .

The above is the process for what are termed "single" loaves, i.e., sugar once refined: but double refined sugar is prepared by a process in which the clarification is effected by the whites of about 200 fresh eggs to each panful of sugar, and with fresh water instead of lime water.

Appendix 2

THE FAMILIES OF JOHN REDPATH AND GEORGE ALEXANDER DRUMMOND

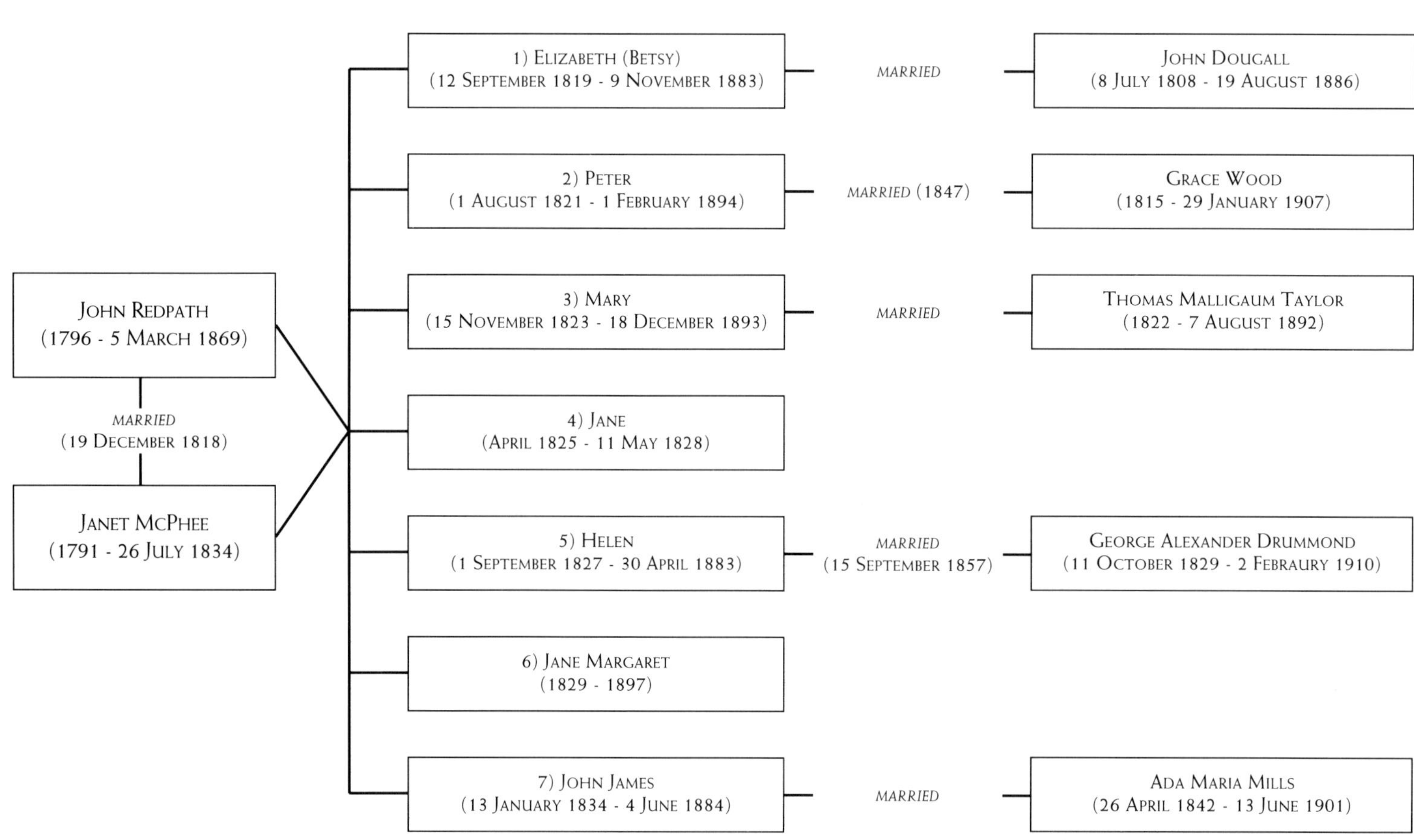

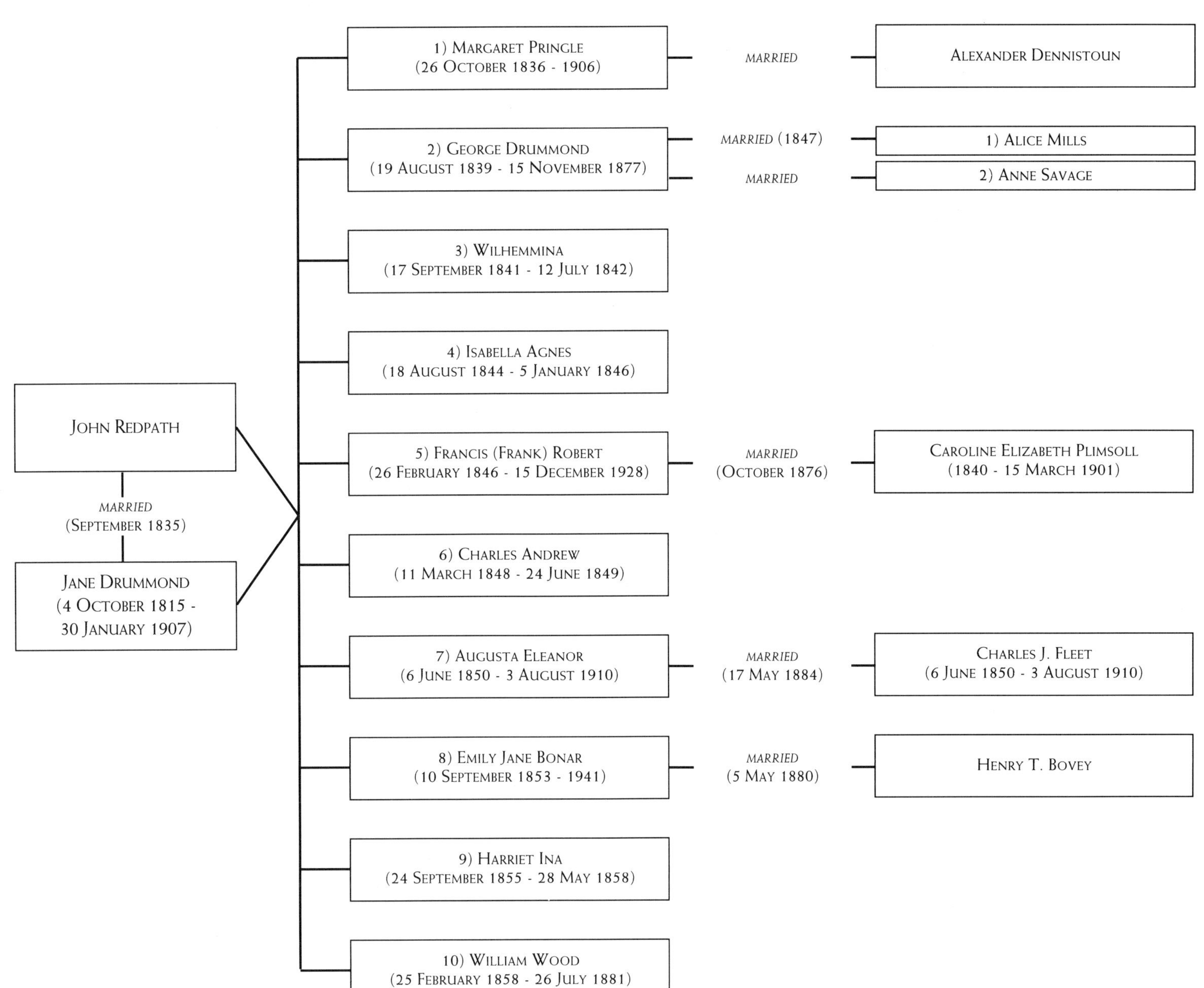
John Redpath
married
(September 1835)
Jane Drummond
(4 October 1815 -
30 January 1907)
1) Margaret Pringle
(26 October 1836 - 1906)
married
Alexander Dennistoun
2) George Drummond
(19 August 1839 - 15 November 1877)
married (1847)
1) Alice Mills
married
2) Anne Savage
3) Wilhemmina
(17 September 1841 - 12 July 1842)
4) Isabella Agnes
(18 August 1844 - 5 January 1846)
5) Francis (Frank) Robert
(26 February 1846 - 15 December 1928)
married
(October 1876)
Caroline Elizabeth Plimsoll
(1840 - 15 March 1901)
6) Charles Andrew
(11 March 1848 - 24 June 1849)
7) Augusta Eleanor
(6 June 1850 - 3 August 1910)
married
(17 May 1884)
Charles J. Fleet
(6 June 1850 - 3 August 1910)
8) Emily Jane Bonar
(10 September 1853 - 1941)
married
(5 May 1880)
Henry T. Bovey
9) Harriet Ina
(24 September 1855 - 28 May 1858)
10) William Wood
(25 February 1858 - 26 July 1881)

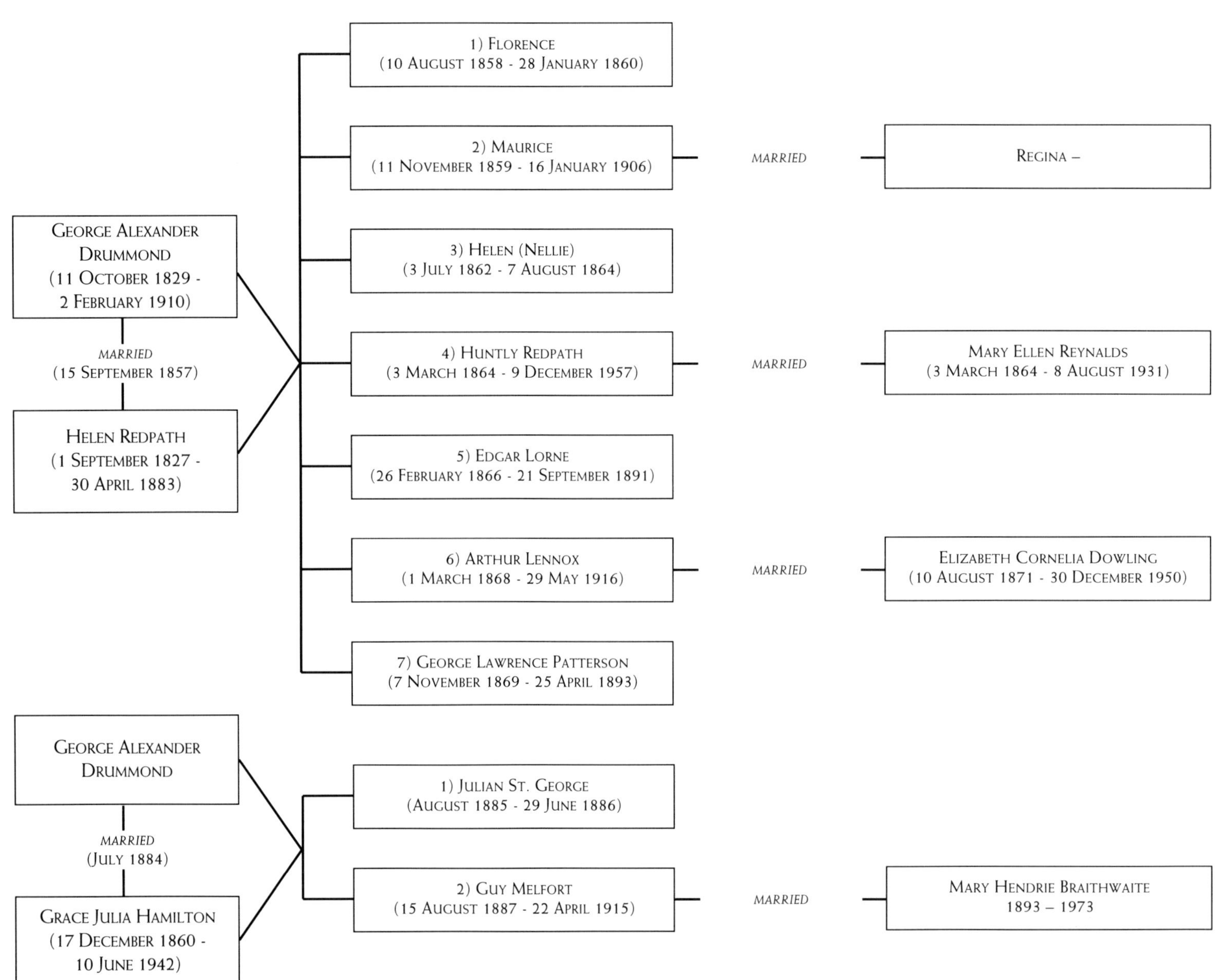
George Alexander Drummond
(11 October 1829 - 2 February 1910)
married
(15 September 1857)
Helen Redpath
(1 September 1827 - 30 April 1883)
1) Florence
(10 August 1858 - 28 January 1860)
2) Maurice
(11 November 1859 - 16 January 1906)
married
Regina –
3) Helen (Nellie)
(3 July 1862 - 7 August 1864)
4) Huntly Redpath
(3 March 1864 - 9 December 1957)
married
Mary Ellen Reynalds
(3 March 1864 - 8 August 1931)
5) Edgar Lorne
(26 February 1866 - 21 September 1891)
6) Arthur Lennox
(1 March 1868 - 29 May 1916)
married
Elizabeth Cornelia Dowling
(10 August 1871 - 30 December 1950)
7) George Lawrence Patterson
(7 November 1869 - 25 April 1893)
George Alexander Drummond
married
(July 1884)
Grace Julia Hamilton
(17 December 1860 - 10 June 1942)
1) Julian St. George
(August 1885 - 29 June 1886)
2) Guy Melfort
(15 August 1887 - 22 April 1915)
married
Mary Hendrie Braithwaite
1893 – 1973

Appendix 3

1920 EMPLOYEE PICNIC, LIST OF GAMES AND PRIZES

Taken from an original programme in the collection of the Redpath Sugar Museum

GAME	1ST PRIZE	2ND PRIZE
Baseball: Mechanical Department and Refinery vrs Office, Yard and Stores	50 cigars to the Winners /	25 cigars to the losers
Boys' Race: 6 - 8 year olds (50 yds):	School Outfit	Running boots
Girls' Race: 6 - 8 year olds (50 yds):	School Outfit	Running boots
Boys' Race: 9 - 11 year olds (50 yds):	Baseball bat	Flashlight
Girls' Race: 9 - 11 year olds (50 yds):	Music Case	6 Handkerchiefs
Thread & Needle race: 9 - 11 year olds (50 yds): (Ladies to run and men to thread the needle - Ladies' prize only)	Ladies Umbrella	Fountain pen
Single Young Men's Race (100 yds):	Pair of rubber boots	Flashlight
Young Ladies' Race (75 yds):	Electric Toaster	Manicure Set/Perfume
Egg and Spoon Race (50 yds): (Married Women - Employees Wives only)	Electric Iron	5 lb Box Laura Secord Chocolates
Married Men's Race (100 yds):	Ham	Load of Kindling Wood
Fat Men's Race (must weigh 200 lbs or over) (50 yds):	Silver Plated Gillette Safety Razor	Box of Cigars
Employees with the largest Family:	(Husband) Case of Pipes/(Wife) Ham	
Gentlemen's Three Legged Race: (75 yds):	2 Fountain Pens	2 Pipes

Putting the Shot:	Gillette Safety Razor	Box of Cigars
Hop, Step and Jump:	Gold Plated Gillette Safety Razor	Book of Street Car Tickets
Married Ladies' Race (50 yds):	$15.00 worth of bed sheeting	6 Table Knives
Sack Race (Gentlemen) (50 yds):	Case of Pipes	Fountain Pen
Smoking Race (50 yds): (competitors must light their pipes after starting and must be smoking when finishing)	Suit of Overalls	2 lbs Tobacco
Human Wheelbarrow Race (30 yds): (change at half way)	2 Shirts	2 Tins Cigarettes
Committee Race: (75 yds):	Set of Carvers	Box of Cigars
Tug O' War: 6 men per side:	One 2½ dollar Gold piece to each man on winning Team	
Swimming Race:	Gents Umbrella	Bathing Suit
Rubber Duck Hunt:	2 Ducks	

1927 EMPLOYEE PICNIC LIST OF GAMES AND PRIZES

Taken from an original programme in the collection of the Redpath Sugar Museum

Soft Ball Game: Yard and Store vrs All other Employees — Cup to Team, Belt Buckles to winning members; 50 Players Cigarettes each to losers

	1ST PRIZE	2ND PRIZE	3RD PRIZE
Boys' Race: 8 yrs & under:	Roller Skates	Running boots	Baseball
Boys' Race: 10 yrs & under:	Ingersoll Jr. Watch	Baseball & Catchers Mitt	Baseball
Girls' Race: 8 yrs & under:	Beautiful Doll	Set of Dolls Dishes	Running Shoes
Girls' Race: 10 yrs & under:	School Outfit	Running Shoes	Eversharp Pencil
Girls' Race: 12 yrs & under:	Pair Silk Stockings	Silk Scarf	Box of Handkerchiefs

Hop, Step & Jump:	Electric Table Lamp	Flashlight	50 Players Cigarettes
Broad Jump:	Silk Umbrella	Pen Knife	50 Players Cigarettes
Putting the Shot:	Carving Set	Fountain Pen	Pen Knife
Sack Race:	Eversharp Pen & Pencil Set	Alarm Clock	Pipe
Thread & Needle Race:	Silk Umbrella	Ivory Brush & Comb	Lady's Compact
Single Men's Race:	Silk Umbrella	Pipe	50 Players Cigarettes
Young Ladies' Race: (Employees Only)	Cut Glass Bowl	Handsome Tray	Set Table Linens
Egg and Spoon Race:	Aluminum Ware	"Pyrex" Pie Plate	"Big Ten" Brush Set
Married Men's Race:	Half Ton Coal	Load Kindling Wood	Safety Razor
Fat Men's Race:	Half Ton Coke	Load Kindling Wood	Safety Razor
Gentlemen's 3-legged race:	2 Pipes	2 Shaving Cabinets with extra Razor	
Employees (100 yds): 20 yrs Service or Over:	Valuable Camera	Load Kindling Wood	Box 50 Cigars
Married Ladies' Race: (75yds) (Employees' Wives):	Half Ton Coke	Half dozen Stainless Knives	Set of "Big Ten" Brushes
Smoking Race:	Cut Glass Sugar and Milk	Flashlight	50 Players Cigarettes
Human Wheelbarrow Race: (change half way):	2 Silk Umbrellas	2 Tins Cigarettes - 100 each	
Committee Race:	50 yards 40 inch sheeting	Fountain Pen	50 Players Cigarettes
Tug O' War (Departments):	$2.50 Gold Piece to each of six winners		
Departmental Relay Race Three Man:	3 Eversharp Pencils		

Appendix 4

THE DEVELOPMENT OF THE MONTREAL REFINERY SITE 1854-1930

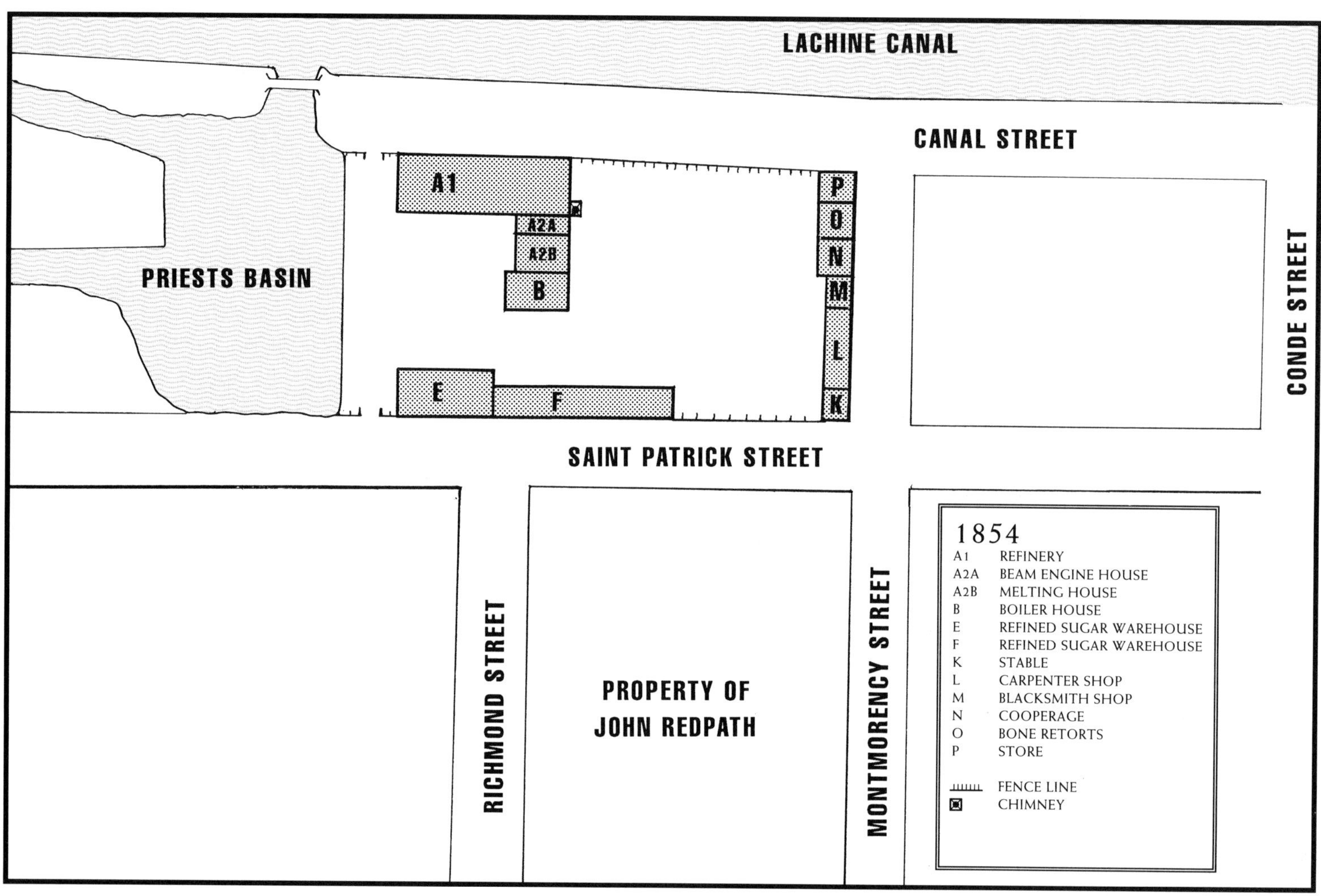

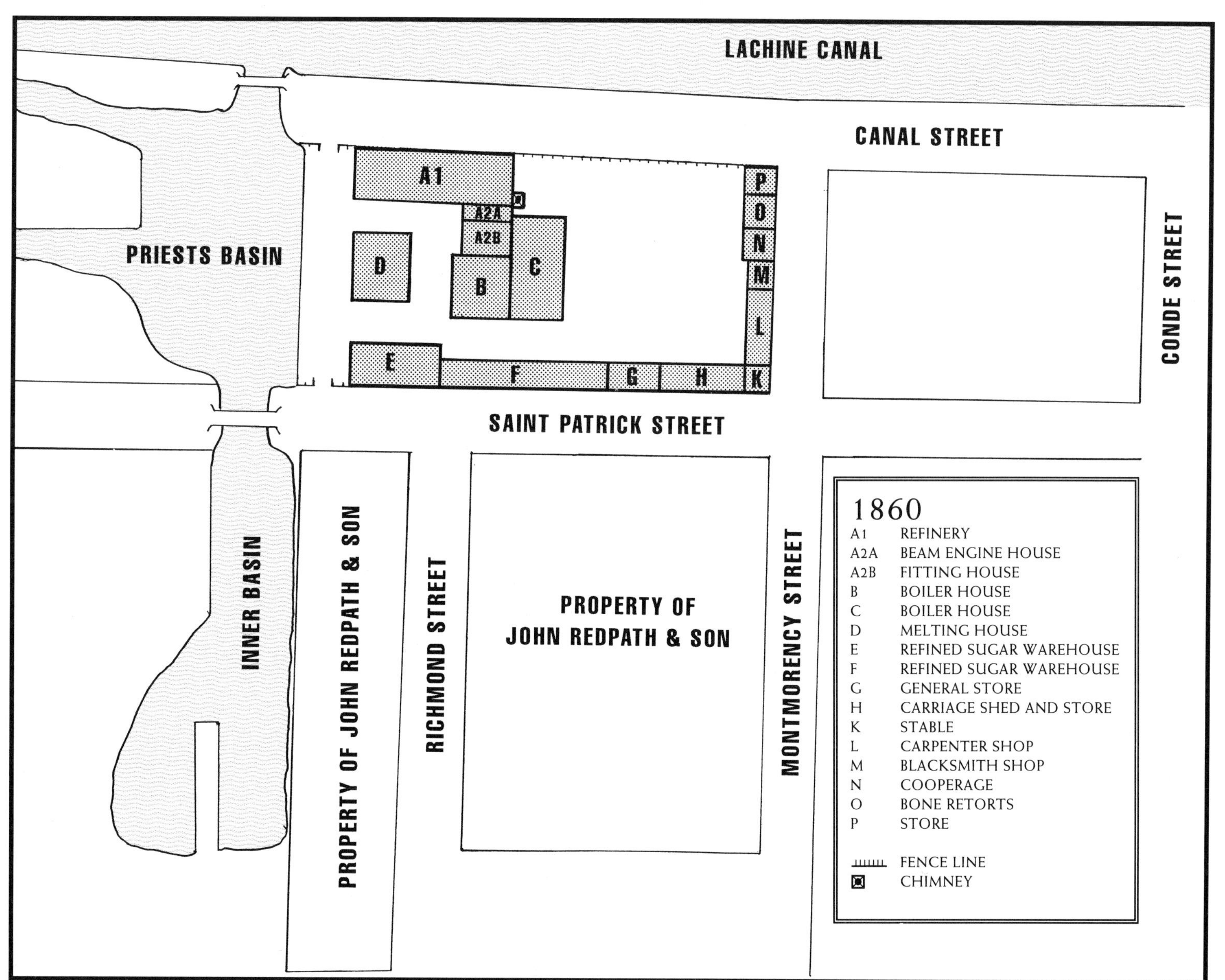
LACHINE CANAL
CANAL STREET
PRIESTS BASIN
A1
A2A
A2B
C
D
B
E
F
G
H
K
P
O
N
M
L
CONDE STREET
SAINT PATRICK STREET
INNER BASIN
PROPERTY OF JOHN REDPATH & SON
RICHMOND STREET
PROPERTY OF
JOHN REDPATH & SON
MONTMORENCY STREET
1860
A1 REFINERY
A2A BEAM ENGINE HOUSE
A2B FITTING HOUSE
B BOILER HOUSE
C BOILER HOUSE
D MELTING HOUSE
E REFINED SUGAR WAREHOUSE
F REFINED SUGAR WAREHOUSE
G GENERAL STORE
H CARRIAGE SHED AND STORE
K STABLE
L CARPENTER SHOP
M BLACKSMITH SHOP
N COOPERAGE
O BONE RETORTS
P STORE
FENCE LINE
CHIMNEY

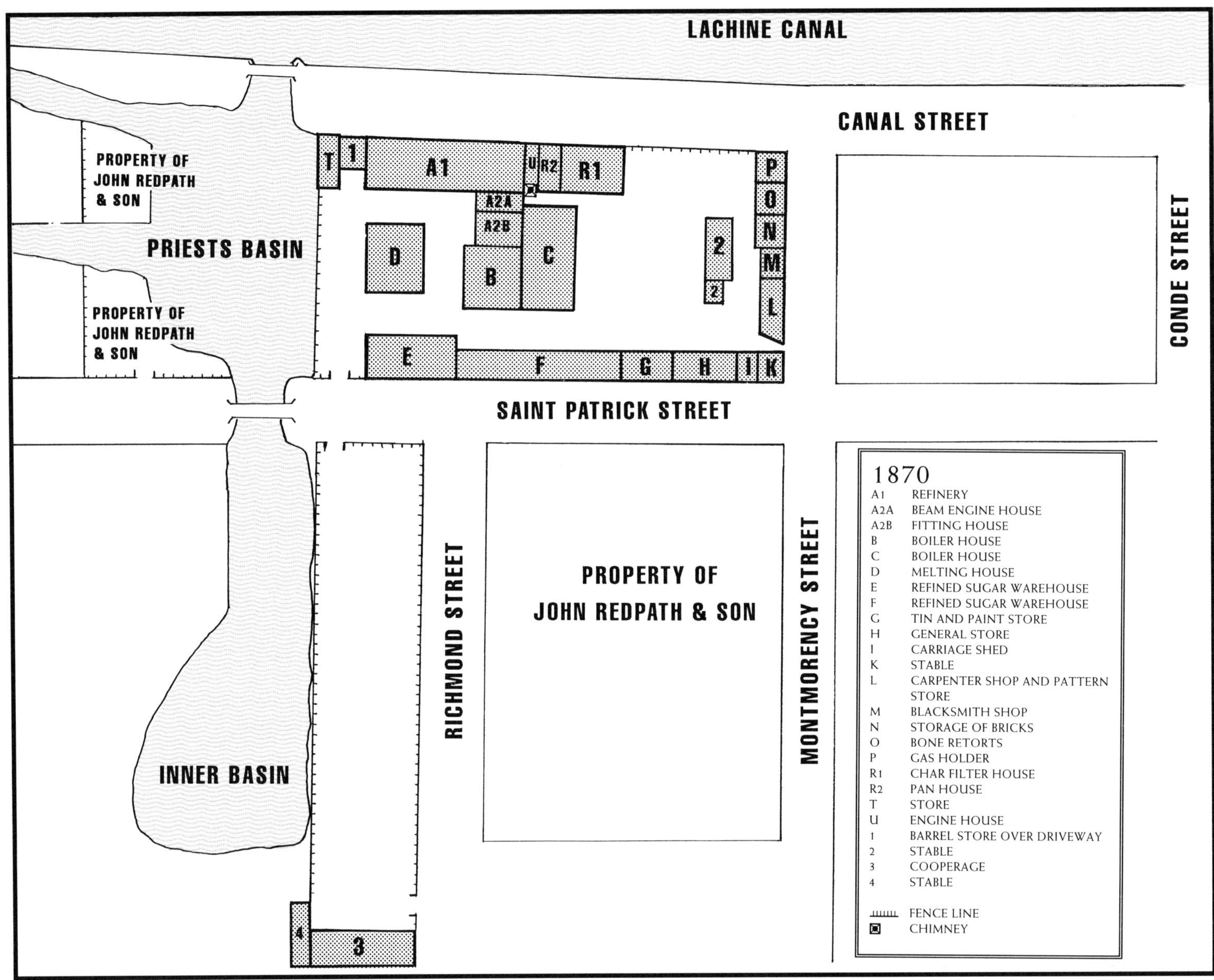
LACHINE CANAL
CANAL STREET
CONDE STREET
PROPERTY OF JOHN REDPATH & SON
PRIESTS BASIN
PROPERTY OF JOHN REDPATH & SON
SAINT PATRICK STREET
RICHMOND STREET
PROPERTY OF JOHN REDPATH & SON
MONTMORENCY STREET
INNER BASIN
T
1
A1
U
R2
R1
A2A
A2B
D
B
C
2
2
P
O
N
M
L
E
F
G
H
I
K
4
3
1870
A1 REFINERY
A2A BEAM ENGINE HOUSE
A2B FITTING HOUSE
B BOILER HOUSE
C BOILER HOUSE
D MELTING HOUSE
E REFINED SUGAR WAREHOUSE
F REFINED SUGAR WAREHOUSE
G TIN AND PAINT STORE
H GENERAL STORE
I CARRIAGE SHED
K STABLE
L CARPENTER SHOP AND PATTERN STORE
M BLACKSMITH SHOP
N STORAGE OF BRICKS
O BONE RETORTS
P GAS HOLDER
R1 CHAR FILTER HOUSE
R2 PAN HOUSE
T STORE
U ENGINE HOUSE
1 BARREL STORE OVER DRIVEWAY
2 STABLE
3 COOPERAGE
4 STABLE
FENCE LINE
CHIMNEY

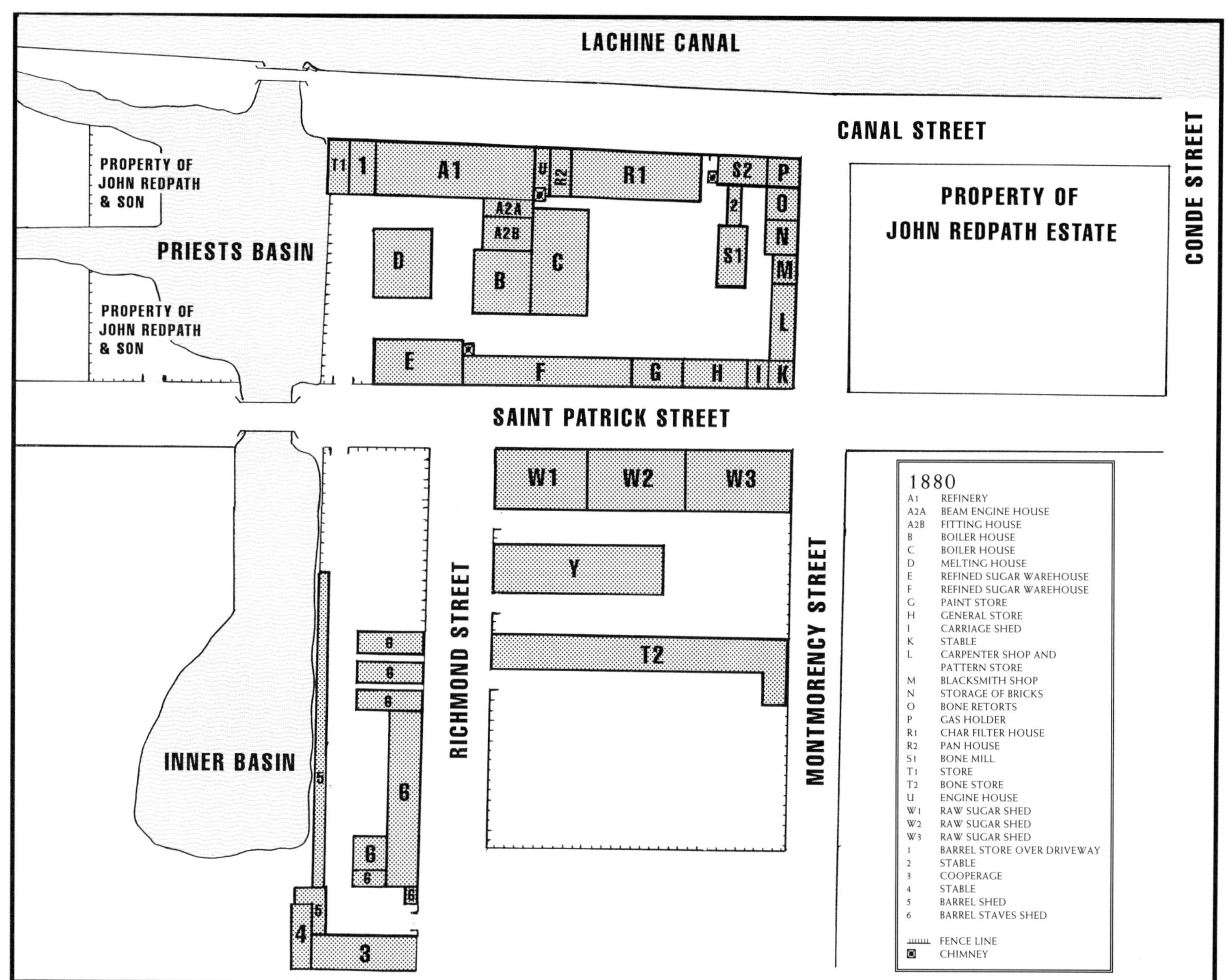
LACHINE CANAL
CANAL STREET
CONDE STREET
PROPERTY OF JOHN REDPATH & SON
PRIESTS BASIN
PROPERTY OF JOHN REDPATH & SON
PROPERTY OF JOHN REDPATH ESTATE
T1
1
A1
U
R2
R1
S2
P
2
O
A2A
A2B
D
C
B
S1
N
M
L
E
F
G
H
I
K
SAINT PATRICK STREET
W1
W2
W3
Y
T2
RICHMOND STREET
MONTMORENCY STREET
INNER BASIN
5
6
4
3
1880
A1 REFINERY
A2A BEAM ENGINE HOUSE
A2B FITTING HOUSE
B BOILER HOUSE
C BOILER HOUSE
D MELTING HOUSE
E REFINED SUGAR WAREHOUSE
F REFINED SUGAR WAREHOUSE
G PAINT STORE
H GENERAL STORE
I CARRIAGE SHED
K STABLE
L CARPENTER SHOP AND PATTERN STORE
M BLACKSMITH SHOP
N STORAGE OF BRICKS
O BONE RETORTS
P GAS HOLDER
R1 CHAR FILTER HOUSE
R2 PAN HOUSE
S1 BONE MILL
T1 STORE
T2 BONE STORE
U ENGINE HOUSE
W1 RAW SUGAR SHED
W2 RAW SUGAR SHED
W3 RAW SUGAR SHED
1 BARREL STORE OVER DRIVEWAY
2 STABLE
3 COOPERAGE
4 STABLE
5 BARREL SHED
6 BARREL STAVES SHED
FENCE LINE
CHIMNEY

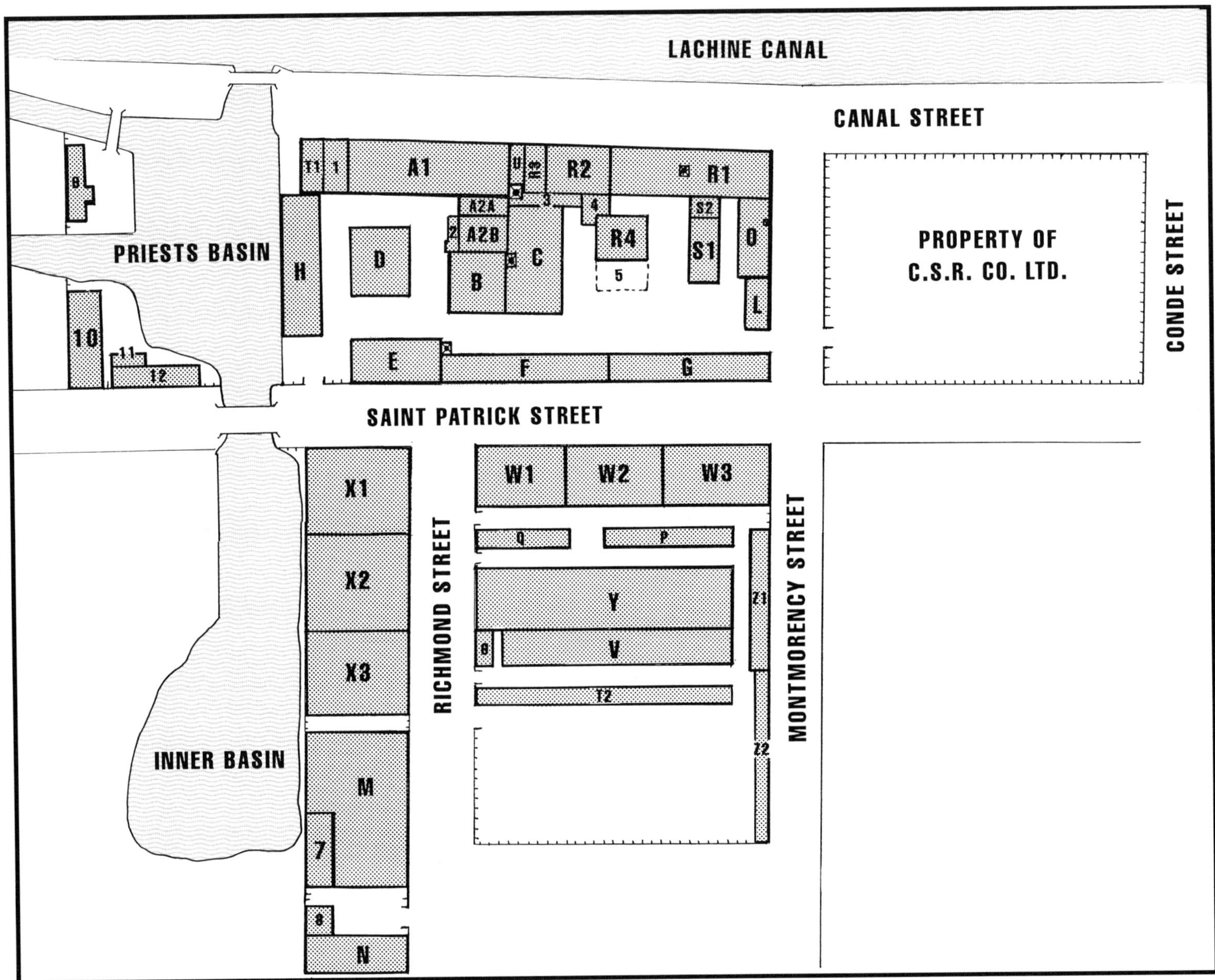
LACHINE CANAL
CANAL STREET
T1
1
A1
U
13
R2
R1
A2A
3
4
S2
A2B
2
R4
S1
O
PRIESTS BASIN
H
D
C
B
5
L
PROPERTY OF
C.S.R. CO. LTD.
CONDE STREET
10
11
12
E
F
G
SAINT PATRICK STREET
X1
W1
W2
W3
X2
RICHMOND STREET
Q
P
MONTMORENCY STREET
Y
Z1
X3
V
T2
Z2
INNER BASIN
M
7
8
N

1890

A1	REFINERY
A2A	BEAM ENGINE HOUSE
A2B	PUMP ROOM
B	BOILER HOUSE
C	BOILER HOUSE
D	MELTING HOUSE
E	REFINED SUGAR WAREHOUSE
F	REFINED SUGAR WAREHOUSE
G	REFINED SUGAR WAREHOUSE
H	MACHINE SHOP
L	CARPENTER SHOP AND PAINT STORE
M	BARREL SHED
N	COOPERAGE
O	BONE RETORTS
P	STORE
Q	STORE
R1	CHAR FILTER HOUSE
R2	CHAR FILTER HOUSE
R3	CHAR FILTER HOUSE
R4	CHAR FILTER HOUSE
S1	BONE MILL
T1	STORE
T2	BONE STORE
U	ENGINE HOUSE
V	SHED
W1	RAW SUGAR SHED
W2	RAW SUGAR SHED
W3	RAW SUGAR SHED
X1	RAW SUGAR SHED
X2	RAW SUGAR SHED
X3	RAW SUGAR SHED
Y	RAW SUGAR SHED
Z1	SHED
Z2	SHED

1	STORE OVER DRIVEWAY
2	STORE
3	PASSAGEWAY
4	TANK HOUSE
5	FOUNDATION FOR CHAR FILTER HOUSE EXTENSION
6	SHED
7	DRY KILN
8	SHED
9	COACH HOUSE
10	SHED
11	SHED
12	SHED

(symbol)	FENCE LINE
(symbol)	CHIMNEY

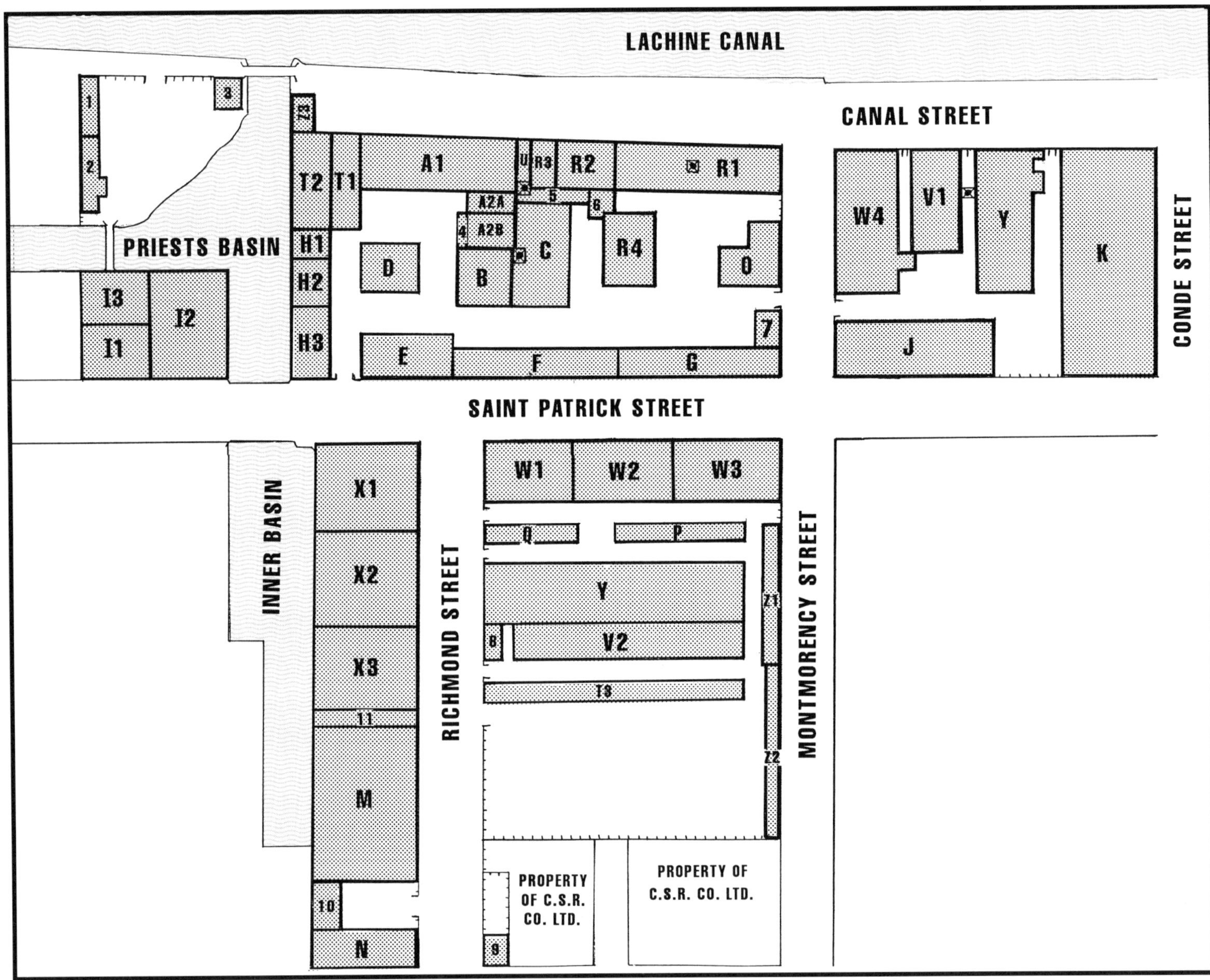
LACHINE CANAL
CANAL STREET
PRIESTS BASIN
SAINT PATRICK STREET
CONDE STREET
INNER BASIN
RICHMOND STREET
MONTMORENCY STREET
A1
A2A
A2B
B
C
D
E
F
G
H1
H2
H3
I1
I2
I3
J
K
M
N
O
P
Q
R1
R2
R3
R4
T1
T2
T3
U
V1
V2
W1
W2
W3
W4
X1
X2
X3
Y
Y
Z1
Z2
Z3
1
2
3
4
5
6
7
8
9
10
11
PROPERTY OF C.S.R. CO. LTD.
PROPERTY OF C.S.R. CO. LTD.

1904

A1	REFINERY
A2A	BEAM ENGINE HOUSE
A2B	PUMP ROOM
B	BOILER HOUSE
C	BOILER HOUSE
E	REFINED SUGAR WAREHOUSE
F	REFINED SUGAR WAREHOUSE
G	REFINED SUGAR WAREHOUSE
H1	PATTERN STORE
H2	MACHINE SHOP
H3	CARPENTER SHOP
J	REFINED SUGAR WAREHOUSE
K	RAW SUGAR SHED
M	BARREL SHED
N	COOPERAGE
O	OFFICES
P	STORE
Q	STORE
R1	CHAR FILTER HOUSE
R2	CHAR FILTER HOUSE
R3	CHAR FILTER HOUSE
R4	CHAR FILTER HOUSE
T3	BONE STORE
U	WATER TANKS
V1	PACKAGING HOUSE
V2	SHED
W1	RAW SUGAR SHED
W2	RAW SUGAR SHED
W3	RAW SUGAR SHED
W4	REFINERY (STEFFEN BUILDING)
X1	RAW SUGAR SHED
X2	RAW SUGAR SHED
X3	RAW SUGAR SHED
Y	RAW SUGAR SHED
Z1	SHED
Z2	SHED

1	COACH HOUSE
2	STABLE
3	FIRE PUMP STATION
4	SHED
5	PASSAGEWAY
6	TANK HOUSE
7	SHED
8	SHED
9	DWELLING
10	DRY KILN HOUSE
11	DRY BAG STORE

MONTREAL PRODUCTS

D	BONDED SPIRIT WAREHOUSE
I1	BONDED SPIRIT WAREHOUSE
I2	BONDED SPIRIT WAREHOUSE
I3	BONDED SPIRIT WAREHOUSE
T1	DISTILLERY
T2	FERMENTING ROOM
Z3	EXISE HOUSE

╧╧╧╧	FENCE LINE
▣	CHIMNEY

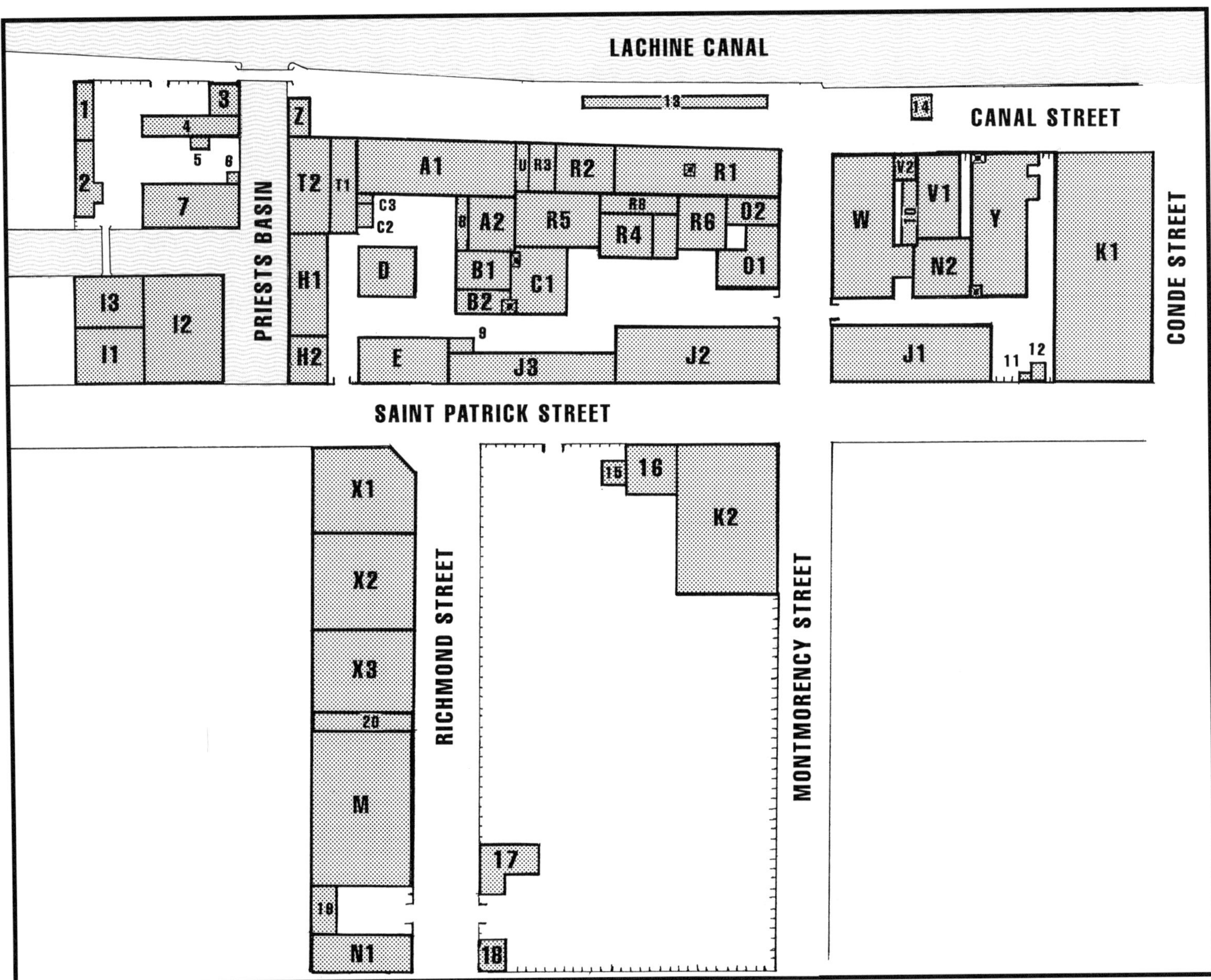
LACHINE CANAL
CANAL STREET
PRIESTS BASIN
SAINT PATRICK STREET
CONDE STREET
RICHMOND STREET
MONTMORENCY STREET
1
2
3
4
5
6
7
13
14
I1
I2
I3
Z
T2
T1
H1
H2
A1
A2
C3
C2
C1
D
B1
B2
E
9
J3
J2
J1
U
R3
R2
R1
R5
R8
R4
R6
O2
O1
W
V2
V1
10
Y
N2
K1
11
12
X1
X2
X3
20
M
19
N1
15
16
K2
17
18

1918

A1	REFINERY
A2	BONE KILN AND BOILER FEED PUMP ROOM
B1	BONE KILNS
B2	TRUCK GARAGE AND DRYER BUILDING
C1	BOILER HOUSE
C2	TANK STORE
C3	SHED
E	PARIS LUMP MILL
H1	MACHINE SHOP AND CARPENTER SHOP
H2	MACHINE SHOP OFFICE
J1	REFINED SUGAR WAREHOUSE
J2	REFINED SUGAR WAREHOUSE
J3	REFINED SUGAR WAREHOUSE
K1	RAW SUGAR SHED
K2	RAW SUGAR SHED
M	BARREL SHED
N1	COOPERAGE
N2	BOILER FEED PUMP HOUSE
O1	OFFICES
O2	POWER HOUSE
R1	CHAR FILTER HOUSE
R2	CHAR FILTER HOUSE
R3	TANK HOUSE
R4	CHAR FILTER HOUSE WING
R5	CHAR FILTER HOUSE WING
R6	CHAR FILTER HOUSE WING
R7	CHAR FILTER HOUSE WING
R8	CHAR FILTER HOUSE WING
U	TURBINE PUMP HOUSE
V1	PACKAGING HOUSE
V2	AIR WASHING BUILDING
W	REFINERY (STEFFEN BUILDING)
X1	RAW SUGAR SHED
X2	BONE STORE
X3	MACHINE SHOP STORE
Y	BOILER HOUSE

1	COACH HOUSE
2	STABLE
3	FIRE PUMP STATION
8	WATER TANK HOUSE AND SHED
9	PAINT STORE
10	COLD WATER PUMP BUILDING
11	CHAIN STORE
12	SCALE HOUSE
13	LOADING PLATFORM
14	COAL TOWER
15	SHED
16	SACK WASHING BUILDING
17	COOPERAGE STORE
18	DWELLING
19	BOILER HOUSE
20	DRY BAG STORE

MONTREAL PRODUCTS

D	BONDED SPIRIT WAREHOUSE
I1	BONDED SPIRIT WAREHOUSE
I2	BONDED SPIRIT WAREHOUSE
I3	BONDED SPIRIT WAREHOUSE
T1	DISTILLERY
T2	FERMENTING ROOM
Z	EXISE HOUSE
5	MOLASSES PUMP HOUSE
6	DISTILLERY PUMP HOUSE
7	BONDED SPIRIT WAREHOUSE

‗‗‗	FENCE LINE
▣	CHIMNEY

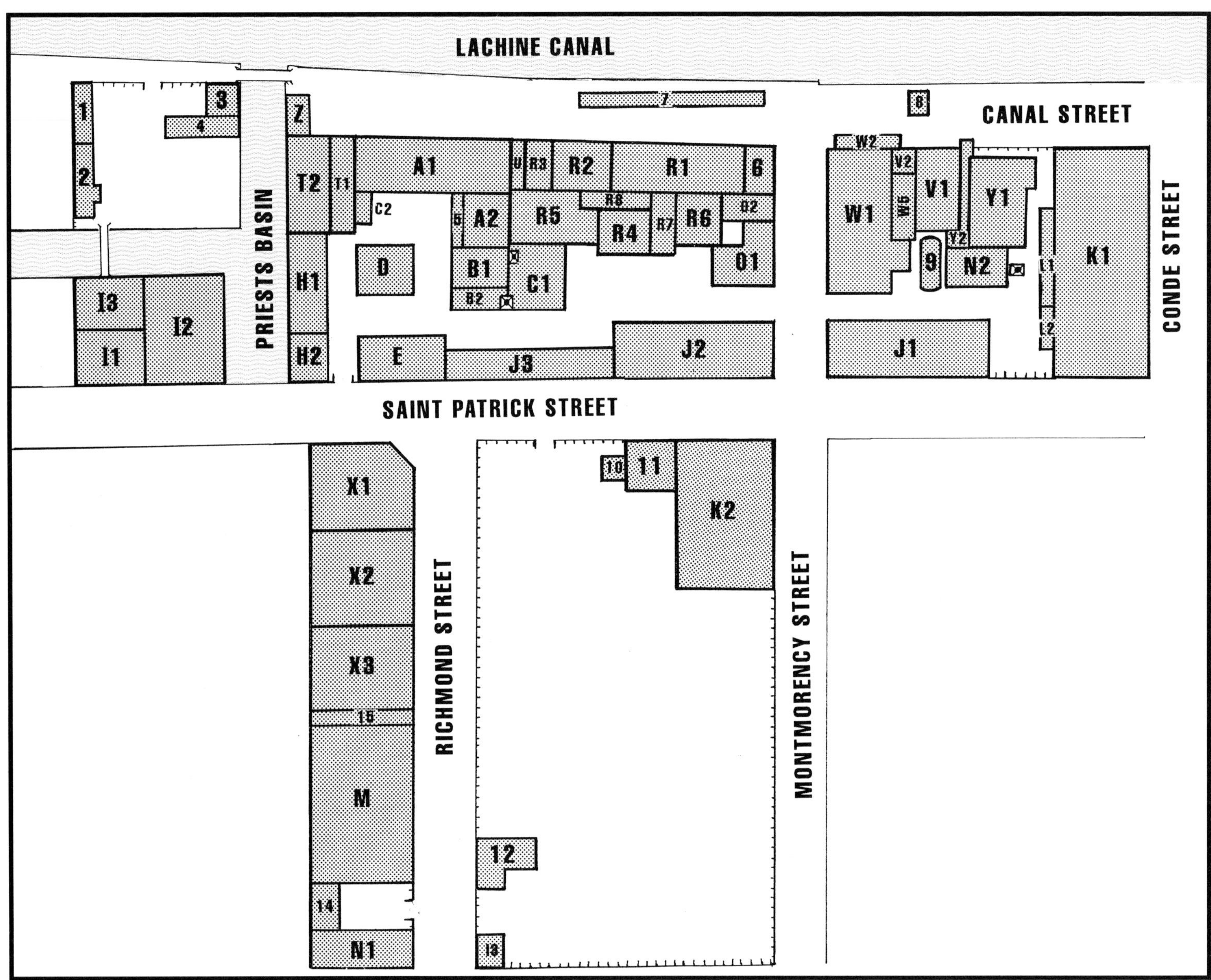
LACHINE CANAL
CANAL STREET
PRIESTS BASIN
SAINT PATRICK STREET
RICHMOND STREET
MONTMORENCY STREET
CONDE STREET
1
2
3
4
7
8
Z
T2
T1
A1
U
R3
R2
R1
6
C2
5
A2
R5
R8
R4
R7
R6
O2
O1
D
B1
B2
C1
H1
H2
I3
I2
I1
E
J3
J2
W2
V2
W1
W6
V1
Y1
Y2
9
N2
L1
L2
K1
J1
X1
X2
X3
15
M
14
N1
10
11
K2
12
13

1929

A1 SPARE REFINERY AND STORAGE
A2 BONE KILN AND BOILER FEED PUMP ROOM
B1 BONE KILNS
B2 TRUCK GARAGE
C1 BOILER HOUSE
C2 TANK STORE
E PARIS LUMP MILL
H1 MACHINE SHOP AND CARPENTER SHOP
H2 MACHINE SHOP OFFICE & PATTERN STORE
J1 REFINED SUGAR WAREHOUSE
J2 REFINED SUGAR WAREHOUSE
J3 REFINED SUGAR WAREHOUSE
K1 RAW SUGAR SHED
K2 RAW SUGAR SHED
L1 ELECTRICAL SUBSTATION
L2 STORE
M BARREL SHED
N1 COOPERAGE
N2 POWERHOUSE
O1 OFFICES
O2 POWER HOUSE
R1 CHAR FILTER HOUSE
R2 CHAR FILTER HOUSE
R3 TANK HOUSE
R4 CHAR FILTER HOUSE WING
R5 CHAR FILTER HOUSE WING
R6 CHAR FILTER HOUSE WING
R7 CHAR FILTER HOUSE WING
R8 CHAR FILTER HOUSE WING
U TURBINE PUMP HOUSE
V1 PACKAGING HOUSE
V2 AIR WASHING BUILDING
W1 REFINERY
W2 REFINERY ANNEX AND LABORATORY
X1 RAW SUGAR STORE
X2 BONE STORE
X3 MACHINE SHOP STORE
Y1 BOILER HOUSE
Y2 HOT WATER BUILDING

1 COACH HOUSE
2 STABLE
3 FIRE PUMP STATION
4 BOAT HOUSE AND GARAGE
5 WATER TANK HOUSE AND SHED
6 LIQUOR GALLERY
7 LOADING PLATFORM
8 COAL TOWER
9 STEAM ACCUMULATOR
10 SHED
11 SACK WASHING BUILDING
12 COOPERAGE STORE
13 DWELLING
14 BOILER HOUSE
15 DRY BAG STORE

MONTREAL PRODUCTS

D BONDED SPIRIT WAREHOUSE
I1 BONDED SPIRIT WAREHOUSE
I2 BONDED SPIRIT WAREHOUSE
I3 BONDED SPIRIT WAREHOUSE
T1 DISTILLERY
T2 FERMENTING ROOM
Z EXISE HOUSE

ıııııı FENCE LINE
⊠ CHIMNEY

Selected Bibliography

Canada's Illustrated Heritage Series:

Atwood, Margaret: 1977 *Days of the Rebels 1815 - 1840* Canada's Illustrated Heritage: McClelland and Stewart Ltd.

Batten, Jack: 1977 *Canada Moves Westward 1880 - 1890* McClelland and Stewart Ltd.

Callwood, June: 1977 *The Naughty Nineties 1890 - 1900* McClelland and Stewart Ltd.

Carroll, Joy: 1986 *Pioneer Days 1840 - 1860* McClelland & Stewart Ltd.

Collins, Robert: 1977 *The Age of Innocence 1870 - 1880* McClelland and Stewart Ltd.

Craig, John: 1977 *The Years of Agony 1910 - 1920* McClelland and Stewart Ltd.

Into the 20th Century 1900 - 1910: 1977 McClelland and Stewart Ltd.

Stephenson, William: 1977 *Dawn of the Nation 1860 - 1870* McClelland and Stewart Ltd.

The Crazy Twenties 1920 - 1930: 1978 McClelland and Stewart Ltd.

Century of Canada Series:

Bennett, Paul W.: 1985 *Years of Promise 1896 - 1911* Grolier Ltd.

Morton, Desmond: 1983 *Years of Conflict 1911 - 1921* Grolier Ltd.

Waite, Peter: 1985 *Years of Struggle 1867 - 1896* Grolier Ltd.

Chalmin, Philippe: 1990 *The Making of a Sugar Giant, Tate and Lyle 1859 - 1989* Harwood Academic Publishers

Collard, Edgar Andrew: 1965 *Call Back Yesterdays* Longmans Canada

Collard, Edgar Andrew: 1976 *Montreal, The Days That Are No More* Doubleday Canada

Deerr, Noel: 1949 *The History of Sugar*, (2 volumes) Chapman and Hall Ltd.

Denison, Merrill: 1966 *Canada's First Bank: A History of the Bank of Montreal* (2 volumes) McClelland and Stewart Ltd.

Francis, R. Douglas and Smith, Donald B.:1986 (2 volumes) *Readings in Canadian History* Holt, Rinehart & Winston

Hugill, Anthony: 1978 *Sugar and All That* Gentry Books

Jenkins, Kathleen: 1966 *Montreal, Island City of the St. Lawrence* Doubleday and Company Inc.

Legget, Robert: 1972 *Rideau Waterway* University of Toronto Press, Revised Edition

MacKay, Donald: 1987 *The Square Mile* Douglas & McIntyre

Masters, Donald C.: 1963 *The Reciprocity Treaty of 1854* McClelland and Stewart Ltd.

Mintz, Sidney W.: 1985 *Sweetness and Power, The Place of Sugar in Modern History.* Elisabeth Sifton Books - Viking

Morton, Desmond: 1979 *Rebellions in Canada* Focus on Canadian History Series Grolier Ltd.

Niccol, Robert: 1864 *Essay on Sugar, and General Treatise on Sugar Refining* Mackenzie & Co.

Schreiner, John: 1989 *The Refiners, A Century of B.C. Sugar* Douglas & McIntyre

Shortt, Adam and Doughty, A.G.: 1913 *Canada and Its Provinces Volume IX and X Industrial Expansion* Edinburgh University Press

Stacey, C.P.: 1963 *Canada and the British Army 1846 - 1871* University of Toronto Press

Strong, L.A.G.: 1954 *The Story of Sugar* George Weidenfeld & Nicolson

Waite, P.B.: 1971 *Canada 1874 - 1896* McClelland and Stewart Ltd.

Woods, Shirley E.: 1983 *The Molson Saga 1763 - 1983* Doubleday Canada

MANUSCRIPTS

McCord Museum

Notebooks, account ledgers, and letterbooks, originally belonging to John Redpath, held in the collection of the McCord Museum, Montreal under catalogue numbers:

John Redpath papers	Items 1 - 21
Garneau papers	Items 20145 - 20175

M. W. Davidson

Research notes and accounts from unpublished drafts by M. W. Davidson.

Notes

Notes: Unless otherwise specified, all quotes and references included in the text are extracted from original documents, account books, articles, and letterbooks within the archive collection held by the Redpath Sugar Museum, Toronto. Where the contents of entire chapters are derived from these items they are referred to below as Redpath Sugar Museum.

Chapter 1 - "That Sweet Comfit Men Call Sugar"

1. Noel Deerr, The History of Sugar (2 volumes) Chapman and Hall Ltd. 1949
2. Ibid.
3. Ibid.
4. Ibid.
5. Ibid.
6. Ibid.
7. Ibid.
8. Ibid.
9. Ibid.
10. Ibid.
11. Ibid.

Chapter 2 - The Making of a Man of Substance

1. Robert Legget, Rideau Waterway University of Toronto Press, Revised Edition, 1972
2. Ibid.
3. John Redpath papers, McCord Museum, Montreal
4. Ibid.
5. Ibid.

Chapter 3 - The Building of a Sugar House

1. Public Archives of Canada, Department of Revenue Records, RG16 Volume 187
2. Public Archives of Canada, Department of Revenue Records, RG16 Volume 188
3. Ibid.
4. Public Archives of Canada, Department of Revenue Records, RG16 Volume 189
5. Ibid.

Chapter 4 - "A Growing Concern"

1. Public Archives Canada, Records of the Governor Generals Office C.R.G. 7, Series G.20, Volume 83
2. C.P. Stacey, Canada and the British Army, 1846-1871 University of Toronto Press, 1963
3. E.A. Collard, Call Back Yesterdays, Longmans Canada, 1965

Chapter 5 - "Growing Concerns"

1. Public Archives of Nova Scotia, R.G.5 Series G.P. Volume 7

Chapter 6 - "The End of an Era"

Redpath Sugar Museum

Chapter 7 - "... A Devil of a Time ..."

Redpath Sugar Museum

Chapter 8 - "... We Are at a Crisis of Our Affairs ..."

Redpath Sugar Museum

Chapter 9 - The Axe Falls

Redpath Sugar Museum

Chapter 10 - "Intermission"
Redpath Sugar Museum

Chapter 11 - "Another Opening"
Redpath Sugar Museum

Chapter 12 - "... A Hard and Anxious Time ..."
1. Merrill Denison, Canadas First Bank: A History of the Bank of Montreal, (2 volumes), McClelland & Stewart Ltd., 1966

Chapter 13 - "Too Many Cooks"
1. E.A. Collard, Call Back Yesterdays, Longmans Canada, 1965
2. Ibid.

Chapter 14 - "A Busy Year"
Redpath Sugar Museum

Chapter 15 - "When Fortune Turns the Wheel"
1. Canadian Pacific Corporate Archives, Book 36, page 785

Chapter 16 - "What You Gain on the Roundabouts"
Redpath Sugar Museum

Chapter 17 - "You Lose on the Swings"
1. George Alexander Drummond Letterbook, courtesy of Bruce McNiven

Chapter 18 - "The New Way"
1. George Alexander Drummond Letterbook, courtesy of Bruce McNiven
2. Ibid.
3. Ibid.
4. Ibid.
5. Ibid.
6. Ibid.
7. Ibid.

Chapter 19 - Cheers and Tears, Ginger Ale and Champagne
1. George Alexander Drummond Letterbook, courtesy of Bruce McNiven
2. Canada First Magazine, Metro Toronto Reference Library

Chapter 20 - The Building of a "New" Sugar House
1. George Alexander Drummond Letterbook, courtesy of Bruce McNiven
2. Ibid.
3. Ibid.

Chapter 21 - "A New Captain"
1. George Alexander Drummond Letterbook, courtesy of Bruce McNiven
2. Ibid.
3. Ibid.
4. Ibid.

Chapter 22 - "Redpath Must Be Everywhere"
1. George Alexander Drummond Letterbook, courtesy of Bruce McNiven
2. Ibid.
3. Ibid.
4. Canadian Grocer, University of Toronto, Fisher Rare Book Library
5. George Alexander Drummond Letterbook, courtesy of Bruce McNiven

Chapter 23 - "A Patriotic Stand"
Redpath Sugar Museum

Chapter 24 - "Big Brother"
1. Interview with Helen Henderson, by the author
2. Ibid.

Chapter 25 - "An Unfortunate State of Affairs"
Redpath Sugar Museum

Chapter 26 - Dance of the Millions
Redpath Sugar Museum

Chapter 27 - Picking Up the Pieces
Redpath Sugar Museum

Chapter 28 - The Final Straws
Redpath Sugar Museum

Visual Credits

National Archives Canada

Page	23	(C 19587)
	35	(P.A. 32453)
	54	(P.A. 22466)
	127	(P.A. 44248)
	167	(P.A. 45941)
	216	(P.A. 110140)
	226	(P.A. 110112)
	272	(P.A. 119390)

McCord Museum of Canadian History
Notman Photographic Archives

	33	(M.P. 040-83)
	43	(6,840 B II)
	51	(35,407 I)
Right	74	(46,387 I)
Left	74	(64,451 I)
	91	(L.R.C.) (64,301 I)
	92	(6842 B II)
Left	100	(M.P. 167.76)
Right	100	(40,163 B II)
	140	(2801 view)
	146	(2458 view)
	170	(2943 view)
	171	(2944 view)
	174	(2938 view)
	194	(8770 view)
	206	(M.P. 163.76)
	207	(no number)
	214	(M.P. 165.76)
	240	(193230 II)

Ontario Archives

26	Burrows Collection Sketch 52
27	Burrows Collection Sketch 57

McGill University

29	John and Jane Redpath

Index